FAMILIAR MYSTERIES

FAMILIAR MYSTERIES
The Truth in Myth

SHIRLEY PARK LOWRY

New York   Oxford
OXFORD UNIVERSITY PRESS
1982

Copyright © 1982 by Shirley Park Lowry

Library of Congress Cataloging in Publication Data
Lowry, Shirley Park.
Familiar mysteries.

Bibliography: p.
Includes index.
1. Myth.   I. Title
BL304.L68   398′.042   80-27792
ISBN 0-19-502925-9   AACR1

Printing (last digit): 9 8 7 6 5 4 3 2 1

Printed in the United States of America

To Jack

Acknowledgments

Joseph Campbell's brilliant explorations of mythology moved me toward my own adventures in that field, and Mr. Campbell's influence pervades my book. Robert Iverson made writing the book possible. A work of synthesis, such as mine, entails journeys into alien fields of scholarship; from the scholars cited individually in the text and bibliography, I learned much that was essential to my purposes. I have tried to express my appreciation by drawing carefully upon their knowledge, crosschecking all ambiguities and controversies that came to my attention. Barbara Kirby, who illustrated the book, taught me what "illustration" means. Colleagues George Herrick, Stephen Statham, David Jones, and T. O. Daniels generously provided information and support. Rabbi Gerrold Goldstein reviewed Chapter 11 for historical accuracy; Marie Anne Mayeski CSJ, Chairman, Department of Theology at Loyola Marymount University, did the same for Chapter 12's section on Christianity. Nancy Brown typed the manuscript with unusual skill. James Raimes, formerly of Oxford University Press, sponsored an unknown writer. Ira S. Lowry freely shared his time and talents. His advice on everything from diction and format to finding an audience for the book raised its chances for success. His sustaining presence was a great gift.

Pacific Palisades, Ca.   S. P. L.
July 1981

Contents

Introduction: What Myth Is and What It Does   •   3

I   THE SYMBOLIC LANGUAGE OF MYTHS

    1   Where We Get Universal Symbols   19

    2   Symbolizing the Sources of Life   32

    3   Symbolizing the Mystery of Death   61

II   THE HERO

    4   What Heroes Do   75

    5   The Heroic Life-Pattern   90

III   THE COMPLEAT HOME AND
      THE MONSTER AT THE DOOR

    6   Images of Cosmos and Chaos   129

    7   Cosmic Centers as Images of Physical
       and Moral Order   132

    8   Monsters as Images of Chaos   177

IV CONQUERING DEATH

   9 The Problem of Death   213

  10 Survival Through Fertility   218

  11 Survival Through a Family Line   253

  12 Personal Survival in Another World   265

  13 Gilgamesh and the Great Secret   299

     Notes   309

     Bibliography   323

     Index   331

FAMILIAR MYSTERIES

Introduction:
What Myth Is and What It Does

May God us keep
From Single vision & Newton's sleep!

William Blake

Waking from a story about Heracles, Perseus, Jonah, King Arthur, or hobbits, we realize once again that no wily serpents or green giants exist; nor golden apples, winged sandals, magic potions; nor people journeying to the underworld or living in fishes' bellies or slumbering in secret barrows or thorn-smothered castles.

Why then do such stories quicken our pulse, haunt our dreams, and encircle the world? The question is particularly puzzling in a time when the notion of truth has so narrowed that for many people "truth" and "scientific fact" are precise synonyms. Any idea or story widely believed but contrary to fact is likely to be called a myth, a usage that trivializes the meaning of the term.

In this book, "myth" will mean a story about a culture's gods or heroes, a story whose vivid symbols render concrete a special perception about people and their world. Many myths embody a people's perception of the deepest truths, those truths that give purpose, direction, *meaning* to that people's life. That myths use concrete symbols to express abstractions accounts for their unrealistic trappings. That they often embody the essence of our experience accounts for their power. Whether or not a particular myth corresponds to scientific fact as presently understood is, in this book, unimportant. What makes a myth important is how it guides our personal lives, supports or challenges a specific social order, makes our physical world a manageable place, or helps us accept life's mysteries—including misfortune and death—with serenity.[1] The examples that follow will clarify the roles that myths have played in human life since earliest historical times.

PERSONAL GUIDANCE

Myths give us patterns of personal behavior that help us to deal with each stage in our lives—childhood, maturity, old age—and to move gracefully from one stage to the next. For instance, modern mythic heroes help children through the inevitable fears arising from their smallness and dependency. Superman and Wonder Woman feed children's natural fantasies of being Strong Man and Strong Lady, fantasies that keep them from being overwhelmed by a world of large and mysteriously powerful adults. Superman's dual identity is particularly satisfying, for it suggests that, even though others may not find oneself imposing at present, one has a secret power that has not quite ripened or that one does not yet choose to reveal.

Similarly, the Incredible Hulk, a popular television monster, expresses concretely the kind of anger that we all, especially as children, sometimes feel—puffed-up, blank-brained, volcanically destructive. Such a feeling terrifies us because we suspect that, once unleashed, it will prove uncontrollable. For a child, watching the Hulk on a rampage is thrilling without being frightening, because the Hulk, though mindless with rage, somehow attacks only bad guys.[2]

Innumerable traditional stories, familiar and unfamiliar, deal with the transition from childhood to maturity. A supernatural helper usually eases the youth or girl through the crisis. Whether the young person is Odysseus' son Telemachus getting help from Athena, the Old Testament Joseph from God himself, or Cactus Flower Girl from her Spider Grandmother (see Chapter 1), the helper's clear message is: Yes, you are an untried youngster moving among powerful, experienced people, some of them malevolent, but because you are young, brave, and pure of heart, I am here to help you. Trust me and your intuition. Take the risk. You are sufficient. Furthermore, though in general you should respect your elders, it is right that you challenge someone older than yourself for his place if he is unworthy of that place.

To the mature person, myths say that people who misuse their power lose it, but those who use power generously and wisely are loved, obeyed, and raised high. Faust squandered his power. Jason's uncle Pelias hoarded it. Herod and innumerable other kings of traditional stories tyrannized over the weak. But Theseus, Jesus, King Arthur, and George Washington spent themselves for their people, and they were richly rewarded with love, emulation, and lasting glory.

And finally myths say: When your light dims, go; grow radishes, like Odysseus' father; teach the little children; die in one last glorious act for your people, as Beowulf did; climb a rope of feathers to join the Great Spirit in the sky. Whatever you do, get off the high seat. Something good awaits you.

SUPPORTING OR CHALLENGING THE SOCIAL ORDER

Remote societies offer many examples of myths that either support a social order or ratify changes in that order. In ancient Egyptian belief, the pharaoh embodied on earth the sun's generative power, and upon his death he became the sun god Re himself. The welfare of all life in Egypt depended on the pharaoh's welfare and—when he died—on his safe arrival in the afterlife; therefore, simple self-interest encouraged all Egyptians to uphold the pharaoh's earthly power and cooperate in building and equipping his tomb. The God of the early Israelites rewarded or punished people on this earth only, and usually as family groups rather than as individuals. Then, as the Israelites' circumstances changed radically from the seventh to the second centuries B.C., so did Judaic theology relating to social roles: God would not punish children for their fathers' misdeeds but would treat each person in accordance with his individual merit.

Myths still perform social functions. One such myth has inspired Americans to see their country as the world's natural moral leader and to defend such principles as freedom of speech, tolerance of diversity, and equality of all before the law that they believe underlie this moral authority. Informally put, this myth reads: God saw what a botch people had made of civilization in Europe. Some people of no natural distinction claimed that God had divinely ordained their rule. While they tyrannized over everyone else and spent their money on cakes and baubles for their mistresses, millions slept on nettles and ate potato peelings. Ordinary people grew poorer and poorer. If someone dared complain, he was packed off to a dungeon where rats chewed his toes and where he died without anyone ever hearing of him again. God decided to start over. Since he had promised never to send another flood, he decided to give people another chance by opening up a New World across the sea. Practically vacant, this glorious land had almost inexhaustible natural resources. Many people came to this New World. They were people of special energy, self-reliance, intuitive intelligence, and purity of heart. God put these people under his particular care, guiding them into the right ways to live and to shape their institutions. The doors of the New World were open to all, and whoever wanted freedom and justice and honest work would succeed there. This nation's special mission in the world would be to serve as the moral guide to all other nations.[3]

One American myth dealt with an awkward problem. In the nation chosen by God to lead the rest of the world toward justice and liberty, in the paradise where every adult male was equal before the law, thousands of slaves toiled. Always embarrassing, that fact became more so as wicked European nations paid it increasingly shrill attention. Deeply religious American Southerners, whose economy depended on slave labor, felt particular distress, but the embarrassment eased when it became clear that the Bible itself ratified slavery. The Bible said that the sons of Ham—that wicked boy who had peered at his drunken father's nakedness—would be, for punishment, hewers of wood and drawers of water. Since blacks did just such work, obviously they were those descendants of Ham.

After that story had been discredited, black people still did not share the privileges granted other Americans. Again, a myth was found to ratify the discrepancy. Black people were a primitive race, not fully enough developed to cope with responsibility, knowledge, and power; therefore, it would be unkind to them and others to give them these things.[4]

Meanwhile, many black people found solace in the belief that they were as much God's children as whites and that God would redress their wrongs by and by. But after three hundred years of work, prayer, and considerable patience had brought mediocre results, some blacks came forth with a new myth explaining their low status and sponsoring radical change. About 1930, a mysterious Wallace D. Fard, known as "God in person," founded a sect called the Black Muslims. When he disappeared, his chief disciple Elijah Muhammad took charge.

The recently incarnate Allah had given Elijah Muhammad this story: Far from being a primitive race, black people were the original people; they had built great civilizations in Africa while white people were still groveling on all fours in the icy caves of Europe. Indeed, before whites even existed, wise black scientists knew so much about eugenics that one of them created an especially strong tribe, the Shabazz, from whom American blacks descend.

The present white dominance came about as follows: Trillions of years ago, not long after the moon separated from the earth, Original Man—black people—founded the holy city of Mecca. About seven thousand years ago, although over two-thirds of the Original People lived in harmony, a small percentage were dissatisfied. Among this troublesome group was the large-headed, diabolically clever Mr. Yacub. Starting school at four, he finished all the universities by the time he was eighteen. When he began successfully to convert too many people, the anxious authorities exiled him and his sixty thousand followers to the island of Patmos. There, in revenge against Allah, he decided to put to an evil purpose his scientific ability to breed races. He would create a race of bleached-out devils. After eight hundred years of controlled breeding, all inhabitants of Patmos were blond, blue-eyed devils who lived in trees. Eventually, these devils found their way back to the mainland. By telling lies, they got the black people to fight with each other, turning what had been an earthly paradise into a hell. Finally, the blacks rounded up the devils and drove them in chains across the Arabian sands to the caves of Europe. Two thousand years later, Allah raised up Moses to civilize these cave devils. The lost Books of Moses correctly prophesied that for six thousand years these white devils would rule; then, in our time, when white civilization was destroying itself through its own devilish nature, nonwhite people all over the world would be rising up. At this time, someone from the black race would be born with infinite wisdom, knowledge, and power.[5]

Myths about women have long supported their lack of power in Western civilization. For instance, according to informal Judeo-Christian tradition, the first man was created in God's image, the woman created as a sort of afterthought from a spare part of the man's body, to be his helper. This frivolous, irresponsible creature fell into deep trouble and then dragged her too-fond husband down with her.

Well, now we know better. Just as Fard stated that blacks were the original people, so do some women affirm that women were the original sex. Indeed, according to Elizabeth Gould Davis, in *The First Sex*, Science tells us that males are botched females, that the male's Y chromosome is in fact a "deformed and broken X chromosome—the female chromosome." The male's maleness is not only derivative; it is actually the result of a genetic error. The first males were "mutants and freaks"; maleness is "abnormal." We also know that long ago, before men usurped the natural authority of the healthier, more intelligent sex, women ruled the high civilizations with men as their servants.[6]

The inferior status of blacks to whites and of women to men had long been ratified by powerful myths. It should not surprise us much, then, that some members of both groups are putting forth equally toxic counter-myths in order to break free of the traditional myths and discover themselves afresh. Elijah Muhammad's tale turns upside down some of the most disheartening notions about blacks—that their darkness signifies a moral taint and that they only recently climbed down from the trees. Davis's version of biology invites the notion that sex chromosomes under a microscope would really look like Xs and Ys, and that the poor Ys have lost an important appendage. So much for Freud's theory of penis envy!

A SENSE OF PHYSICAL ORDER

Some of our most enduring myths tell us how the cosmos was created. The cosmos is an image of the universe as an organized, sanctified arrangement of earth, sky, plants, animals, and people, through all of which pulsate plan and meaning. Its opposite, chaos, is disorder, confusion, wilderness, absence of structure or significance. Myths about the creation tell us our place in the grand scheme; they comfort us with the sense that we are part of and contributors to some larger plan; and they warn us against carelessly, selfishly, or pridefully tearing the fragile web of natural or social order. Chaos lurks at the edge of the cosmos, awaiting its chance.

One of the most electrifying accounts of the transformation from chaos to cosmos occurs in the first two chapters of Genesis. All creative energy is concentrated into a single majestic God who pulls form after form out of the void, infuses the emerging arrangement with intense meaning, and, when the whole system is almost complete, perfects it by making two creatures in his own image, man and woman, and placing them at the center.

The importance of myth's cosmological function cannot be overstated. Consider the following story: Before British technological culture moved into Australia, the aboriginal people, the Aranda, wandered in small tribes over the land. They had no agriculture. They possessed virtually no arts or crafts. They gathered such food as seeds, grubs, and small animals. What few weapons and tools they had were of stone or wood, for they had no metals. Even the making of pottery, one of mankind's earliest skills, was unknown to these isolated people. They moved through the bleak, sun-blistered wastes, one of the harshest, most stultifying environments in the world. But they did not go mad and die. They endured. In some way, the Aranda were equal to this impossibly demanding environment. They endured because they believed that a wise, beneficent Supreme Ancestor, Numbakula, had made this their particular place and had put here whatever they would need. Their cosmology, in other words, gave them the confidence to survive.

A myth of the Achilpa, a dominant totem-group of the Aranda tribe, tells that after Numbakula had made the important rivers, plants, and animals, he cut a eucalyptus pole and erected it at the center of the cosmos. Anointing the pole with blood, he climbed it into the sky. His important work on the earth completed, he was never seen again. This pole, the "Kauwa-auwa," holds somewhat the same place in Aranda tradition as the Cross holds in Christian tradition. A large model of it is erected for the most sacred ceremonies, and a smaller model, the "Kauaua," for lesser ceremonies. Like a cross, the "Kauaua" is, wherever it may be, the center of the cosmos, the pole that joins the earth to the sky, infusing the world with meaning, transforming it from chaos to cosmos. This pole is the movable cosmic axis, the "path" of the sky-spirits who validate and sanctify the earth.

The importance of cosmological confidence is underlined in a poignant Achilpan legend. Long ago the Ancestors always took the "Kauaua" wherever they went. The stick guided their journeys by bending in the direction they should take. It also indicated to them where to stop for the night. The carrier would plunge it into the earth at the proper spot, and for that night this spot and none other was their home. When the Ancestors lay down to sleep, they lay in a circle around the sacred pole. Once they had to wander for a long time and had grown extremely tired. One evening during this ordeal, they happened to implant the "Kauaua" very deeply. As they were pulling it out the next morning, the old man leading them accidentally broke it off just above the ground. In consternation, they picked up the broken pole and stumbled on, but now aimlessly and without heart. Breaking the pole meant the end of the cosmos, the return of chaos. Finally, they lay down upon the ground together and quietly waited for death.[7]

In a cruel environment, serenity and harmony within a group are essential. Often myth consolidates the wisdom that makes survival possible. It may indeed be argued that all cultures and all individuals that survive do so with the aid of a "Kauaua," that is, a device that shapes and validates their environment, gives them a purpose and direction, suggests constructive patterns of behavior. For instance, a person who chooses to immigrate to the United States because he sees it as a golden land of opportunity for the bold and hardworking is, upon arrival, likely to be especially alert to "opportunities" and likely to call forth his own reserves of boldness and industry. His confidence is by no means based on a lie, but this confidence does help him to complete the truth about the United States. His mythic vision is a co-creator of some facts about the United States.

The immigrant's mythic vision helps to orient him in a foreign place, helps him to make it a "cosmos." To orient oneself means to get one's bearings, to put oneself into the proper relation with one's surroundings, to become familiar with the facts or with one's circumstances. The word "orientation" itself illuminates the concept of cosmos. As the word "Orient" still does, "orientation" once referred to the east. The churches and cathedrals of Europe face east. For many centuries, people in English villages have been buried with heads positioned so that when the dead awaken and arise they will be facing God—who apparently resides in the east. The pervasive idea that east is the direction of godhead goes back to prehistoric times when many agricultural peoples quite reasonably worshiped the sun as the source of light and of life itself.

Whenever a person walks in on the middle of a film or a conversation, or starts a new friendship, opens a book, takes a new job, or moves to a new city, his first need is to orient himself. We all must know, in a general way, what to expect so that we can plan and respond intelligently and feel comfortable. And although all animals work with their senses and brains to orient themselves, human beings do something unique. We live less simply and directly in the world than do other animals. Instead, like the immigrant, we make a version of a world, an interpretation of it, and then we live in that. The degree of comfort and success that we achieve in our lives depends on how well that interpretation suits our circumstances. Myths bend, over time, as circumstances change.

Another way to state this idea is that genetically built into people is a special *organizing* mode of perception. The philosopher Susanne Langer calls this mode *transformational*: We are co-creators of our own perceptions. In the very act of physically perceiving, we interpret; we transform the raw data gathered by our senses into complex symbolic meanings. We literally cannot function and survive without seeing in our world evidence of order and purpose. We take nothing at face value; we systematize, explain, weave a large network of connected meanings. [8]

This network causes absurd behavior—that is, behavior that Robert Frost's horse in "Stopping by Woods on a Snowy Evening" or Jonathan Swift's Houyhnhnms and other sound-minded animals would find absurd. No self-respecting nonhuman animal would take it into his head to endure the discomfort and danger of a polar expedition of blast off to the moon or spend years learning chess, or, as the Mormons did, march cheerfully into a bleak and forbidding desert, fight the wilderness and the natives, endure every sort of defeat, stubbornly insisting upon the preposterous notion that they could turn a hellhole into a garden—and do it.

While the sound-minded, that is, nonhuman, animals toil for their lives, play, or lie in the sun—do whatever is suitable for the moment—only people fret and practise and struggle to achieve distant or abstract goals. We are the only animals who live partly removed from our immediate physical circumstances. This extravagance, this seemingly inappropriate or even lunatic behavior is, of course, the source of our language, art, science, music, religions, philosophies: those things we value most. Aside from such direct physical causes of death as hunger, exposure, old age, or disease, the one circumstance we truly cannot survive is living in a raw, uninterpreted place—in chaos. Each of us either finds a meaning in some traditional religion or philosophy or patches together one of his own, or else, like the Achilpa in the story, he panics, loses the will to live, and, in one way or another perishes.

We need a sense of cosmic order, and our myths are one of its major sources.

ACCEPTANCE OF LIFE'S MYSTERIES

Myths help people accept life's great mysteries with serenity rather than with horror. What am I? Why am I here? Is Someone in charge? If so, what will be asked of me? What will happen if I don't do it? Why do some people who obey suffer, and some that disobey enjoy good fortune?

What happens to us when we die? This book's last section treats these issues in detail.

For now, a sketch of familiar folk beliefs will show how we achieve composure in a world of potentially terrifying mysteries. We are the children of God, put here, first, to serve him by making this world a better place and, second, to improve ourselves so that when we die we may join God and the angels in heaven. That a child whom we love dies is no accident, but the event is not necessarily a punishment either. God may have wanted that child to enjoy bliss now because the child was so special. He is in heaven preparing a place for us. An earthquake or flood that kills thousands of people is no senseless calamity. Not only is it an act of God but the *purposeful* act of a *benevolent* god. Of course the event may be a punishment, for we sinners all deserve punishment, but more likely God needed all those people for some mysterious good purpose. When he causes a person to suffer, say, multiple sclerosis or cancer, the disease could be a blessing in disguise, perhaps a way to help that person improve spiritually so that he may be rewarded with a particularly blissful eternal life. Furthermore, by bearing affliction well, a patient sufferer inspires the rest of us to bear up under our lesser troubles.

This scheme explains reassuringly what we are, why we are here, why we suffer and die, and what will happen after we die. Against apparent evidence to the contrary, it shows that our God is attentive, purposeful, strong, benevolent, and just. In Alexander Pope's words, "God sends not ill; if rightly understood, / Or partial Ill is universal Good."

Other people have offered very different answers to the ultimate questions. For instance, the ancient Sumerians explained that the gods created people not out of love but as a solution to the servant problem. As long as a person served the gods well, both through work and through ritual, he would live. A person's death signified not that the gods wanted him in their realm with them but that they had discarded him as aristocrats might discard an enfeebled or impertinent servant. Since the Sumerians were an unusually vigorous, creative people, we can assume that their harsh answers to the big questions did not devastate them. Apparently we do not need flattering or gentle answers so much as we need believable ones. We need to know where we stand.

SOME FINE DISTINCTIONS

These, then, are the functions of myth: to guide people in their personal lives, in their social roles, in their efforts to make an orderly image of their world, and in their responses to life's great mysteries. But do we really want to make such large claims for all myths? What of some trifling tale told of Theseus or Apollo? If it appears to have no function beyond entertainment, should we insist that it is a myth? And how are we to distinguish between myths, legends, and folk tales, to say nothing of the modern pop fantasies? But why bother? Such distinctions seem easy enough when one is dealing with the familiar stories in the European tradition, for instance, with sublime Prometheus, on the one hand, and apple-kneed Hansel and Gretel, on the other. Few would quarrel with the labels of "myth" for the story of Prometheus, "legend" for Charlemagne, and "folk tale" for Hansel and Gretel. But the distinctions blur when one encounters the traditional stories of the Australians, the Hottentots, or the American Indians; and, in fact, the stories from these groups are more nearly typical of myths throughout the world than are the Greek stories. The Greek stories, in their forms familiar to us, have been systematized and many of them infused with ever more meanings by a series of highly sophisticated poets. The functions of the Greek stories that we know sometimes differ radically from the functions of their earlier versions. Sometimes the newer meanings are trivial or lighthearted, as with the tales of Zeus' philandering and Hera's revenge. (Gone is the awesome fertility god whose power is the source of plenty in field and barn and family.) Sometimes the newer meanings reverberate even more richly than the old. (An Aeschylus or Sophocles may infuse a story with profound "mythic" meanings that it never had before.) The story may continue, through centuries of interpretation from new viewpoints, to evoke fresh insights. These insights then become part of its value. The stories of the original garden, of Oedipus, and of Faust have thus become infinitely precious.

And what about such stories as the "legends" of Alexander and Paul Bunyan, not shaped by tradition at all but simply made up by an Egyptian storyteller on the one hand and a self-promoting lumber company on the other? What about the comic-book and television fantasies that engross our children? Myth, legend, and folk tale are not very precise concepts. One "myth" may have a very different kind and degree of meaning from another. Certainly it is important to know a myth's sources and history before trying to interpret it. But, after all, the reason we confuse ourselves when we try to define "myth" and to distinguish between myth, legend, folk tale, and such modern "mythic" stories as *Star Trek* is that they share a very large element of fantasy. They all come closer to dreams than to realistic narrative, both in shape and content.

They may be disjointed, extravagant, highly imaginative, indifferent to such natural laws as gravity, spatial exclusiveness, and consequentiality; they often express common human preoccupations through vivid but mysterious symbols.

Still, we can make some useful distinctions between types of fantastic narrative. In European folk tales, the point of view is unsophisticated, lowly; in Graeco-Roman myths, the point of view is aristocratic. In the folk tale, simple wish fulfillment is a strong element. The main character's struggle or quest has no broad significance, and the resulting benefit is likely to be merely personal: A bird bestows upon him a magical wishing ring that makes him rich, or she becomes a queen. In classical myths with human heroes, the hero is a noble person whose quest or struggle tends to be highly significant and whose personal reward, if he gets one, is much less important than the boon that he bestows upon a large group of people. As an example, Theseus' winning the maiden Ariadne is far less important than his slaying the Minotaur that has been devouring Athenian youths and maidens. In European folk tales, characters often have generic names, such as Ash Boy (the protagonist of many Scandinavian tales) and Little Red Riding Hood; they are not individualized. In the Greek myths, the characters are well-defined individuals with family histories.

G. S. Kirk, a professor of Greek at Cambridge University and an astute thinker on the subject of myth, cuts through some of the muddle about what myths are and do. Although he emphasizes that his distinctions between myths and other folk stories are only tentative, his distinctions are useful, particularly because he looks beyond the rather atypical European tradition. Myths, says Kirk, are traditional stories with a strong element of "free-ranging and often paradoxical fantasy," characteristically used for purposes that go beyond entertainment—such purposes as "establishing and confirming rights and institutions or exploring and reflecting problems or preoccupations." Their main characters, often superhuman, belong to an era of divine and cultural creation, a distant timeless past. The presence of the supernatural often drastically affects the outcome of the action. If contemporary life intrudes much, as in *The Odyssey*, legend has filtered into the story. Legend is an imaginative treatment of events that are at least believed to be historical. Thus, *The Iliad*, about the Trojan War, is legendary material given a strong mythic aura by the frequent, pointed interventions of the gods.[9]

What is "grave and constant" in human experience is the subject of the richest myths.[10] Much of our satisfaction lies in these stories' broad, open-ended meanings, their way of illuminating a wide range of experience, thus telling us much about ourselves, whoever we are and whatever our circumstances. And as our own experience grows, these myths illuminate that new experience, too. The stories of Gilgamesh, the Fall, Oedipus, and Medea are never "over" for us.

Like poetry and dreams, myths often give the sense of charged compression. Through cryptic symbols, they suggest far more than what they say. These symbols are the universal language of fantasy. When we speak of an aura of the mythical in a film, short story, poem, dream, even an occasional comic strip, we mean that through a release of fantasy it explores emotionally the permanent meaning of life.

Kirk tentatively defines folk tales as traditional tales "not primarily concerned with 'serious' subjects or the reflexion of deep problems and preoccupations." Their main appeal lies in their narrative interest, the ingenious ways in which they answer "And then what happened?" Although witches, ogres, magical objects, and other supernatural elements may appear, the main character, Kirk observes, is human, often of humble origin, and achieves strictly human purposes. Although recurrent social dilemmas, especially those concerning family life, are frequent, they are never, as in myth, profoundly treated. Noting that these tales abound with the use of trickery and ingenuity, Kirk thinks that perhaps the use of ingenuity is the "most striking and consistent characteristic of folk tales" throughout the world. Much of the audience's satisfaction lies in the "neatness and finality with which an awkward situation is resolved or an enemy confounded." That quality contrasts utterly with the open-ended quality characteristic of myths; but many Greek myths contain large elements of the folk tale and, in other contexts, would be termed folk tales.[11]

A cluster of folk tales often springs up around a deeply serious myth. The solemn liturgical dramas of the medieval Church eventually became so freighted with popular additions of coarse humor that the Church dissociated itself from them. Given free rein, the folk imagination then contrived ever more elaborately absurd behavior for such favorite characters as the drunken Noah, his nagging wife, and the ranting Herod. A similar group of popular stories grew out of the solemn Osirian cult in ancient Egypt. Some of these tales reduced the profoundly significant battle between Osiris' son and Set to a series of Looney Tune tricks played on each other. Some Greek stories present Theseus and Heracles behaving like a couple of sophomoric fraternity pals. European tales fondly tell of plain folks who outwit the Devil, but this is not that fearsome archangel who rose in pride against the High God—not that Satan whose reeling fall from heaven cast batlike shadows over the shining planets. This is the village cheat or the tyrannical husband given his comeuppance by a shrewd merchant or a snappy young wife.

And yet some of the same symbols that give myths and legends their peculiar power appear also in folk tales and widely shared contemporary fantasies. The next chapter takes up these charged symbols.

I

THE SYMBOLIC LANGUAGE
OF MYTHS

1

Where We Get Universal Symbols

The dark forest, the giant, the strange visitor, the magic seed, the abandoned child, the transformation, the collapse of order, the monster, the death-struggle between parent and child, alien heights and alien water, unusual sexual acts, burial and other entrapments—these are a few of the themes familiar to people who read the myths and folk tales of any culture, and to people who monitor their own dreams and fantasies.

The human imagination speaks a language whose peculiar symbols bear little apparent relation to the everyday world. Yet the same symbols continue to arise everywhere as if spontaneously, bubbles out of the deep, to haunt us with their strange power.

SOME EXAMPLES

1. "This is my neighborhood, but nothing looks quite right. Finding a phone booth, I dial my parents' number several times but get no answer. After a long search, I find my parents' house, but inside everything is different from what it's supposed to be. The decor is old-fashioned. Although my mother and father are nowhere to be seen, an old man and woman sit by the fireplace. The way they smile makes me uncomfortable." [Abandonment, transformation, collapse of order, strange visitors.]

—A *dream* [1]

2. After some time, the brothers found a way to kill the fish and struggle out of its belly. They swam up to the surface of the lake and walked home. But there they found weeds and vines grown high all around the dwelling. Their father had vanished.[2] [Monster, water, entrapment, abandonment, collapse of order.]

—A Wichata myth

3. "I was driving alone through a murky forest, my tires bumping over huge tree roots. Large limbs kept looming in front of me and scratching the paint off my car." [Forest.]

—A dream

4. Yellow Corn Girl would not marry any of the boys in her own pueblo or the neighboring ones, even though they all wanted her. One day she went out into the pine forest to gather pine nuts. A boy appeared whom she had never seen before. He told her that he would throw a pine nut into her mouth, and, if she did not swallow it, it would make many more. She caught the pine nut in her mouth and, when she got home, she threw it into a storeroom. A little later the entire room was full of nuts.

After a while she had a baby. The men in the pueblo wanted to know its father. They took the baby to the kiva [the circular temple of Southwestern Indians] and put it in the middle of the floor. Each man held up a flower in his hand. Whosoever flower the baby reached for would identify the father.

But the baby did not reach for any flower. The sun came in through a little hole in the roof, and the baby sat in the ray of light, paying no attention to any of the flowers.

The men began to be mean to Yellow Corn Girl and say that she must throw the baby into the lake. She tried to obey, but every time found that she could not. She would sit down and suckle the baby instead. Finally, knowing that she must obey, she went to the lake and, without looking, threw her baby in.

The Sun caught the baby.

Some time later, Yellow Corn Girl's child, now a well-grown boy, appeared at the lake and told her that he was the Sun's child. This news made her very happy.

Later when the boy came to the pueblo with his mother during the ceremonial dance, the other girls said that he did not belong there. Then he said that, because the people had made Yellow Corn Girl throw her baby into the lake, it was clear that they did not want many people here. They might all die, he added. Then he took his mother to live with the Sun, and the rest of the people in the pueblo did die. [Forest, special seed, abandonment, water, strange visitor.]

—A Southwestern American Indian myth

[In another version of the story, Yellow Corn Girl conceives the baby when grinding corn in front of a little window. Old Man Sun streams in through the window, "and from him she got a baby."][3]

5. "I was upstairs in my room. Mom and Dad were outside by the pool, arguing. As I put down my book and got up to go get something to eat, I glanced down at the pool. There was my mom swimming laps, unaware of a dark thing swirling madly in the deep end. It was going to kill her, and my dad either had conveniently departed or had turned into the monster. I ran out frantically to warn her. At first she didn't get the message. When she did, she rushed to the steps at the shallow end. The thing, a snakelike creature but with spiky hairs, thrashed toward her. Just as she reached the top step it grabbed her. I jumped into the pool to try to save her." [Water, transformation, monster, death-struggle between parent and child.]

—A dream

6. Mamuru's enemies came at him from all sides. He jumped around so much, dodging their spears, that his motion gradually made a depression in the ground. Finally it got so deep that only his head showed. Just as his head disappeared into the earth, one of his enemies speared him right through the earth from behind.[4] [Burial, entrapment.]

—An Australian myth

7. Ages ago, a chief and his wife lived with their people on the tip of the island. They had only one child, a son, and because he was their only son, they loved him above all other things and worried over him. But when he was a well-grown youth, he became very sick, and they could do nothing. Their son died.

After removing and burning his intestines according to custom, they laid him upon his bed in the loft of their dwelling and mourned him for a long time.

One morning when the chief's wife climbed the ladder to wail over her son, she found not her son's body lying there but a youth bright as fire. She called out to her husband that their son had come back to life. After much rejoicing, the shining youth told everyone that heaven had sent him down to comfort the chief, the mother, and the whole tribe.

For a long time, despite coaxing, the shining youth ate almost nothing. The chief's wife worried and worried. One morning when she was away from the dwelling, the chieftain happened to climb up the ladder into the loft, and there he found the corpse of his son.[5] [Strange visitor, transformation.]

—A Northwestern American Indian myth

8. "I was standing in front of our apartment, waiting for my father. He drove up and started to open the car door for me. But just then, a rhino bigger than the whole building sprouted out of the ground and swept me up on his horn. He started dangling me high above the ground by my stretchy sweater and shaking me around. I could see my father way down below, just standing there staring in a kind of detached amazement. Then he got into the car and drove away." [Monster, alarming height, collapse of order, abandonment.]

—A dream

9. Ilya of Murom, after sitting in a helpless stupor for thirty-three years, crippled in arms, legs, and mind, was aroused by Christ himself and two apostles. As begging holy men, they insisted first that he fetch them a drink of water. Ilya was amazed to find that he could perform the task. Then they said that he must drink the bowlful himself. After complying, he felt superhuman strength surge through his body. The strangers told him that he was now one of the strongest men in the world and would be a great fighter against pagans.

Shortly afterwards, he went walking in the green woods. There he saw a huge white linen pavilion. Soon the giant Svyatogor came riding in the distance on his great horse. Ilya climbed a tree to be out of sight and to get a good view. Svyatogor carried his comely giant-wife along

with him in a crystal box. Stopping at the pavilion, he unlocked the box
so that she could jump out and prepare a meal.

As soon as the giant had fallen asleep, his wife, having spied Ilya in
the tree, forced him to come down and dally with her. When the giant
began to wake up, she quickly hid Ilya in the giant's own pocket. [A
reader's half-conscious sexual fantasies might suggest simply leaving him
in *her* "pocket." One even surmises that a similar flash of fantasy in the
narrator's mind was responsible for the comically inappropriate hiding
place that the lady did choose.]

But soon enough, putting his hand in his pocket, Svyatogor understood all that his wife had been up to and, without much ado, he
chopped off her head.

Then the two men rode off toward the mountains, the older and
much larger one teaching the younger his skills as they went along.
Svyatogor explained that because the damp Russian soil could no longer
hold his enormous weight and strength, he now had to spend most of his
time on the rocks of the high Holy Mountains.

As they rode up into the deserted passes where the wind blows, they
came upon a huge iron coffin lying beside the way. As if joking, the
giant suggested that Ilya lie down in it to see if it fit. Ilya complied, but
got out quickly. [Despite the narrative blandness, one imagines how uneasy Ilya must be, all this time.]

Then, laying himself down in the coffin, Svyatogor jokingly invited
Ilya to close it. Ilya refused, so Svyatogor closed the lid upon himself.

To Svyatogor's astonishment, when he was ready to end the joke the
coffin would not open. For the first time, he found that his enormous
strength was of no use. Beginning to suffocate, he called out to Ilya for
help.

Ilya tried, but his best efforts could not open the lid. Now frantic,
Svyatogor instructed Ilya to lean down to the crack between the lid and
the box and draw into himself Svyatogor's own tremendous strength. Ilya
did so and, feeling his own strength tripled, he hoisted Svyatogor's huge
sword and brought it down so hard on the iron coffin that blue sparks
flew. But the coffin would not open. The heroes tried a second time,
Svyatogor again forcing his own strength into Ilya's body through the
crack, expending his superhuman life-breath in the frantic hope for more
life. Ilya's already tripled strength tripled once more, but the lid would
not yield.

The third time, Svyatogor cried out, "Young brother, I am dying!

Bend down again, and I shall breathe into you all my great heroic strength." But at this point, Ilya replied, "My present strength suffices me. Had I more power, the earth could not carry me."

Faintly came the reply: "You do well not to heed my last command, younger brother, for I should have breathed into you the spirit of Death, and you would have fallen dead beside me. Take my sword, and good luck to you. But tie my horse to this coffin to die with me. He is mine, and I want no one else to ride him." [6] [Strange visitors, transformation, forest, height, giant, unusual sexual act, entrapment and burial, death-struggle between father-substitute and son.]

—*A Russian legend*

[Here, writ small, is the inevitable struggle between the generations, with its inevitable outcome. The older man has shared and lost all to the younger one—wife, fighting skills, strength—and the usurper is coolly guiltless, satisfied, detached, ready to begin his own time of power.]

10. Cactus Flower Girl would not marry. Her father, needing help with the work, kept urging her to marry, but she would not even leave the dwelling. One day, however, when her hearth-fire went out, she went to one of the other dwellings to find some live coals with which to restore it, and there, in the otherwise deserted place, she found an old man lying down. She lay down beside him and played with him. But the old man's wife returned, and berated the girl. When the woman told Cactus Flower Girl's parents what their daughter had done, they turned her out, saying she was no longer their daughter.

No one would have anything to do with her. She thought she would die. Then a tiny voice from a spider sitting upon her shoulder said, "I am your Spider Grandmother, and I shall protect you."

They came, after a while, to a big lake with two poles rising from the center. As Cactus Flower Girl watched them grow, she realized that they were a kiva ladder. [Kivas are often built partly or wholly underground.] A woman came up the ladder. "I have been expecting you for a long time," she said. Calling herself the girl's mother, she was very eager that Cactus Flower Girl enter the lake. When the woman threw a cornmeal ball from the lake's center to the shore, a dry path appeared, just long enough for Cactus Flower Girl to cross to the ladder. Then the water closed over the path.

Down inside the chamber, a large number of people greeted Cactus Flower Girl, telling her they were her new family. Although they all sounded very friendly, the tests through which they presently put her would have killed her without her Spider Grandmother's help. She was asked to smoke a certain long pipe and to inhale. Luckily, the girl's grandfather, an inconspicuous gopher that had been present the whole time, quickly dug a small tunnel under her so that the smoke could pass through her body and out the tunnel. No one could understand how a human girl could smoke this pipe and live. Next, the girl was given a large quantity of "corn" to grind. Actually it was ice and not grindable at all. But Spider Grandmother melted it, and the strange family was satisfied. Then, with a great display of hospitality, the family showed Cactus Flower Girl to her bed.

It was nothing but a solid block of ice. Cactus Flower Girl knew that if she lay on that, she would be dead and frozen solid by morning. Of course she was frightened, but again Spider Grandmother protected her by providing a blanket of soft turkey down. Cactus Flower Girl slept warmly and well.

Only when she awoke in the morning did she see that the block of ice had been placed on the very edge of a cliff and that down below lay many bones of girls. As she stared at them, she heard someone say off-handedly, "She must be dead by now. I guess I had better go and throw her away." [7] [Unusual sexual act, abandonment, water, entrapment, death-struggle between parent-substitutes and daughter, alarming height.]

—*A Southwestern American Indian myth*

THE DIFFUSION OF SYMBOLS

A person steeped in the folk tales of northwestern Europe will find uncannily similar plot-sequences in ancient stories from India, Arabia, and Persia, as well as the same images of magical fruits, enchanted gardens, and spirits of the dead embodied in birds.

About a century ago, scholars began to gather and study traditional stories from all over the world. Anthropologists were much struck by the recurrence of themes and symbols in these stories. The pioneers in psychiatry became interested when they observed that these same themes and symbols appear in dreams. All wondered why.

One proposed answer was that plot-patterns and symbols from one culture are often borrowed by its neighbors. Some anthropologists held that the sharing of customs, tools, symbols, and so on, among cultures could usually be explained as having diffused from a few highly inventive "culture centers." Other anthropologists, asserting the similarity of the human mind in all times and places, held that shared elements could usually be explained as having been independently invented. Most scholars today agree that neither view alone makes sense, that *both* diffusion and independent invention occur.

Diffusion does explain the widespread occurrence of many symbols and plot-patterns in traditional stories. For instance, it explains some of the similarities in European and Oriental folk tales. Many familiar tales came into Europe during the Crusades of the twelfth and thirteenth centuries, the first really massive encounter of Europeans with the Islamic world. Many of the stories, originating in India, entered Europe as Latin translations of Hebrew and Arabic tales. The other great source of familiar tales was Ireland. Its gloriously imaginative fairy tales, with their enchanted princesses, solitary castles in deep forests, and lurking dragons, entered the mainstream of European lore in the late Middle Ages. At the same time, the Arthurian romances, also of Celtic origin, were flowering in France, England, and Germany. They spread many of the same themes as did the Irish fairy tales.[8]

But diffusion has more general implications. Rarely does a brilliant culture develop in geographical isolation. Most great cultures of the ancient world were trading centers that shaped the ideas and technology of diverse peoples into inspired new patterns. These centers then seeded their neighbors with these patterns—and with their best stories. Readers are sometimes perplexed to find that such biblical symbols as the garden, the fountain from which the four great rivers flow, the tree of life, the snake that deprives humankind of eternal life, and the great flood do not appear exclusively in the Bible but also in Mesopotamian poetry. The fact is that the first great civilization, even before that of Egypt, arose in Mesopotamia, and the poetry of this region had dealt with these themes for well over a thousand years before the earliest parts of the Bible were written down, about 850 B.C. The symbols that we know through the Book of Genesis were widely used in the Middle East by 2000 B.C. What makes Genesis special is not the originality of its symbols but the profound wisdom and pathos with which it infuses symbols widely known when it was written.

That the motif of a great flood should appear in Greek myth is not so mysterious, even though the idea is geographically alien to Greece. In the river-valley cultures of Egypt and Mesopotamia, the motif was founded upon experience. But so compelling is the notion of a great flood that it may have detached itself from its origins and diffused widely. The Mycenaean Greeks (ca. 1600–1100 B.C.) had strong commercial ties with the Canaanites and Hittites, and through these peoples learned much of Mesopotamian beliefs, rituals, and literature. Chapters 2 and 3, however, suggest why even people dwelling in dry, rocky lands may invent stories of a great flood.

The issue of diffusion is complicated by the fact that seemingly primitive, isolated mythic traditions often derive partly from some other, more highly developed, tradition. Plot-patterns that we know from the medieval Christian or classical tradition may pop up in the legends, even religious rites, of places as remote as Samoa or the Venezuelan Orinoco Basin.

Consider a Warao Indian story recorded in the Orinoco Delta between 1932 and 1942, when, according to Johannes Wilbert, an authority on the Warao, European influence had only begun. Hoasoro was a crippled water carrier and as poor as a man could be. One day while he was resting on his water barrel, a handsome young man dressed all in gold rode up on a white horse. He told Hoasoro to stand up. Hoasoro said that, with his crippled legs, that would not be easy. The stranger dismounted, touched Hoasoro with his hand, and commanded him to walk. Hoasoro found that he could. The stranger was Ka-Nobo, the Old One, who lives in *heobe* (heaven) and sometimes comes down to earth looking like a Warao. Ka-Nobo told Hoasoro that any time he wanted to walk or get water, if he would just ask, it would happen. Very humbly Hoasoro said he would, and Ka-Nobo galloped back to heobe.

So here in a remote South American swamp is a story echoing the Russian one about Christ, in disguise, visiting the crippled Ilya, begging a cup of water, and making the humble man strong and well. Reading on in the Warao story, one comes to a part similar to the North American story about the village men encircling Yellow Corn Girl's baby in a ritual to determine the baby's father. In the Warao story, the girl with the baby is the chief's daughter. The chief commands that the disgraced girl and Hoasoro, the supposed father, be put in a large box. The chief himself nails the lid shut and has it hoisted onto a passing schooner from which it is to be dumped into the sea. This part echoes the ancient Greek story of how Danaë's father put her and her infant son Perseus into a chest and had it thrown into the sea.

This Warao story was recorded by a Capuchin missionary from Spain. Wilbert notes that the missionary was a careful recorder, but that many of the stories he recorded were told by mission Indians, a fact "clearly reflected in the material."[9] And Elsie Clews Parson, who recorded Yellow Corn Girl's story, notes that the part about seeing which flower the baby would reach for is a Spanish element, not a native one. Diffusion surely accounts for some widespread plot-patterns. Later chapters suggest why certain patterns are appealing enough to borrow.

The theories of Freud and Jung on the "unconscious" kindled other efforts to account for some seemingly universal human thought-processes by exploring possible innate patterns of mind shared by people in all times and places. The anthropologist Claude Lévi-Strauss and others have posited basic "structures" in the mind. The linguist Noam Chomsky believes that an innate grammar underlies the human ability to learn and use language. The psychologist Jean Piaget has shown certain perceptual patterns evolving in the minds of very small children as they conceptualize their world with greater and greater accuracy. Piaget's work offers strong evidence that these patterns—duality, classification, causal connections, and so on—are nonarbitrary, noncultural, but *inevitable* in the child's progressive organization of experience. Because the present discussion concerns how we invent symbols, Carl Jung's theories on patterns of mind are of great interest to us.

"ARCHETYPES"

Carl Jung, one of the great pioneers of psychiatry, focused attention on the fact that the symbol-forming and myth-making tendency is common to all people. He asserted that the same cluster of symbols arise spontaneously in the myths of Egyptians, Greeks, Chinese, Peruvians, and modern Americans, as well as in the dreams of individuals of any time and place. Dreams, he said, may be thought of as individuals' myths.

The psychiatrist Erich Fromm also noted the similarity between myths and dreams. Their symbols, he wrote, are a kind of universal language "in which inner experiences, feelings and thoughts are expressed as if they were sensory experiences, events in the outer world."[10] Another psychiatrist, Rollo May, agreed: "People communicate their most meaningful experience in symbols." Myths and, to some degree, dreams express the quintessence of our experience through concrete, compressed symbols. [11]

For instance, a sense of freedom, with its attendant exhilarations and dangers, is often spontaneously represented as flying; frustration or helplessness, as trying to swim in some such stuff as mud or gelatin; the fear of abandonment, as one's parent disappearing while one struggles with a monster. Jung called these powerful, widespread images "archetypal images" or simply "archetypes." Some of his own examples are the visions of paradise and hades; of woman as virgin, mother, temptress, and destroyer; of the formidable father with whom one must come to terms or overthrow by trick or luck; of a "divine child" (Christ-child, Tom Thumb, dwarf, elf), an inexplicable child separate from, transcending, his human origins; of the unacknowledged, unexplored part of oneself, as one's shadow, double, or daemon; and of ritual initiations as dying and being reborn. Archetypes, Jung wrote, are not specific symbols such as shadow, temptress, or elf but, rather, the more general symbols that lie behind them.

Jung asserted that archetypes are universally the same and that some archetypes are independent both of all tradition and of the individual's own past experience. Therefore, he reasoned, we must assume as their source a genetically inherited cluster of mental patterns arising from some repository in ourselves that he called the "collective unconscious" of the human race. [12]

Without underrating Jung's enormous contribution to the understanding of myth, psychology, art, and literature, one may say that this particular notion was accepted far too uncritically by many students of myth and literature, resulting in the publication of much nonsense. Although few psychologists still subscribe to Jung's theory of archetypes in its original form, scholars of art, literature, and other fields that draw upon the imagination have found Jung's general idea very valuable. The word "archetype" has come to mean a powerful image, symbol, plot-pattern, or character type that persists in myths, religion, folk tales, dreams, and art throughout the world. When individuals of any culture encounter a particular archetype, it leaps up at them as if from out of their own buried selves.

But where do these universal symbols, charged with such power, come from? If cultural diffusion does not adequately account for the worldwide use of certain symbols and we are not persuaded that they arise from a racial memory or a collective unconscious, how are we to account for their existence?

For instance, what about the American Indian story of Yellow Corn Girl impregnated by a ray of sunlight? It seems to echo the Greek story of Zeus visiting Danaë in a shaft of light or a shower of gold. The Spanish had been in the American West for a long time when anthropologists started collecting Indian stories; the Spanish had certainly passed on some of their own favorites, and they surely knew Danaë's story. Thus, cultural diffusion may account for the similarity. But may we not also assume that the Indians of New Mexico understood the generative powers of the sun as well as the Greeks did?

When we encounter the Russian giant Svyatogor trapped in a coffin designed especially for him, we may reflect that the same fate overtook Osiris in an Egyptian myth at least five thousand years old. Here, cultural diffusion would be a perverse explanation. In the natural course of life, fantasies about being tricked into entering boxes or cages or other traps, are likely to occur to individuals anywhere that know of such objects. Folk stories from Ireland and France to Africa, India, and China tell of such trickery. Because a coffin is the ultimate box, fantasies about it are especially likely.

Erich Fromm stated the view of archetypes widely held today: "There is no need to speak of a racial inheritance in order to explain the universal character of symbols. Every human being who shares the essential features of bodily and mental equipment with the rest of mankind is capable of speaking and understanding the symbolic language that is based upon these common properties."[13] Put simply, many of our most powerful symbols arise out of nearly universal human experiences. For instance, we are all born small and helpless into a world of giants. Since most of us are born into a family, our earliest experience includes a mother-goddess and father-god. We all know hunger, thirst, heat, cold, darkness, sleep. We observe that falling feels peculiar and that landing hurts. We see that some creatures can fly and some can stay under water indefinitely. We see that babies come from bellies, dogs have a large number of sharp teeth, the sun goes away and comes back.

But part of the shared "bodily and mental equipment" that Fromm mentions is the human habit of reasoning by analogy. This propensity to see one thing as like another goes a long way toward explaining why different minds independently invent so many of the same symbols. We are particularly prone to help ourselves comprehend abstract concepts, including the deepest and most unsettling of life's mysteries, by drawing analogies between them and familiar things. For instance, when Einstein described the universe as limited but without boundaries, the seeming contradiction baffled some of us until clearer minds suggested imagining the universe as a hollow doughnut with an ant walking around inside it: Although his journey would be limited to an enclosed space, the ant would never meet a boundary.

Other chapters deal in detail with many of the symbols and motifs mentioned here. But to show how each individual, locked within the labyrinth of his own mind, discovers there so many of the same powerful symbols that others find in their minds, we might trace some ways in which we think about two clusters of our experience: life's sources and conclusions. These phenomena, though a sure part of every life and of urgent concern to us all, remain essentially mysterious. We express that mystery in vivid, compressed symbols.

2

Symbolizing the Sources of Life

In the beginning the earth opened in the middle of Perigundi Lake, and from it emerged one [clan totem] after another. They lay in the sunshine until they were strong. Then they arose as men, and scattered across the country.

An Australian myth [1]

That life makes more life is easily observed. But where did life come from, or what stirred matter into life the first time? What can be done to strengthen life? What makes it grow and multiply? How can it be restored after it has begun to wane? An essential mystery remains. People have come to terms with this mystery through a profusion of symbols. Examining some of them can suggest how separate minds happen to invent so many of the same symbols.

Again and again, this pattern emerges: Our visions move from the small, familiar, and concrete to the cosmic; they move by the process of analogy; and they usually combine personal observation with culturally transmitted ideas. For instance, the Sumerians surmised that the living earth was engendered by a mingling of sweet and salt waters; the first gods by a third watery element, probably clouds. These speculations

are obviously based upon observation of the way in which new land is actually formed in Mesopotamia. Mesopotamia is an alluvial country. It has been built through thousands of years by silt which has been brought down by the two great rivers, the Euphrates and the Tigris, and has been deposited at their mouths. This process still goes on; and day by day, year by year, the country slowly grows, extending farther out into the Persian Gulf. It is this scene—where the sweet waters of the rivers meet and blend with the salt waters of the sea, while cloud banks hang low over the waters—which has been projected back into the beginning of time. Here still is the primeval watery chaos . . . and here the silt—represented by the first of the gods, Lahmu and Lahamu—separates from the water, becomes noticeable, is deposited.[2]

LIFE FROM WATER

One answer often given to the mystery of life's beginning is water. Anybody who has ever seen the shimmering grass come up after a rain, planted seeds, found water in a parched place by searching for a band of green winding down a ridge, or kept a geranium knows the power of water. In a less scientific age than ours, one might well have believed that water was magical or a blessed gift from the gods who kept the world alive. That would be particularly so if, as in the Nile valley, the cause of the sudden, regular, life-giving flood remained unknown or, as in Greece, springs gushed gratuitously from hard limestone.

In the beginning, according to the cosmogonies (creation stories) of many cultures, water covered the whole earth. Life sprang directly or indirectly from that water. In these stories, an emergence from water signifies the coming of land, light, life, and consciousness. A single culture sometimes envisions creation in several ways, each vision emphasizing one of these elements. Still, most cosmogonies start with water.

In the great river-valley civilizations from which so many of our richest symbols arose, one could not avoid seeing that water makes life. Each year the land would dry up and die. Then the river would flood, and, from all the places it had touched, grass would spring. Similarly, in places that get only periodic rains, the effect of water is dramatically clear. In the American Southwest, a downpour turns the desert into a garden.

Sometimes water even appears to generate animal life. Along the Nile, for instance, tiny frogs used to hatch so quickly after the flood receded that the water and earth themselves seemed to have spawned them. The same was true of insects. In other climates, countless earthworms appear after a heavy rain. Although in fact the earthworms have come from underground to avoid drowning, they seem to have fallen with the rain.

The springs, pools, wells, and fountains that appear so often in myths are not intended as realistic parts of the landscape. They are symbols from the mysterious source of life itself, but their origins *as symbols* are not mysterious. The ancient well or fountain was a stone cylinder built around a spring to protect the water and ease the task of drawing it out. In the most literal, dramatic way, such a spring meant life, which gathered and flourished around it. If the spring brought forth much water, it became the source and center of a village, the whole life of the small cosmos radiating from the spring. For instance, Jericho, the oldest known town in the world, which flourished about 8000 B.C., grew around a spring. Much later, the city of Mecca gathered around the holy spring of Zamzam. According to Arab tradition, when the biblical Hagar and her infant son Ishmael had been cast out and were about to perish in the desert, an angel saved them for a distinguished fate by showing them this spring.

In some parts of the ancient world, people made pilgrimages to springs believed to be sacred. To see fresh, cool water gushing from a rocky cliff or mountainside is an impressive experience. At Delphi, a sacred spring called Castalia flows from the reddish cliff above the town. According to ancient mythic tradition, before the Hellenic-speaking people arrived on the Aegean peninsula and placed the oracle of their sky-god there, Delphi was the site of Mother Earth's oracle. Lending credence to the tradition, the remains of a cavern stand in the steep wall of the red gorge, the route to the place polished by the hands and feet of many agile climbers. Before the cavern's roof collapsed, tradition asserts, eerie noises and vapors arose from this "mouth" of Mother Earth. Castalia's water seems a gift from no ordinary source.

In Sweden, a sacred spring flowed beside the great temple at Uppsala, and in the pre-Christian image of the cosmos, a sacred well watered the cosmic tree.

Whatever is linked symbolically with the source of life is often linked with sexuality and procreation. In stories from the Middle East, China, India, and medieval Europe, people destined for marriage chance to meet at a well. Of course, the public well was for centuries the place where a respectable girl was most likely to encounter a stranger, but in myths the well is far more than a stage prop. The Greeks consciously associated springs, as sources of life, with marriage. The Greek word *nymphē* means both "young bride" and "nymph," in the familiar sense of "lower goddess." Nymphs, the deities residing in springs, were the goddesses of marriage, and at wedding ceremonies brides were sprinkled with spring water. In Rome, the protective structures around springs eventually became large buildings, and marriages took place in these temples.

In the folk tale "The Frog Prince," the frog emerges from a well to introduce the princess to sexuality, that is, to the mystery of creating life. In medieval versions of the tale, the princess is required not only to let the frog eat from her plate and sleep in her bed but to let him have sexual intercourse with her. In related Celtic stories, the disgusting creature by the well or pool is an ancient, evil-smelling hag. Several young men treat her rudely. When at last a compassionate youth speaks kindly to her and fetches her a drink of water, she turns into a beautiful young princess who marries him. The story of Sleeping Beauty opens with the queen bathing in a pool and fervently wishing for a child. A frog hops out of the water to promise that she will have a child within a year.

In the creation myth of the Tsimshian Indians of the Northwest Pacific coast, Raven, the Tsimshian culture-hero, flies to heaven to steal light for the earth. He lies low by a spring until the daughter of the chief of heaven approaches for a drink. Then he transforms himself into a cedar leaf and floats upon the water. As the princess drinks, she swallows the leaf and becomes pregnant. The infant will be Raven in his human form. (The obvious symbolic connection here between the spring and procreation is only one small aspect of Raven's life-enhancing power. Like Moses "found upon the water" and raised within the house of the chief whom he will subvert, Raven is reminiscent also of the incarnated infant Christ and of Prometheus. He will bring both light and life-sustaining fish to the earth.) The mythic savior of the Tlinket Indians— related to the Tsimshians—is conceived when a woman, barren till then, swallows a pebble with sea water.

In Polynesian myth, the god Eel impregnates a virgin when she swims in his pool. In our own culture, girls sometimes hope that mothers will believe one can become pregnant from swimming in a public swimming pool.

People troubled by sterility, other sexual problems, and the infirmities of age have from time immemorial sought cures by drinking spring water. The distributors of the bottled mineral waters much consumed in Europe claim for them an imposing array of medical benefits, as do owners of health spas. One recalls the Fountain of Youth sought by Ponce de Leon, among others, and the waters of the Styx into which Achilles' mother dips her son to render him invulnerable.

Like the later, more familiar Venus, born of the ocean foam, the Mesopotamian fertility goddess Ishtar was associated with water. She bathed in the fountain in Dilmun, the gods' sacred garden. Once when she perished, the goddess of the underworld washed her with the waters of life to revive her.

Considering how often myths point to water as a vitalizing agent, one begins to understand why fish so often symbolize life and fertility. These eerie, jewel-like creatures arise directly from the source of life. Moving with careless grace through a medium alien to people, they seem to possess peculiar knowledge or powers. Thus, in folklore one finds wishing rings or cryptic messages in their bellies, messages such as we now seek in analyzing rocks from Mars and radio waves from outer space. Furthermore, as the hungry Pilgrims of the Plymouth colony soon observed, fish are indeed concentrated sources of life or bringers of fertility: With good results, the Indians regularly buried small fish in the fields before planting seed. Fish fertilizers are widely used today. A diet high in fish has long been supposed to promote human fertility.

Ironically, because springs and wells are concentrated sources of the life-force in myths, they are represented as very dangerous places. Ancient Mediterranean peoples saw the earth as a mound that had arisen from the original watery chaos or as a disc floating upon this water. (The Sumerian cosmos was born from a primeval sea. Then the god of sweet waters had to cast a spell upon those waters to keep them from rising up to overwhelm the earth.) A well plunged all the way to this moiling source of life as if a plug had been cut out of the solid earth. Who knew what forms of brutal, untamed energy might lurk in those depths?

In myths, as one peers into the alien, hypnotic waters, one might either fall in and be drowned, be lured in by a water spirit, or be snatched by a monster risen from the deep. The Loch Ness monster is a modern version of a widespread ancient notion that in deep bodies of water lurk mysterious beasts older than the world itself and likely to seize the unwary. The swimming-pool monster of Example 5 (p. 21) near the beginning of Chapter 1 echoes the idea.

But few of the modern small children frightened of draining bathtubs and flushing toilets can be acquainted with the ancient image of the world as a disc upon monster-infested waters. Nor are they likely, at that age, even to have encountered TV's monsters of the deep. Has some "racial" memory of water symbols implanted their fear in them? Adults who suppose so might try to imagine themselves as very young and small and still a bit confused about relative sizes and distances. Then they might feel that tub water sucking at them, pulling them toward some echoing, mysterious chamber beneath the floor, and they might watch the toilet water lunge and listen to it roar. Who is to say whether the water is feeling friendly that day and, if it is not, whether the mother-goddess's power can match the water's power? In short, although small children have not yet learned the symbols that express adults' complex feelings about water, they certainly have observed some of its behavior that gives rise to those symbols. They know that it is an enigma, that though it can be sumptuous and caressing, it sometimes leaps, snorts, pushes people about, even chokes them. And children create symbols quite as spontaneously as do adults.

The dragon symbolizes life-giving powers through the agency of water. The symbol is common to Babylonia, Assyria, India, China, Japan, and America. Some anthropologists think it originated in Sumeria, or possibly Egypt, and spread to these other cultures. An all-powerful deity, it controls every form of water. The Oriental dragon is associated with thunder, lightning, sinewy rivers, raging floods, and new life. Although it manifests itself in energetic, sometimes destructive ways, it is a beneficent power. Confusingly, in Western myth and legend, dragons usually embody evil, for they are associated with the serpent and Satan. But in Greek myth, a dragon guards the apples of immortality, the Golden Apples in the Garden of the Hesperides; and in widely dispersed myths, dragons and other such monsters guard treasure. (See the discussion of monsters as guardians in Chapter 8.)

That water promotes life helps account for its use in religious rites marking beginnings. Birth itself is an emergence from "water," that is, from the amniotic fluid protecting the child in the womb. According to Zuni Indian tradition, the first people emerged from the dark inner earth into the upper world through a spring or lake whose waters parted for them. In initiation ceremonies, water symbolizes rebirth or renewal and purification. To purify is to make fresh, to wash away blame and blight, to restore a thing to its original state of perfection. Thus, symbolic purification is close to the ideas of birth and regeneration. In early Egyptian myth, the hero Horus visits his father Osiris in the underworld with the news that the evil Set has been vanquished; then Horus arises from the waters of the underworld to reign as his father did, in justice. Horus's descent into the waters is both a symbolic purification and a prelude to a rebirth, for the Egyptians often viewed Horus as the reincarnated Osiris.

In the religions of ancient Greece and Rome, people purified themselves with holy water upon entering the temple. The custom survives in the Roman Catholic and Moslem faiths. The Christian baptism, whether by total immersion or by sprinkling water on the forehead, initiates into life the person being baptized and washes away his sins, opening to him the possibility of eternal life. Medieval baptismal fonts were meant to symbolize the fountain of life in paradise, "transmitting the waters of God's grace to earth."[3] According to medieval and Catholic doctrine, even newborn babies are tainted with the Original Sin of Adam and Eve and are thus, before baptism, ineligible for heaven. In the words of Christ, "Except that a man be born of water and of the Spirit, he cannot enter into the kingdom of God" (John 3:5). Although in Jesus' day, Jews had long used water in rites of purification, the practice of baptism, then as now, sometimes stressed a person's embracement of a religious heritage or his formal dedication to a holy purpose.

Each year the king of Saudi Arabia ritually washes the Ka'ba, the sacred black stone in the Moslem holy city of Mecca. In modern Japan, general election campaigns usually begin at a Shinto shrine, where the candidates ritually wash their hands in holy water.

In India, the Hindu Jar Festival (Kumbh Mela) links water with beginnings, purification, the underworld, and energy—including demonic energy. Although Hindus bathe in the Ganges at any time to wash away their sins, the spiritual potency of its waters is considered to be greatest every twelve years, especially where the Ganges and another river, the Yamuna, converge. According to an ancient Hindu legend, the Ganges also converges there with an underground river of tremendous sacred power. Once, long ago, the gods lost their strength through a curse. To get it back, they had to enlist the aid of their more energetic enemies, the demons, in making a life-giving nectar. In the gods' struggle with the demons over the jar of nectar, a bit of the liquid spilled there. It returns every twelve years. During the Jar Festival of January 1977, according to some holy men, the sun, moon, and stars stood in the same relative position as at the creation of the world, making that the best time in the world's history to bathe in that place.[4]

The human imagination works wonders with water, but its persistent association of water with beginnings and returns to beginnings arises from water's own properties.

LIFE FROM EARTH

People often associate the earth with the beginning of life. God made Adam from the dust of the ground. In the story of Gilgamesh, the goddess of creation Aruru made Enkidu, Gilgamesh's noble companion, of clay. According to myths of the American Southwest, the first people were made of sand and saliva or of clay. People do not much resemble the earth, but the earth brings plant life out of itself, and plants do not look like the earth either. That the earth might originally have brought forth animal life, too, makes some sense, all the more so in those regions where one can see many small creatures swarming out of the mud as if generated by it.

In neither the account of Adam's nor of Enkidu's creation does dust or clay seem to have pejorative meanings. And in both stories people are, in their noncorporeal properties, very like gods. The God of Genesis created man and woman in his own image. Before taking a pinch of clay to shape Enkidu, the goddess Aruru "conceived an image in her mind, and it was of the stuff of Anu of the Firmament."[5] Anu is the god of the heavens. That men are made of earth seems just a way of suggesting that men are heavier and more solid than air, explaining why men cannot, like gods, make themselves invisible or move off into distant spheres.

Both stories suggest that men are a joining of earth and spirit. Our sense of possessing a mind distinct from the body is much older than Descartes and the Renaissance. In fact, we have always and universally felt in our mysteriously supple, invisible minds and our lumbering bones that they are distinct. The mind, especially the imagination, often feels itself moving at great speed, as if it is something birdlike or godlike; not so the body.

Both main strands of Western thought, the Judeo-Christian and the Greek traditions, find the body a limitation on the perfection of the spirit. *Dirt, soil,* and *dust,* words for this stuff of which we tell ourselves we are made, also mean "dung." We are ashamed of our clumping earth-body, so clearly like that of the "lower" animals in its needs—and in its pitiful, stinking conclusion. Yet try as we might to repudiate the mind's connection with the body, the body keeps insisting upon it, pulling the mind earthward, yammering for food, a good scratch, a tickle in the sack, and sleep. At least three of the so-called seven deadly sins—gluttony, covetousness, and lust—are rooted in material, bodily cravings that tend to overwhelm judgment.

In the Ptolemaic cosmos, to be sure, the earth sat importantly at the very center of the universe; on the other hand, the earth, its inhabitants, and the moon—the nearest of the spheres circling the earth—were held to have been tainted by the Fall and thus were composed of a greater proportion of the heavy, gross "element" earth than were the spheres beyond the moon. Only the "sublunary" part of the universe, that part "under the moon," including the earth and moon, was imperfect, subject to change and susceptible to death. The mainstream of our culture still distinguishes sharply between the nonmaterial and the material, reserving its greatest admiration for the nonmaterial and holding in contempt the materialistic.

Words suggesting height and air, as opposed to lowness and earth, we associate approvingly with our minds, our souls, with our "spiritual," nonmaterial selves. In expressing approval, we say that a person is "high-minded," "stands tall," is a person of "stature," or is capable of "elevated" thought.

Even such phrases as the complimentary "down-to-earth" belong to this set of values. What we approve in a person who is down-to-earth is his modest recognition and acceptance of human limitations. He is sensible, realistic. A person "with his head in the clouds," because his mind does not keep in touch with his earth-body, is likely to plunge even lower than the rest of us. We say that he has gone off the deep end. In cartoons he tumbles into manholes or falls off piers.

But another cluster of symbols shows that we do not always shrink from the idea that people came from the earth. This cluster, centering on the earth as the "mother" of all life, implies a tranquil acceptance of humanity as a part of physical nature.

A striking instance of this attitude occurs among the Southwestern American Indians. One of the most sacred places in their cosmos is the hole through which they emerged from Mother Earth. In the Navajo version of an Indian myth, the First People lived for a long time within Mother Earth, without light. They finally emerged into the upper world by making their way through a hollow reed. Clearly, the emergence of people from inside the earth is analogous to the birth of mammals, journeying from the womb through the birth canal and emerging from the vagina.

The sacred hole through which people climbed is the "Sipapu" (Hopi) or "Shipap" (Rio Grande Pueblos). In every village, in the center of the kiva floor is a corresponding hole, the "sipapu." Just as the cross in any Christian church not only stands for the Cross on Calvary, the sacred center of the Christian cosmos, but actually shares in it, so does the village sipapu share in the sacred center of the Indian cosmos, the Sipapu. But whereas the cross directs devotion toward the sky, the sipapu directs it toward the earth.

Formalized reverence for the earth is most often found in fairly simple agricultural societies, including, for instance, some of ancient Asia Minor, of Northwestern Europe, and of Greece (before the semi-nomadic Hellenic people swept in with their sky-gods). And rural people everywhere tend to revere their land and think of it as female. By analogy with female animals, the earth brings forth the plants and, with these, nurtures all animals, including humankind. The analogy may seem inconsistent because Mother Earth, unlike most observable animal mothers, eventually takes back whatever she has borne. But maternal animals must be nourished in order to nourish in turn, and since, unlike other mothers, the Earth has made all, it is necessary that she be nourished by her own children. Besides, she takes them back only for a time, sending them into the world again, refreshed, in new forms.

In stories from widely scattered cultures, the first inhabitants of a region or a particular city sprang long ago right from the earth of that place, and the people telling the stories assert that they themselves are the direct descendants of these "autochthonous" men. The word *autochthon* today usually means an aboriginal inhabitant of a region or a native of a place. But the Greek word, comprised of *auto* (self) and *chthon* (the earth, land, or ground), means "of the land itself." The social function of these myths is to express the absolute bond between the people and their native place—their sense, as we say, of roots—and to ratify their claim to that place.

A closely related idea is that either within the earth or within something emerging from it—a tree, a rock outcropping—lies an ancestral energy-bank. Each member of the family, clan, or tribe comes from that perpetual store of life and, upon his death, returns to it. Often mistakenly called ancestor-worship, the idea expresses one's sense of belonging to, being an organic part of, one's familiar land and people. Enterprising Americans have repeatedly taken native Indians' ancestral land for homesteads and, more recently, for reservoirs, freeways, and atomic testing sites—resettling the Indians on land "just as good." Some people would rather not understand that such forced moves may rupture an Indian community's stored past, its meaningful future, its collective self. That patch of earth is sometimes truly that community's source of life.

FIRE

Water, earth, and air (the media in which we observe life thriving) plus fire constituted in the ancient world the four "elements," the basic stuff out of which all things were supposed to have been made. And upon examining fire as a symbol, we discover that it, too, has a rich history of association both with earthly life and with what lies beyond that. Especially as ancient peoples settled into agricultural village life, the sun and its earthly representative, fire, became central elements in their religions. The Celts' early summer festival of Beltane and Midsummer, promoting fertility, involved kindling a fire, often after all the district's fires had been snuffed. Priests sometimes lit the fire around a tree, representing the vegetation spirit, or a pole covered with greenery, the Maypole of later times. People danced sunwise around the fire, and the livelier the dance, the better the harvest was supposed to be. Since contact with the divine flame was thought to promote health and fertility, people drove their cattle through the fire or between two fires and they themselves darted through it.[6] The Greek story of Demeter putting the baby in the fire to render it immortal derives from a similar impulse. (Borrowing the whole story, the Hellenized Egyptians told it of Isis.)

The upward rush of fire suggested to the Zoroastrians that it was the lightest, most "spiritual" of the four elements. For the Zoroastrians, the perpetual altar flame signified the pure life imparted steadily by Ormazd, the supreme source of life. In many faiths, a candle or lamp near the altar symbolizes the concentrated presence of the divine. For the Greeks, the torch signified the continuity of noble human effort, a secular, collective "immortality" achieved when, as in a relay race, gifted individuals passed on their gifts to others. The early Christians transformed this symbol into one of personal eternal life. They also adopted the phoenix as a symbol of resurrection and immortality. (In the best-known version of the pre-Christian legend, the phoenix is an asexual bird that, after living five hundred years, builds itself a nest of fragrant boughs that is also its funeral pyre. Consumed in the flames, the bird rises anew from its own ashes and, on the third day, flies off to live for another five hundred years.)

LIFE FROM THE BODY OF A PRIMEVAL BEING

Many stories say that either humankind, the earth itself, or the plants and animals that sustain life came from the body of some primeval being—a giant, monster, or god. Although, unlike most origin stories, these seem at first tedious and arbitrary, their range and persistence suggest that they once symbolized important ideas. In Babylonian myth, the god Marduk created the cosmos by slaying Tiamat, the goddess of the terrifying, chaotic ocean, and then making the earth, heavens, and heavenly bodies from her corpse. (Here again, in a sense, water is a source of life that must be tamed, and land comes out of water.) The Aztec story of the earth's creation shows a similar conceptual origin. The gods made the earth's mountains, valleys, plants, and so on, from the body of a great toad. Again, toads appear after rain as if emerging from the water. The Talmud suggests that the earth was formed from the body of Adam. In one Greek version of the creation of man, Zeus established his dominion by burning to death the gigantic Titans—the savage gods who ruled despotically before his reign—and the first men sprang from their ashes. In Norse myth, three gods slew the giant Ymir, the first living thing to emerge from the primordial ice, and created earth and heavens from his body. (In one Norse version of humankind's creation, the first man and woman popped from the warm hollow of Ymir's left armpit. A rather blurred analogy with the normal manner of human birth seems to have suggested this amusingly inelegant origin: An armpit is warm, moist, concave.) East Indian myth also suggests that the first man and woman came from the body of a primeval being. As commanded by the sun, the Persian god Mithra slew a primeval ox, from whose seed came all the animals of the earth and from whose marrow came numerous kinds of grains and healing plants.

Because most of these stories are either from Mesopotamian cultures or from cultures of another common origin—the prehistoric Indo-European people whose descendants comprise virtually all the present peoples from India in the east to Ireland in the west—the similarity of motif is not particularly surprising. The question is why the motif of creation from the body of some original creature appealed to enough people to persist. Much of the answer belongs to the discussion of monsters in Chapter 8 and of fertility in Chapter 10, but some possibilities relevant here come to mind. New life can be observed to come from mutilated or dead and decaying organisms. Many plants can be chopped up and their fragments rooted to produce several offspring. Upon the moldering remains of long-fallen pine trees can be seen a sprinkling of small trees. Mushrooms grow out of rotten wood. The two halves of a severed earthworm wiggle competently away as two worms. And, until recently, anyone had ample opportunity to observe that rotting animal carcasses seem to generate animals of other kinds. But within all the stories of life generated from the body of some primeval being lies the perception that all animal life sustains itself by destroying other life.

EATING SEEDS, NUTS, AND FRUITS

A people engaged in agriculture almost inevitably draws an analogy between animal and plant reproduction. "Ploughing" and "planting" become sexual allusions, and the belief arises that having intercourse in a newly planted field will increase the vigor of the crop. The same analogy accounts for the fact that seeds, nuts, and fruits are worldwide symbols of fertility and, by extension, of regeneration. Thus Yellow Corn Girl, Example 4 (p. 20) at the beginning of Chapter 1, ate a pine nut and became pregnant. In Middle Eastern stories, the magical nut is often an almond, a particularly good symbol of regeneration because almond trees blossom earlier in the spring than do most other trees. In ancient Irish stories, nuts and apples from a faraway land renewed youth, freeing those who ate them from time's bond. In the Norse *Volsunga Saga*, a woman conceived a child by eating an apple. The Norse gods maintained their youth by eating magical golden apples. The Norse stories may have been influenced by the Irish ones, or by Greek mythology, as were some Norse myths in their late form known to us. For the preclassical Greeks, the Golden Apples of the Hesperides restored youth to those who ate them. The apples of the gods are a very old motif from the Near East, where the apple tree was first cultivated.[7]

In Greek myth, Demeter, goddess of grain and an Aegean earthmother from pre-Hellenic times, had a beautiful virgin daughter, Persephone, who was carried off by the god Hades, ruler of the underworld. Distracted by grief, Demeter allowed all fertility to cease; the fields stopped bringing forth food, and animals and people starved. In order to allow the earth's creatures to survive, Hades was finally made to give up Persephone, but each year she had to return to him for several months because, while in his realm, she had eaten a pomegranate seed.

A pomegranate seed? Without explanation, the story seems either charmingly whimsical or silly, depending on one's taste. But seemingly artibrary details in myths often point to symbolic meanings that once needed no explanation and were then retained after the meaning had slipped away because "that's how the story goes." The pomegranate is a very old fertility symbol of Semitic origin. Certainly the abundance of juicy, bright red seeds packed into a protective bellylike skin would suggest fertility to more than one lively imagination. The story of Demeter and Persephone is an "etiological" myth, that is, one that explains symbolically the origin of a phenomenon—in this case winter, the earth's recurrent but never permanent "death." That Hades persuaded Persephone to eat the pomegranate seed suggests, in the language of myth, that he awakened her to sexuality after which he had some real claim upon her. Like Eve, Persephone had eaten from the tree of knowledge. In the realm of death, Persephone had become part of the great round of life. And it is no accident that in the story of Adam and Eve, too, awakening sexuality was linked to the eating of a fruit—by long tradition, an apple.

Why does folklore connect eating with pregnancy? One answer is the universal association of a full belly with having eaten something. When a woman explains to a small child that her belly is big because a baby is inside, the child quite reasonably wants to know if the woman ate the baby. (The association goes far to explain the extraordinarily frequent theme of cannibalism in folklore.) Another answer is suggested in the perennial question that worried girls ask advice columnists: Will kissing with my mouth open make me pregnant? The mouth is a highly erotic part of the body—like the vagina, a warm, wet opening, penetrable and ringed with responsive muscles. Throughout the world, by obvious analogy, people associate the two. The vagina is even called the mouth of the womb, and timorous medieval monks, among others, fantasized about its having teeth.

SUN AND MOON

The first creatures came from a hidden world beneath the earth where they were neither warm or cold, happy or sad, starved or

well fed. They became truly alive only after they had seen the sun
which caused them to burst into life like tufts of grass.

An Eskimo story[8]

From earliest times, in all known cultures, people have so well understood the dependence of life upon sunlight that they have very often identified their chief god, symbolically or even literally, with the sun. In Egyptian myth, the sun-god created life and then battled tirelessly to maintain it. In Genesis, God made light before he made life. Raven, of the Northwest American coastal Indians, promoted life on earth by bringing light from heaven. In the stories of the Southwest American Indians, emerging from the earth into the world of sunlight greatly enhanced life. In addition to feeling the sun's generative powers, all people feel an elemental life-quickening joy in the presence of sunlight. "The sun's in the sky, and all's right with the world": Sunshine symbolizes for us the regular, orderly processes of life.

Many cultures see the sun as male and the moon as female. Why the sun and moon are seen as having gender is probably related to the facts that animals do and that the sun and moon seem, like living animals, to have regular periods of activity and rest. The sun is by far the more effective, bold, and dramatic of the two spheres; thus it is male. Furthermore, if by analogy one sees the earth itself as feminine and has observed the connection between sexuality and procreation, one will, in extending the analogy, expect to find the earth's partner in procreation. The two phenomena to which the earth's productivity responds most clearly and dramatically are the sun and water. Thus, most early cultures symbolized these vital powers as male, and the sun-god or the rain-god, depending partly upon the climate, became their chief deity. In sunny, arid Greece, the power of rain is of more concern than the power of sunshine; thus, Zeus the Thunderer, not the sun-god Helios, was the chief god. Egypt gets virtually no rain; its life-giving water comes from the Nile. During most of its ancient history, the god Re (or Amon-Re), associated with the sun, and Osiris, associated with the Nile waters, vied for supremacy. Sometimes they were viewed as aspects of the same deity, for Egyptian theologicans well understood the mutual dependence of sun and water as life-forces.

The moon almost universally symbolizes the life-giving powers of women. Its twenty-eight-day cycle of waxing and waning parallels the menstrual cycle, and the phases of the moon suggest the swelling of pregnancy and subsequent birth. Unlike the sun, the moon never over-powers, never turns harsh and cruel. The moon suggests the softness and gentleness often associated with women. Its perpetual cycle also suggests cycles of death and resurrection.

BIRDS, WORDS, THOUGHT, AND LIGHT AS SYMBOLS OF LIFE'S SPIRITUAL SOURCES

Many stories of creation emphasize the part played by some nonmaterial force. According to an Egyptian myth, in the dim past the "Benu" bird flew from a distant place of everlasting light, the Isle of Fire. Perching upon a staff in the watery abyss, this bird opened its beak and broke the primeval silence, thus stirring life into being upon this earth. The Benu bird, represented in paintings as a blue heron, is a manifestation of God's soul; its life-stirring call is the Word, as in the biblical statement, "In the beginning was the Word . . . and the Word was God" (John 1:1). The Word is the nonmaterial divine Presence that turns chaos into cosmos. In myths of the Keresan-speaking Indians of New Mexico, Thought Woman created all things by thinking them into existence. To create Gilgamesh's friend, the Mesopotamian goddess Aruru first conceived an image in her mind. In one Egyptian creation myth, Ptah, the mind of Re, thought the world into existence. These creation stories grow out of the observation, available to us all, that before we make a thing, we often conceive an image of it in our minds and model the thing upon that image. (Plato's conception of a world of Forms owes much to the same observation.) And we know that words, as nonmaterial as thoughts, possess the same power to make material things happen.

In the Benu myth, at least five thousand years old, three symbols of creation converge in a highly sophisticated way: light as a generative force; flight as a symbol of "soul" or "spirit," the mysterious, intangible essence of life; and the word as an activator of life. Because life can leave matter and does so invisibly, life seems to be some nonmaterial thing that came from somewhere outside of matter and infused matter with itself.

The Benu myth is a symbolic expression of the mysterious leap of inert matter into life. In 1953, two scientists at the University of Chicago carried out an extraordinary experiment: By sending electric sparks through a sealed container of water vapor, ammonia, and methane, they produced amino acids, the building blocks of protein out of which all living organisms are made. It may be that during a long period in the earth's development, when these conditions prevailed, what became life made its first appearance. One imagines the Benu bird perched there upon his staff in the warm ammoniac fog, electrifying the wastes with his cry. "And the Spirit of God moved upon the face of the waters."

Raven flew, like the Benu bird, from a lighted world to our own when our world was still dark. To bring light to our world, he then flew up to heaven and, in the form of a baby, tricked the chief of heaven into giving him the precious box of light, analogous to a flint box, to play with.[9]

Mexican legend pictures the god Quetzalcoatl—himself a feathered serpent—putting into the human body a bit of the divine, symbolized as a rich feather. Shamans from Alaska to Siberia mystically ascend to the upper world as birds.

In the Christian tradition, the part of the Trinity called the Holy Ghost is represented as a bird, a white dove. According to a medieval notion, this dove impregnated the Virgin by flying into her ear. Taken literally, this idea is a gentle absurdity. Taken symbolically, it conveys with brilliance and sophistication exactly what is intended. In stories, many women impregnated in a nonsexual way swallow the "seed" by mouth. But the mouth, as the upper door to the belly and the one through which gluttony waddles, is associated with physical appetites. The tellers of the Virgin's story wanted to stress the spiritual nature of the conception. The ear opens symbolically to the nonmaterial mind or spirit; the Virgin's *mind* receives the "seed," God's nonmaterial essence.

Birds almost universally symbolize the spiritual and the Other World. The dove returning to the Ark with the olive branch has long been interpreted as a message of God's willingness to make peace with humankind. Sometimes Christ himself is depicted as a dove with human face, wings spread in the shape of a cross or cupped in a tender, protective gesture suggesting Christ as Savior. The dove expresses the idea that the Holy Ghost and Christ are benevolent, loving visitors from the Other World, the world of sacred power that makes life in our world, infuses lumpish life with meaning, and provides us with the means to journey to the Other World ourselves. (Of course the dove, long associated with Aphrodite, also represents erotic love, and the elaborative courting ritual of common doves shows why.)

Knowing about these symbolic birds leads one to ponder a curious stone relief in the Coptic Museum in Cairo. The Copts are the native Christians of Egypt, and their church dates from the earliest centuries of Christianity. At that time, Egypt was a part of the Roman Empire, and Graeco-Roman culture flourished there. This stone relief depicts a familiar scene: Zeus, in the form of a swan, raping Leda. In this particular rendering of the scene, Leda is no girl dallying with a swan; she is being raped in the full sense of the word, overpowered and stunned by a great muscular bird. It is a brutal act. And to the left, very much an approving member of this scene, stands a winged angel! Perhaps the figure is simply a towering Eros, god of love. But perhaps this early artist saw a parallel between the Christian story of the Annunciation and the pagan story of Leda. In the pagan tradition, the rape of Leda is not just a tale demonstrating the high god's lust; it is the opening event in a cycle of holy legends.

The Iliad and The Odyssey (ca. eighth century B.C.) narrate the events set in motion by this act of Zeus. These stories consolidated in permanent form the ideals that defined the Greeks to themselves. Rather as the New Testament defines "Christian" in the term's permanent, ideal form, so did these epics define "Greek." The Greek belief in the dignity and intrinsic worth of human beings, whatever their status, is expressed for all time in The Odyssey. For Homer and his audience, it is often esteem for oneself and one's species—not fear of divine judgment—that promotes generosity, respectful treatment of others, and compassion for the unfortunate.[10] It is impossible to know how much the sculptor understood. On one level, his vision is naive and deeply offensive to the modern moral sensibility. Yet, on another level, he may have guessed that the Greek and the Christian influence on Western civilization would be similarly momentous.

THE EGG

Of all life-symbols, probably the most nearly inevitable one is the egg. Although a common object, the egg is arrestingly beautiful and mysterious. More lovely in shape than even the moon, an egg is silent, smooth, serenely uninformative, complete and self-contained; above all, inanimate. Yet an egg can crack itself, and when it does, out comes life—confused, demanding, busy, and, like all creatures, capable of generating another and yet another. An egg is a miracle indeed. But that people in widely separated cultures have found it so and have symbolized the beginning of all life as an emergence from a primordial egg is surely not a miracle.

In one early Egyptian version of creation, four primeval beings "with the heads of frogs and serpents—creatures of mud and slime," produced the primal egg. The bird of light emerged from this egg. In another version, the divine goose Geb laid the egg containing the light. The most haunting Egyptian version of the cosmic egg pictures the egg as the cosmos itself, not a solid object but a bubble of light and air protecting the earth-disc, the bubble immersed in the primeval dark waters.[11]

In a myth of the Greek Orphic cult, the cosmos emerged from an egg. In an ancient Hindu myth, the high god hatched from an egg generated by the primordial waters. The Easter egg of the Christian church, especially the Eastern branch, symbolizes the triumph of life over death, both in Jesus' own return to life and in the promise of an eternal life available to all after death.

FERTILITY: THE RABBIT, BULL, RAM

As the earth returns to life after a hard, frightening winter, it manifests and promotes life through the renewed fertility of animals and fields. The rabbit—the Easter Bunny—is one of many animals that, because of their dramatic procreative powers, symbolize the triumph of life through fertility. A Mexican stone figure depicts a hare giving birth to the sun-god. The figure represents the daily rebirth of the sun from the Earth's womb. The strength and virility of the bull have made it a very common fertility symbol. In one of the oldest known towns in the world, the Anatolian Çatal Hüyük (seventh millennium B.C.), the enshrined fertility goddess gave birth to a ram above a mounted group of bulls' heads. Millenniums later, at one of Egypt's main cult-centers, the sun-god Re—maker and maintainer of all life and father of all pharaohs—was worshiped in a series of living bulls thought to be the creatures in which Re had incarnated himself. In predynastic times, Osiris, once a fertility god, was worshiped in the form of a bull. Apis, another sacred bull, was long worshiped as the incarnated form on earth of the creation-god Ptah and later as the incarnated form of Osiris; or as Horus, the son of Osiris, who restored Osiris to life. Much farther north, in Scandinavia, the bull symbolized the sun because both are generative forces. The Hellenic Greeks associated bulls with their generative god Zeus. The Greeks sacrificed bulls to Zeus because, according to their early beliefs, the concentrated power of these bulls increased Zeus' power to generate life. In Egypt, Greece, and Rome, as in Turkey earlier, the ram, like the bull, symbolized procreation and fertility, and for the same reasons.

BLOOD AND WINE

Blood is for obvious reasons a pervasive symbol of life. Anyone who has witnessed wounds sees the intimate connection between blood and life. As the blood flows out, a wounded creature becomes more and more quiet, sinks into unconsciousness, and, if the flow is not stopped, dies. In the Western tradition, very "lively" people, whether courageous, jovial, or energetic, have been thought to possess a superabundance of this liquor of life. Such an important substance will surely figure largely in myths and rites around the world.

In Greek myth, the blood of Prometheus, mankind's special benefactor, protected life. Medea gave Jason an ointment that rendered invulnerable for a day the warrior rubbed with it. This ointment came from the plant that sprouted where the blood of Prometheus fell into the earth during his long ordeal. This story combines sacrificial blood with two other life-symbols, the earth and a plant.

Drinking the blood of other people was once a widespread practice thought, accurately enough, to strengthen the drinker, that is, to impart more life to him. The symbolic drinking of Christ's blood in the Christian Eucharist is a spiritualized version of this very old practice. Drinking Christ's blood imparts to the worshiper some of Christ's own purity, strengthens and renews his determination to bend his life toward Christ, and celebrates the idea that Christ's blood-sacrifice has made permanent life possible.

Much blood has been spilled upon altars everywhere. Such sacrifices have probably been more often the rule that the exception in human societies, and the purpose has ever been to secure life. Reasoning by analogy probably accounts for the fact that most known primitive agricultural societies have practiced blood-sacrifice. To get more wheat, rice, maize, or whatever, one gives up some of the precious grain harvested from the preceding crop, throwing it back into the ground. If one refuses to give it up, the next crop will be paltry. Nor does one choose the broken or blighted grains; one gives the best. To secure human life, the reasoning goes, some of it, too, must be given up.

Two familiar examples of blood-sacrifice show how the imagination sometimes works upon the connection between blood, life's symbolic essence, and the continuation of life. The Aztec gods, like people, could not survive without nourishment; and if the gods did not survive, neither would the world. Thus, the Aztecs slaughtered thousands of people, vigorous young men and women when possible, by ripping open the victims' chests and laying their still throbbing hearts upon the altars. To save the world from one day to the next by renewing their gods' vigor, the Aztecs had to make constant war against neighboring tribes to obtain victims.

The Norse followers of the battle-god Odin hanged victims in trees, sometimes hundreds at once, punctured their bodies in prescribed places, and caught the blood in bowls to offer to Odin. Odin demanded much blood and, if warriors failed to provide it before they went into battle, he would not hesitate to take their own during the fighting.

Wine has long been important in myth and ritual because it symbolizes blood. Like blood, it is red and, in moderate quantities, its effect is to warm, cheer, and "enliven" the drinker. Many people have believed that it strengthens or enriches the blood. Furthermore, it can enhance life by helping one transcend his present time, place, and self. It can free one from habitual boundaries of thought, quicken the imagination, plunge one into the depths of the unconscious mind, put one in touch with the dream-world, the world of permanent truth, the Other World.

The question has often arisen of how to propitiate the gods by offering what one values most—life or the means to life—and yet not give it up. At issue over the millenniums has been survival itself. The answer is to offer symbolic substitutes. Wine is one of many such substitutes. In place of people, animals have been offered or parts of people representing their vital essence (for instance, foreskins, menstrual blood) or even dolls and effigies. In ancient Egypt and many other cultures, the gods consumed the nonmaterial "essence" of the food offered, leaving the substance for the hungry people. According to Greek myth, Prometheus tricked Zeus into choosing the bones and fat as the gods' portion of meat, winning for humankind the right to save the good parts for people.

MILK

Like blood, milk is a powerful natural symbol of life and restoration. As if by magic, when a mother makes life, she also makes the substance to nourish it. According to an ancient Hindu myth, the gods and demons brought forth the elixir of immortality by churning a great primeval ocean of milk. In Norse myth, a primeval cow licked into being Ymir, the ancestor of both gods and men, and then suckled him. Figures of mother-goddesses often cup one of their breasts in a hand, demonstrating this gift of milk.

Sometimes in representations of the Virgin Mary, the Lady stands upon a crescent. As early as five thousand years ago, this same crescent symbolized the great Middle Eastern mother-goddess of many names. The crescent signified both cow horns and the new, swelling moon, that is, the "pregnant" moon. Hathor, one of ancient Egypt's mother-goddesses, is often represented as a cow. Nut, the goddess whose body makes the protective pillars and roof of heaven, is also sometimes represented as a cow sheltering many people beneath her belly.

Plants that exude milky substances often become associated with mother-goddesses. These plants range from the fig (Egypt's sycamore fig, India's "Asvattha" or Bodhi) to the hazel nut (Scotland, Ireland) to the coconut (Indonesia, Polynesia) to maize (the Zunis and other North American Indians) to the maguey (the pre-Columbian Aztecs). The goddess is often shown in the form of the plant.

TREES

Egyptian paintings show a woman high in the branches of a sycamore fig tree directing the milk streaming from her breast to the mouth of a kneeling figure below. Sometimes the woman in the branches offers fruit from a tray and pours liquid from a jar into people's cups. In one such painting (Fig. 1), the tree appears to be standing in a little aquarium full of fish and plants. The woman is the Great Mother, perched in the afterworld's tree of life, distributing the food and drink of immortality to the newly arrived. The tree, planted in the primeval waters of life, renders the gods immortal and enables people, also, to become virtual gods.

This celestial tree is not always represented as standing in water, for its roots can bring up the vital waters by plunging deep and wide into the earth. It is these waters that the goddess in the branches pours down to the people gathered under the tree. In a crude but fascinating sketch from the burial chamber of Tuthmosis III (ca. 1500 B.C.), the pharaoh is suckled by the sycamore goddess. She is represented simply as a tree with a human arm attached to the upper trunk and a hand offering a breast

Fig. 1. The Egyptian mother-goddess (variously Nut, Isis, and Hathor), in the branches of the sacred life-giving tree, nourishes inhabitants of the afterworld. The tree grows out of the waters of life. The life-giving tree was a widespread symbol in the ancient Middle East. In art, animals with special powers—here birds—often flanked sacred sources of life. *Detail, an Egyptian painting, thirteenth century* B.C. (Roger Cook, *The Tree of Life: An Image for the Cosmos* (London: Thames and Hudson, 1974), Fig. 33.)

that grows from one of the tree's branches. The vision seems less bizarre after one discovers from other drawings the custom that suggested it: When Egyptians worked in the fields, they took with them a supply of water in an animal-skin bottle and hung this bulging skin in a nearby

Fig. 2. In this impression from a prehistoric cylinder seal, a human figure bearing branches is flanked by Dinka sheep. In historical times, this motif of the plant flanked by virile animals represents a sacred source of life, often a cosmic "center" from which divine power infuses the earth. Such scenes are often shown occurring on stylized mountains. The central figure is usually a god. *Sumerian, late fourth millennium B.C., Vorderasiatisches Museum Berlin.* (Eva Strommenger, *5000 Years of the Art of Mesopotamia,* trans. Christina Haglund; photographs by Max Hirmer (New York: Harry N. Abrams, 1964), Pl. 17, bottom row. Copied by courtesy of Hirmer Fotoarchiv München.)

tree at a height convenient for drinking. A waterskin with its four legs distended strongly suggests a cow's full udder.

An astonishing number of sacred trees flourish in myths: the tree of life and the tree of knowledge in the Judeo-Christian heritage; the Bodhi under which Buddha received his great revelation; Zeus' oaks at Dodona and Apollo's laurel grove; Yggdrasil, the great world-tree of the Norse; the Arandas' "Kauwa-auwa"; Thor's special tree, the oak; sacred trees of the Assyrians, the Celts, the Chinese, the Siberians, the American Indians, and, it begins to seem, of everybody everywhere. What do they mean?

Many of these trees stand near a sacred well or pool; sacred birds fly or perch at the top, and a serpent lies at the base. Tree, birds, serpent, pool—these four images appear together in such widely dispersed areas as the Fertile Crescent, Iran, China, southern Borneo, and Scandinavia. The earliest known combination of tree, bird, and serpent occurs in the

Fig. 3. Horned beasts, symbols of fertility, grow from the trunk of the "Asvattha," the long-venerated Indian fig tree. *Indus Valley, before 2300 B.C.* (Heinrich Zimmer, *The Art of Indian Asia: Its Mythology and Transformations*, ed. Joseph Campbell. Bollingen Series XXXIX, Vol. 2. Copyright © 1955, 1960 by Princeton University Press. Line drawing after Pl. 2e. Copied by permission of the publisher.)

still poorly understood Sumerian story of Gilgamesh and the huluppu tree (third millennium B.C.). Three mysterious creatures set up residence in a tree that Inanna, queen of heaven, had planted in her sacred garden: coiled about its base, the snake "who knows no charm"; at its crown, the Zu-bird, a monstrous storm-bird; in the middle Lilith, "the maid of desolation." When Inanna wished to harvest the wood to make a fine chair, these intractable creatures made felling the tree impossible. The hero Gilgamesh settled the matter by killing the serpent for Inanna, putting the other two creatures to flight.[12]

Although this particular story remains puzzling, the images of tree,

Fig. 4. At the center of this East Indian tree of life, a cobra shields the lotus, symbol of eternal generation, the womb of the universe. That snakes annually shed their skin suggests that they can renew their lives and thus possess the "secret" of immortality. The multiheaded snake in Indian art is an immortal guardian of life. Two bulls, fertility symbols, flank the tree, and two monkeylike creatures cling to its trunk. Birds perch on the tips of the boughs. *Bronze, India, ca. 1336–1546 of our era. Nelson Gallery—Atkins Museum (Nelson Fund), Kansas City, Mo.* (Roger Cook, *The Tree of Life: An Image for the Cosmos* (London: Thames and Hudson, 1974), Pl. 19. Copied by permission of the museum.)

bird, and serpent established themselves very early in the Middle East as symbols of life. So did the pool. The date palm, an important source of nourishment that the ancient Mesopotamians made their symbolic tree of life, grows in oases near springs. The emerging visions of an eternal

Fig. 5. The logo of the San Diego County Zoo neatly expresses the unity of life in, on, and above the earth. All these forms of life are life symbols of ancient origin. The elephants, probably least familiar as symbols to Westerners, represent fertility in East Indian myth and ritual. (Copied by permission of the Zoological Society of San Diego.)

realm—the gods' realm, paradise, heaven, the cosmos itself, whatever—often included the tree with its birds, serpent, and pool. For instance, in the Pyramid Texts of the Egyptian Middle Kingdom, the life-giving fig grows in the sky-world on a sacred island in a lake or beside a sacred pool. Swallows representing the immortal gods fly overhead. Although absent from this particular scene, the serpent was by this time a long-established symbol of life in Egypt.

The Norse world-tree probably derived partly from the ancient Middle Eastern image as well as from the Germanic world-pillar and the world-trees of the Finno-Ugric tribes and other peoples to the east.[13] As it happens, a simple sketch of the Norse tree duplicates, on a vastly enlarged scale, the tree described in the Egyptian Pyramid Texts. The island in the lake on which the Egyptian tree grew corresponds to the whole Norse earth-disc in the vast sea. The resemblance probably derived from common observations to be discussed in Chapter 6, among them that whatever land we know, whether island or continent, is bounded by water and water makes trees grow.

Moslem legend tells of the Sidra tree in paradise. It holds as many leaves as there are people in the world; each leaf bears the name of a living person. On a certain day in autumn, when the tree is shaken, the leaves of all who will die the next year fall. The legend derives from the Egyptian tradition of Thoth, the divine scribe who wrote the names of kings and the blessed dead on the leaves of a holy tree in the Other World.[14]

The motif of a tree flanked by two animals—paired bulls, griffins, birds, lions, snakes, dragons—reaches back in an unbroken tradition to five thousand years ago (Figs. 1–5). It has appeared on seals and official documents, plaques, vases, door panels of temples and churches, paintings, fabrics, heraldic enamels, Pennsylvania Dutch cabinets, and so on. The San Diego County Zoo uses the motif as its logo. The flanking animals usually embody some life-promoting quality such as virility, strength, fecundity, mastery, or regeneration. A Christian variant shows the first man and woman standing on either side of the tree, ready to scatter their seed over the face of the earth.

But what of the sacred trees apparently unrelated to the Middle Eastern composite life-symbol? The tree is simply the most imposing manifestation of vegetal life. According to Arnold Whittick, an authority on symbols, the sacred tree is the most widespread of all visual symbols. It may represent knowledge, as with Semitic, East Indian, Prussian, and Greek oracle-trees; or the whole universe, as with the Norse tree. But most often it represents life itself, especially in the sense of regeneration and immortality.[15] The appropriateness of trees for such a symbol seems obvious. They live long. Some of them go into winter dormancy and then return dramatically to full vigor with the "rebirth" of the year; others, conifers, are almost the only vegetation that appears not to perish in the long northern winters.

Whittick notes that the sacred tree was usually of the species most valued or most imposing in a region. For Mediterranean peoples, it was the date palm, cedar, pomegranate, or grape vine; for northern peoples, the ash, oak, or elm.

Thus do our minds transmute common experience into the vivid, compressed language of symbols to express the ineffable mystery of life's beginning, growth, multiplication, and survival. Our own observations, our human propensity to reason by analogy, and our fund of lore work together. Quite predictably, whatever our time and place, our minds converge on the same major life-symbols: water; earth; light, especially sunlight; creative thought; the egg; animals of special fecundity or power; blood and wine; milk; seeds, fruits, trees, and other dramatic or vigorous forms of vegetal life.

Because death, life's dark twin, is our other most nearly universal concern, we should expect to find an equally abundant and highly charged cluster of symbols associated with it. So we do.

3

Symbolizing the Mystery of Death

It is astonishing that the idea of survival after death is almost universal in human history, astonishing because no one ever returns from death to tell us about the Other World or even sends us a sign from it that people outside our own faith and tradition will accept as true. The belief in an afterlife is not of the same order as a belief in, say, Japan; for, though many of us will never go to Japan, we know people who have been there and objects that come from there, and we are assured that, given the money for a ticket, we could fly there ourselves and then return home. Japan belongs to a whole continuum of experience; numerous details point to its existence as a place with the same type of reality as wherever we happen to live. The Other World does not belong to such a continuum.

Leaving aside all questions of how factual truth relates to particular sacred books and traditions, the question here is what experiences might be common to ordinary people of whatever time, place, or religious tradition, to predispose so many of them to believe in survival after death. A cluster of such experiences does exist.

HOW PERSONAL EXPERIENCE PREDISPOSES US
TO BELIEVE IN AN AFTERLIFE

First, the idea of death as total erasure is both repugnant and, for oneself at least, nigh incomprehensible. One cannot readily conceive of one's own self as nothing because, in the act of struggling with the idea, the self is grunting noisily over the task, very much present. One can see in imagination the empty spot where one used to sit, but all the while one is, like Tom Sawyer, peering at the spot from the gallery.

Second, when one is asleep, one often finds oneself moving in a strange, intense world where delights are purer, terrors more horrible, confusion deeper, and the threat of chaos more palpable than in the waking world—and while one is there, one's solid body lies inert. The surmise that a part of one's being detaches itself and actually goes to another world beyond the waking world is surely inevitable. One speculates that perhaps death, so often similar to sleep in observed process and appearance, consists of remaining permanently in that other world.

Third, we know deeply in our earliest years the daily dying of the sun, the snuffing of all our shimmering world, when our wail brings the gods—our parents—to our side only tardily, dimly. When they come, they may be cold or lurching and fuddled; or they may not come at all, leaving us to howl in empty blackness. Sometimes, indeed, in this dark time we hear strange cries as of beasts struggling, and in these cries we recognize the voices of these two gods who alone keep all safe and whole. Can we really have forgotten all this enough to wonder over the Eygptian myth that every single night the sun-god Re must battle Apep, the monster of chaos, subdue him, and create the cosmos anew? And yet, like the Egyptians, we did find again and again, as children, that we had endured, that the sun and the world of familiar objects had returned, that the gods were restored. The end was not the end.

Fourth, in most climates the earth itself seems to die annually, but it, too, always returns to life. In the fertile river valleys of the Middle East, where human history began, the searing summer desolates the land, but not forever. In other parts of the world, frost blackens the meadows; trees turn to skeletons; the earth grows cold, the water stiff, the sun dim. Snow turns the familiar into treacherous blank space. Living creatures almost disappear—but not forever.

Again and again in our experience, the end is not the end.

Of course, a person observing all these cyclic "deaths" also observes that a dead body, whether it be lizard, dog, or one's beloved child, does not after a time come alive again but, instead, decays and disappears permanently. However, it seems reasonable that, just as the dreaming self goes about its affairs independent of the inert body, the Other-World self would not need the body and this is why the body decomposes.

In short, when our teachers introduce us to the idea of a return to life after death, that idea joins its shadow-twin already there within us.

And as for the nature of the afterlife, as conceived in various cultures, it parallels what we know of the dream-world. We find in the dream-world familiar things leavened with a peculiar yeast. An uncle who, in the day-world, disturbingly throws one into the air only when one's parents are absent, may appear in the dream-world as a pouncing fiend so cleverly disguised that he fools even one's parents. Spiders and geese of gigantic size, humanoid tractors, typewriters, or street sweepers run amok, detached heads or hands—these may be the monsters of one's dream-world. One may be spurned, mocked, humiliated, wounded in ways more sharply horrible than are remotely likely in the day-world. One may even be killed and chopped up—whereupon one finds that, even when one wishes to lose all consciousness, one never does. Indeed, often, at the moment of death in the dream-world, one is returned immediately to the day-world, still vulnerable to the monster waiting behind the dream-world wall, but given another chance to get away.

We also readily observe that, in the dream-world, delights can be complete and unalloyed. We may zap a platoon of thugs with ease, engage without reproach in remarkable sexual experiments, eat all we want, stay under water for hours, give birth to small, exquisite animals, or with a flick of an ankle rise twenty feet in the air. In sleep, our imagination ranges far beyond that of our waking selves; the laws of day, both social and natural, that limit our possibilities, are gone. This is a world of the greatest conceivable terror and delight. Naturally, many of us have toiled to ensure that when we go there permanently, the joys and not the terrors will await us.

Where is this place? What part of us shall go there, and how shall it travel?

COMMON IMAGES OF THE AFTERLIFE AND HOW WE INVENT THEM

We often picture the afterlife as inside the earth or in the sky. In our common experience, the media in which life is possible are three: air, earth, and water. Because those who die do not move visibly among us in the air on the earth's surface, we imagine them to be in some part of the earth, sky, or, less often, the water; this Other World is inaccessible to a living, waking person without supernatural help and, even with help, his journey to the Other World would be extremely perilous.

Because we often bury our dead in the earth and we cannot see inside it, we may reason that those not among us are in some sense living there. But from our miserable experiences of small, dark rooms, of caves, of stuffy tunnels, we tend to dislike the idea of an underground afterworld, much preferring a fair land in the sky. In one Egyptian myth, Osiris, even though he has become the Universal Savior and King of the Underworld, nonetheless complains of his dark, constricted fate. In *The Odyssey*, the hero Achilles makes a similar complaint.

Although people of virtually all known cultures have invented images of the afterlife,[1] the Egyptians imagined it in much richer detail than did other ancient peoples. Indeed, the visions of this single people stand almost as a catalog of known afterlife-images.

THE EGYPTIAN AFTERLIFE

As in our own tradition, Egyptian priests accommodated descriptions of the afterlife to unsophisticated minds, and it was possible to believe in two or more distinct notions simultaneously. During most of the third millennium B.C., one version of the afterlife had a dead person joining his ancestors in the cemetery at the desert's edge and, so long as his relatives faithfully tended his tomb, living a carefree life modeled on the earthly one. According to another notion, the soul rose to join the sun, moon, and stars in their daily round.

Later visions were elaborations of the earlier ones. Sometimes the dead were pictured as hunting, fishing, playing chesslike games, and banqueting in a faraway earthly paradise. At the same time, the idea of rising to the sky was much expanded. In order to succeed, the soul had to undergo a series of difficult spiritual transformations.[2] Often the blessed immortals were pictured as sailing daily across the sky in Re's boat. In some visions, bodies of the dead remained in the tomb while their souls moved about freely. The souls could stroll among the pleasant, varied sections of an extensive afterworld so long as their entombed, mummified bodies remained intact. Later still, righteous souls could live even if their earthly bodies perished. Often, the righteous dead were pictured as becoming immortal by assimilation with the god Osiris.

It was the Egyptians who elaborated the idea of dark, perilous, monster-infested caverns and fiery lakes as compartments of the Other

World or as perils from which souls needed protection on their journey there.

CAVES AND TUNNELS

Most ancient peoples of the Middle East and Europe invented far less elaborate images of an afterlife. They usually pictured it as a dreary, silent half-life in dim caverns inside the earth; the dead, usually disembodied, reached it by some combination of boat, bridge, or tunnel.

One may question why so many peoples have associated the afterlife realm with caves or the journey there with tunnels. Of course caverns, wherever at hand, have been the choice of many cultures for disposing of their dead, and in them people could conceivably, if without much enthusiasm, abide indefinitely. Yet caves and tunnels as symbols are rooted in a phenomenon both more and less obvious than burial customs. Especially in the presence of fire, human eyes perceive the world at night as either a cave or a tunnel, depending on whether one is at rest or moving; and for reasons already explored, we associate night with the afterworld.

ALTERNATIVES TO GLOOMY CAVERNS

Several ancient peoples at least considered a paradisiacal alternative to gloomy caverns, but viewed it as a place reserved for a very few. In the Babylonian version of Gilgamesh's story, only one man and one woman were ever saved from the wormy, dust-choked underworld. In Greek tradition, a handful went not to Hades but to the Elysian Fields, probably a pre-Hellenic paradise, according to H. J. Rose, that the Hellenic Greeks melded with their own Islands of the Blessed.[3] In neither the Babylonian story nor in Greek stories is superior virtue the cause for singling out an occasional person for paradise. Greek writers also occasionally allude to the land of the Hyperboreans, where the inhabitants spend their time banqueting and dancing in the sunshine, and to the Garden of the Hesperides, in which a tree bears golden apples of immortality. But it is never suggested that real people might go to these paradises after death.

Nobody today knows whether Valhalla, the Norse hall of heroes in the gods' realm, was a real mythic vision or a poetic convention created after the advent of Christianity. In any case, Valhalla was open only to those followers of Odin slain in battle; apparently all women and the vast majority of men, if they believed in an afterlife at all, believed they would go straightway to Hel, a realm hardly distinguishable from the grave itself.

For centuries, Christians held more or less simultaneously two views of the afterlife. They sought comfort in the analogy of death to sleep, and envisioned the dead as sleeping in their graves until Gabriel blew his horn to awaken them all on Judgment Day; then the righteous would arise and live forever in an earthly paradise. But as the centuries stretched on beyond everyone's predictions, that conception gradually gave way to the other common one, of an immediate, individual judgment and translation either to the airy realm of heaven or to hell within the earth. In addition to abolishing the tediously long sleep, this notion better suits our association of air with virtue, earth with evil.

SOULS

James Thayer Addison, who has studied various beliefs concerning life after death, remarks that the folklore of Africa, Scotland, China, Greece, and other areas, reveals a striking unanimity about the nature of the soul, the part of the self that we think of as surviving. It is a thin, vaporous duplicate of the person himself. Many languages—among them Sanskrit, Hebrew, and Latin—use a single word for the concepts of breath and soul. Addison notes that, when we look at a dead person, pondering what makes him different from a living person, the fact that he lacks breath readily comes to mind; the breath or soul, we infer, has left the dead body. Some languages use a single word for the concepts of shadow and soul. In many traditions, souls cast no shadows, for they themselves are shadows.[4] Homer calls the souls of the dead "shades." For Cheyenne Indians, the word *tasoom* means both the shadow of any animate thing and the part of a person that goes to the sky after his death.[5] Souls may hover in caves, graveyards, deserted places. They may wander home to warm themselves at the hearth, may move in the wind or fire.

Because in human experience flying is the freest form of motion and birds are the most conspicuous flying creatures, we often picture the soul as flying like a bird. In some ancient Egyptian accounts, this soul-bird could fly out of the tomb and come back to comfort the quasi-conscious yet inert, mummified body with news of the day-world.

In Judeo-Christian tradition, angels such as Gabriel and Michael and other Old Testament messengers of God are demigods who have always existed. But by at least the late Middle Ages, the souls of extraordinarily virtuous Christians were sometimes envisioned as arising after death to become angels. Winged angels of this tradition probably derived from Assyrian art through post-Babylonian Hebrew theology and through the art of the Greeks and Romans depicting their gods.[6]

In Islamic tradition, although most of the dead must await Judgment Day to be consigned to paradise or hell, souls of martyrs go straight to heaven, where they stay in the crops of green birds around God's throne. Green is associated with heavenly bliss.[7]

Not all visions of mythic sky-travel, of course, involve the sprouting of wings from shoulders, but all are based on analogies with familiar things. Sometimes people are swooped up by enormous eagles. Often common forms of earth travel are simply equipped with wings and transferred to the sky, as with winged sandals, horses, and chariots. Because chariots suggest both dignity and personal passivity, they are a favored means of ascension to heaven. Finally, in some stories—Egyptian, Hebrew, Polynesian, aboriginal Australian, Siberian, American Indian—people climb ladders or trees to reach the sky.

WATER AND BRIDGES

If the Other World is not imagined as within the earth or beyond the earth in the sky, it may be imagined as upon the earth's surface far, far to the west—the west because the sun's daily journey ends there. The Other World is less often envisioned as within water, except by people who spend much of their lives on the water, such as the Warao Indians of the Orinoco Delta and the New Caledonians of the South Pacific. In folklore, living people entering water are often symbolically struggling with death: the brothers in Example 2 (p. 20) and Cactus Flower Girl in Example 10 (pp. 24–25) at the beginning of Chapter 1; Jonah, Beowulf, and the European folk heroines that fall into wells. These people are not, or not yet, entering an afterlife.

But precisely because water is for most peoples an alien medium, a natural barrier, the separateness of the Other World is often symbolized by a boundary of water. Ancient Mesopotamians journeyed to the underworld in the boat of the West. Rock carvings from the Norse Bronze Age (1600–450 B.C.) show a ship of the sun sailing nightly through the underworld after the sun has dipped beneath the western sea. The Norse sometimes launched dead heroes in boats; the less eminent they often buried in graves marked by stones set in the shape of a boat. Like the Egyptians, who also traveled much by water, the Norse envisioned certain privileged dead people as traveling in the sun's ship to the Other World. In the legend of King Arthur, three mysterious women appear in a barge to take the dying king out upon the water. The suggestion that these women may have taken the king to the otherworldly island of Avalon to cure his wounds is consistent with the vision in pre-Christian Celtic myth of the Other World as an island. Especially among people close to the sea, the Other World is often seen as an island. We often daydream about tropical "paradises," where food, water, and beautiful girls are abundant, and about steaming, disease-racked "hells" such as Devil's Island.

To get from our world to the Other World, one often must cross a perilous bridge. Most of us are familiar with bridges, and from an early age we perceive that, unlike birds, people do not belong in empty space and will be hurt if they fall from high places. Any bridge is perilous to the imagination, all the more because what lies beneath it is that other dangerous medium, water—and sometimes rocky chasms. Although few of us have experienced a bridge disaster, imagining one is easy. We have seen threads, wires, ropes, and spiderwebs break. Our minds' eyes have no trouble envisioning a delicate, swaying footbridge snapping under our weight; a troll chewing through a bridge's vine tether; a giant or a mad dog planted menacingly in the middle of the bridge that we must cross to flee some equal danger behind us or to accomplish some heroic purpose on the other side; monsters popping up to hack the bridge's two ends after we have started across; villains setting dynamite and sneaking away just before our train roars helplessly into what will be, in three seconds, empty space. Equally easy to imagine are the bridge thin as a needle or sharp as a razor's edge, the bridge of spikes or of fire, the electrified bridge. All vividly symbolize the terrible vulnerability of man in space or, beyond that, of man between two ordered realms.

A bridge, then, is a natural symbol of a dangerous boundary but, for the same reason, a symbol of special opportunity for the courageous. It is the means to leave one's native "island" (hometown, region, country) for the big world. It is a natural symbol for venturing from any comfortable, familiar state into one of risk and opportunity, for example, from small child to school child, dweller in parents' house to chooser of one's own roof, student to jobholder, single person to married. The ultimate bridge, one that can never be recrossed, is that between our world and the Other World. But in a sense, in the act of crossing any of our bridges, we burn them because crossing them transforms us into creatures different from what we were. For instance, once adults, we can never return to our childhood or to the world where we lived as children. Those places no longer exist. The world rolls up behind us. The bridge is a powerful symbol, then, for a series of boundaries that we cross only once, and especially for the last, greatest boundary.

In Norse mythology, Bifrost is a rainbow bridge or a bridge of fire (probably suggested by the aurora borealis) separating our world from Asgard, the realm of the gods; only the gods and their potent enemies, the giants, are able to cross this bridge. Another bridge separates Midgard from Hel, the underground land of the dead.

WALLS AND GATES

Other almost inevitable symbols associated with the afterlife are walls, gates, and guardians of the gates. Most modern Americans probably have had more direct experience with enclosed realms than they realize. To a very small child whose domain heretofore has been the house, a walled backyard is a veritable kingdom. Later, still at a profoundly impressionable age, the child is likely to encounter many sealed enclosures and monstrous watchdogs leaping at fences in order to get at him. He plays in the fenced schoolyard, peeks through cracks at a rich family's elegant lawn and tiled pool. He climbs the mountainous steps of the library, courthouse, or church and sees the great doors yield. We all see the glass wall at the supermarket or the air terminal divide as we approach, and we watch the massive corrugated doors of packing plants and warehouses roll back with a terrible screech. We see the armed sentries at military bases, border-patrol points, and prisons.

Because death is a boundary crossed only once, the notion that the dead stay in an enclosed realm follows. For the conception of heaven as a walled city, one need only consult the histories of old cities. These centers could not have survived without walls to hold back the casual marauders, hostile armies, and barbarian hordes drawn by their treasures. In the ruins of Troy, Jericho, and Angkor and in such long-lived modern cities as Istanbul, Cairo, and innumerable towns of France, Germany, and Spain, stand the remains of these walls. Every night and in times of trouble the gatekeepers locked the massive gates. Once one imagines the

Other World as a splendid city, the gate and its watchful keeper who questions every unfamiliar face necessarily follow.

Sometimes even heaven is not safe. In the North, where people felt life to be especially precarious, they envisioned the gods as waging a constant battle against the savage frost-giants; all knew that the frost-giants would finally breach the walls of Asgard, the gods' heavenly city, and destroy it forever.

An idea widespread in the ancient Middle East was that the dead must cross Ocean, the circular river surrounding the earth-disc, to reach the Other World. A grim ferryman took them across in his boat. Given the human bent toward analogy, several circumstances together account for this conception. First, many cities were built on the banks of rivers, and, to safeguard their lives and goods, ancient city-dwellers sometimes made islands of their walled towns by rechanneling part of the river so that it would encircle the town. Second, thoughout most of human history, the customary means of crossing a wide river has been a ferry. Third, if we move in any direction upon our flat-looking earth, we do eventually come to the ocean. Just as the city became a walled island-enclave of order surrounded by danger and chaos, so the earth itself could be seen as a larger island of relative order, the great waters holding back a thousand possibilities.

FIRE

For some of the same reasons that fire is a colorful symbol of vigorous life, it is associated with death. Fire is a dramatic form of energy—but energy squandering itself with ferocious speed. Fire does not simply kill. It obliterates. Annihilation is what we fear most, and in common experience fire is the quickest, most nearly complete annihilator. That fact should go far toward explaining why, when people imagine complete destruction, personal or cosmic, their minds often symbolize it with fire. By the third millennium B.C., much earlier than other peoples, the Egyptians had developed the concept of a judgment after death followed by reward or punishment. They sometimes envisioned the evil as being tossed into fiery lakes or pits that reduced them instantly to ashes. Later, other cultures may have borrowed the vision of the fiery pit.

To Westerners, fire's compelling beauty and its apparent whispers and hisses, its seemingly gleeful destructiveness, above all, its association with damnation strongly suggest demons within, luring people to destruction.

On the other hand, because flame consumes the physical quickly and leaps as if eagerly toward the sky, it has suggested to many imaginations the freeing of the soul from the body. Almost as many cultures have burned the dead on pyres as have committed them to the earth.

COSMIC DESTRUCTION

The destruction of the world itself is a very widespread image in mythology. The envisioned destruction of the cosmos is almost a consequence of having envisioned its creation. Once one has pictured chaos turning into an orderly arrangement infused with meaning, that vision plays itself backward. If the cosmos arose from a great flood, it may be obliterated by a great flood. If it freed itself slowly from solid ice, that ice may encroach upon it again. If the cosmos is a bunching and cooling of hot gases into a solid mass even now seething within, it may one day fly apart or crack and spew forth its fires. The cause for destruction in myths is usually punishment for noisiness, disobedience, or other sins, analogous to punishment by parents or social authorities; or the cause is decrepitude, analogous to each living body's progressive decline and slide into death.

But just as it is scarcely possible to envision the true, final dissolution of oneself and one's kind, so with the world's end. Again and again, we watch birth, struggle, triumph, loss, death—and birth. Individuals die, but new ones are born and flourish. Villages emerge from the valley, the desert, or the swamp; grow into brilliant civilizations; and then fall into decay. But somewhere else, new ones emerge. Always in myth, the return to chaos is only the end of one realm, one age, or one dispensation. Noah's family stepping off the Ark, the dewy young man and woman awaking among flowers after the Norse gods' catastrophe; the unfallen American Adam planting seeds in the New World—the end is never the end. In a currently popular vision, when we have worn out the earth, a wise and hardy few will push off to a glorious new life somewhere in outer space.

Long, long ago, say the myths, a cosmos took shape. It will perish. But another world-egg will stir.

MAKING SYMBOLS: A SUMMARY

Our mothers and fathers, grass, rain, pools, fish, the earth, seeds, apples, the sun, the moon, birds, eggs, bulls, blood, milk, trees, night, caves, islands, bridges, walls, gates, fire: these are but a few of the familiar symbols to which we turn for help throughout our lives when we confront some momentous thing that we can neither tame with our rational minds nor discount. These are universal symbols, the language of our deepest experience, the language of our myths and dreams. Using as examples some widespread symbols connected with life's sources and conclusions, I have shown that we come to terms with even the greatest mysteries by seeing them as analogous to familiar things. So it is that the minds of people in different times and places converge upon many of the same symbols. Those that we do not make for ourselves, we borrow from our neighbors; but even borrowed symbols reflect our sense of their rightness.

I suggest that examining other powerful, widespread symbols will reveal the same mental processes at work. The next section treats the mythic hero, and these processes can be seen there also.

II

THE HERO

4

What Heroes Do

THE DARK FOREST

> *Little Red Riding Hood's grandmother lived away in the forest, a half-mile from the village. One day Little Red Riding Hood's mother said to the child, "Here are some cakes and a flask of wine to take to your grandmother, for she is ill, and they will do her good. Set out early and walk briskly and mind that you do not trip and spill the wine." Little Red Riding Hood assured her mother that she would be careful. As soon as she came to the wood, she met the wolf, but, having no idea that he was a bad animal, she did not feel frightened.*
>
> Adapted from *Household Stories,*
> *from the Collection of the Bros. Grimm* [1]

> *Wandering about, starving, in the woods where their parents had abandoned them, Hansel and Gretel tried to find their way back to their father's house, but the more they tried, the further into the dark forest they found themselves. At last they came to a little house built entirely of gingerbread and roofed with cakes.*
>
> Adapted from *Household Stories* [2]

Almost every child knows these stories and is likely to seek in his early years a blood-quickening dark forest of his own. Sometimes it is only one great, shadowy pine tree down the road from the housing tract or the sycamores of the city park, but he makes do with what is available. He plunges into his dark forest, and he does of course find danger there: old hunched men who spit or horrible-looking beetles in the grass and craw-dads in the muddy pond. All his mother's admonishments leap out at him: Always come straight home; never talk to strangers, take shortcuts, linger in secluded places, play alone near water, or eat food that someone has abandoned. But he does, despite his thumping heart, stay long enough to find a treasure, a discarded Cracker Jack box, maybe, with the prize puzzlingly still in it. Then he hurries home to sit on his bed and examine the treasure, pondering whether he dare eat the crumbs of candy-coated popcorn. Already he knows, like Midas, Phineus, Ti-thonus, and Cassandra, that the gifts of the gods should be viewed with suspicion.

Innumerable stories, from the Babylonian epic *Gilgamesh* of the sec-ond millennium B.C. to the tales of our own day, begin with the questing hero's plunge into a perilous dark forest. Although Gilgamesh's friend Enkidu warns him against the dangerous expedition, Gilgamesh insists on going into the great cedar forest that the god of the earth Enlil has put under the protection of the ferocious giant Humbaba. Over three thou-sand years later, Dante's *The Divine Comedy* begins:

> Midway in our life's journey, I went astray
>   from the straight road and woke to find myself
>   alone in a dark wood. How shall I say
>
> what wood that was! I never saw so drear,
>   so rank, so arduous a wilderness!
>   Its very memory gives a shape to fear.
>
> Death could scarce be more bitter than that place!
>   But since it came to good, I will recount
>   all that I found revealed there by God's grace.[3]

In the Arthurian cycle and the Robin Hood stories, countless dangers lurk in the forest. Edmund Spenser's *The Faerie Queen* begins with Una and the Red-Cross Knight, under a blackening sky, seeking shelter:

> A shadie grove not far away they spide,
>   That promist ayde the tempest to withstand:

Whose loftie trees yclad with sommers pride,
Did spred so broad, that heavens light did hide.

Almost immediately they get lost in the labyrinthine wood:

They cannot finde that path, which first was showne,
But wander too and fro in wayes unknowne
. . .
That makes them doubt, their wits be not their owne.

These forests are always alien places that baffle and confuse. Una, like so many wise mothers, warns of "the danger hid, the place unknowne and wilde."[4] But the Red-Cross Knight fails, like so many rash youths, to heed her advice; soon, like Dante before him, he finds himself face to face with a "monster vile."

In Coleridge's poem "Christabel," Christabel in the forest at midnight comes upon what appears to be a distressed maiden, but what is indeed a monster vile, probably a blood-sucking vampire, whom the innocent, tenderhearted Christabel takes home with her to her own bed.

Again, it is in the wood beyond the village that Nathaniel Hawthorne's Young Goodman Brown sees or thinks he sees the Satanic baptism, the vision of universal evil that blasts his whole life. It is there, too, that Hester Prynne strays pridefully from village wisdom and begins a life of solitary trial. She gains from her ordeal a kind of wisdom different from that of the village; later, after settling at the edge of the village to live on its terms, she is curiously respected, welcome, but never intimate with its members.

James Dickey's novel *Deliverance* tells about four ordinary men who, seeking a weekend's adventure, canoe down a wild river in north Georgia. As they are camping deep in the woods far from help, decadent mountaineers who keep no laws slink forth and terrorize them. The adventurers, all unready, must learn heroism or die.

THE HERO'S LIFE: WHAT THE DARK FOREST MEANS

The dark forest is the wilderness full of peril, the "chaos"—the unsanctified, unordered place—beyond the little "cosmos" of one's home or village. The person who enters it will have an adventure; he will be wrenched from the comfortable, familiar patterns, the conventional life and conventional wisdom. He will be tested, thrown upon his own resources. He will suffer, and, especially if he is not yet ready for this demanding adventure, he may well perish. For he has moved into the unforeseeable—all props kicked out from under him—and that necessarily involves risk and danger. On the other hand, he is getting the chance to grow or the chance to discover possibilities that he has not dreamed existed. A great boon may await him if he meets the test.

Quest, boon, and return: This is the essence of the heroic life-pattern. The hero leaves the safety of home, ventures into the wilderness, finds something there that is mysteriously dangerous or valuable—often both— and returns home in triumph.[5]

The dark forest symbolizes exactly the same as, in the stories of Melville and Conrad, the open sea and the jungle; the same as, in Genesis, the land outside the garden; in the Old English epic *Beowulf*, the wild, misty fens far from the roaring fire and good companions of the mead-hall; in Irish tales, Scottish romances, *Wuthering Heights*, and some of the novels of Thomas Hardy, the open moors; in *Huckleberry Finn*, the Mississippi; and in *Star Wars*, outer space. One has moved beyond the community circle, beyond everyday demands, assumptions, possibilities.

THE CITIZEN'S LIFE

An alternate life-pattern, the citizen's life, the "nest" as opposed to the quest, is most vividly symbolized in our culture by the Christmas card cliché that still moves us, believers and nonbelievers alike: the tiny village at dusk, snow heaped heavily upon it; a church in the center, its radiant light and warmth pushing back the bluish snow; clusters of happy people converging upon the church. This picture is a vision of the cosmos, the magic circle of peace, order, harmony, comfort, safety, and support, both human and divine, that keeps the sterile blankness of the snow from burying the whole creation. The steeple with its cross on top is, of course, the magic pole, the "Kauwa-auwa" under whose protection the people thrive. Furthermore, the light glowing from the church suggests the triumph of life, even of life stretching into eternity. Thus, the scene's power lies in its compressed representation of beliefs, attitudes, and goals familiar and profoundly inviting to many, many people.

These feelings center on human brotherhood. For instance, in this idealized village, if old Mrs. McGurney does not appear at her kitchen window one frosty morning, her always watchful neighbors will notice and seek an explanation; and if they should find that she is sick, they will rally around, with pots of broth and stewed apples. This is a homey instance of the mutual aid that all may rely upon in a stable, traditional community.

THE HERO VERSUS THE COMMUNITY

The hero's adventure is likely, at the very least, to confuse him. His physical "be-wilderment" is accompanied by and often symbolizes psychic confusion. Another way to express his state is to say that his adventure disorients or "disconcerts" him. Examining the etymology of "concert" further clarifies the relationship between the two life-patterns. As the term "concerted effort" suggests, "concert" means more than a performance by a group of musicians. It implies people acting together in harmony. Its Latin meanings are "together" (con-) and "settled," "certain" (certus). The people in a community guided by a powerful myth are, unlike the solitary hero, certain of the Truth and certain of how to act; these matters are settled. And in a sense it is the warmth generated by this certainty that enables the community to hold back the blank, death-dealing snow.

It would be foolish indeed to dismiss as naive or trivial the settled truths by which a traditional community lives. These truths protect the community from chaos: from ignorant, tinkering do-gooders as much as from the alien and the wantonly evil. What has lasted, worked, helped generations of people to survive together with some kindliness and decency must contain a very rich wisdom. Little Red Riding Hood is not the only person who came to grief because she stepped into the dark forest ill-equipped. Anyone who steps forth had better possess a pair of winged sandals, a cloak of invisibility, or the gifts of unusual personal courage and good sense. His own brain and bone will have to be his "Kauwa-auwa." If he ventures far from the conventional wisdom or the society that affirms it, for survival he will need either the rock-hard faith of Noah upon all that deep, sloshing void, the resourcefulness of Odysseus, or an almost incredible integrity in all senses of the word. Otherwise, he is likely to collapse or, like Melville's Ahab or like Joseph Conrad's Kurtz in *Heart of Darkness*, to go fiendishly mad, becoming himself the monster of chaos that he has set out to destroy.

Furthermore, if the hero is able to acquire the boon he seeks and returns to his community to offer his gift, he had better be prepared to find all doors closed to him or his place usurped. In sending his young cousin Jason on a dangerous quest, Pelias really wanted Jason's death, not the Golden Fleece, and he certainly was not prepared, when the unwelcome hero returned, to relinquish the throne now rightfully Jason's. When Agamemnon returned from sacking Troy, weighted with glory and treasure, Clytemnestra, far from being thrilled, promptly murdered him in his bath. When Odysseus returned, he found his very house stuffed with louts yearning for nothing so much as his death. Nor had Polydectes, the evil wooer of Perseus' mother, planned for the young hero's return with the great prize of Medusa's head.

Nor were the Israelite slaves in Egypt pleased when Moses returned from the desert wilderness with his stunning gift of freedom for them. They had long since adapted themselves to the meager but sure comforts of slavery—the privileges of whining, of helplessness, of sly passivity—and here came this nuisance, this cosmos-cracking monster calling upon them to leave their nest and behave like heroes. A miserable nest, for most of us, is still preferable to no nest at all. Indeed, Moses had to push the whole pack of freed slaves, many thousands of them, month after month through the wilderness. The Israelites had been so demoralized by slavery that, though they could be bullied into accompanying the hero into the desert, their first generation could not become heroes. They were the doubly dispossessed, so blasted first by the generations of servitude and then by this second uprooting, that they could not take up the gift of adulthood, of personal responsibility. Far from thanking Moses for their freedom, they never truly forgave him.

In short, the hero is often too disruptive, his effect too momentous, to be utilized by those who must stand directly in his white light. It is appropriate that Semele, the only one of Zeus' mortal lovers to see him in his full glory as king of heaven, instantly perished from the sight—but that her child alone, of all the children Zeus sired by mortal women, became a god, and a god of the utmost importance.

Most people know, if not from myth then from the human observations out of which myths grow, that the very great, the heroes, the originals, are often unrecognized as such by their own families or their own people. When Dionysus returned to Thebes, the town of his birth, to make his godhead known, the king yawned. William Faulkner's brother was not quite sure why people made all that fuss over Bill. Recently in a small Irish town, a dignified official dismissed the importance of two of the best, most original writers in English in this century. Of Yeats, he said, "Oh, he wrote a few pretty pieces, but we Irish don't think much of him," and of James Joyce, "Tell me, now, would you want your sixteen-year-old daughter reading him? Ireland isn't like that. Goldsmith, now there's a true Irish writer." Sometimes, as Joyce did, the hero understandably decides not to return to his community.

If the hero returns from his journey, real or psychic, bearing a gift extraordinarily precious, the townspeople may do him the ultimate honor of toasting him twice, first upon a spit and then forever afterward with their best wine. That is, the usual sequence is to nail him to a cross and then, after a suitable period of bashing each other in disputes over his significance, raise that cross to their highest place and live in harmony for a while beneath its protection, its light. As bitter as the contemplation of this pattern may be, it is often necessary. Confronted with a possible insight of tremendous power, the community is thrown into consternation. It sometimes tears the hero apart, then tears itself apart and puts itself together again in accordance with its understanding of this new Truth. Eventually the community may accept the hero's gift, gratefully reshaping itself to adapt to his contribution, but not without upheaval. Thus a settled community quite sensibly greets a fresh insight with alarm, and some wise members try sensibly to destroy it. Its bearer is one form, indeed, of the chaos-monster, the monster that so often in myth appears upon the heretofore peaceful scene to threaten its harmony and order.

In discussing the word "concert," above, I stated that it implies people working together in harmony. But not all of its root-meanings refer to harmony and cooperation. The Latin verb *certare*, related to "certain" and "settled," means to decide by debate or warfare. Precisely. Those community values did not spontaneously leap together into harmony. Again and again, heroes reentered the community's magic circle and were ignored, expelled, laughed at, or stoned. Often enough, they in some sense deserved that treatment, for they set neighbor against neighbor, ruined the peace, exposed the long-buried grievances, the "strife closed in the sod." The conflict between the community seeking stability and the hero seeking a potentially constructive change is the conflict of two kinds of wisdom, two valid life-patterns. The community's way is a gift, a composite boon bestowed by the heroes of old and handed down through time. That village on the Christmas card, for instance, represents the combined gifts of Moses, Jesus, the seventeenth-century Pilgrims, the eighteenth-century shapers of the United States, and others—heroes able to leap free of their own communities' assumptions and conventional wisdom, dive into the deep, find there something of great value, and force their way back into the group.

THE DISCONSOLATE WANDERER

One need not weep long for either the solid citizens or the heroes. Both know what they are about. Both can shape highly satisfying lives for themselves. Both tend to die good deaths, deaths of comfort or glory or knowledge of their efficacy. The true unfortunates are those who can neither embrace the community's values nor formulate clear purposes of their own. They wander disconsolately near the fringes of the community, trying one way to shape their lives and then another—a wonder diet or drug supposed to put everything in perspective; the guidance of gurus or astrologers; a creed of self-fulfillment. They may find the patterns offered by the traditional community sterile, yet they cannot find a coherent and sustaining alternative.

Matthew Arnold poignantly describes this state. In "Stanzas from the Grande Chartreuse" (1866), he pictures himself as "wandering between two worlds, one dead, / The other powerless to be born, / With nowhere yet to rest my head."[6] In "Dover Beach" (ca. 1851), he likens the Christian world-view to a shimmering band that for centuries protected the world (the magic circle again) but does no longer, leaving the earth once more a senseless wilderness:

> The Sea of Faith
> Was once . . . at the full, and round earth's shore
> Lay like the folds of a bright girdle furled.
> But now I only hear
> Its melancholy, long, withdrawing roar,
> Retreating, to the breath
> Of the night wind, down the vast edges drear
> And naked shingles of the world.
> . . .
> . . . the world, which seems
> To lie before us like a land of dreams,
> So various, so beautiful, so new,
> Hath really neither joy, nor love, nor light,
> Nor certitude, nor peace, nor help for pain;
> And we are here as on a darkling plain

Swept with confused alarms of struggle and flight,
Where ignorant armies clash by night.[7]

In "The Scholar-Gypsy" (1853), Arnold contrasts life inside the traditional cosmos—serene, informed with a unifying purpose—with life in what he saw as the spirit-shattering modern world. The poem is an explicit comment on the spiritual ills of people living in an age of doubt and rapid change. What kills such people, he says, is their indecision, their attempts to live too many lives, their inability to pursue any one purpose with conviction.

> . . . What wears out the life of mortal men?
>   'Tis that from change to change their being rolls;
> 'Tis that repeated shocks, again, again,
>   Exhaust the energy of strongest souls
>   And numb the elastic powers.
> Till having used our nerves with bliss and teen,
>   And tired upon a thousand schemes our wit,
>   To the just-pausing Genius we remit
> Our worn-out life, and are—what we have been.
>   . . .
> Thou waitest for the spark from heaven! and we,
>   Light half-believers of our casual creeds,
>   Who never deeply felt, nor clearly willed,
>   Whose insight never has borne fruit in deeds,
>   Whose vague resolves never have been fulfilled;
>   For whom each year we see
>   Breeds new beginnings, disappointments new;
>   Who hesitate and falter life away,
>   And lose tomorrow the ground won today—[8]

Arnold spoke eloquently for the person unable to embrace the community's purposes or the myths that shape them and yet unable to blast off to explore outer space.

THE FUNCTION OF HEROES

In pondering how a person gets caught in such a miserable plight, one might question what it is about community life that makes his plight possible. One may reasonably argue that *every* relatively long-lived community, whether shaped by Osiris, Moses, Buddha, Jesus, or the founders of the American Dream, possesses mankind's single most fruitful insight. Far from being a great secret, it is a cliché: "Do unto others. . . ." Sometimes the idea is rephrased: View other people, animals, plants, the earth itself as part of a divine whole, treating them with respect, even reverence; or, think of your acts as pebbles thrown into a pool and consider the rings of consequence emanating from those acts; or, treat all men as your brothers.

The precise words hardly matter; the insight is the same. And since we possess it, what is wrong? Why are we not all tingling incessantly with conviction, purpose, and brotherly love? A world that has had this golden egg laid upon its doorstep again and again, we might think, would have achieved almost perfect harmony by now. None of us should need to wring his hands or ride off into the dragon-infested forest searching for the Great Answer or wait for a hero to bring it back in his magic pouch.

In short, who needs heroes?

The community does. Great insights keep getting lost, and only a hero, able to see beyond a particular community's muddle, can retrieve them. Mrs. McGurney's neighbors start arguing over whose turn it is to take her the pot of broth. Or she dies, and when peculiar folks who live the wrong way move into her house, everybody argues over what to do. Sometimes the neighbors even plant a cross on the new folks' lawn and set aflame this symbol of ultimate acceptance, ultimate love.

To say that a community possesses an insight is not to say that all its members absorb the essence of the idea and bequeath it, unchanged, to their children. Since only rare people can perceive the insight directly and steadily, it reaches most people through powerful, yet ephemeral, metaphors. That is, the insight is usually embodied in a myth, and people tend to believe the myth literally or quasi-literally. As they revel in the insight itself and strive to live by it, they enthusiastically embellish the story that solidifies the idea for them. The mythological George Washington is a case in point. For nineteenth-century Americans, this figure crystallized a valuable group of insights. The process begun by Mason Locke Weems was continued by the people who snapped up Weems's "biography" of Washington; finding their own perceptions seemingly perfected there, they passed on the glorious details, with some new embellishments, to their children, pupils, and constituents. (Additional stories tend to attach themselves to a hero because his admirers want his qualities demonstrated and explored to their uttermost limits.) Nor is the mythologized Washington false; it is true both to the character of the historical man and to the ideals that he still represents. It simplifies, heightens, and compresses the facts, making the wisdom that underlies those facts accessible to large numbers of people.

However, as the stories grow more extravagant, they tend to smother the very insight from which they have grown. When people begin to doubt that a cherished myth is in keeping with the facts, they begin to lose faith in its validity. If the myth has stood at the center of their lives, this loss of faith may well devastate them. That is what happened to Matthew Arnold and other intellectuals of his time. The new astronomy, geology, and then biology had undermined the literal interpretation of the biblical stories upon which they had founded their deepest purposes. Because we usually perceive human brotherhood through myths, if the myths collapse, then the insight itself gets lost for a time, and only another hero can recover it.

An additional irony arises from the fact that most people perceive this insight only through its metaphorical or mythical expression. Again and again, two groups who possess different metaphors for the same basic insight of brotherhood insist on their own metaphors. They cannot do otherwise. Philip Roth's short story "Eli, the Fanatic" illustrates the point. The story takes place in a very pleasant, mostly Protestant American suburb shortly after World War II. The Jews there have had to underplay their Jewishness in order to gain admittance to this place where their children can grow up in wholesome serenity. When a conservative Orthodox rabbi sets up a yeshivah in an old house up the hill and moves in with eighteen young charges—all survivors of Hitler's Europe—their presence so threatens the position of the local American Jews that the latter want them out. The American group, also scarred by bigotry and the nightmare of the war, believe that the welfare of their children—and in that sense, their survival—lies in blending with the gentiles. But for the immigrants, the welfare of the eighteen children and the survival of their badly cracked cosmos lies in their highly visible exotic customs. The two groups, so profoundly brothers, inevitably clash because the metaphors through which brotherhood comes alive to them clash.

Always, some members of a community must pay a high price for the community's peace and safety, compromising their needs for the sake of harmony. Sometimes the price is too high: What constitutes a necessity for one segment of the community may constitute the chaos-monster for another. One solution is to do battle, which destroys that community. Another is to reinterpret the conflicting myths. For example, in an early

Greek story the goddess Artemis demands that Agamemnon sacrifice his daughter Iphigenia; in the later version of the story after the gods had come more and more to represent the humane and rational, Artemis, far from really insisting on the horrible act, whisks Iphigenia off to safety.

For a time, the "Jews" slew Jesus; later, when Christians decided that brotherhood should extend to Jews, they determined that a small group of fanatics was responsible. The Mormon Church long forbade intermarriage between whites and blacks, and refused blacks full participation in the church on the grounds that they are descended from the accursed Cain. In the 1960s and 1970s, that position became more and more embarrassing. Recently, "God" revealed that he had at last lifted the curse. For millenniums, women were "Adam's rib," created as man's helpmate, adjunct, inferior; now the Mary Magdalene story is cited as evidence that Jesus was the first great feminist. But to reinterpret too frequently raises doubts about the validity of any version of the myth that once held the community together.

A third way to resolve conflicting views within a community is for a hero to stumble upon a social ideal that not only *shelters* diversity but also informs that diversity with *mythic value*. For example, because the American ideals of respect for diversity and for freedom of speech, worship, and so on, run counter to the homogeneity that helps to bind a community, this respect itself has to be powerfully mythologized through such folk heroes as Washington and Lincoln and through such binding rituals as Thanksgiving and the Fourth of July. Still, as a community tries to come closer and closer to its ideals of tolerance, it is always in danger of shattering, and a significant number of its members become restless, confused, dissatisfied. In this seeming jumble of contradictions, they are seeking a meaning that will propel them into action. Some may become heroes, quasi-heroes, villains; and some will wander and wait.

A community that has already lost its binding purposes may subsist for a time on the traditional attitudes engrained in its members by the lost insight's once supporting myths. But growing numbers of people, obscurely unhappy, will behave in perverse ways. Again, a hero may be needed to restore the insight.

Finally, even in the most favorable circumstances, the elemental principle of brotherhood simply is not always compelling. We frequently forget that all people are our brothers—and whenever we forget, the statement ceases to be true. Here is a truth only true to the degree that large numbers of people believe it, live by it, and trust their neighbors to do the same. The truth actually must be created again and again. Yet the myths, rituals, and admonishments that help a community to re-create it gradually lose their efficacy. One is struck by the seemingly electrifying ritual of the Mass, in which the devout absorb symbolically—even literally, according to the Roman Catholic doctrine of transubstantiation—the body and blood of the Hero, and yet the effect is often neither deep nor permanent. A modern reader is struck, too, by the vigorous preaching of brotherhood in medieval literature, for instance, in Chaucer's *The Canterbury Tales*—incessant cajoling, wheedling, badgering—and by the intermittence of the response. The thoroughly believable Pardoner, consumed by greed, describes in lurid detail how he cheats the gullible in order to line his own pockets and then tells a shudderingly convincing story about the trap that greedy people set for themselves. The daily betrayer of plain, poor people and of his own humanity, he knows what he is, and laughs. The biblical account of Judas, Robert Browning's poem "Soliloquy in a Spanish Cloister," and Flannery O'Connor's short story "Revelation" present other vivid instances of people who are conscious members of communities centered unequivocally upon the insight of human brotherhood and who simply do not feel it.

Frequently, a person forgets his own past self so readily that he cannot understand his children and feels so little kindness toward his own future self that he willfully condemns himself to grinding debts, lung cancer, or a life otherwise blighted. Thus it should be no great surprise that he does not always feel a warm bond between himself and *other* people.

Furthermore, if in the great cosmic myths the insight is always that all men are brothers and that all life should be honored, the opposing insight is equally valid: All men are singular. The first brothers, after all, were Abel and Cain. The nest does keep going up in flame, and those who set it afire are not always monsters from without who have breached the magic ring. If all men are brothers, then all, too, are potential Cains.

> Lizzie Borden took an ax
> And gave her mother forty whacks;
> When she saw what she had done
> She gave her father forty-one.

But in trying to puzzle out the paradoxical relationship between the communal life and the solitary quest, and the mystery of why the quest is ever appropriate at all, perhaps one need only look at a typical family.

Each new partner in a marriage remembers vividly the mistakes that his mother and father made in their marriage and in their rearing of children, and he vows passionately to avoid these. Just as vividly, he remembers their great successes and vows to emulate these. One might suppose, then, that over a few generations an almost perfect marriage would evolve and that, indeed, by the present time, each child, as the product of his parents' and his parents' parents' wisdom, would be almost the perfect human being—no more problems, every hurdle leapt, all major issues settled, the prize of wisdom clasped in his dimpled fists like lightning bolts.

Even should there have been some small error somewhere, rendering one's mother or father not quite wholly wise, one still has the accumulated wisdom of all the other mothers and fathers, the whole race, to draw upon. Yet we do not see in each new life perfect ease and wisdom. Instead we see the same old struggles and indecisions, the same old problems.

The cause, again, lies in man's singularity. We cannot *be* each other; thus we cannot learn perfectly from each other. In a sense, we cannot learn from each other at all. The mother and father fought dragons and, often, after much fear, pain, and toil, conquered them. In conquering them, the parents made a cosmos for their children, just as in Norse mythology the gods slew Ymir and then made out of him the world-nest for the child-people. But the child cannot live forever in that nest. To every family comes the twilight of the gods, the faltering of the parents' wisdom, the return of chaos and old night. Parents can raise their children to become good dragon-fighters, but parents can never fight their children's dragons for them. The children must be ready to leap free of the collapsing dome of their parents' cosmos into their own dark forest to meet their own dragons. The dragons that the children must fight—the I-am-insufficient dragon, the world-is-too-complicated dragon, the how-shall-I-make-the-world-pay-me-or-respect-me dragon—these are some of the same dragons that the parents fought in order to make their own nest. So in a real and profound sense, the "call to adventure" in the heroic life-pattern is the call to every young person to leave that nest to make his own order out of the world's chaos. The heroic life-pattern in mythology and other folklore is an emblem, a blazing vision, of what each one of us must do, and therein lies its enduring power.

Most of us, indeed, will be called upon to enter that forest and fight a dragon not just once but again and again. And as for the two basic life-patterns, the one of cooperation within the community and the other of solitary adventure, very few of us today live consistently by the one or the other. The conditions in which we live are so complex and diversified, so bewildering, that the community itself may almost be viewed as a wilderness. Most of us follow some of its blurred patterns and reject or modify others. We have many more choices than do people who live in stable communities, but, because both the criteria for making choices and the consequences of our choices are much less clear, we must endure the strain of far greater uncertainty. In a sense, we are all heroes, willy-nilly.

The next chapter tells about heroes in myth and legend.

5

The Heroic Life-Pattern

The essential heroic pattern is a simple one of four parts: The hero (1) enters the unknown, (2) struggles with what lies there, (3) finds something of value—a boon, and (4) returns with that boon to his community. Parts 3 and 4, of course, do not always occur in the story. Many an adventurer's bones lie bleaching in the wilderness; many a community locks its gates against the returning adventurer; many a prize, when unveiled before the throng, is found to have turned to dust; and many a hero is so transformed by his experience in the forest that home is lost to him forever. Indeed, it is these tragic possibilities that keep the basic pattern meaningful; without real risk, that pattern would become mere cliché.

The pattern is known to us all, for it is not only the plot of many stories but is also, in enlarged, dramatic form, the pattern of our own experience. Again and again, we find ourselves facing the unexpected, with its risks and opportunities, and we either turn back or discover something that helps us to deal with it and with similar challenges in the future. Small wonder that we want stories about people under stress and that we follow their responses so eagerly. These stories help us to create and interpret our own lives.

Even if we grope in confusion when asked to name some modern heroes in the news—John Wayne? Joe Namath? Timothy Leary? Douglas MacArthur?—we have little trouble naming the heroes of myth and legend or their modern counterparts. We generally agree on Hercules, Ulysses, Theseus, Achilles, Alexander the Great, Samson, David (the killer of Goliath), King Arthur, Joan of Arc, George Washington, and dozens more. We agree on the Lone Ranger, on Superman, and on Captain Kirk, Mr. Spock, and other members of the *Star Trek* crew.

DEFINITIONS

What these personages have in common is, above all, courage; in addition, all undertake a difficult task that is comprehensible to ordinary people and whose successful outcome is believed to enhance the lives of many. Simply defined, the hero is a brave person who undertakes a large, constructive task and is, in the minds of his people, effective. An important secondary characteristic is glamor, panache.

Almost as interesting as what a hero is, is what he need not be. For instance, he often is not very clever. Hercules, or Heracles, as the Greeks themselves called him, had boundless physical strength and energy, but he lacked good judgment. This kind of hero is often a favorite as much for his human limitations as for his excellence. The strongest man on earth and helper even of the gods, Heracles frequently killed people by accident. The first unintended victim of his heedless strength was his music teacher; later victims were his beloved wife and three sons. The Hindu god Indra, a great warrior, hacked up demons and got drunk with equal gusto. The only one of the early Aryan gods imagined as human in characteristics and morals, he had addressed to him by far the largest number of hymns.[1] The biblical Samson, another swashbuckling hero, could bring down a huge temple with his bare hands but could not guess that Delilah, a Philistine and therefore an enemy of his people, might have married him in order to help her people undermine his strength. Although Thor, the most popular god among the Norse—the one whom ordinary farmers and fishermen took to their hearts as their personal champion—was not staggeringly stupid, he was easily fooled, and his effectiveness lay not in his intelligence, compassion, or creativity, but in his brute strength. Like Heracles, he did not plan or question; he simply slugged enemies with his hammer. The Russian hero Vasili Buslayevich was so strong and, like Heracles and Thor, so fond of drinking that, heartily seizing a man by the hand, he tore his arm from the socket; hugging another, he broke him in two. Like Heracles and Thor, he ate with immoderate gusto and wielded a club. He brought about his own death when, against all warnings, he dove across a great stone from sheer exuberance, slipped, and bashed his brains.[2]

Nor are all heroes modest, much to the distress of some modern readers. Indeed, in many traditions, an important preliminary step in the heroic act is the boast; before a large, gaping audience, usually in a banquet hall, the hero outlines his impressive genealogy and the great deeds that he has already accomplished, and then, with stunning eloquence, asserts his sure victory against the next day's seemingly invincible foe. The literary function of the heroic boast is to review the hero's qualifications and to increase dramatic tension. The social function is to thrill the audience into admiration, wind up the hero's courage, and bind him to the task. The boast is like a ritual incantation, assuring both the onlookers and the hero himself that he can do the job. One finds such boasts in *Gilgamesh, The Iliad, The Odyssey,* and *Beowulf.* Even in the United States, whose people would scorn bragging in a serious would-be hero, Daniel Boone and other frontier heroes boasted in the traditional way, but playfully. Combining outrageous bragging and playfulness renders such heroes not only acceptable but irresistible to their audiences.

Nor do all heroes insist on winning fair and square, as they do in the American Western. In fact, the trickster hero is one of the most ancient of all heroic types, and once widely loved. "Wily" Odysseus is probably the all-time favorite. His extraordinary mental agility is as thrilling as his physical prowess, and much more dependable than his sense of justice. Even in seemingly hopeless predicaments, Odysseus is, as most translators put it, "never at a loss." He works his way out through startlingly ingenious tricks. He and his audience clearly enjoyed a good trick for its own sake, even if some of these tricks are morally unacceptable to modern readers. The same is true of Old Testament heroes, especially in Genesis. Although Yahweh did not congratulate them on cheating their fathers, brothers, husbands, and cousins, these heroes qualified as good guys, and their clever exploits were often meant to delight the ancient audience.

Nor do heroes always stride about, asserting themselves. Sometimes the sacrificial savior, a heroic sub-type, simply lies down and dies with little ado. It is his death, rather than the deeds of his life, that ensures life to others. He originated in prehistoric vegetation-gods; he might die annually in the fall, or his death be ritualized at that time, the year's death, and he be resurrected in the spring, as the life of fields, flocks, and homes quickens. The best-known examples are Middle Eastern and Mediterranean gods—the Babylonian Tammuz, the Egyptian Osiris, the Greek Dionysus, the Phrygio-Roman Attis. Christ is a highly spiritualized, sophisticated conception of the sacrificial savior. Not only did he cooperate in the events leading to his death; to a large degree, he engineered them, precisely as if he were acting out a painful but urgent ritual.

Nor do heroes always embrace their roles with confidence and enthusiasm. When chosen by God for the appalling task of uniting the Israelite slaves and leading them out of Egypt and into the sizzling wilderness, Moses sensibly protested, Who will believe that *you* have told me to do all this? And I am not an eloquent man. What shall I say? How could I persuade people? Moses clearly lacked heart for the task. Yet he not only took up the job but persisted at it for long, bitter years; he did so without much cooperation or thanks from the beneficiaries and without clear rewards from God.

Because great heroes are almost by definition rebels, it goes without saying that they are not always good citizens. But a distinct sub-type, the outlaw hero, emerged long after the establishment of civil law, as a recognition that civil law and justice are not the same. Robin Hood, the most vivid traditional example, battled both civil authority and injustice. So do the modern Hipshot, the Beat heroes such as Neal Cassady, Han Solo of *Star Wars*, and, above all, the Humphrey Bogart character. This disreputable heroic type appeals particularly to Americans because the discrepancy between law and justice gives Americans particular pain. The type appeals keenly to the young while they are discovering the discrepancy for themselves. Huck Finn, better than any other outlaw hero, embodies that poignant moment in all our lives when we see, yet cannot allow ourselves to understand and forgive, the community's shabby compromises.

Again, the defining qualities of the hero are few and simple: courage, basic good intentions, recognized effectiveness. Styles and preferences vary with time and place; what one people loves, another may disdain. But these three attributes endure.

This plain statement of the hero's attributes helps clarify two other concepts, the villain and the anti-hero. Like the hero, the villain is outstanding, often glamorous or grand. He may be courageous, his intentions are destructive, and he is only too effective. One thinks of Satan wheeling through the air on gigantic bat wings; of tall, beetle-browed wizards brewing dreadful potions; of Hitler able to understand and manipulate the basest, most hidden inclinations of millions. "Anti-hero" is a term coined in the 1950s for a protagonist most of whose attributes are the opposite of the traditional hero's attributes. The anti-hero lacks glamor. He may be cowardly, inept, stupid, or dishonest; whatever his intentions, his effect is trivial. He is often a collection of self-canceling, short-lived impulses, of doubts and raveled purposes. Meursault, the anti-heroic protagonist of Camus's *The Stranger* (1942), is insipid, arid, irresponsible, untouched by love, a feeble human being. One may well ask why anyone would find such an uninspiring person worth attention, yet Meursault has fascinated the Western world for four decades.

Although the anti-hero has turned up occasionally in stories for thousands of years, especially in the loose-jointed picaresque novel, what is most striking about him is his sudden emergence as a major character-type in the 1950s, in such postwar English novels as John Wain's *Hurry On Down* (1953), Kingsley Amis's *Lucky Jim* (1954), and John Osborne's play *Look Back in Anger* (1956).

Earlier in the century, Hemingway's stories had judged the whole modern world as a wilderness. Because no other world existed, Hemingway's heroes had no choice about whether to inhabit that wilderness, but they did choose how to live in it. They strode through the rubble with that old stiff upper lip. They embodied such traditional heroic values as courage, grace under pressure, endurance, and personal loyalty. The anti-hero, on the other hand, is a plain, inglorious citizen, dazed, resentful, groping about alone, willing to consider just about any scheme to put himself in a more comfortable spot.

A well-known American anti-hero is Yossarian, of Joseph Heller's anti-war novel *Catch-22* (1961). The situation of Yossarian goes far toward answering the question of why such characters interest us. Many Americans loved Yossarian in a special prickly way. His name evoked wry laughter, but anyone who called him a jerk, a bum, or a no-good was likely to have a fight on his hands. Yossarian clarified for millions their sense of an important truth, in this case, that they lived in such an insane society, such a wilderness of twisted values, that a sane man's efforts in any direction would be thwarted. The story was a judgment of a society, not of Yossarian. Many people felt canceled out by a community too disordered to appreciate its sane members and too heavily patrolled for them to escape into the dark forest. The inevitable symbol for this perception of walled-in chaos is the insane asylum, a symbol developed in Ken Kesey's enormously moving, popular novel *One Flew Over the Cuckoo's Nest* (1962).

The anti-hero clarifies our sense of powerlessness, of futility, in times of social confusion. The hero, on the other hand, tells us about acquiring power and using it well, and that is what we all want most. That is adulthood. Because stories about heroes of every time and place share this purpose, we might expect to find some similarities among the stories. But this sober expectation cannot possibly prepare us for the astonishing similarities that we do find. These cannot but come as a puzzle and a revelation.

THE HEROIC LIFE-PATTERN

Traditional heroic stories from most of the world tend to elaborate themselves in such similarly bizarre ways that scholars have long discerned a general life-pattern of about nine peculiar elements into which fall the lives of such varied individuals as Moses, Heracles, Alexander, Charlemagne, and Davy Crockett. Furthermore, this peculiar life-pattern for heroes is very ancient and very persistent. It had begun to form by the third millennium B.C., that is, as early as written literature, and still flourishes. Although some scholars trace the elements of this widespread pattern to particular Middle Eastern myths, the question still remains *why* the pattern arose and why it spread.

Here is the pattern:[3]

1. The hero is born under unusual or mysterious circumstances, such as the following:
   a. The mother is a virgin of noble birth.
   b. The father is a god.
   c. The father is an animal, often a god in disguise.
   d. The child is conceived in incest.
   e. A magical nut or fruit is responsible for the child's conception.
   f. The child's birth is unnatural: For instance, the child is born by Caesarian section; springs from a thigh, forehead, armpit, or some other nongenital part of the body; or is born of a male.

2. The child is marked early for greatness by some special sign.

3. The child is endangered—often exiled or placed where he is likely to be killed—but is rescued and reared in a dramatic way far from his place of birth.

4. The youth must prove his fitness for the heroic role by a test.

5. The hero fights a monster or does other great deeds involving dramatic risks; magical helpers often assist him with magical gifts.

6. The hero wins a maiden.

7. The hero journeys to the land of the dead.

8. Banished in his youth, the hero returns to triumph over his enemies.

9. The hero's death is mysterious, ambiguous.

Before listing examples or trying to account for this strange pattern, so unlike the lives of people we know, it might be useful to show how the pattern works itself out in a particular story. Consider the story, then, of a favorite Greek hero, Perseus.

PERSEUS, A TYPICAL HERO

King Acrisius of Argos heard from the Oracle at Delphi that not only was he never to have the son that he wanted but that a son of his daughter Danaë would kill him. Unwilling to incur the gods' wrath by slaying a relative, he nevertheless wished to ensure that the princess Danaë would remain a childless virgin. [Element 1a.] Thus he imprisoned her in an underground chamber made of bronze. Only a small opening at the top provided Danaë with light and air. But one day Zeus himself, struck by Danaë's beauty, contrived to visit her by turning himself into a shower of gold. [Element 1b.] Their child was Perseus, and Danaë kept his existence a secret for four years. Upon discovering the child, Acrisius had mother and son thrust into a chest and tossed into the sea.

Instead of drowning, as Acrisius had intended, Danaë and the boy were washed up on a little island. A kindly fisherman rescued them and gave them shelter in his home. [Element 3.] About the time that Perseus grew to manhood, the fisherman's tyrannical brother Polydectes, who ruled the island, asked Danaë to marry him. Protected by Perseus, she refused. Eager to get Perseus out of the way, Polydectes maneuvered the proud but poor young man into a commitment to bring him a glorious gift: the head of Medusa. Medusa was a winged monster whose very look turned men to stone and whom no one could possibly kill unaided. [The hero's rash promise is a common motif in folklore.] Perseus would probably wander about, never finding Medusa, and, if he did, of course she would instantly turn him to stone. [Element 4.]

Determined to fulfill his pledge but lacking any notion of how to do so, Perseus was pacing a lonely part of the island when both Hermes and Athena appeared. First, said Hermes, Perseus must journey to a strange land beyond the Ocean, at the World's End; neither sun nor moon ever shone there, so the land lurked in perpetual gloom. [Though not Hades, this land certainly evokes the ancient Middle Eastern notion of the afterworld. Element 7.] Upon arriving, Perseus was to seek out three withered gray women in a cave. He must trick them into telling him how to find another stange land, that of the Hyperboreans, for only there were to be found three magical gifts that he would need for success in his perilous undertaking.

The gray sisters did tell Perseus the way to the shimmering, faraway land of the Hyperboreans, a land that evokes another, and quite different, notion of a timeless afterworld. The forever-young inhabitants sang, danced, and banqueted in the perpetual sunshine. Here the nymphs graciously gave him the three essential gifts: winged sandals so that he could fly; a pouch that shrank or expanded to whatever size was needed; and a cap that made the wearer invisible. In addition, Hermes lent his own sword, to be used against Medusa's tough scales, and Athena lent her shining bronze breastplate, instructing Perseus to use it as a mirror, a means of not looking directly at Medusa. [Element 5.]

Equipped thus with magical gifts, instructions, and his own singular persistence and courage, the young man did succeed in winging down upon Medusa and, peering at her reflection only in Athena's breastplate, in slaying her. Eyes averted, he popped the head into the pouch.

On his way back to Polydectes' island with this peculiar gift, Perseus touched down in Ethiopia. There he came immediately upon a beautiful princess, Andromeda, in a horrible plight. Her father the king had chained her to a rock on the sea's edge, as a sacrifice to a ferocious sea serpent. The subjects of Andromeda's father had forced him to do this, for only she herself could appease the monster that had lately been slithering out of the deep to feast upon the local citizens.

By now Perseus needed no coaching from Hermes. In his winged sandals, he swooped down, chopped off the monster's head, and freed the beautiful princess. As her savior, he had won Andromeda's love and her parents' consent for them to marry; but before marrying her he had to fight almost single-handedly Andromeda's uncle, to whom she had been betrothed, and the uncle's many armed followers. [Elements 5, 6.]

Furthermore, Perseus still had to deliver Medusa's head to Polydectes. Returning to the island, he found that, while he had been gone, Danaë had taken refuge from the tyrant at an altar. Perseus approached Polydectes' palace, where Polydectes and his cronies were gathered for a banquet. Sweeping into the hall and flashing Athena's brilliant breastplate to rivet all eyes upon him, he then plucked Medusa's head from his pouch and brandished it high in the air. All the evil men instantly turned to stone. [Element 8.]

Although Danaë and Perseus were reconciled with Acrisius, Perseus did later kill him accidentally. [In myth, prophecies come true despite all efforts at countervention.] But Perseus and Andromeda lived happily for many years as the king and queen of Mycenae.[4]

One can see that, though the story mentions nothing of Perseus' death, his life is a good example of at least seven of the nine elements in the pattern. The lives of only a few heroes include all of the elements listed, but a great many include several.

QUESTIONS

How could such an unnatural collection of events engage people's attention in the first place, then spread so widely, and last so long? If stories that help people interpret their own lives are most compelling to them, surely, one thinks, they would not choose to hear about people who are born of virgin princesses, fly through the air wearing winged shoes, slay magical monsters, and journey to preposterous, imaginary lands. And on the other hand, if these tales please people because they are *not* reflections of people's own mundane lives, why do the tales fall so often into the same pattern, millennium after millennium? If they spring up spontaneously in widely scattered cultures, should we suppose that all people are genetically programmed to invent or at least to accept such tales? If the elements are handed down from culture to culture, does mere lack of inventiveness or some felt value account for their proliferation?

Although the reader may know or find many examples of the behavior of heroes, it will be useful to name some here. Since most of the examples to be discussed have been chosen for their relative familiarity, they will only suggest the copiousness and range of the phenomenon. The discussion's purpose is twofold: to show that such a pattern really exists and to account for it.

ELEMENT 1: THE HERO'S CONCEPTION AND BIRTH

Consider the Egyptian hero Horus. In the central and very early myth of ancient Egypt, the great king Osiris (who was born already crowned) was murdered and his body chopped up and scattered by his evil brother. Isis, one of the most devoted, resourceful wives in all mythology, found, assembled, and embalmed all the pieces—except the penis, eaten by a crab. Finding a skilled craftsman to make a wooden phallus, she then used all her considerable arts of love to enable the body of Osiris to beget upon her the holy child Horus. To protect the baby, Isis made her way stealthily to the delta marshes to bear and nurture it. Like many infants who later become heroes, Horus was born in a humble, secret place. This child would become the avenger of his father and would be the supernatural father of every Egyptian pharaoh for thousands of years.

The Greek god Cronus, while in the shape of a horse, begot the centaur-hero Chiron. Zeus, in the form of a great swan, raped the Spartan queen Leda. The result was twins destined to become Polydeuces, the hero, and Helen, the world's most beautiful woman. The father of Alexander took the shape of a serpent in begetting his great son. The conception of God's son Jesus occurred when the Holy Spirit, an aspect of God in the form of a dove, entered the Virgin's body through her ear. Not a princess, Mary was nevertheless special. She was a member of the great family long before chosen by God as the people through whose seed all the nations of the world would be blessed. Some declared her a descendant of King David. Later, she was declared to be the purest of all people ever born, "more" sinless even than the unfallen Adam.

The virgin mother of the Phrygio-Roman god Attis conceived him by eating an almond or by putting an almond or pomegranate between her breasts. One recalls the Tewa Indian tale of Yellow Corn Girl, impregnated with Old Man Sun's child when she put a pine nut in her mouth. The mothers of Heracles, the Irish Cuchulainn, the Indian Karna, the Finnish Väinämöinen, and of many other heroes were virgins. In Germanic mythology, the barren Hunnish queen finally became pregnant after eating a magic apple sent to her by Freyja, goddess of fertility. After carrying the child for six years, the queen asked that it be cut from her body. The strapping child Volsung later founded the dynasty celebrated in the *Volsunga Saga*. The Tlinket Indians of the Pacific Northwest tell of a village in which all the people except two women died of sickness or were carried away by some malevolent being that lived in the forest. When the two women were gathering roots in the forest, one of them swallowed some of the root juice, which created a baby in her. The boy, Root-stump, grew very fast and was tough. When he was playing on the beach one day, the malevolent being came to grab him, but the boy grew roots in every direction, pulled down the thing that had been killing his people, and broke it in pieces.[5] Quetzalcoatl's mother conceived him by swallowing an emerald; the god Huitzilopochtli's mother, by finding a white feather in the temple and putting it between her breasts. (The Aztecs often symbolized the divine, immortal part of a human being as a precious stone or a feather.)[6]

Some additional heroes whose fathers were reputed to be gods are the Greeks Heracles (fathered by Zeus), Theseus (by Poseidon), and Dionysus (by Zeus); Romulus, the founder of Rome (by Mars); the East Indian Karna (by the sun god); the Irish Cuchulainn (by Lug). Early Egyptian pharaohs were the incarnated god Horus, son of Re. (This Horus and Osiris' son Horus came to be viewed later as the same god.) Many great families are descended from gods, for example, the Volsungs from the high god Odin.

Just how the Chinese hero No-Cha was conceived is not clear. His mother dreamed that a Taoist priest forced his way into her bedroom, barked out "Woman, receive the child of the unicorn," and before she could reply, pressed an object to her bosom. Waking in a cold sweat, she was seized with labor pains and, that same night, bore a ball of flesh that rolled on the floor like a wheel. Her husband, not at all pleased, struck the ball with his sword. Out popped a baby, surrounded by a red halo and already wearing red silk trousers and a magical gold bracelet.[7]

Two American Indian heroes who rid the earth of such evils as cruel sons-in-law and the monster Wind-Sucker (tuberculosis) are Afterbirth Boy, grown from another boy's afterbirth, and Blood Clot Boy, from a blood clot that an old man found in a newly killed buffalo. Hare, the great hero of the Manitou Indians of the Great Lakes region, went down to earth and entered a virgin's womb. The supernatural energy and compassion with which he would later destroy evil people and bestow the gift of reincarnation on good people were already fully formed, for when he heard the people weeping, he burst prematurely from his mother's womb, killing her.[8]

To be conceived in incest might not seem to confer honor upon the child, but heroes and heroines so conceived include the Greek Antigone, by Jocasta and Jocasta's son Oedipus; the Greeks Castor and Clytemnestra, by Tyndareus and his daughter Leda; the Norse Sinfiotli, son of Signy and her brother Sigmund; Cuchulainn, by Conchobar and his daughter Dechtire; Pope Gregory the Great, by noble twins; and King Arthur, by King Uther Pendragon and his sister.

The story of Sinfiotli suggests a partial explanation for this motif. Signy tricked her brother into begetting a child with her because she knew that only a full-blooded Volsung would have the strength and courage to avenge a great wrong done to the Volsungs. The story underlines the idea that the virtues of the Volsungs were far greater than those of other family lines; incest concentrated these virtues instead of diluting them. But, more simply, incest also offers the dramatic contrast so characteristic of heroic stories. Incest is taboo; as with a lowly birth, an incestuous one renders a hero's later glory more dazzling.

A great many heroes are born in unnatural ways. Buddha was born from the right side of the fertility goddess Maya after she dreamed that a white elephant had descended from Heaven and entered that side. Mamdhar, also in India, was born from his father's side. Like Volsung, the Persian Rustum and the Welsh Tristan were born by Caesarian section. Dionysus was twice-born: When his pregnant mother Semele perished upon the sight of Zeus in his full godly glory, Zeus saved the child and carried it in his own thigh until the proper time of its birth. Athena, the Greek goddess of wisdom, was not born of a female at all, but of Zeus alone, springing full-grown from his forehead.

ELEMENT 2: THE SPECIAL SIGN

The special sign that marks the nascent hero may be the aid of gods, as with Perseus and as with the Egyptian Horus. Set, in the form of a poisonous snake, slithered into the marshes and bit the infant Horus. Isis found the baby writhing in pain. As the frantic mother watched her child slip toward death, the high gods came to her aid. Thoth, the messenger of Re, descended. This child is so special, he declared, that were it to die, the sun itself would stop. This is Re's son, who from this day on will enjoy as much protection as the sun. The Norse Odin, as a cloaked stranger, usually appeared at a hero's birth to leave the child a special weapon.

Sometimes cosmic wonders, such as comets, meteors, brilliant stars, and great colored lights herald the child's birth. Or the child possesses astonishing precocity. When Hera sent two mighty serpents to strangle the infant Heracles, the baby rose up and strangled the serpents. On the day of his birth, Hermes jumped out of his cradle, invented the lyre, and, feeling hungry, stole Apollo's cattle. Apollo himself was very young when he killed the dragon Python. At only five years old, the Irish Chuchulainn simultaneously battled 150 strapping boys. Immediately after his birth, the infant Buddha ascended to the world's summit. Later, when his parents took him to the temple, the statues of the gods bowed before him.[9] At seven years old, No-Cha was already six feet tall and, by hurling his magic bracelet, was killing people who treated him rudely.

At first glance, most of these stories may seem childish fantasies or lies, but they are far from that. They symbolically express the sense that the hero is from the very beginning extraordinary. The view is not so different from every parent's sense that his child is special, a veritable miracle. And it could be argued that the parent is right. A child's conception, birth, and development are so essentially mysterious, so astonishing, that no sober person would believe in the process if it were not everywhere so familiar. And it seems natural enough to express one's sense of how extraordinary one's child or lover or hero is by seeing him as a child sired by or singled out by the gods.

Nor is it symbolically absurd for a people's life-giving god, the god of the rain or the sun, to manifest himself in the form of an animal widely associated with male procreative power. Furthermore, in patriarchal societies, where women and women's bodies are viewed as inferior and tainted, the singular excellence of a hero is sometimes conveyed by assigning the female function to the male. Still further, people for whom sexuality carries some taint may remove their hero from a sexual conception.

ELEMENT 3: DANGER AND RESCUE OF THE CHILD

Among the most frequent patterns of danger-and-rescue for destiny's child is, as with Perseus, being tossed into a river or sea in a basket or chest and rescued by an unexpected person. Colorful contrasts help to make a story memorable and, by their improbability, suggest that supernatural powers think the case important enough to step in. If the child is high-born, the rescuer is typically low-born, and vice versa. The prince Perseus was rescued and raised by a lowly fisherman; the slave Moses, by a princess.

Although mythologists call the general pattern the "Moses motif" after its most famous case, the first-known hero about whom the story was told was the historical Sargon, a great Mesopotamian king who ruled about 2550 B.C., roughly twelve hundred years before Moses' time. In the Sargon story, the child's father was unknown. His low-born mother set the baby adrift upon the Euphrates River in a basket made of bulrushes. In this story, although the child was found and raised by a farmer, the great goddess Ishtar protected him, and it was through her favor that Sargon eventually became an emperor. In one version of the story about Sigurd, the greatest Scandinavian hero, the boy's father Sigmund, believing his wife to be unfaithful, killed her, put the baby in a glass vessel, and cast it into a stream.

Some other heroes whose stories include the Moses motif are Dionysus, Alexander, Romulus and Remus, and the Welsh Taliesin. Another story of an abandoned child who reaches greatness is that of Chandragupta, the founder of a Hindu dynasty in the fourth century B.C. In this story, a herdsman working near a cowshed discovers the child stuffed into a clay jar, and rescues and raises it. In a modern twist on the Moses motif, the infant Superman, born on the doomed planet Krypton, is launched into space by his brilliant father, lands on earth, and is adopted by the Kents, an ordinary American couple.

A frequent cause for abandoning the child is that the father or some other older male who enjoys power correctly sees the young boy as a threat. The man is sometimes an uncle, grandfather, or king. It may seem bizarre that, although sympathy always lies with the child in such stories, the older male's fears are always correct. The child always does grow up and overthrow, castrate, or kill him, either accidentally or with good cause. The underlying subject of these stories explains the tone, for, however indirectly, they are about the inevitable tension between father and son, between the "king" and the ultimate usurper. In the course of human life, the son is the natural victor.

As in the story of Perseus, the threat is usually expressed in a prophecy. In the story of Oedipus, the oracle told Laius that some day his

infant son Oedipus would kill him and supplant him as husband of Jocasta, Oedipus' own mother. Laius directed that the child be killed. The
infant was not killed outright but left in a remote place to die. Similar
stories are told of Krishna in India, of Cyrus in Iran.

Zeus, as an infant, was almost eaten by his father Cronus, who had
eaten all his earlier children to avoid fulfillment of the prophecy that one
of his children would overthrow him. In the story of Moses, the pharaoh
feared not one male child but the male Israelites collectively. As their
numbers swelled, he began to worry that they might rebel and join the
military forces of Egypt's enemies. With an eye to future safety, he ordered that all male Israelite infants be drowned in the Nile. As often
happens in the dramatic world of myth, it was the seemingly insignificant
exception that was destined to make the big difference: Only one mother
contrived to save her child, but that child was Moses. With predictable
irony, Moses was nurtured as a prince in the pharaoh's own household,
as if Moses were his grandchild. Again, the "son" smote the "father."

In the story of Jesus' birth, the powerful male who believed himself
threatened was not, of course, Joseph but Herod the Great, king of Judea,
Samaria, and Galilee. Herod was king of the Jews under the Roman
rulers. When he heard that magi from the Orient had seen a great star
portending the birth of the Messiah and had come to worship the child,
Herod was naturally alarmed. He was all the more uneasy because, under
Roman dominion, his people had split into factions, not all of which
supported his family line. A proclaimed Messiah would mean political
trouble. Learning that the child had been born in Bethlehem, Herod
sent soldiers there to slaughter all males under two years old. But one
survived. Miraculously, an angel had warned Joseph just in time to take
Mary and the fated child to Egypt, and there they stayed until the angel
told them it was safe to return.

In Hebrew legend, Abraham's infancy was attended by similar dangers. Nimrod, the Canaanite king, had read in the stars that a child
would be born who would reveal Nimrod's religion as a lie. Nimrod built
a large house where all women were to go to bear their children. There
he had all boys killed. But when Abraham's birth drew near, his mother
fled alone to the desert. As she bore her child in a dark cave, the light in
the child's face illuminated the whole cave. Rather than take her baby
back to the city to be killed, she left him in the cave. Gabriel, sent by
God, caused nourishing milk to flow from the baby's own finger.[10]

Several Polynesian tales tell of a child born and reared under circumstances very similar to those of the Greek Theseus: A high chief or god marries far from home, fathers a child, and leaves gifts that will establish its identity. In the Hawaiian version, a great personage from a land in the clouds fathered a child, Namaka-oka-pao'o, in a village on Oahu. Before disappearing, the personage left a feather cloak and other gifts for his son. While still a baby, Namaka-oka-pao'o pulled up all the potato vines his supposed father had planted. Furious, the pseudo-father tried to kill the baby with an ax. But the baby said a chant, causing the ax to slip and chop off the man's head. When the alarmed chief of Oahu and his warriors tried to kill Namaka-oka-pao'o, it was they who died. According to the version told in the Marquesas Islands, when the other village boys mocked the boy for having no father, the mother sent him to his father's land. There, before the boy was recognized as son of the ruler, he was tossed into an oven (or thrown into a hole). His father rescued him. In the Tonga version, the boy's jealous sky-brothers killed and ate him. They were given an emetic, and the boy was put back together.[11]

Often the fated child is reared apart from its father for safety, and, when the prospective hero returns to his father's city, the youth is again threatened or hostility again flares. As Oedipus walked along the highway toward his native Thebes, his unrecognized father tried to strike him down. Theseus went to Athens, where his father Aegeus nearly poisoned him accidentally. Later, even though Aegeus apparently did not send Theseus to Crete to fight the Minotaur, Aegeus allowed him to go to his probable death there. And, of course, both Oedipus and Theseus were responsible, through heedlessness, for their fathers' deaths.

The danger to the nascent hero may come from older brothers jockeying for power rather than from a father-figure whose power is already established. As if following some law of dramatic tension, in such a case of unestablished power, the number of enemies usually increases. Ten older brothers ganged up on the Old Testament hero Joseph, first deciding to murder him outright and then instead abandoning him in a desert well. In the mythologized story of the eighth-century Frankish hero Charlemagne, several older brothers persecuted the young prince, driving him out of France into Moslem Spain.

Sigurd's enemy was his guardian. A posthumous child of the royal Hunnish line and destined to become the greatest of all Germanic heroes, Sigurd was reared in exile by the Danish king's master smith Regin. Hoping that Sigurd himself would be slain, Regin urged Sigurd to slay the dragon Fafnir.

Frequently, as with Perseus, the danger to the young hero comes in the form of a quest upon which the father-figure sends him, a quest that can reasonably be expected to end in the boy's death. The story of the Greek hero Jason is a case in point. When Aison's throne was usurped by his nephew Pelias (the motif of treachery between the old and young again), Aison's infant son and rightful heir Jason was sent off to rustic safety. Meanwhile the evil Pelias enjoyed the throne. When Jason returned as a young man, generously suggesting that Pelias keep much of the wealth rightfully Jason's but turn over the scepter to Jason, Pelias seemed to agree. But then he claimed that an oracle had told him one of them should go to a certain distant, savage land to bring back the Golden Fleece, owned by that land's king and guarded by a watchful serpent in a sacred grove. Jason, so much the younger, would be the logical one. Jason took the bait, and that appeared to be a tidy way to dispose of him forever. The lovely princess Medea, a sorceress, became both Jason's magical helper and prize. In Irish tradition, Cuchulainn's future father-in-law sent the hero on the perilous journey.

Jason's early protector Chiron, half-man and half-horse, brings to mind another common element in a hero's boyhood. Although shepherds often rescue and rear the endangered child (as they do Krishna, Zeus, Cyrus, Heracles, Oedipus), many times animals first play some interesting part in protecting it. King Priam of Troy, hearing that his son Paris would one day destroy the kingdom itself, directed that the child be left in the hills to die. Until shepherds found the baby, a bear nourished it.

The animal, often a fierce one mysteriously solicitous of the child, sometimes imparts to it the animal's admired qualities. An eagle nourished Gilgamesh in the Babylonian version of his story. Goats nourished the Babylonian Nebuchadnezzar and the Greek Zeus (goats are symbols of the procreative power, and Zeus was originally a fertility god); a bear suckled Atalanta; a wolf, Romulus and Remus. Other heroes have been reared by does (for instance, Siegfried), dogs (for instance, Cyrus), and so on.

Familiar European folk tales resemble heroic stories in often presenting children threatened by their natural protectors whose own power the children endanger.[12] In the folk tales, however, both the threatened child and the parent-figure are usually females, not males, for the sphere is the peasant household, and here the mother, not the father, is perceived as exerting primary power over the children. Like the mother in Mediterranean myths who often objected to the father's plan to kill or abandon the child, Hansel and Gretel's good father objected to their stepmother's plan to abandon them in the woods so that wild animals would kill them, but he yielded to her. In a European folk tale, when the child survives, the audience is intended to be pleased not because the child is destined to bring succor or glory to mankind but because it is a good child. Instead of wary kings trying to rid themselves of their presumptive successor, one finds wicked stepmothers pushing the husband's real daughter out of the nest. This daughter is usually younger, prettier, more obedient, industrious, and sweet-tempered than the stepmother's own daughters, and the stepmother aims to nullify the girl as a competitor of the clumsy, mean stepsisters for eligible husbands and as an inheritor of the father's goods. And though one seldom reads of wizards in European folk tales, wicked witches, usually disguised mother-figures, abound. In the French version of "Sleeping Beauty," from which the English version came, the mother-in-law of the Sleeping Beauty is a gourmet ogress who aims to eat her two grandchildren and then her daughter-in-law, baked and served with Sauce Robert. The witch in "Hansel and Gretel" who lures the children into her house is the traditional northern European grandmother, but as seen in a nightmare.

These stories involving great danger to the child are again not so fanciful as they may seem. Many children have in fact been rejected, abandoned, thrust out, even killed by their parents. And although most parents watch with pride as their sons grow to vigorous manhood, a father naturally also feels twinges of jealousy, sometimes bitter ones, as a son, once dependent and worshipful, promises to equal or outshine the father's achievements, just when the father's own strengths begin to wane. It is also common for a parent to feel pangs when a child appears to have supplanted him or her in the other parent's affections. Attributing maternal harshness to stepmothers, in folk tales, recognizes, without unduly frightening children, that mothers are not always ideal and that most mothers sometimes seem cruel. Making the mother a stepmother comfortably accounts for her "wickedness" ("real" mothers are good), for her insecurity (she is the second wife, not the first choice, not the love-bride), and for the father's particular attachment to the child (a reminder and a part of the love-bride).

In short, whether in myth or folk tale, the main source of the threatened-child stories is the tension built into family structure and into the biology of human beings. Human children remain vulnerable and helpless far longer than do other young animals, while their brains develop and while they acquaint themselves with the enormously complex human world into which they are born. In these circumstances, part of reaching maturity must be to repudiate the parents' protection and in some sense to supplant them. The parents must give way. Human adults enjoy great power and then, inevitably, lose it and die. The old king must die before the shining prince can become the new king. *Of course* the king mistrusts the prince. *Of course* the child, sent to his room without supper, dreams of putting his mother into a little box and nailing it shut or of accidentally burying his father in the sand.

Furthermore, as generations of loving parents know, childhood is always very risky, and the more special the child seems, the more miraculous seems his survival of these risks.

ELEMENT 4: THE TEST:
THE CHILD MOVES INTO ADULTHOOD

In heroic stories, the next event in the life of the young man aspiring to the heroic role is a test to prove himself suitable for such a role. It is no more appropriate to bestow sword or scepter on the mythic hero until he has demonstrated his readiness to use it well than to bestow car keys, college degrees, or high political office on people until they have demonstrated a similar readiness. In folklore, as in real life but more dramatically, passing the test certifies that the youth is ready for power; in other words, he has moved successfully from adolescence to adulthood.

At a wedding feast of the Volsungs and the Goths, in the presence of many brave young men longing to begin heroic destinies, a mysterious stranger strode into the hall, plunged a glorious sword into a heavy oak pillar, and announced that the sword would belong only to the one who could dislodge it. The stranger was Odin, the Norse battle-god himself, and he was honoring someone there, choosing him for one of his own warriors. Many men pulled at the sword without success, but for Sigmund it yielded easily. A similar story is told of the Celtic Arthur, an apparently insignificant young yokel whose achievement confounded many youths of noble blood.

Theseus, reared in relative obscurity like Arthur and many other mythic heroes, had to find a way to lift the great stone under which, before the boy's birth, his illustrious father had left for him a special sword and pair of sandals.

The prospective hero often suddenly emerges from an obscure childhood to demonstrate, through the test, who he "really" is. The pattern provides dramatic contrast and feeds happy fantasies of moving from obscurity, shame, or ineptness into admired mastery. The transformation of Clark Kent into Superman and the Ugly Duckling into the elegant swan tap the same fantasies. So do the advertisements for the Charles Atlas body-building course: The ninety-eight-pound weakling endures humiliation on a public beach when the bully kicks sand in his face; but, after the course, he terrifies bullies and attracts beautiful girls.

The emergence of the hero catches the essence of moving into adulthood. Like the newly recognized hero feted by kings, any youth entering adulthood is moving into a more spacious world. Kings and aristocratic warriors represent the power of adulthood in its most vivid form. In European folk tales, Cinderella is perhaps the most famous of innumerable girls similarly tested and brought forth into a life of splendor. The same essential meaning is conveyed in "Jack and the Beanstalk" and other tales of seemingly stupid or inept sons, often the youngest of three, who suddenly and dramatically demonstrate their sufficiency in a world even larger than that of their parents. The many Scandinavian tales about the Ash Boy—an apparently feckless son who, before his transformation, lounges on the hearth aimlessly sifting the ashes—are of this type. So is the cliché of the pigtailed tomboy who goes upstairs, dons a long dress, sweeps up her hair, and descends the stairs to be recognized by the audience below as a great beauty.

During a trial at the threshold of the adult world, one might expect from a boy some mixture of boldness and timidity, rashness and caution; on the part of the mature witnesses, some mixture of pride ("See what a fine thing we have produced!"), anxiety ("What if he doesn't make it?"), and alarm ("Just who does he think he is?"). In the story of Perseus, two elements of these mixed attitudes separate out and take extreme forms: Polydectes exploits the youth's rashness in order to preclude any threat to himself.

The test that Telemachus, the son of Odysseus, must undergo reveals superbly what the trial of the young hero means. This story is so brilliantly conceived that here formula and profound psychological truth merge completely. The reader recognizes Telemachus both as an individual and as the symbol of everybody's perilous, difficult move from childhood to adulthood.

Telemachus' boyhood can hardly have prepared him less well for a heroic role, that is, for aristocratic adulthood. His father left for Troy when Telemachus was a baby. Lacking older brothers, uncles, or cousins who could serve as models for the skills and attitudes that make heroes, Telemachus is reared wholly by women. Hearing of his father's feats for twenty years without ever having had the benefit of Odysseus' day-to-day guidance could produce little more than a yearning to turn into his fabulous father as if by magic. His mother's suitors have made Telemachus' chances to develop all the more dim. Not only are these men grossly unfit models, but their presence puts the boy and his mother in such peril that, however much these insolent spongers infuriate him, he cannot act against them. The small trials and errors that teach good judgment and effective self-assertion are denied him. Through no fault of his, then—indeed, through a clear understanding of his position and extraordinary self-control—he has not taken up the tasks that would have helped him become an adult. He cannot afford the only actions by which he might grow.

Like many a child of an illustrious parent, Telemachus doubts himself so much and sees such a distance between himself and Odysseus that he wonders if he really can be the hero's son. And if Odysseus ever does return, will he not find Telemachus an unworthy one? One thinks of the modern child's silent question, "Am I adopted?" and his nightmares in which his father shouts contemptuously, "You're no son of mine!" In Telemachus, Homer presents in the clearest, most definitive form, that is, in its *classic* form, an experience that most readers, whenever and wherever they live, have shared. All parents seem to young children extraordinarily gifted, and the transition into effective adulthood seems impossible.

At this point in the story, the wise Athena steps in. The two-week trial that she invents for Telemachus is exactly right: It is difficult but within his ken; it breaks at last the magic circle of his mother, the suitors, and the watching townspeople that has penned in the young man; it will toughen his assertiveness and confidence without tipping his mother into disaster or getting Telemachus himself murdered. One small, gemlike detail demonstrates the value of Telemachus' test. Arriving in Sparta to seek information about his father, he is graciously bathed and feasted, as is the custom, before his royal host and hostess ask his name or the purpose of his visit. Naturally, during the meal, in speaking of their own eventful lives, Menelaus and Helen mention the glorious Odysseus who has played such a large part in their lives. Then Helen, turning to their young guest, remarks upon his striking resemblance to Odysseus. One can imagine how such a comment would nourish the boy's spirit: A total stranger sees Odysseus in me; so I *am* my father's son!

Thanks to this two-week trial during which he makes important decisions and finds that impressive people respond to him with respect, Telemachus is ready when Odysseus does return and needs the boy's help in the riskiest imaginable action. To be sure, his inexperience makes him far from perfect, and indeed he almost brings the whole plan to tragic ruin; but, even at the awful moment, he is brave enough to tell his father the truth and, without losing time gnashing teeth, to help repair the damage. The behavior of both son and father, here, is classic in the essential meaning of the term: at once warmly believable and yet a veritable model of behavior. It is a combination that must inspire pride and confidence in human potential and thus must also inspire emulation. Telemachus' test is the definitive test of the youth on the threshold of adulthood.

Telemachus' story is incomplete, but he acquits himself so well under his father's tutelage in this action that we can think of him as ready for the deeds of the mature hero. These so often center on the slaying of a monster, and the subject is so rich, that Chapter 8 is devoted entirely to it.

ELEMENTS 5, 6: SLAYING MONSTERS AND WINNING MAIDENS

Like Perseus, Telemachus, and Odysseus, innumerable heroes are honored by supernatural aid. The Greek gods threw themselves into the Trojan war to help their personal favorites. The ancient Mesopotamian god Shamash trapped the monster Humbaba in fierce winds so that the heroes Gilgamesh and Enkidu could slay him. In the Old Testament, Yahweh repeatedly intervened on behalf of the Israelites. Cactus Flower Girl's Spider Grandmother and Gopher Grandfather belong to a host of helpful animal spirits in American Indian stories. In Christian lore of the Middle Ages, God performed miracles for his champions Charlemagne and Arthur against the pagans. Talking birds in the forest and fairy godmothers on the hearth protect the young against treacherous guardians. An ace fighter-pilot of World War II wrote a book called *God Is My Co-Pilot*. In *Star Wars*, Ben Kenobi and the Force come to Luke Skywalker's aid at desperate moments.

Such stories suggest that, as attentive parents protect good children, the gods and other supernatural beings protect deserving people. When we seem to be alone, fighting against overwhelming enemies, we are not really alone. Particularly if we stay deserving under stress—alert, faithful, whatever—supernatural aid will come to us as a magic pebble, a special sword, a thunderbolt, a vision, a hunch, a renewal of confidence.

The next element in the heroic life-pattern, winning the maiden, is almost too familiar a theme to need examples. It is usually connected with slaying a monster. After subduing the serpent and other monsters, Jason won Medea; Theseus slew the Minotaur and won Ariadne; Oedipus outwitted the Sphinx and won Jocasta; Sigurd, after slaying the dragon Fafnir, won Brynhilde; Moses killed a man for abusing Israelite slaves, went to Midian to escape the pharaoh's revenge, and married the priest's daughter. In American Indian stories, a youth proves his right to a special wife by unusual grace, prudence, and ingenuity under pressure.[13]

ELEMENT 7: THE JOURNEY TO THE REALM OF DEATH

More puzzling is the hero's journey to the afterlife, the land of the dead, or some similarly mysterious place. The story of Orpheus is probably the best-known example. On the day of his marriage, his bride Euridice, bitten by a snake, died and went to Hades. So great was Orpheus' love for her that, in order to try to bring her back, he chose to take what was for a living mortal the greatest possible risk: He went to Hades. Through his extraordinary courage and his skill as a musician, he contrived not only to get to Hades alive but to persuade the god of the underworld to release Euridice—on the condition that Orpheus lead her out of Hades without looking back at her. Hero though he was, Orpheus was still human; like many people, he behaved impeccably during a nerve-shattering ordeal and then, a sliver of a moment too soon, gave way. On the rim of the upper world, so close as to be virtually there, he was overcome by the fear that his beloved might have lost her way. He glanced back, and thus Euridice had to return to the underworld forever.

One of the earliest known journeys of a hero to the Other World is that of Osiris' son Horus in Egyptian myths of the third millennium B.C. In some stories, Horus' purpose was to tell Osiris that the disastrous reign of Set was over, that order had been reestablished; in other stories, his purpose was to "open Osiris' mouth," that is, to reactivate Osiris' dormant soul, and to receive Osiris' "Ka," his vital powers, so that Horus could reign with Osiris' own excellence. In a slightly later version of the story (Coffin Text 330, ca. 2200 B.C.), not Horus but the "Divine Falcon" undertook the journey. He was apparently a primeval being created long before the present dispensation.

The Divine Falcon sought to spread the news that Set was vanquished, Horus triumphant. If he could bring his news to Osiris, Osiris would be released from his death-torpor and, by implication, become ruler of the Other World. The Falcon's journey was full of struggle and danger. Even Nut, the sky-goddess, refused him passage. But again and again, because of the great importance of the Falcon's task, the high god himself intervened to help him. The persevering Falcon, traversing Earth, Sky, and Underworld, succeeded in arousing Osiris, and the triumph of justice rang through the cosmos.[14]

The motif of the perilous journey to the underworld was also common in Sumerian literature of the third millennium B.C. One of the richest versions of the ultimate journey is Gilgamesh's journey in the Babylonian story from the second millennium B.C.

Searching for his dead friend Enkidu and for a way to subvert death, Gilgamesh reached the margin of the known world, the high mountain into which the sun disappeared at night. Its twin peaks touched the very wall of heaven, and its paps reached down to the underworld. Monsters guarded its entrance. Groping for many leagues through the mountain's pitch-dark tunnel, Gilgamesh emerged into the dazzling, bejeweled garden of the gods. There a mysterious woman directed him to a ferryman. The ferryman took him far out into the Ocean, where no man, only the sun, had been before. "Eastward of the mountain," Gilgamesh came to a static paradise, Dilmun, where Utnapishtim and his wife, the only people whom the gods had ever granted everlasting life, lounged in the sunshine. Although they assured him that neither he nor any other man would have everlasting life, Utnapishtim casually mentioned where to find a life-restoring plant in the deep, swirling waters. Hearing only what he craved to hear, Gilgamesh persuaded the ferryman to row to the place and, tying stones to his feet, plunged to the depths to pluck the plant. On his way home, while the exhausted hero bathed in a refreshing pool, a snake from the pool's bottom rose up and snatched the plant. The plant was gone forever.[15]

Gilgamesh's journey was not to the land of the dead. But it was the prototype of the ultimate quest undertaken by numerous later heroes, the quest for the truth about what lies beyond the grave and for the means to accept or subvert that truth. Gilgamesh's journey also contained many features that have appeared in the afterlife journeys and paradises of later cultures, for example, the guardian monsters, the dark tunnel, the dazzling garden, the water journey with a ferryman, the pool, the life-giving plant, the serpent.

This story was widely known in the Middle East. How directly and to what extent the preclassical Greeks knew the story is still an open question, but it seems reasonable that many thoughtful people would independently view death as life's most fearsome mystery and would find a voluntary exploration of it the supreme act of courage. Because the journey to the realm of the dead signified for the Greeks the highest courage, with time the legends of many beloved heroes incorporated such a journey.[16] Often the hero's specific purpose for making the journey seems a bit flimsy, and none of the Greek stories has nearly the richness of the Babylonian one. These stories are better viewed as folk tales than as myths. For Heracles, the journey was the grand finale of the twelve labors imposed on him, a stunt of no particular social value. He had to go to Hades and bring back Cerberus, the ferocious three-headed dog that devoured all who tried to leave. After accomplishing the feat, Heracles simply returned the dog to Hades.

While in Hades, Heracles rescued his friend and cousin Theseus. How Theseus got there is another story, one that presents this generally wise, judicious, compassionate man as uncharacteristically rash, ready out of sheer bravado to kidnap the child Helen and to help a friend kidnap Persephone. If the story had a point, it seems to have been that the supreme act of daring presented little difficulty to Theseus.

More seriously, Heracles was willing to go to Hades on another occasion to bring back an excellent wife, Alcestis, to her grieving husband. Odysseus undertook the journey ostensibly to consult the seer Teiresias, but his act, like that of the others, was for the most part just a symbol of the utmost courage. In a Roman story, Psyche, the only woman in classical literature to undertake the journey, did so to demonstrate the depth of her love for Cupid and the depth of her remorse for not having trusted him.

The Roman poet Virgil, writing roughly seven hundred years after Homer, admired and consciously imitated Greek heroic poetry; thus it is not surprising that, wishing to glorify Rome, he chose to signalize the courage of its founder—here, Aeneus—by having him journey to the Roman underworld Avernus. Dante, about thirteen hundred years later, in *The Divine Comedy*, indicated his profound admiration for Virgil by making Virgil his fictive guide through two of the three realms of the dead, the Inferno and Purgatory.

The journey to the underworld appears also in the story of Jesus. Although *none of the four Gospels mentions it*, by about A.D. 500, it had become an article of faith for Christians. According to the Apostles' Creed, so-called because tradition ascribes it to the Apostles, Christ "was crucified, dead and buried; He descended into hell; The third day he rose again from the dead; He ascended into heaven."

Why did he go to hell? Both the meaning of the words and Jesus' purpose are variously explained. Generally, where the King James Bible uses the word "hell," the Revised Standard Version uses the original words: "Sheol" in the Old Testament, written in a Hebrew dialect, and "Hades" in the New, written in Greek. "Sheol" was the Semitic word for the rather vague underworld that the Israelites long shared with other Middle Eastern peoples, including the Homeric Greeks. The place was much like the grave, although the dead, all of whom went there, did possess a dim, sporadic consciousness. It is true that in the second century B.C., the notion of a final judgment appeared in Israelite doctrine, but in Jesus' own day, the ideas of an immediate judgment, of damned souls, and of hell had not fully emerged. (Only the Lazarus story in Luke 16 clearly implies such beliefs.) Thus, that Christ "descended into hell" may once simply have meant that he died, not that he walked among the damned.

According to one early view of Christ's descent, God required that Christ literally take upon himself the punishment intended for sinners. If Christ was to suffer for people's sins, he must do so not just on earth but in hell itself, the place of greatest torment. By using himself as payment, Christ the Redeemer freed sinners of the obligation to pay for their sins— a legalistic interpretation. But this interpretation was gradually abandoned as repugnant. Its God appeared to be too much the harsh judge, too little the merciful Father. According to a later tradition growing out of a brief biblical passage (I Peter 3:19–20), Christ made the journey in order to preach the Gospel to those who had died before his ministry, so that they too could have a chance at eternal life in heaven.

A medieval legend explained Jesus' journey as a mission to rescue his "parents" Adam and Eve and take them to heaven. The story echoes the one about Dionysus going to Hades to rescue his mother Semele and take her to Olympus. Some writers even claimed that, just as Heracles rescued Alcestis by wrestling Death himself, Christ fettered the ruler of Hades, either Death or Satan.

In short, the idea that Christ went to hell is treated seriously by all, as if it has significance, but the nature of that significance is much less firmly established. As in the Greek tradition, the journey seems prior in importance to the specific purposes offered for it.

However, the heroic tradition itself should put in focus this particular hero's journey. Christ's journey, like that of other heroes, revealed him as courageous to the utmost degree, willing to steep himself in death, to know it to the greatest possible extent. But the special grandeur of the story lies in Christ's basic purpose. He did not go, like other, earlier, heroes, out of boyish bravado or for love of a friend or a bride or to acquire instructions or advice or even as an anguished attempt to repudiate man's mortality. He went out of compassion for all humankind.

As with other serious myths, a literal-minded view of this story is inappropriate. One might say, He suffered only three hours on the Cross, and maybe during those three days in hell; but he knew he'd get to spend the rest of eternity in glory. Plenty of people have chosen to suffer much longer than he for their friends, their families, their countries, even for total strangers—and without knowing they'd get a big reward for it, either. Some might even say that poor old Judas is the real sacrificial hero of this story, set up for the dirty, necessary job and destined to suffer forever for having done it, while Jesus relaxes on the right hand of the Father, sipping mint juleps. In Stephen Spender's poem "Judas Iscariot," Judas himself offers this view. Of course, it badly misses the point. No earlier hero's purpose had the grandeur, the scope, of Christ's purpose. No other story of the journey presents compassion in such a vivid, compelling way, and thus no other possesses such power to civilize. To take a literal-minded view of the story is simply to fail to understand it.

In Norse mythology, such a journey was also undertaken for a profoundly serious purpose. The most loved of all gods was Odin's son Balder. An exquisite youth with a mild, generous spirit, Balder was killed in an accident arranged by the spiteful giant Loki. The loss of Balder devastated the gods; furthermore, Odin, who had prophetic vision, recognized Balder's death as the first catastrophe in a chain that would conclude with the destruction of the earth and all its people, the sun, and finally the gods themselves. It was imperative, then, that someone go to the place of the dead and persuade the dark goddess Hel to return Balder. Hermod, another of Odin's sons, undertook the journey, a long, dangerous one through dark dales and over a mysterious river. Although Hermod nearly succeeded, Loki contrived to thwart Balder's return, and the terrible destruction began.

The story strongly suggests that neither courage nor goodness nor all the power of the high god himself is any match for evil and destruction, that when the time for death and darkness comes, no power can hold them back. It is the same bitter truth learned by Gilgamesh and Orpheus, but underscored. For the inhabitants of northern Europe, living in a land where darkness and life-snuffing winter always lurked, the story expressed the plain truth and came to terms with it.

An Aztec story tells that, after the first generations of people had perished, Quetzalcoatl went to the underworld to gather the bones of a man and a woman. Bringing these back to the upper world, he ground them and sprinkled his own divine blood upon them. They became the new first man and woman, this time possessing an element of divinity lacking in the earlier generations.[17] American Indian journeys to the Other World fairly often involve young men or women straying from the group or young men seeking their recently dead brides. Although the protagonists usually lack great heroic purpose, they do tend to be more curious, bold, enterprising, or independent than their friends. Examples 2 and 10 (pp. 20, 24) at the beginning of Chapter 1 illustrate the point.[18]

Chinese literature of the Middle Ages tells of various people descending into the ten hells. Most notable are a particularly admired emperor and a Buddhist monk who rescued his mother.[19] The nineteenth-century Finnish poem *Kalevala*, based on traditional Finnish stories, tells of the hero Väinäinöinen making the underworld journey.

In addition to literal journeys to the land of the dead, folklore and literature abound with experiences that bear a striking symbolic resemblance to such journeys. That is, these experiences suggest more than the heroic quest into the dark forest, with its attendant risks and opportunities; they suggest dying and, sometimes, being reborn into a more spacious life, even into a kind of paradise. In Genesis, when Joseph's jealous older brothers cast him into the dry well in the desert wilderness, his life as the son of a Hebrew patriarch ended. He was rescued and carried off to Egypt, a rich, alien land where he achieved a new life of perfect fame, wealth, power, and wisdom.

The flint-hearted, recalcitrant prophet Jonah, pitched from a boat, sank to the depths of the sea. The seaweed tangled horribly about his head, as if strangling him and pulling him down. He sank to Sheol itself, to "the bottoms of the mountains," where, he feared, God would never hear his cries or find him, and the bars of the earth would hold him forever, locked away from God's love and mercy. Swallowed by a whale and held fast for a harrowing three days, he began to learn obedience and mercy.

Several American Indian heroes, including Blood Clot Boy of the Blackfeet tradition and Afterbirth Boy of the Wichata tradition, were also swallowed by great fish. In the Blackfeet story, the fish had swallowed many earlier victims. By an ingenious trick, Blood Clot Boy killed the fish and rescued those of the earlier victims who had not perished. In the Wichata story, the motif is of special interest. Although mere children, Afterbirth Boy and his brother had done many great deeds and slain vicious monsters. One day, while running in the course of playing a game, they found themselves unable to stop. They ran toward a large lake and suddenly found themselves inside a gigantic fish. Afterbirth Boy remarked that this was the first time anything had ever mastered them so unexpectedly. When their father returned to their isolated lodge that night to find them gone, he was so sure that they were in trouble or dead that he straightway left the earth, becoming a star in the sky. When Afterbirth Boy finally managed to free them from the fish and they returned home, they found the dwelling long deserted. But as night came, they recognized their father in the sky, followed his earth-track till it ended, then shot two arrows into the sky, climbed these, and joined their father.[20] The sequence strongly suggests the helpless surprise and darkness of death, the sense of having been abandoned by one's ultimate protector (father, Father, whatever), and then the spacious serenity of an afterlife.

A very vivid instance of symbolic death and rebirth occurs in *The Odyssey*. Odysseus has left his own estate, his "nest," to fight in a foreign land and then, with fewer and fewer companions, who keep failing the requisite tests, he fights several monsters. The only survivor, Odysseus is trapped by the goddess Calypso and forced to dwell with no companion except her on her small island far from any known place. Calypso lives in a snug, vine-covered cave, and caves have from earliest times been associated with the earth-mother, at once womb and tomb. Calypso hums and spins contentedly, the pot abubble on the hearth, the fire crackling fragrantly, the lap-rugs cosy. Outside, the wild parsley nestles against the door, the birds twitter, and four springs gush among the violets. Though not a garden, this place resembles the ancient Middle

Eastern paradise with its remoteness from time and events, unbreakable hermetic isolation, opportunity to live forever, and four springs.

To perfect Calypso's domestic bliss, here is Odysseus, her sexy baby-lover safely trapped in the playpen of this constricted feminine nest. What more can this mythic Woman want?

When, after eight years, Athena and Zeus finally force Calypso to release Odysseus, he goes through an experience that strikingly suggests a birth, death, and resurrection. First, he takes a long water-journey, during which he endures chaos and dissolution—formless, roaring waters that strip him naked and then attack his flesh. After washing up on the rocky Phaeacian shore, bruised, brine-soaked, half-flayed, more nearly dead than alive, he manages to dig for himself a gravelike hole in some leaves, crawl in, and sleep. Later Odysseus is "resurrected," much refreshed, by a maiden, and is purified by a ritual bath and anointing.

After a short time in the Phaeacian paradise—once again a small but complete, perfect world, unknown to ordinary travelers—Odysseus experiences still another quasi-death. The Phaeacians pile a boat with treasure for Odysseus and then enchant him: "There fell down upon his eyelids a balmy sleep, / Unwaking, most sweet, nearest in semblance to death."[21] The Phaeacian sailors row the comatose hero from their isle to his own home. They lay him upon the shore, heap the treasures in a nearby cave for him, and then suddenly are turned to stone forever by the angry Poseidon: They will never retrace the way. When Odysseus awakes, he does not at first recognize his own land.

The boat, the strangely silent water-journey, the uncrossable boundary, the heaped treasure, the cavern, the disorientation upon return—these motifs, if somewhat disordered here, are all familiar to a person steeped in myth and legend. They suggest the heroic funeral customs and beliefs of the prehistoric Greeks, Scythians, Celts, Germanic peoples, and others.

Why is the motif of the underworld journey and the successful return so pervasive, and why does it persist? Certainly the sequence, with its dramatic contrast and pleasing conclusion, makes a good story, but the answer surely does not end there.

Many scholars have sought the answer by exploring rituals. Although attempts to bind all myths to rituals, or vice versa, are misguided, rituals and myths often arise from similar needs and are often linked in practice; thus it seems reasonable to view rituals as a possible source of insight into some mythic patterns. The mythic journey to the realm of the dead is a case in point. A ritualized death and rebirth into a fuller life appear in most initiation rites, ranging from the extremely popular mystery religions of ancient Greece and the Hellenistic world to those of recently observed tribal cultures, Masonic orders, and college fraternities. Some myths involving symbolic deaths may have very ancient connections with the initiation rituals of once-tribal cultures. In some tribal cultures, the initiation rites of young men, including a symbolic death and rebirth, end in pairing the youths with wives. Clearly, in these cultures, the rite marks the end of childhood and the beginning of adult privileges and responsibilities.

In the often tremendously difficult, frightening, and painful tasks of the hero's life, scholars speculate, may be embedded the ritual ordeal that initiates a boy into manhood. The hero's trip to the underworld may correspond to or echo the symbolic death in the initiation rite. The beautiful maiden that the folkloric hero so often wins may echo the choosing of wives for the young initiates. Possibly. In heroic legend, however, the test of the youth is seldom a journey to the realm of the dead. That journey comes later, after he has been tested and has won the maiden.

On the psychological level, the mythic journey into the realm of death and back makes a great deal of sense. We have probably all experienced personal crises during which we felt ourselves and our comfortable world disintegrating, times of disorientation, panic, profound depression, from which we emerged feeling refreshed, in possession of some valuable new understanding.

The answer to why the underworld journey is so appealing may be stated even more plainly. All people know hard times, and the hope that we may pass through them and go on to something even better helps us to cope with them. Reminders in the form of compelling stories of trouble and happy endings are always welcome. For most of us, the hardest of all our hard times are our encounters with death. What a compelling story, then, is one suggesting that a person meets his own death and, instead of being annihilated or knowing endless anguish—both fearful possibilities—passes through this worst experience into a state even better than before. I submit that this simple, natural fantasy is at the core of all stories involving a person's encounter with death, symbolic or literal, and his return.

Many, many stories both sacred and secular say, in effect, be less afraid to lose yourself in death. Helpers will see you through, or you will find and develop resources in yourself that you do not know you have, or you may not lose yourself at all but move into a better life.

So the hero's journey to the underworld not only resembles both ancient, widespread initiation rites and a natural, probably almost universal, human psychic experience; it satisfies a basic human need. In ancient literature, the motif of death and rebirth—disintegration and recovery, the dark journey and revelation—is often a literal journey to the land of the dead and back. In more recent literature, the journey is likely to be symbolic. To peruse this literature is to be struck by the continuing elemental power of the theme.[22]

ELEMENT 8: THE TRIUMPHANT RETURN

The glorious moment when Perseus flashed into Polydectes' banquet hall and brandished Medusa's head moved the sculptor Cellini to freeze it forever in bronze.

In myth and other folklore, the triumphant return frequently includes a terrible revenge on powerful enemies. Medea, Jason's wife, cooked his evil cousin Pelias in a vat. Odysseus and Telemachus made such mincemeat of the presumptuous suitors that the hall had to be thoroughly washed down after the battle. Dionysus returned to his native Thebes not just as a hero but as a god, and when the king refused to believe in Dionysus' power, Dionysus sent the king's own mother into a Dionysian frenzy during which she ripped her son to pieces and fed upon him. The Old Testament Joseph, in triumphing over his murderous brothers, did better than return to his home and family. As humble suppliants, the brothers journeyed to Egypt and found there a magnificent person, second only to the pharaoh himself in power and grandeur. This person was Joseph. Although he dealt with them far more generously than they once had with him, their lives were now in his hands and he made them sweat. The young Charlemagne, after fleeing from his brothers, served the Saracen king nobly, converted the beautiful princess to Christianity, and returned to his own land to defeat his evil brothers and become a great king.[23] In the Polynesian story of the boy mocked as a bastard, sent away by his mother, and eaten by his sky-brothers, the boy enjoyed a similar triumph. After the brothers were forced to disgorge him, their hatred turned to such devotion that they followed him back to earth. There he became a great ruler.[24]

The triumphant return of the mythic hero is the glamorized version of an almost universal childhood fantasy, at least in Western culture. What child, humiliated or in his view unjustly punished or unvalued by his "bad" parents, has not healed his spirit with the dream of himself grown tall, elegant, *effective*, returning from afar to punish those who have so mistreated him? Like Joseph, he may, of course, magnanimously forgive his now miserable repentant abusers, providing that they grovel satisfactorily.

The powerful fantasy that the myth memorializes is the special property of the young, for it is they who most often find themselves helpless and in need of solace against disdainful elders. When young, most of us dream some version of local-frog-proves-prince, starring ourselves, particularly if our personal aspirations outstrip others' estimates of our potential. But the need to see oneself as effective and successful is of course important to people of all ages. When other people do not see one that way, the dream of future triumph is often what keeps one from dissolving in the acid bath of others' scorn and often enough propels one toward success.

A striking modern instance of the future-triumph fantasy and its function concerns the American general Douglas MacArthur in World War II. Early in the war, when Americans were still stunned by the attack on Pearl Harbor, the Japanese routed MacArthur and his troops from the Philippines, inflicting another humiliation on the United States. But as MacArthur hurried away, he managed to pause long enough to declare grandly, "I shall return!" It was a public gesture of the utmost importance. Instead of drowning in the calamity, a grateful nation focused on MacArthur's response to it and sought to emulate that response. Within weeks, newspapers carried colored, full-paged pictures of the hero in a dignified pose, eyes steely, jaw determined, the magic words printed at the bottom. The covers of dime writing-tablets—the rage among children—carried the heroic portrait of MacArthur. Significantly, the public idolized this hero not for victory but for his victorious response to defeat. He saved the national dignity. It is the *fantasy* of a glorious return that the myths feed, and the darker the hero's temporary defeat, the more exquisite the fantasized triumph.

ELEMENT 9: THE HERO'S MYSTERIOUS, AMBIGUOUS DEATH

General MacArthur, that most self-conscious of heroes, declaimed at the end of his career, "Old soldiers never die. They just . . . fade away."

Forty years after Amelia Earhart's plane vanished in the South Pacific, theories still circulated that Japanese soldiers had captured her and held her secretly throughout World War II. Many mythic heroes do not plainly die. They may vanish in the desert, as one Persian hero did, or disappear in fire, air, or water. Heracles, too strong to be vulnerable to any human or natural danger, was finally, through magic, made to suffer unendurable agony. To end his torment, he immolated himself on a funeral pyre atop a mountain. However, almost at once he was apotheosized; that is, he arose to Mount Olympus to live forever with the gods. Romulus disappeared without a trace. Elijah arose in a chariot of fire. Moses vanished from a mountaintop. American Indian heroes, often relatives of the Sun, may go to the sky or fly away to Eagle land.[25] When a high public official indisputably dies but dies unexpectedly or under dreadful circumstances, clouds of controversy continue to surround his death. Not only do such clouds continue to swirl around the Kennedy and King assassinations; they still surround the assassinations of the Russian Czar's family in 1918 and of Abraham Lincoln over a century ago.

Often a hero's legend suggests that he is not dead at all or may be reborn or may return from death at some future time when he is much needed. Charlemagne arose one hundred years after his death to lead a crusade against the Saracens. Mortally wounded, King Arthur went to the mysterious Avalon, and some day he will return and reign once more. Rather as Christians await the return of Christ, the Moslems of one of Islam's two branches, the Shi'a, await the return of the Hidden Imam, the true spiritual leader of Islam. According to Shi'a belief, not long after Mohammed's death, the true, divinely appointed "imams"— spiritual leaders—lost the political succession through a series of murders. Two centuries later, one of the twelve imams then living disappeared mysteriously into the mountains instead of dying. Still alive in the world, he will one day return, restore the true faith, and lead the world to social harmony. During the Iranian revolution of 1978–79, some Iranians declared that the Ayatollah Ruhollah Khomeini, who led the revolt against the Shah, was the Twelfth Imam. When Napoleon invaded Egypt, the Bedouins thought that he was the reincarnated "Iskander," that is, Alexander the Great, who for nearly two millenniums had been a major Islamic mythic hero.

In Aztec belief, although the snake-bird Quetzalcoatl, high god and creator of all life, was driven away by another god, the Aztecs for centuries awaited his return from the east. In this case, the myth had tragic results. Aztec sentries, always on watch for him, spotted the huge, seemingly supernatural vessels of the Spanish explorer Cortez sailing in from the east. When the sentries could see the Spaniards' plumed helmets and their armor that resembled snake scales, the sentries naturally inferred that Quetzalcoatl had returned. The Aztecs soon realized their mistake, but by then the Spaniards had seized power in the land.

The legends that arise concerning a hero's death have obvious personal and social functions. These legends ease the loss, the sense of abandonment, and the sense of the hero's (and by extension, all people's) tragic ephemerality. And by encouraging hope, the promise of the hero's return keeps alive the ideals represented by him and extends his influence. For Jews, the promise of the coming Messiah and, for some Buddhists, the promise of another Buddha serve similar functions.

HEROIC STORIES REFLECT THE STAGES IN ORDINARY LIFE

The persistence and pervasiveness of the heroic life-pattern in folklore cannot be attributed to one simple cause. Some details pass from one hero to another because they are entertaining or honorific. In addition, many details reflect underlying social purposes: to dramatize the divine sponsorship of the hero and to dramatize the value of such life-enhancing qualities as courage, endurance, and self-reliance; love of justice and willingness to act on that love; compassion, altruism, the wish to serve mankind. The hero is a dazzling personification of the qualities that a people admires and wants to emulate. Whether or not the heroic life-pattern arises in part out of ancient rites of passage is almost beside the point, for in the seemingly arbitrary, bizarre pattern, one recognizes the stages in *every* life. Any ordinary life adumbrates the heroic pattern.

It is common for parents to see their own children as extraordinary. Their child comes from a special bloodline and has a special kind of birth (Element 1). At a remarkably early age, he shows some uncanny ability (Element 2). He is barely but miraculously snatched from death or disaster. People who either do not recognize his value or who do and envy it almost ruin him. (Element 3.) Despite very unfavorable odds, he wins important contests (Element 4). Nor are these claims ludicrous; they are often, in the natural course of childhood, true.

The same is so of normal adulthood. Attaining adulthood is comparable to a second birth: We must leave the nest, reject parental protection and guidance; we must sever life-supporting ties. We find ourselves, as adults, only too frequently in the dark forest, making important, necessary choices without access to sufficient facts and experience. We fight a great many monsters, internal and external—incomprehensible forces that, if we were not provided with seemingly gratuitous, even miraculous help, would crush us (Element 5). We marry, that is, formally become sexually active and commit ourselves to the welfare of the resulting children (Element 6). We almost inevitably know many times the "dark night of the soul," the panic, despair, sense of utter futility, the crushing grief of discovering our essential, irrevocable solitude and the emphemerality of ourselves and all that we love (Element 7). And we often return from this devastating experience at once subdued and refreshed, hugging some comforting or otherwise valuable piece of knowledge or sense of sufficiency. Often, too, no matter how much we long to share this insight with other people so that their own underworld journey will be easier, the knowledge refuses to be shared with the uninitiated. Its magic does not reach across our own singularity to the person we are trying to help. (Element 8.) Finally, in our minds we almost all mitigate the absoluteness of death, often even apotheosizing a person whom we admired and whose qualities we wish to survive: "Daddy is up in heaven with God and the angels, and he is watching us and feeling proud of us for going on. He is hoping that you will do such-and-such. And we'll all be together again some day up there." (Element 9.)

In traditional cultures and cultures more rigidly stratified than our own, only a few parents have seen the nascent hero in their own child and only a few children have been invited to follow the heroic model; but even the humble proudly join in exalting those within their culture who represent its most important values, and even the humble feel the connection between themselves and the heroic.

It is clear that despite the glamorous, extravagant details, the stories of heroes are about the lives of ordinary people, indeed about the most important and most nearly inevitable events in their lives. It is this fact, combined with the glamor, that makes the stories so compelling.[26]

III

THE COMPLEAT HOME
AND
THE MONSTER AT THE DOOR

6

Images of Cosmos and Chaos

In the stony wilderness of the new world, God made a sumptuous garden for Adam and Eve. Here grew figs, apricots, melons, cucumbers, and all manner of shady trees. Birds warbled on the boughs, and sleek animals from A to Z peered with gentle eyes from among the leaves. A fountain overhung by a great tree sang at the garden's center. Fish shimmered in the four streams that flowed from the fountain. Within this garden nestled all delights—and also an evil snake, awaiting his chance.

In the wintry wastes, the Danish chieftain Hrothgar raised a mead-hall for his warriors. Returning from the day's labors, a man could dump his fifty pounds of armor in a corner and warm his bones before the great fire. The sweet mead flowed, and the board bent beneath the savory meats. A man could sit at ease, tell tales among friends, sigh to the harpist's song, and burrow at last into a snug, furry bed. But in the night, the monster Grendel—mean, hungry, powerful beyond all reckoning—came clawing at the door.

The Persian god Ormazd made the iron sky-dome in the form of an egg. "The top of it reached to the Endless Light; and all creation was created within the sky—like a castle or fortress in *which every weapon that is needed for the battle is stored, or like a house in which all things remain." He made the shell especially strong "as a bulwark against the Destructive Spirit," the evil Ahriman whom Ormazd knew would try to destroy this fortress. At its center, Ormazd made the earth. At the center of the earth, on the banks of the river Daitē, he fashioned Gayōmart, a glorious man. Outside the shell, Ahriman watched and waited.* [1]

The three little pigs built their houses—walls, roof, door, lock; and the wolf snickered upon the doorstep.

The image of a protected, complete space enclosed within a wilderness gives us deep satisfaction: The Sumerian cosmic bubble of air and light immersed in black waters aswirl with monsters; the Sleeping Beauty's castle locked within the impenetrable thornbush; the nuclear submarine, equipped with gym and first-run movies, winding stealthily through the crushing murk of the deep seas; Leisure World, with its full garden-maintenance, its yoga and ceramics classes, safe behind a guarded wall; the modern spaceship with its recycled oxygen, its neat packets of Jello and aspirin, zinging through the interplanetary silence; the goose-down sleeping bag and foam mattress, snug within the translucent tent, while rain, wind, and lightning turn the High Sierra night into a howling madness.

These vivid contrasts may at first suggest the images discussed in Chapter 4, the village and the dark forest. There, however, the images contrast two *life-patterns*, that of the citizen and that of the hero. The present images emphasize not life-patterns but the *settings*.

In myths, the gods make, furnish, and hold intact the enclosed space where people live. Just as the life-patterns of countless traditional heroes, beneath the embellishments, can be seen as variations of a "monomyth," so can the actions of the multitudinous gods be seen as following a single pattern. Within a primeval wilderness, where organized, sane life is impossible, the gods make a great sealed house with floor and domed roof. This is the cosmos, the physical and moral sanctuary within which life can thrive. The gods stock this dwelling with life and with all that "proper" living things need. The notion of a cosmos implies that which is both *whole* (complete, perfect, enclosed) and *holy*. That the words "whole" and "holy" come from the same Indo-European word suggests their close connection in the human mind.

In the myth-inspired art of many cultures, the cosmos is suggested by framing a symmetrical scene within an oval, circle, dome, or occasionally a square. At the center stands a pole or tree, sometimes rising out of a mound. The god or chief teacher often sits beneath the axial pole (Buddha) or hovers above it (the Sumerian Enlil, the Egyptian Horus, the Christian God or Christ or the Virgin as Queen of Heaven, the Norse Odin, the Delaware Indian Gicelemukaomg) or is incorporated in it (Krishna, Christ). Unless the god himself is represented as a bird at the top of the pole, two winged creatures may hover on either side of it, symbolizing his omniscience.

But often outside the frame or within it, near the bottom, monsters skulk. Indeed, an evil serpent may coil itself right up the axial pole.

Because the cosmos lies within the original chaos, chaos always threatens to invade and destroy it. In the original chaos prowl grotesque monsters of tremendous energy—unchanneled energy, senseless, intractable. Like deep-sea creatures bumping their snouts against the thick window of a bathyscaphe, these monsters keep ramming against the walls, oozing through cracks, clawing the protective membrane, climbing down the chimney. Often in creation myths, the gods kill one of these monsters and from its body make either the cosmos itself or the first, ancestral, creatures of the cosmos. Thus, even if none of the mysterious forces beyond the cosmos gets past the guards, some of that wild, appalling stuff lurks within each "proper" creature and may unexpectedly erupt. ("I can't understand how Bill could have done such a horrible thing! He was always so neat and polite, and so gentle with the little kids in the neighborhood.")

Thus the struggle between the forces of cosmos and of chaos persists, not just at the cosmic boundary but within the individual, within society, within the natural world, even within the gods' own realm.

Most mythic systems agree on this basic point: What promotes cosmic order, harmony, and life is good, and what promotes chaos, disintegration, and death is evil. Two widespread symbols arise from this basic perception: the *cosmic center* from which the regulative power of the high god radiates; and the *monster*, personifying the forces of chaos. Chapters 7 and 8 explore these two symbols.

7

Cosmic Centers as Images
of Physical and Moral Order

From earliest times, people scattered over the amorphous lands of the earth have thought of the earth as having a center. Each group envisions its own land as surrounding this spot or its people as having come from this spot. The Chinese name for China is "Center-country." For the ancient Egyptians, the exact center was the mound of earth that had arisen first from the primal waters; for the Babylonians, the great ziggurat of Babylon; for the Jews, the foundation rock in Jerusalem; for the Greeks, the *omphalos* (navel) at Delphi; for the legendary founders of Rome, the *mundus*, a pit at the center of the city where the souls of the dead resided as an energy bank for successive generations; for medieval Christians, the hill of Golgotha where the Cross had stood; for Moslems, Mecca—the birthplace of Mohammed, the place where Allah had spoken to man, the site of the sacred well Zamzam and of Allah's house on earth; for the Inca, the city of Cuzco; for the Maya, a legendary place called "Tulan"; for the Tsimshians of the North Pacific coast, a pole on which the earth turns; for the Southwest American Indians, the Sipapu, the hole in Mother Earth from which humankind emerged and into which a person's soul returns when he dies; for the Trobriand Islanders of New Guinea and other Oceanic peoples, a similar hole. If the group moves about, as did the Aranda of Australia, the cosmic center may move, too.

Common experience suggests to us that the cosmos comprises three levels: earth, sky, and underworld. The center is the place where the earth connects with the sky at a high place (hill, tree, pole) or with the underworld at a low place (pit, hole, cave). Metaphysically, it is the most sacred place in the cosmos, the place where the divine flows into the world. This center is the source of all order: natural, social, moral.

A modern reader, noting more than one cosmic center in Egypt, Palestine, or Greece, might conclude that ancient peoples could not even keep their own ethnocentric geography straight. That would be unfair. The cosmic center is a spiritual concept, not a geographical one. Four observations may clarify the concept.

First, a culture possesses not only a main cosmic center but also many auxiliary centers. The modern Christian community recognizes the Church of the Holy Sepulcher in Jerusalem as its spiritual center, but every small church with its own cross upon its altar is also a center. For many Christians, a cross is not just a reminder or token; the presence of God or Christ is actually concentrated in it. Each cross is a spiritual lightning rod through which divine power flows into the world.

Second, communities do not view their own cosmic centers as the only true ones. For instance, when one people conquers another, the invaders often do not build a new temple for their gods; they set up their own gods in the temple of the conquered people, partly to obliterate the earlier gods, but partly, too, to seize the divine power still clinging to that holy place.

Third, people who well know that their culture is not the glorious center of the world often affirm that their ancestors came from such a place and replicated the center's laws and customs in their own land. They are proclaiming that their cosmic center is a true model of the earlier center. In the version of Norse mythology that we know from the *Prose Edda* (early thirteenth century), the earth-center is not this late northern outpost of civilization. Instead it is Troy, a magnificent city in Asia where the earth yields an abundance of good things, from food crops to gold and gems. The northern peoples traced their origin to the royal line of this glorious civilization and believed they had replicated its customs and laws in Scandinavia.[1] The English traced themselves to one Brutus, a descendant of the Roman hero Aeneas, and affirmed that the legendary King Arthur was descended from Brutus. Similarly, an ancient Greek legend traced the Athenians to an Egyptian leader Cecrops and his people, and Mohammed traced himself and his people to the biblical Abraham and Hagar. A slight variation is the Mormon belief that, between Christ's resurrection and ascension to heaven, he preached in the western hemisphere. All these stories not only add luster to the new place; they make it a holy earth-center. And they do not snatch the center away from the older cosmos. The relationship between the two centers is analogous to starting a flame from an established holy flame. Both are holy, and the new takes from the old without diminishing it.

Fourth, the cosmic center is similar to the secular vision of the city as the hub of activity, the place where people's lives converge and from which power flows. If, for a particular person, the City happens to be Gary, Indiana, he can still recognize that Los Angeles, Buffalo, Paris, and Cairo are for other people the City.

In short, the cosmic center is a symbol, the place where the divine enters the world, not a geographical place.

This chapter explores why we tend to think of the cosmos as having a center and why the visual symbol of a pole or hole is so similar from one culture to another. Then it explores myths about the cosmic center as a conduit of divine power and myths in which the chief god dwells at the cosmic summit.

WHY WE THINK OF THE COSMOS AS HAVING A CENTER

> *I placed a jar in Tennessee,*
> *And round it was, upon a hill.*
> *It made the slovenly wilderness*
> *Surround that hill.*
>
> *The wilderness rose up to it,*
> *And sprawled around, no longer wild.*
> *. . .*
> *It took dominion everywhere.*[2]
>
> Wallace Stevens

Wallace Stevens's poem "Anecdote of the Jar" recognizes with amusement the human craving for images of order, images in which wilderness leaps almost visibly into a pattern with a special object rising in the center. We are fond of plunking poles into the sand, building cairns upon hillocks, and embedding brass plaques in marker stones. Sometimes simply because many eyes can spot an object from a distance, it becomes a focus for attention. For practical reasons, we meet at landmarks and often settle important issues there. We sign treaties under imposing trees and arrange to meet atop mountains or beneath clock towers. Over time, we often invest such places with special significance. To help us re-create in our imaginations some momentous event or idea, we like a marker that we can touch, kiss, gape at, or photograph. For instance, in Genesis the patriarchs customarily set up pillars as markers of graves, boundaries, agreements, and direct encounters with Yahweh. Chartres Cathedral soaring over the wheat fields, Plymouth Rock, Big Ben, innumerable Founders' Oaks, the American flag raised on Mount Suribachi on Iwo Jima and on the moon—all mark crucial events or ideas.

But such customs alone do not account for the electrifying image of the *cosmic* center so pervasive in myth. Some of its sources are less obvious than these customs and yet more nearly inevitable in human experience. First, it is clear from many ancient peoples' notions that, if innocent of science, people tend to think of the whole world as shaped like the part of it that they can see. As H. J. Rose suggests, unless we are closed between long lines of hills or confined to an island or group of islands, what we see, roughly, is a flat disc. We also observe that the sun and moon always rise on one side of the horizon, travel across the sky-dome, and set on the other. It is natural to suppose that, when they are out of sight, they are making the same sort of journey beneath the disc.[3]

Second, each person does perforce look out upon the world from his own center. He is a pole with eyes and ears; things become real as they move within his range of perception. Like a lighthouse, he stands at the center of a circular "world," beaming its features into reality (Fig. 6). Commonly, as a child begins to develop a sense of the world beyond himself, he sees it as a series of roughly concentric zones, with himself at the center. In James Joyce's A *Portrait of the Artist as a Young Man*, for instance, the young Stephen writes in his geography book

> Stephen Dedalus
> Class of Elements
> Clongowes Wood College
> Sallins
> County Kildare
> Ireland
> Europe
> The World
> The Universe[4]

In Thornton Wilder's play *Our Town*, a child goes through a similar exercise. However sophisticated we become, however aware of our limits, the basic physiological fact that each of us stands at the center of his own

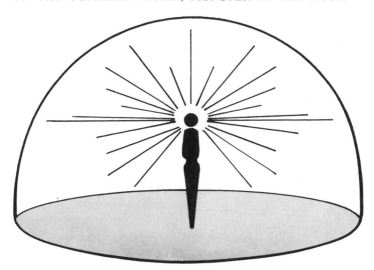

Fig. 6. Each person stands at his own cosmic center. For him, reality radiates from this center, especially from his head, which is the source of sight, hearing, speech, and understanding. Most conceptions of the divine cosmos start with this basic image of axial pole, dome, and plane. Knowledge, power, reality concentrate at the pole's top and radiate from there.

reality predisposes us to think of reality in its larger sense as circular and as most intense at the center.

A third important source of the cosmic center as an image is our almost universal childhood experience of home, a place where we indisputably belong and are protected by parent-gods. They have created that place, and their power holds it together. Only through their love and grace do we live at all, but this love and grace flow abundantly. These parent-gods welcome, bless, and validate us. Later, out in the exciting but perilous world beyond the original dwelling, we are always seeking the pattern of home and parents. We conceive of invisible gods who, like good mothers and fathers, give us permission to step out into this world and who hold over us an invisible protective canopy. These gods make a cosmic home for us by transforming part of the wilderness into a sane place.

Fourth, just as a child's personal world consists of concentric zones that the parents organize and patrol from the center, so has the cosmos such zones, the whole system organized and patrolled from the center by gods.

SKY-PROPS

> *One day Henny-Penny was pecking up acorns in the woods when—whack!—something hit her on the head. "Goodness gracious!" said Henny-Penny, "the sky is falling. I must go and tell the king."*

We insist upon a vision of the world as a shelter, a safe "internal" space. Many ancient peoples took this idea of internal space literally. For most of them, because the sky was truly a canopy, it needed such props as poles or pillars. These props sometimes later became the cosmic axis up and down which the gods traveled. Pillar cults, well known to scholars, thrived in Bronze Age Egypt, Crete, and Greece. A little stone pillar found in the niche of a domestic shrine at Jericho (Palestine) suggests that such cults go back at least to the eighth millennium B.C.

The notion that the cosmos needs a prop seems reasonable enough in its context. If one has not been told that the sky is open space, one is likely to see it as a great blue dome. Domes often do need props. Whether one is a member of an isolated tribal culture in the distant past or a modern camper setting up a rain shelter, one's first architectural efforts are likely to produce the hut or tent, stabilized by a central pole. For obvious reasons, in ancient times this pole was usually of wood. Scholars have puzzled over the widespread mythic theme that, in the time of creation, the sky had to be forcibly separated from the earth in order to give people a living space. Assuming the notion of a roofed space, I think that a possible explanation for the theme is an analogy with early architecture. Furthermore, long after ancient peoples had mastered complex architecture, they still generally used pillars to support roofed space; thus, if the cosmos were to be seen as an interior, it would almost necessarily be seen as needing support.

Sky-props are prominent in ancient Egyptian art. Although in Egyptian art the props are not usually cosmic centers, they do often convey universal dominion of the pharaoh—the high god's son or incarnation. The "Djed" or "stability" column is an upright pillar representing the resurrection of Osiris' soul; by extension, the column represented eternal life, for the Egyptians believed that they would achieve eternal life in Osiris' soul. But R. T. Rundle Clark shows that, from Old Kingdom times, the Egyptians used the column to represent also a cosmic pillar or sky-prop. He cites several stelae on which "the *Djed* Columns are world pillars, holding up the sky and so guaranteeing the space and air in which the king's authority holds good." In all ancient royal symbols, according to Clark, "kingship is universal; it means rule over the whole earth and all that is beneath the vault of the sky." Thus, the frame in which the pharaoh Zoser's name appears contains, to the left and right of the name, a Djed column, and outside these two columns the hieroglyph for totality, a coiled rope . The Djed columns delimit the world vertically, the coiled rope horizontally, symbolizing that "Zoser is master of all that is beneath the sky and to the ends of the earth."[5]

In ancient Egypt, the notion of sky-props appears in other forms, as well. The hieroglyph for sky   is a stylized picture of a beam atop gates. The Egyptians sometimes thought of this sky-roof as resting upon four pillars. These pillars were probably suggested by the corner pillars of a simple rectangular room. In Egyptian religious art, the sky-goddess Nut leans over to make the sky-roof of her back and the roof's four supportive pillars of her arms and legs. The mother-goddess Hathor, in cow form, is also sometimes represented as making the cosmos of her body, with her four legs as the pillars. The earth itself is a platter ringed by mountains, an image suggested by the Egyptians' awareness that beyond their own flat land lay mountains. The sign for the earth is . The joined sky-roof and mountain rim make an enclosed shelter.

Several pre-Columbian Mexican manuscripts represent the world as a cross, with the sky-god at the center and four trees or mountains in the arms of the cross. The four tips of the cross are the cardinal points. Probably the most widespread Mesoamerican religious symbol is the quincunx , which represented the cosmic cross with the center and the four cardinal points emphasized.

Also in Mesoamerican art, according to the anthropologist Hermann Trimborn, a double-headed serpent symbolizes the sky-arch. At one end, representing the gate from which the morning sun emerges, is a living head; at the other, representing the gate into which the sun falls, is a death's head. In Mayan cities, this sky serpent was pictured as a canopy over the king's throne, over representations of kings, and over doorframes of temples. But one day, this serpent, with the help of hostile gods, might destroy the known world by flood. In other Mexican myths, the sun might fall and the earth be consumed by fire. To prevent such a catastrophe, the Creator had placed a guardian jaguar at each of the four cardinal points to support the heavens.[6]

THE WORLD-TREE

The image of a cosmos supported by one central prop is more widespread than that of a cosmos supported by four props. Many peoples have imagined that great pole as a tree. Such a notion seems natural enough to a person who can remember the first time he flopped directly beneath a tall pine in the woods, stared dreamily upward, and was suddenly startled by a wonder: All the other treetops converge on that pine like spokes of a wheel. One is staring directly up at what appears to be the true center of the world.

But for peoples who live in very simple dwellings, the notion of a tree as world-pillar has an even more immediate source, the dwelling itself. In *Shamanism: Archaic Techniques of Ecstasy*, Mircea Eliade writes that the shamanistic cults common among hunting peoples generally envision a cosmos with three levels connected by a central axis. The gods travel up and down this axial pole through holes analogous to the holes in a tent's floor for the central pole, and in the roof for drawing off smoke. The shaman's soul, as the community's messenger to the sky and underworld, travels in mystic trances up and down the pole. For the Samoyed, the pole is the "Sky Nail," an image shared by the Lapps, Finns, and Estonians. For the Mongols, it is the "Golden Pillar," for the Siberian Tatars, the "Iron Pillar," and so on. For Greenland Eskimos and many other northern tribal peoples, the central pole of their dwelling is the earthly counterpart of this sky-pole. For the Ostyak of central Asia, the smoke hole in their circular, portable dwellings corresponds to the hole in the "Sky House." Nor is the correspondence between the earthly dwelling and the world itself confined to northern peoples. Eliade cites the Khasi of northeastern India, the Galla of Ethiopa and Kenya, and others.

Many peoples have identified the cosmic pillar as a tree. In children's imaginations and in widely scattered stories, people who want to climb to the sky, and find no mountain, rainbow, or eagle handy, climb a tree. Sometimes in myth, the images of mountain and tree are combined, no doubt partly because the two together raise one higher than would either alone, and perhaps also because the conical or domed dwelling with a protruding central pole suggests a mountain topped by a tree. In any case, Eliade offers many examples of the image among nomadic tribal peoples of Siberia and peoples from central Asia and Oceania.[7]

Linguistic evidence suggests that Indo-European peoples also thought of the cosmic prop as a great central tree. The Indo-European word-root *bheu-* means "to exist, to grow." From this root comes "beam," first in the sense of a tree or wooden pillar and later also in the sense of a beam of light. (The Norse gods traveled up and down the world-tree. The gods of many peoples manifest themselves in a beam of light joining heaven and earth.) Such words as "booth" (from Old Danish for dwelling), "building," "bower," and "byre" (stall, hut) come from the same root. So does "husband." To "husband" is to bring things to life, to make them grow and thrive, to cultivate and conserve. The master of a house husbands the life within it just as the gods husband the life within the sealed cosmic shelter. The world-tree, then, is like a living house. Even the shapes of such trees as the oak, the beech, and the fir suggest the ancient cosmic dome or cone.

Traces of the sky-prop appear in ancient Greek art as a mere pillar, sometimes with a few stylized leaves at the top suggesting its origin. During the Hellenistic period, similar pillars stood at cult-centers in Italy and northwestern Europe. The Scandinavian tribes, whose development was slower than that of the peoples farther south, provide more direct evidence of the sky-prop as a tree.

First, the northwestern Europeans venerated trees as guardians. In *Gods and Myths of Northern Europe*, H. R. Ellis Davidson notes that the idea of a guardian tree standing beside a dwelling place was once widespread in northwestern Europe. Sometimes the house itself was built around the tree. (In the *Volsunga Saga*, the Branstock, a huge oak, is such a tree.) Not only family houses but the gods' house, the temple, had such a guardian tree. In stories of northwestern Europe, the oak was sacred, especially to Thor, and often had a sacred spring beneath it. Swedish settlers of Iceland customarily brought to the new land the sacred Thor pillars from the temple at home and used the high-seat pillar to help support the new temple.[8] One speculates that the symbolic support of the Thor pillars helped the settlers stabilize their new "cosmos."

In about A.D. 1070, the German chronicler Adam of Bremen described the great temple and its grounds in Uppsala, Sweden. Near the temple stood a sacred grove within which scores of human and animal sacrifices were offered every nine years; but according to a marginal note, one tree in particular arrested the attention of visitors: "Beside this temple stands an enormous tree, spreading its branches far and wide; it is ever green, in winter as in summer. No one knows what kind of tree this is. There is also a well there, where heathen sacrifices are commonly performed."[9]

The tree and its well resembled Yggdrasil, the cosmic axial tree described in the Icelandic *Prose Edda of Snorri Sturluson*. According to the tradition that Snorri knew, a great ash tree, Yggdrasil, spread from earth to sky and underworld, and the realms of people, frost-giants, gods, the dead, and so on, lay along the trunk, branches, and roots of this tree (Fig. 7).[10] Although Snorri describes three sacred springs, one beside each root, modern scholars think the older conception probably included only one spring.

The pre-Christian Norse probably did not envision Yggdrasil exactly as Snorri did later; yet clearly it was a guardian tree, its fate intimately bound to the fate of the gods over whom it watched. Furthermore, it was a world-tree, spreading its limbs over all lands and linking the realms of gods, giants, people, the dead, and so on.

The pre-Christian Saxons venerated a wooden world-pillar, the "Irminsul," and set up models of it at various cult-centers. According to Arthur B. Cook, in *Zeus: A Study in Ancient Religion*, in A.D. 772, Charlemagne destroyed a Saxon cult-center in Westphalia, toppling a great tree trunk venerated by the natives as the Irminsul was venerated. Cook recounts a sixth-century instance when the Saxons, upon conquering a town in Thuringia, immediately erected and worshiped an Irminsul. He cites several stories in which central Europeans of the Middle Ages feared that the sky might literally fall upon them. According to the Roman historian Livy, an entire army of these people fled a thunderstorm in the belief that the sky was falling.

Cook goes on to show traces of such a fear in the poetic images and folklore of Italy and Greece during the same period. Indeed, in modern Greek folklore, the Callicantzari are pagan gnomes that spend the whole year between New Year's Day and the following Christmas underground, trying to gnaw through the great tree or column on which the world rests. But at Christmas time, when only a threadlike fiber of the trunk

Fig. 7. A tree sometimes represented the cosmic axial pole for ancient Egyptians, Indo-European peoples, and, more recently, for Finno-Ugric peoples, Siberians, and American Indians. The thirteenth-century Icelandic writer Snorri Sturluson described his conception of the pre-Christian Norse cosmos. A great ash tree, the axial pole, had branches reaching over the whole upper world. The watchful eagle of the high god Odin perched in the upper branches. People dwelt on Midgard, the central disc. Beyond the sea encircling Midgard, arose Jotenheim, the cold mountain range of the frost-giants. Above Midgard, the gods built their walled citadel, Asgard. In the underworld, the queen of the

remains intact, the Callicantzari assume that the trunk will topple by itself and, abandoning their work, come above ground. Here they stay until New Year's Day or Epiphany. But when they return to the underground, they find the tree whole and strong again.[11] In Snorri's account of Yggdrasil, a great serpent and its brood gnaw perpetually at the tree's main root.

Trees as sky-pillars occur also in American Indian myths. In Mayan tradition, a sacred ceiba tree rose through all levels of the universe. The Mayan name for the ceiba means "first tree." In Mayan art, this sacred tree "bears buds from which the head of the maize god emerges, its horizontal boughs end in reptilian jaws, and the top of its trunk has the features of the sky god." In a famous relief from Palenque, a Mayan city, the "first tree" rises above "the corpse of a human sacrificial victim, which in turn rests on the head of an earth monster. On top of the tree sits [a sacred bird associated with the sky-serpent], and round its trunk the double-headed sky serpent coils itself."[12] In myths of the Southwest United States, people long, long ago left the earth itself for the lighter, more spacious world by growing an extraordinarily tall tree and then climbing up it and through the opening. As mentioned earlier, the kiva, the round temple of the Pueblo Indians, has no door at ground level. People enter and leave it by ladder through a hole in the roof. The analogy of the kiva with the original mythic home is quite conscious.[13]

CONDUIT OF DIVINE POWER

Most tribal cultures have had deities who dwell in a particular impressive place, such as a spring, cave, tree, or mountain. Sometimes all of a

---

dead reigned from her stronghold. The tree's three great roots, one in Asgard, one in Jotenheim, and one in the underworld, held the tree in place. A sacred spring bubbled up beside each root, nourishing the tree. Four dwarfs held up the sky-dome. In the ocean surrounding Midgard lurked a great hooped serpent biting his own tail. Another serpent, a constant threat, gnawed at the tree's main root in the underworld. *This drawing is a modern artist's simplified illustration of the cosmos described by Snorri. (The Prose Edda of Snorri Sturluson: Tales from Norse Mythology*, trans. Jean I. Young (1954; rpt., Berkeley and Los Angeles: University of California Press, 1964), pp. 35–47.)

people's deities who dwell in, say, mountains come gradually to be related, even become manifestations of the same deity. Later, if that people recognizes a universal deity, the image of his original mountain or the mountain of important earlier gods remains associated with him. The realm of the gods becomes some inaccessible mountain, as with Mount Olympus of ancient Greece and as with Sumeru of ancient India. Or a god's early locale becomes an image of the cosmos itself, as with Yggdrasil. Thus the cosmos is often an enlarged version of an early local deity's sphere of influence.

The cosmic center is the place where the gods' power flows into the cosmos; here the gods' presence is most concentrated.

People sometimes associate their city with the cosmic center because cities, like the cosmic axis, are centers of highly organized power and energy radiating into the land beyond them, and because, throughout most of history, they have tended to be islands of relative order within a wilderness. In Plutarch's account of Rome's legendary founding, Rome corresponded to the cosmos, and its center was a circular pit. In digging this pit, the founders followed the instructions of Etruscan priests. The settlers cast into the hole as a sacred offering the first fruits of all plants important to human welfare; each man added a bit of soil from his native land. The founders called the pit the *mundus*, Latin for the world, the heavens, the cosmos itself. With a plow drawn by a bull and a cow, Romulus marked out the city's boundary in a circle around the pit. Other men followed the plow, turning all the broken clods inward, toward the mundus.

Upon this circular boundary, the city wall would be raised. The boundary was regarded as so sacred, Plutarch writes, that nothing sacramentally unclean must ever cross it. Thus, when the plow came to the places where the gates were to be erected, it was lifted out of the ground so that ordinary, unclean things could routinely pass through the gates without offending religious scruples.[14]

In this story, with the help of local priests, men themselves transformed the wilderness into a cosmos. The pit seems to have had two ritualistic purposes. First, the settlers were seeding this new place with the established sanctity of their former homes. Second, by casting native soil into the pit, these men—many of them wanderers and adventurers of dubious repute—were solemnly binding themselves to the sacred laws of this place.

According to legend, the Romans covered the mundus with a great stone, called the "soul stone." The ancestral spirits dwelt in the shaft, and when on certain days the stone was removed, the spirits arose.[15] The legend seems related to the notion in many cultures of a people's ancestors as the source and guardians of its vital energy. The ancestors constitute the energy bank from which each new life draws; at death, each person returns his energy to that place.

Plutarch also recounts a legend of a sacred cornel tree. One day, trying his strength in a spear-throwing exercise, Romulus threw a spear whose shaft was of cornel wood. The spear landed near the Circus Maximus, and so deeply did the spear embed itself that no one could dislodge it. After a time, the fertile earth, cherishing Romulus' spear, sent shoots up from the shaft. The spear grew into a great tree that generations of Romans revered.[16]

Clearly this story is about a *symbolic* cosmic prop, a stabilizer of the Roman social order. The godlike Romulus created a small cosmos; the very earth honored him; the pole representing his power sprang to life and arched protectively over those who walked beneath it. The personal power of Rome's founder lived on in the tree, reinforcing the ideals by which Romulus had consolidated the Roman people.

The Romans actually made Romulus into a kind of god, Plutarch writes. They held that Romulus did not die, but simply disappeared one day without a trace. The story went on to tell how the sky grew black and a great storm ensued. A short time later, a sensible, intelligent man of high reputation reported having seen Romulus in shining armor. Romulus had explained to this impeccable witness that, having completed his earthly task of founding the city destined to be the greatest on earth, he had "returned" to heaven. The witness also brought a final message from Romulus: His people must continue to practice valor and self-restraint. (Plutarch notes dryly the very similar tales—recorded by the Greek historian Herodotus, ca. 484–25 B.C.—that the Greeks had long spun about people whom they admired).[17]

What is especially striking about the Romulus legend is how consciously and purposefully the Roman storytellers seem to have built a cosmos from motifs many centuries old. Here is the holy enclosure within which the supernatural guardians of earth and sky establish order both physical and moral. Here is the divine center, the continuing source of the community's well-being.

Islamic tradition affords another example of the cosmic center as a conduit of divine power. In medieval Islamic legend, the earth had been "stretched out" or "spread out" (Mohammed's words) like a carpet, and a ring of mountains cast down as tent pegs to hold the cosmic roof in place on the primeval waters.[18]

Mecca is the navel of the earth. In the city's central courtyard rises the great mosque Al Haram, enclosing the holy well Zamzam. One recalls from Chapter 2 that wells are often regarded as openings into the primordial waters surrounding the earth-disc and on which it floats. In the same countryard stands the Ka'ba, the shrine said to be an earthly model of Allah's own house in paradise, built by Adam himself and restored by Abraham and Ishmael. Allah created Mecca two thousand years before the rest of the world, and when he sent the flood, it did not cover the Ka'ba.[19] Most important, it was at Mecca that Allah spoke directly to man. In this legend, in the Roman one, and in others, the correspondence between the sacred center of a particular earthly city and the holiest spot in the Other World is explicit.

A medieval Christian legend placed the Cross at the exact center of the earth, directly over Adam's grave; the blood of the Savior percolated down through the ground to wash the bones of the father of mankind, redeeming him.[20]

In Jewish tradition, Jerusalem is the navel of the earth. In *Legends of the Bible*, Louis Ginsberg tells the story of an extraordinary rock, "the foundation rock" (*Eben Shetiyah*). As King David himself was digging the foundation of the great temple, he discovered a stone very deep in the earth. When he started to move the stone, it spoke, warning him not to disturb it. The rock explained that long ago, when God's voice was speaking from Mount Sinai, the whole earth began to shake and sink into the abyss. Only the quick-thinking rock, by plopping itself into the hole, had prevented the entire earth from disappearing into the abyss.[21] In another version of the story, recounted by George Every in *Christian Mythology*, this rock is "the foundation stone of all creation, the stone that God threw into the abyss to divide the waters from the waters, and so indeed [it] is 'the navel of the earth.' "[22] As in the Roman story, the earth-center, where power is concentrated, needs plugging. As in the Islamic story of the great flood's waters covering all but the sanctuary of the Ka'ba at the earth's center, only the will of God day by day holds back the watery chaos.

In the seventh century, an Islamic leader designated a particular rocky outcropping with caves beneath it as the site of Solomon's temple and as the exact spot from which Mohammed ascended by ladder to paradise.

The famous building called the Dome of the Rock, erected near the end of the seventh century and restored many times since, marks this holy place. For Moslems, it is a kind of auxiliary earth-center.

Still another image of the cosmic center in Jerusalem is a large human navel carved into the bedrock upon which the Church of the Holy Sepulcher stands. This image, Every asserts, goes back at least to the middle of the eleventh century but may be much older.[23]

In some versions of the Pueblo Indians' creation story, the earth-center Sipapu is a pit filled with water. (The Hopi sometimes think of the Sipapu as a particular large natural mound in the gorge of the little Colorado River. At the top of the mound bubbles a hot spring.) Four rivers flow into it from the cardinal points, and the water level in the Sipapu rises and falls rhythmically. In Pueblo versions of the great flood, the Horned Water Serpent usually caused the flood. (These Indians used to irrigate their crops by flooding the fields. In such circumstances, a gentle flooding would make the crops grow, but of course a vigorous flooding would wash them away.)[24] The replicated earth-center in each kiva, also called the sipapu, is usually closed with a stone. During religious ceremonies, the dancers stamp loudly on the stone so that the dead in the underworld can hear. But at the most solemn ceremonies, the hole is left open so that the dead can participate.[25]

THE MOVEABLE COSMOS

The Old Testament story of Moses on Mount Sinai is about divine order flowing into the world from a high place. The mighty Yahweh descended from the sky in a blaze of flame, and the whole mountain trembled. Moses, the Israelites' earthly leader, climbed alone to the peak to commune for forty days with Yahweh. Then Moses returned with the Laws that Yahweh had instructed him to give to the Israelites. Thenceforth, so long as the Israelites bound themselves to Yahweh by keeping his laws, wherever they journeyed and in whatever wilderness, they would travel under the canopy of his divine protection. During the Israelites' long journey, the concentrated presence of Yahweh guided them in the form of a cloud. When the cloud stopped, they camped in that place, whether for a night or a year. At each camp, following Yahweh's complex instructions as to the proper offerings and purifications, Moses had the "tabernacle" raised. The tabernacle was a collapsible temple upon whose altar stood the most holy tablets with the Laws written upon them (Num. 9:15–23).

In rough outline, the story resembles that of the Australian ancestor-god Numbakula (p. 9) descending to earth to shape the physical world and his people's social world in accordance with his will and their needs. In both cases, an awesome supernatural being singled out a people for his parental concern and descended from the sky to bestow upon them

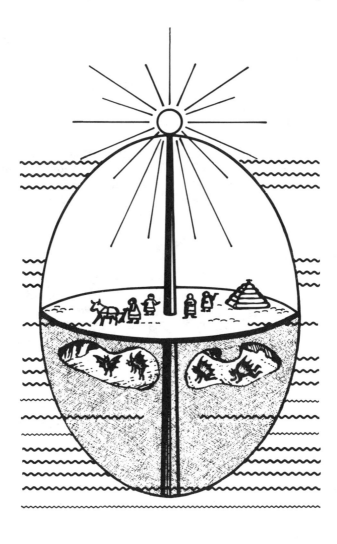

tremendous gifts in return for their conformity to his will. Although both stories tell of a particular high place that first served as a divine path, the import of both is that the god gave his semi-nomadic people a moveable cosmos within the wilderness.

THE COSMIC BUBBLE

The Sumerians viewed the cosmos as a bubble or tent engendered in the primeval sea and still immersed in it. Within the vaulted roof lay the flat earthen disc, and between earth and this heavenly roof circulated the air (Fig. 8). Samuel Noah Kramer, a distinguished scholar of Sumerian culture, speculates that the Sumerians pictured the vault as of tin, for they called tin the metal of heaven. This wall extended beneath the earth, too, completely sealing the cosmos. Directly beneath the earth-disc, between it and the sealing wall, stood a kind of cellar, the murky land of the dead. This general image of the cosmos came to be shared by the whole ancient world—Egyptians, Hebrews, Greeks, Persians, Hindus, and so on.

THE COSMIC MOUND

In a frequent modification, the earth was a platter with a holy mound at its spiritual center. Indeed, the most pervasive symbol of the spiritual

Fig. 8. The Mesopotamian cosmos resembled a bubble or inflated bladder immersed in watery chaos. At the center lay the earth-disc, and at the top of the axial pole hovered the all-knowing high god. Directly beneath the earth-disc lay the murky land of the dead. The dead seem to have been imagined as ugly winged creatures who gradually turned to dust. Other ancient Middle Eastern images of the cosmos share the main features of the Sumerian one and are probably based upon it. (Drawing from descriptions by Samuel Noah Kramer, *History Begins at Sumer* (1956; rpt., Garden City, N.Y.: Doubleday Anchor, 1959), pp. 77–78; E. A. Speiser, *The Epic of Gilgamesh*, Tablet VII, 31–39, in *Ancient Near Eastern Texts Relating to the Old Testament*, ed. James B. Pritchard, 3rd ed. (Princeton: Princeton University Press, 1969), p. 87; Thorkild Jacobsen, in Henri Frankfort *et al.*, *The Intellectual Adventure of Ancient Man: An Essay on Speculative Thought in the Ancient Near East* (1946; rpt., Chicago: University of Chicago Press, 1977), pp. 171–72.)

center is a mound of earth, stone, or brick. This image appears on Sumerian cylinder seals from as early as 3500 B.C., on Egyptian pillars and walls, on Greeks coins, medallions, and reliefs, in Buddhist sculpture and architecture, and in Christian art.

The Mesopotamian symbol, much represented on early cylinder seals, looks like a cone with a scalloped design, suggesting a cairn (Fig. 9). A human figure, tilted at a gravity-defying angle, sometimes walks up this cone, but since the cone appears to be only a few feet high, he does not seem to be in great danger. Cuneiform texts accompanying this symbol call it a mountain and identify the figures near it as gods. Scholars used to call the cone the World Mountain and interpreted it as an actual image of the Mesopotamian cosmos. Now, having considered that neither Mesopotamia's landscape nor early literature support such an interpretation, they are less confident of it.

The cone symbol does apparently stand for a cosmic center, a place of concentrated divinity. In the second millennium B.C., the Mesopotamians began to build terraced, brick mountains, called ziggurats, that

Fig. 9. The Mesopotamian scalloped mound symbolized a sacred earth-center up and down which the gods traveled. As here, it is often shown topped by a tree. Gods are often shown climbing it. Here a human figure and a bull-man subdue bulls. *Cylinder seal impression, Akkadian, ca. 2300 B.C. British Museum, London.* (Copied by courtesy of the Trustees of the British Museum.)

Fig. 10. Ziggurats, terraced brick "mountains" in ancient Mesopotamia, were built as dwellings for a city's chief deity. The ziggurat was a spiritual cosmic center, a holy way-station for the god where the realms of heaven and earth united. The chamber at the top was furnished as a resting chamber for the deity. This restoration drawing depicts the famous ziggurat of Nippur (ca. 2050-1950 B.C.) as it looked in the Late Sumerian period. It was dedicated to Enlil, at that time the high god.

had that significance (Fig. 10). Again, the once common view among scholars that ziggurats represented for Mesopotamians the actual shape of the cosmos, with the terraces as orbits of major heavenly bodies, is now disputed.[26] But the Mesopotamians did view each of their city-states as the earthly manor of one of the gods. So literally was each temple seen as a god's house that most of the twenty-five presently known ziggurats contained furnished apartments for the city's chief deity and for his or her divine attendants. Although only priests ascended to these chambers, each ziggurat, apparently even from the earliest period, contained a lower temple into which the deity descended on special days. Here he received the worship of the people and bestowed boons. Thus, the ziggurat was the man-made channel between gods and people, between the spiritual and earthly realms.[27]

In the Babylonian creation story *Enuma elish* (ca. eighteenth century B.C.), soon after the high god Marduk created the earth and people, the other gods honored him by building him an earthly house with a sanctuary and throne at the top. That building is the great ziggurat at Babylon, at the time, Mesopotamia's principal city. Babylon was regarded as the foundation and center of the earth, and the city's ziggurat not only as the channel between earth and sky but as the counterpart of Marduk's heavenly abode.[28] A charming if impractical "map" from the seventh or sixth century B.C. shows Babylon as the earth's center; the earth, consisting of Babylonia and Assyria, is ringed by the ocean. (The map is on a clay tablet in the British Museum.)

The ancient Egyptians posited a primal mound, the first part of the earth to emerge from the primordial waters. This was the place most favored by the high god and the place of his most concentrated presence.

(Its most common signs, ⌐▢ and ⌂ , closely resemble the most common Sumerian cosmic images.) In Egypt of the third millennium B.C., each of the four great cult-centers claimed that it own temple stood upon that first land.

The ancient Greeks saw Delphi as the cosmic center, the navel of the world. They venerated Zeus' birth-cave on the Island of Crete, his sacred grove at Dodona, and sacred spots throughout Greece connected with Zeus and other deities. But when the Greeks wanted most urgently to learn Zeus' will, they turned to Apollo, god of light and wisdom. Delphi was Apollo's seat, and Apollo was the true, unerring spokesman for his father Zeus.

At Delphi stood a very holy stone that the Greeks called the *omphalos* (navel), designating the center of the cosmos. According to Hesiod (ca. ninth century B.C.), this is the stone that saved Zeus from his tyrannical father Cronus. Hearing that he would be overthrown by one of his children, Cronus had swallowed each infant shortly after its birth. Zeus' mother and grandmother conspired to save Zeus by substituting a wrapped stone for Zeus, and Cronus gobbled it whole. Later, when Zeus attacked Cronus, Cronus was forced to disgorge all his preceding children—and the stone. In saving Zeus, the stone made it possible for Zeus to establish a world of justice and harmonious order. Zeus placed the stone at Delphi as a sign of that new order. On representations of the Delphic omphalos and others in Greece, the symbol of Ge, Mother Earth, often appears, just as, in the Jewish legend of the foundation rock, David's counselor marked God's name on the rock that protected the cosmos from the watery abyss. The most famous of the Delphic omphaloi is a stone object about three feet high that suggests an upended egg with its bottom sliced off. It is covered with an abstract design of intertwined fillets. Often depicted in Greek art, this omphalos was an object of awesome sanctity in the ancient world.

Representations on coins and other objects show that the omphaloi of lesser Apollonian centers in Greece were sometimes bases for pillars. Arthur B. Cook, who has studied omphaloi extensively, sees a connection between the omphaloi and the Hermes pillars and Diana pillars, columns that drew these deities to them and in which the deities dwelt. The felt power of these pillars was probably somewhat similar to that of the Cross in the Christian tradition. The divine presence is especially concentrated in models of the Cross. The pillars rising from the omphaloi are probably also related to the ancient sky-props.

Often the omphalos is shown in art with two eagles perched on it (Fig. 11). The eagle is Zeus' bird, not Apollo's. According to a Greek myth, when Zeus wished to find the center of the cosmos, he let fly two eagles, one from each extremity of the earth. Flying at exactly the same speed, the birds met at Delphi. Also, the eagles are consistent with the idea in both Egyptian and Indo-European cultures that the sky-god who haunts the sky-pillar comes and goes in bird form.[29]

The repeated references in ancient literature to the cosmic center as a navel seem more than conventional metaphors. The human navel lies at the center of the belly-mound; when a belly bulges, most dramatically during pregnancy, the navel protrudes. Equally important is the idea that a child in the womb is nourished by his mother through the umbilical connection. The earth-center is, in culture after culture, intimately associated with symbols of fertility, procreation, and life: with the womb and birth canal (for example, the Sipapu), with the primal waters of life (the Arabian well Zamzam; the Jewish foundation rock), with the Middle Eastern tree of life, with the sexually suggestive union of the earth-mound and the sky-god's pillar. The gods make and nourish life. Associating the cosmic center with the umbilical connection seems consistent with the logic of myths and dreams.

The Delphic omphalos, according to Cook, may once have been related to a cult of the great civilization of Crete in the second millennium B.C. The Cretans had a holy center called Omphalos, "where it was said that the navel-string of the infant Zeus had fallen to the ground." Cook notes that, especially in tribal cultures, an infant's navel cord has often been thought of as a special sign of life for that child and has been buried

Fig. 11. The Greek "omphalos" (navel) symbolized the earth's spiritual center. Shaped like the bronze cosmic dome of Greek mythology, the omphalos was often depicted in free-standing stone and on bas-reliefs, coins, and other objects, especially those associated with Delphi. Zeus' eagles often flanked the symbol or perched upon it. In many peoples' images of the cosmos, one or two birds near the top represent the high god or his messengers.

in some sacred, protected place. What better place, he asks, for Zeus' own navel cord than at the earth's center, further protected by the network of fillets?[30] The notion that people could be the custodian of a high god's navel cord would be a heady one. By protecting what once plugged the god himself into life and, through some magic, still does, the custodians of the cord would be protecting their own lifeline and that of their people. More generally, the umbilical cord is one of the main connections, both anatomical and mystical, between two human lives. In the story of Zeus' infancy, earth and sky are joined; the young sky-god is protected in a cave of "mother" earth.

THE COSMIC MOUND SURMOUNTED BY A POLE

> *First there was a bare rock. The falling of the rain on this rock made moss. The worms, helped by the dung-beetles, made soil from their castings. Down from the sun came a sword handle. It grew into a large tree . . .*[31]

Kayan myth, Borneo

The Greek omphalos is not the only image of the cosmic mound sometimes surmounted by a pole. Very often in mythic art, the cosmic mound is shown with a staff, tree, umbrella, sword, or cross rising from it. Although these objects may not appear to have much in common, they all symbolize the divine power that creates or guards the cosmos. For instance, one Egyptian symbol of creation is the primal mound surmounted by the staff upon which the Benu bird landed when it brought light and life to the earth (Fig. 12). The Benu bird on the staff conveys the infusion of the divine into the world. An eagle or dove perched on a pole conveys the same general idea. The staff, like the tree, joins sky and earth. Furthermore, the staff is a worldwide symbol of power whose primary source is probably military weapons such as clubs, spears, and swords. The staff as a symbol was also early associated with the shepherd's rod or staff. As early as the Gilgamesh cycle, a king was referred to as the shepherd of his people, implying that he was both their guardian and their regulator.

It is a natural leap of mind to think of the high god as carrying a staff tipped with a symbol of the divine, such as a bird, or with a symbol of life. The high god is the protector of life within the cosmos. The god's staff was sometimes surmounted by a lotus, pinecone, or leafed branch. A tree or leafed branch atop the cosmic mound conveys a similar idea. Although imposing trees must have been rare in ancient Mesopotamia, a stylized tree often surmounts the scalloped conical mountain of Mesopotamian art, as in Fig. 9.

According to Arnold Whittick, in such parts of the Orient as India, the umbrella atop the mound came to convey the god's power over all the cosmos because of the umbrella's association with royal power and

Fig. 12. In Egyptian myth, when the world was still a watery abyss the Benu bird flew from a faraway land of immortal life, the Isle of Fire. A bit of land emerged, surmounted by a staff. Here he perched, bringing light and life. *From the so-called* Book of the Dead, *Coffin Text* 335. (R. T. Rundle Clark, *Myth and Symbol in Ancient Egypt* (1959; rpt., Thames and Hudson, 1978), p. 247. Copied by permission of Thames and Hudson.)

dignity. Princes customarily used the umbrella for protection from the sun. Sometimes on ceremonial occasions the umbrellas carried by attendants were so elaborate as to be in fact canopies.[32]

Finally, a familiar related symbol is the orb surmounted by a cross (Fig. 13). The orb probably originally symbolized the vault of heaven. One thinks of the Mesopotamian cosmic bubble that became the cosmic

Fig. 13. The orb represents the cosmos. Surmounted by a cross, it may be held by Christ as Savior or by God as Creator, meaning that God reigns over all. In the hand of a monarch, it signifies that the monarch reigns as God's vicar on earth. Before the Christian era, Roman emperors used the orb to signify their universal sovereignty, and artists sometimes showed divinities with the orb at their feet or in one of their hands.

image throughout the ancient world. Zeus and then Jupiter were often depicted with the orb at their feet or in one of their hands. Sometimes Jupiter was shown handing it to his earthly representative.[33] The first human ruler to use the orb as a symbol of his power, Whittick writes, was the Roman emperor Augustus. He held it in his hand to signify his dominion over the whole world. The emperor Constantine added the cross to show that he ruled the world under God's sponsorship. On church steeples, domes, and even personal monuments, the orb and cross assert that God rules the whole world.

As part of the regalia of European monarchs, the orb with the cross on top is called, oddly, the mound. Although Whittick thinks the term is from the French *le monde,* meaning "the world," most dictionaries trace the word, instead, to the Indo-European root *man-* (hand) and to words meaning "defense" and "protection." *The American Heritage Dictionary,* for instance, traces it to the Old Norse word *mund,* meaning the "(protecting) hand." No source relates it to "mountain."

Across the world in northern New Mexico stands an extremely imposing peak, Mount Tsicomo, from whose summit, high above timberline, one can see for many miles. "In the exact centre of the summit," writes Werner Müller, ". . . is a mound or cairn of loose stones . . . from which rises a long barkless spruce trunk. For the Indians of the Río Grande valley [Taos, San Juan, and neighboring pueblos] and for the Navajo to the west, this mound is the centre of the world, the middle point between the four cardinal points and between zenith and nadir." A little below the summit stands the "shrine of the middle," an oval ring of rocks about eighteen by thirteen feet with seven short, stone-bordered paths, the "rain paths," each pointing toward one of the pueblos that share the shrine. "A pool beside the ring of stones holds the water of the world."[34]

GOD AT THE COSMIC SUMMIT

> *He sees you when you're sleeping,*
> *He knows when you're awake,*
> *He knows if you've been bad or good,*
> *So be good for goodness sake!*

Even though the position of the Pole Star in ancient times did not permit the Egyptians to see it, they knew that the stars wheel around a point in the northern sky. According to R. T. Rundle Clark, the amazingly orderly passage of the stars around this point was, for the Egyptians, striking evidence of a divine controller of the universe. This point, they reasoned, "must be the node of the universe, the centre of regulation." Sometimes, the Egyptians called this point "the great city"; at other times, they saw this sky-center as a tree with stars (souls) perched in its branches or as a "tower or pole, with guide-ropes."[35] In the great cycle of stories about

Osiris (see Chapter 8), a god travels along this pole to the cosmic summit to proclaim the return of health and harmony in the world after a period of decay and sterility (Fig. 14).

The image of the god or of his winged messenger peering birdlike from the summit of a great heavenly vault is familiar to many cultures. This symbol embodies a profound need for a sense of cosmic order maintained by a compassionate but firm moral agent. The image of generous,

Fig. 14. The ancient Egyptians sometimes thought of the "sky-center," the point around which the stars moved, as a tree or great pole held in place by guide-ropes. In Osirian myth, the great hawk soared to the top of this pole to proclaim Osiris' vindication and the reestablishment of divine order. Even though the Egyptians could not actually see the North Star, their image closely resembles the cosmic tent of recent northern hunting peoples (Drawing from description by R. T. Rundle Clark, *Myth and Symbol in Ancient Egypt* (1959; rpt., Thames and Hudson, 1978), p. 58.)

undeceivable Santa Claus at the North Pole preparing to reward children at the end of the year in accordance with their behavior is a child's version of this agent. The pyramid printed on the American dollar bill expresses a related idea. The American union, a little cosmos, will be firm and enduring; that the structure is unfinished suggests that it will grow and develop. The all-seeing eye of God shines from the top, favoring and protecting ("Annuit Coeptis") this new order of the ages ("Novis Ordo Seclorum").

The Sumerians of the third millennium B.C. thought of the high god as peering from the cosmic summit. Although the Sumerian god of the heavenly roof, An, seems once to have ruled the pantheon, by about 2500 B.C.—the time of the first known records on the subject—the air-god Enlil did so. According to Samuel Noah Kramer, by this time, Enlil was called "father of the gods" and "king of heaven and earth." Kings asserted that Enlil had given them dominion and made the land prosperous for them. It was Enlil who had planned and made the daylight, seeded the earth, established abundance, made prototypes of the pickax and plow, and who watched "over the safety and well-being of all humans, particularly the inhabitants of Sumer." In an important hymn to Enlil, the god's "lifted eye scans the lands . . . searches the heart of all the lands." He does not tolerate the arrogant, the oppressor, the informer, the breaker of agreements; he catches the evil in a big net. Enlil's special temple, "the great mountain," stands in the city of Nippur. He sits upon his throne at the top in his lapis lazuli house.

> The temple—its divine laws like heaven cannot be overturned,
> Its pure rites, like the earth cannot be shattered
> . . .
> Its shadow is spread over all the lands
> Its loftiness reaches heaven's heart.

Enlil's holy laws are all-embracing. "Without Enlil, the great mountain," no cities or settlements would be founded, "no king would be raised, no high priest born," no foreman supervise workers, no rivers bring water, no animals bear young. "In field and meadow the rich grain would fail to flower."[36] Clearly, from his lofty seat, Enlil was both the moral guardian and the regulator of the physical cosmos.

In the Bible, too, appears the image of the high god reigning from the summit over a harmonious cosmos. The prophet Isaiah (eighth cen-

tury B.C.) envisioned a time when "the mountain of the house of the
LORD / shall be established as the highest of the mountains . . . / and all
the nations shall flow to it. . . . Out of Zion [that is, the Lord's moun-
tain] shall go forth the law . . . / He shall judge between nations
. . . / and they shall beat their swords into plowshares, and their spears
into pruning hooks" (Isa. 1:1–4). In Isaiah's vision, the Lord God declared that the evil would be punished, and the scattered Israelites would
converge and be ruled by a wise, righteous, compassionate ruler, the
Messiah. This leader would guide even the Gentiles. "The wolf shall
dwell with the lamb, and the leopard shall lie down with the kid
. . . / and the lion shall eat straw like the ox . . . / The suckling child
shall play on the hole of the asp . . . / They shall not hurt or destroy in
all my holy mountain; / for the earth shall be full of the knowledge of
the LORD as the waters cover the sea" (10:1–11:9). Although this vision
was set in the future, it is similar to the earlier vision of Enlil at the
summit, establishing a harmonious realm.

In the Vedas, the earliest Indian religious writings (ca. 2000–1000
B.C.), the god Varuna lived in a golden mansion at the sky's zenith.
Accounts disagree on whether Varuna established the cosmos, but in all
early accounts his essential function was to maintain it. As director of the
physical world, he regulated the heavenly bodies and the rain, presiding
over sky, air, and water. As moral guardian, he witnessed every action
and knew every secret thought.

The Norse god Odin was quite a different sort of god. When actually
worshiped, from about the second through the tenth century of our era,
Odin was a bloody battle-god, unyielding and often treacherous against
his own followers. He had little to do with justice or mercy. Kindly father
he was not! But several centuries later, when the Christian Snorri Sturluson undertook to record the pre-Christian Norse myths as he knew
them, he envisioned Odin "All-father" as peering from his high seat at
the top of the gods' heavenly realm with his "very knowledgeable" eagle
perched nearby.[37] At dawn each day, this transformed Odin, guardian of
order, sent out his two ravens to fly over the entire world. By breakfast
time, they would return and, sitting on his two shoulders, tell him everything that they had seen and heard.[38] Ceaselessly, Odin battled the frost-
giants to forestall as long as possible their final victory over world and
heaven; he sought wisdom to help him in his task; and he gathered as
many human warriors as possible to fight with him in the final battle
against chaos.

Snorri's romanticized conception of Odin very likely reflects Snorri's Christian orientation. However, the evolution of Odin from merciless warrior to compassionate All-father does echo a widespread pattern in myth: A religious figure of limited appeal and of limited power and compassion evolves into a loving universal savior. The prehistoric fertility god Osiris became lord of the dead and later became the high god himself, ruling from a radiant land in the sky. Zeus, bringer of rain and fertility, became the father of the other gods and the wise, just lord of all. Jews reshaped the exacting Yahweh, protector of the tribe of Abraham, into a universal god of justice, and then Christians reshaped that god into a universal god of love. The mortal teacher Buddha became the all-knowing, loving guardian of heaven and earth; the gentle Galilean prophet Jesus became Christ Pantocrator, universal ruler and final judge of all mankind.

Just as people's heroes tend to acquire ever more extravagant powers, so do their noblest heroes sometimes become demigods, and so do their gods grow in compassion and dominion. The idea that *somebody* understands all, wields great power, and is compassionate but morally demanding is not just profoundly comforting: *This idea, when shared by many people, makes a cosmos.* The need for such a figure illumines some of the seemingly bizarre stories and images in the Buddhist, Islamic, and Christian traditions. The following examples show the repeated tendency of the devout to move the revered figure to the center of the cosmic stage and then up.

The man Gautama—later, the Buddha—taught compassion and good works as ways to mitigate life's inevitable suffering. Many myths about the Buddha underline his compassion. For instance, in a popular story, his tenderness for all creatures was so great that he ended one of his earlier lives by plunging from a high rock in order that some hungry tiger cubs could feed upon his body. In another story, his moral perfection and mastery of all knowledge were expressed in the idea that before the Buddha's last human birth, he had dwelt in the highest of the thirteen heavens.

The story of the Buddha's enlightenment under the Bodhi tree is the chief story of Buddhism. Having discovered suffering and having lived the ascetic life for a time, the prince Gautama knew that a great moment in his spiritual life was at hand. He sat down under a tree, determined to stay there until he achieved the supreme enlightenment. Accounts differ as to how many days or weeks he sat there, but the tree shielded him from the hot sun while he did. Mara, the Evil One, knew that if the prince discovered the essential Truth, he would be able to achieve great good in the world. To forestall such a boon, Mara tried to distract Gautama by hurling whirlwinds, stones, and live coals at him. When these tactics failed, Mara sent his beautiful daughters to seduce Gautama. Again no success. Deep in the night, Gautama succeeded in breaking all barriers to knowledge: He saw perfectly the past and future; above all, he saw the causes and cures of suffering. From that time forth, his knowledge and his love encompassed the universe. He had become the Buddha. The tree under which Gautama attained this state is venerated as the Bodhi tree, or tree of enlightenment.

Botantically, the Bodhi tree is the *Ficus religiosa*—in Sanskrit, "Asvattha"; in English simply the Indian fig tree. From earliest historical times, the Asvattha has been in India a sacred tree. In Indian myth, it was the very first tree, appearing on a hill to shade the hot earth; the gods in one of the heavens sit under an Asvattha; an Asvattha grows on a certain mythical island; and so on. In the ancient poem *The Bhagavad-Gita*, the Asvattha symbolizes or prefigures the cosmos itself; its aerial hanging roots, like those of the related banyan, support the whole tree, producing the effect of a pillared hall. [39]

In the Buddha story, the tree is neither a sky-prop nor the cosmic axis, and no god ascends the trunk to peer from the top or to enfold the sky-dome in his great wings. Yet the story expresses very nearly what those motifs express. Symbolically, the story presents the creation of the *spiritual* cosmos. Just as a child's sense of his parent's power and goodness makes of a house a home—the parent and home inseparable—so is the cosmos inseparable from the god whose mind encompasses it. And symbolically, the tree's trunk is the channel of divinity, the tree's shading canopy the sky-dome (Fig. 15). In some illustrations of the story, the evil Mara even hacks at the tree with an ax, reminding one of the Norse world-monster and the Greek Callicantzari.

Of the various myths about cosmic centers, the story of the Buddha under the Bodhi tree best illustrates that the cosmic center is less a geographical place than a mystical point where what were meaningless ephemerae are infused with divinity and permanence. (Jacob's dream of the ladder reaching to heaven expresses a similar revelation. At this point, the spiritual center is created for Jacob personally and, through him, for all his descendants, the Israelites.)

A stupa is a dome-shaped monument to the Buddha. The earliest

Fig. 15. The Buddha's attainment of enlightenment (total understanding, total compassion) under the Bodhi tree, the Indian fig, symbolizes creation of the spiritual cosmos. The tree's shading canopy represents the sky-dome, its trunk the channel of divinity.

stupas, built at Sanchi in central India during the third century B.C., are solid brick mounds containing sacred relics and surmounted by three flat umbrellas rising sequentially from a central pole (Fig. 16). Although some historians speculate that stupas may originally have been artificial hills symbolizing a sacred hill in which a god dwelt, most think that stupas symbolized the universe itself, imitating the vault of heaven.[40] In *A History of Far Eastern Art*, Sherman E. Lee states that all early stupas followed "the same plan: a mound of earth faced with stone . . . surmounted by a three-part umbrella." The umbrella symbolizes the Buddha himself, his Law, and the cosmic order. Lee thinks that the small railing around the pole at the dome's top may go back to an old idea in Indian art, the sacred tree with a protective railing. Thus, this pole may be a highly stylized image of the Indo-European axial tree.

Around the mound of the Great Stupa at Sanchi a path was laid out so that pilgrims to the holy spot could take a ritual walk around the stupa, "walking a Path of Life around the World Mountain."[41]

The pagoda, an Oriental temple topped by a pole bearing several concentric discs, or by a series of roofs, derives from the stupa. The temple replicates the cosmos itself. A widespread cosmic image among Siberians and American Indians strongly suggests a link with the stupa.

Fig. 16. The stupa, a dome-shaped monument to the Buddha, is not a temple but a solid mound. It probably represented the cosmos itself. Some scholars think that the three umbrellas at the top symbolized the sacred tree of early Indian art. A railing usually enclosed the tree. Umbrellas came to be more directly associated with royal power because princes customarily used umbrellas as protection against the sun. Thus, the umbrellas surmounting a stupa conveyed the god's power over the whole cosmos. *The Great Stupa. Sanchi, central India, first century of our era.*

This image represents the cosmos as a series of discs held in place by a central pole. Although the Chukchi, a Siberian people, sometimes posit as many as thirty-three discs and the Pawnee nine, the number is usually three, the middle disc the earth. [42]

In Islamic tradition, several images suggest supernatural consciousness emanating from the cosmic zenith. Allah sits enthroned upon the waters in the highest part of the seventh heaven. A remnant of the tree-of-life symbol appears in the story of the "Sidra" tree, the noblest tree in paradise. The Sidra bears a leaf for each living person. Once a year, the tree is shaken, and if a person's leaf falls, he will die the following year. A pre-Islamic legend that became attached to Sufism, a mystical branch of Islam, pictures a hierarchy of saints culminating in the cosmic axis. The activities of these saints maintain the cosmos. [43]

But Mohammed is by far the most vivid, concrete figure in Islam, and thus, despite the doctrine that he was no more than a mortal man, he does share some of the functions of the omniscient god. It was his famous Night Journey that equipped him for this role.

One night, some time after he had begun to preach, Mohammed was awakened by the angel Gabriel, who led him outside and put him upon Buraq, a winged white animal, half mule and half donkey. Each stride of this miraculous beast carried it as far as the eye could see. In a very short time, Mohammed and Gabriel arrived at the great temple in Jerusalem. Gathered there were Abraham, Moses, Jesus, and the biblical prophets. Gabriel praised Mohammed highly as a true prophet, and Mohammed led the holy gathering in prayer.

In some accounts, the Prophet then returned to Mecca. But in later, more detailed, accounts recorded by his followers, Mohammed describes Abraham (startlingly like himself in appearance), Moses (tall, thin), and Jesus (reddish hair and heavily freckled). He asserts that the event was a fully fleshed fact, not a dream revelation as some commentators have said, and offers as proof such details as empty water jars and bolting camels in the caravans that he passed between Mecca and Jerusalem. As these caravans arrived in Mecca in succeeding days, the traders confirmed Mohammed's assertions.

Furthermore, says the Prophet, according to these detailed accounts, "After the completion of my business in Jerusalem a ladder was brought to me finer than any I have ever seen. It was that [ladder] to which the dying man looks when death approaches." Mohammed tells that Gabriel climbed the ladder with him to one of the outer gates of heaven and assured the angel in charge that Mohammed should be admitted. This angel was so important that he had under his command twelve thousand angels, each of whom in turn had twelve thousand angels under his command. All the angels except one smiled and welcomed the distinguished guest. Gabriel explained that the somber angel, Malik, was in charge of hell. Upon Mohammed's request, Malik took the lid off hell so that Mohammed could peer at the high-leaping flames. Alarmed lest they burn up everything, Mohammed asked that the lid be replaced immediately.

Mohammed watched Adam judging the spirits of Adam's own descendants as they filed past. Some of the evil people would be cast into hell; some were being punished in other terrible ways. Mohammed found the freckled Jesus dwelling in the second heaven, Moses in the sixth, and "my father Abraham" in the seventh, sitting "on a throne at the gate of the immortal mansion," apparently paradise itself.[44]

In short, during his Night Journey Mohammed traveled to Jerusalem, an earth-center longer established than Mecca, and from that center toward the summit. He was honored with a tour of the cosmos, and though he did not achieve full omniscience, he did achieve direct knowledge of the Other World. He saw the worst that humankind could suffer and the bliss in store for the righteous.

Many images and stories in the Christian tradition also suggest the omniscient god at the cosmic summit and the cosmic axial tree. Innumerable medieval religious paintings are domed or arched at the top, and there, centered, presides God, Christ Pantocrator (all-ruler), or the Virgin. Often two angels hover above the figure, recalling Zeus' eagles flanking the omphalos and Yahweh's cherubim flanking the ark in the first tabernacle (Num. 7:89) and, later, in the great temple.

In centered images of Christ Pantocrator, Christ appears within a heavily outlined oval, suggesting the cosmic dome. He sits majestically enthroned, right hand raised, index and middle fingers extended in the gesture of sovereignty (Fig. 17). Sometimes, indeed, he peers down upon the Nativity or Crucifixion. This image, frequently of great size, often dominates the apse—the high concave vault over the altar—of medieval churches. The apse represents the cosmic vault itself. Often, fluffy clouds float behind the figure. A fourth-century mosaic in the apse of St. Prudenziana in Rome shows Jesus enthroned thus, with a very stylized image of Golgotha behind and above him. Golgotha is the familiar hemispherical mound topped by the pole—in this case, the Cross.

Fig. 17. Christ Pantocrator (all-ruler) sits enthroned, right hand raised in the gesture of sovereignty. In early Christian art, the mandorla, an oval or almond-shaped frame, signified the cloud in which Christ arose to heaven. Later, it became the aureole emanating from a divine being. In art and architecture from the Renaissance onward, it is often much enlarged to enclose a great panoramic scene. Used thus, it represents the cosmic vault itself.

The Virgin as Queen of Heaven often sits enthroned in a domed space, the Child on her lap (Fig. 18). The concept of the Virgin as universal queen is occasionally conveyed by a simple cone, the Virgin's crowned head at the apex. Here the Virgin and the cosmos are one. A complex expression of a similar theme is the Virgin standing on the cosmic orb, treading on the serpent wrapped around the orb. The image signifies that, although sin pervades the cosmos, the Queen of Heaven has the power to conquer it (Fig. 19).

In all these images of Christ and the Virgin, the divine sovereign peers from on high, ready to guide, judge, and succor.

In the Nativity scene, God's holy Star often casts a cone-shaped light,

Fig. 18. The Virgin enthroned as Queen of Heaven presents her Son. Christian art often modifies the old motif of the high god's winged messengers atop the cosmos. Here, four angels support the mandorla. *Detail from a door panel, Spain, twelfth century. Vich Episcopal Museum.* (Based on Pl. 18, *Spanish Frescoes*, published in the Unesco-Mentor Art Book series. Copyright © Unesco 1962. Copied by permission of Unesco.)

Fig. 19. The crowned Virgin, on the cosmic orb, treads upon the serpent. The serpent wreathing the orb signifies the pervasiveness of sin; the Virgin's stance signifies not only her universal reign but her conquest of sin, that is, her ability to cancel its effect. The horns of the moon are a very ancient Middle Eastern symbol associated with mother-goddesses and fertility. *After a Tarascan altarpiece, Muséo Nacional de Anthropologia, Mexico, D.F.* (Copied by permission of the museum.)

suggesting the widespread image of the protective cosmic tent. Sometimes, reflecting a pre-Christian tradition concerning the birthplace of important gods, Christ's birth occurs not in a shed but in a grotto within a conelike mountain. The fir tree, a symbol of renewed life from pre-Christian Europe, often repeats in Christmas art the shape of the Nativity scene, including the star at the top (Figs. 20a, 20b). Some Christmas cards bear a simplified tree—an isosceles triangle topped by a star—that calls to mind the Nativity scene almost as readily as it does a tree.

Medieval legends and images of the Cross also treated the theme of the god at the cosmic center. As the aged Adam was about to die, he begged his son Seth to return to the Garden of Eden to seek a healing balm. Seth easily found the way by following the scorched footprints that Adam had left upon the earth long ago when he had been cast from the garden. Although the angel Michael would not let Seth into the garden, Michael kindly allowed him to take a peek. In the center of the garden, Seth saw a great crystal fountain and, in front of the fountain, a mighty tree. A huge serpent wreathed its trunk. Seth could see a terrifying chasm beneath the tree, for the roots stood in hell. But looking up, Seth could also see the top of the tree in heaven. Here the tree was covered with

Fig. 20a. In the Nativity scene, a favorite Christian emblem of the cosmic center, God's holy Star often casts a cone of light, its vertical beam suggesting the cosmic axis. Sometimes, reflecting a pre-Christian tradition concerning the birthplace of important gods, Christ's birth is shown occurring not in a shed but in the grotto of a conelike mountain.

Fig. 20b. The Christmas tree, the same general shape as the cone of light in Nativity scenes, usually bears a symbolic Star of Bethlehem at the top. A recent Christmas emblem on greeting cards and in advertisements combines the two symbols, Nativity and Christmas tree, in a plain isosceles triangle bisected by a vertical line and topped by a star.

leaves, fruits, and flowers. High in the branches shone the "fairest fruit," a little child in the arms of a woman "more lovely than the moon." Doves fluttered over the heads of mother and child. (The reader will recognize the fruits, flowers, and doves as symbols of the ancient Middle Eastern goddess of love and fertility, and will be reminded of the Buddha peering down, before his final birth, from the highest heaven.) Although Michael said that Adam must die, he gave Seth three seeds from the tree of life, instructing Seth to place these under Adam's tongue before burying Adam upon a hill at the earth's center. In time, a great tree, rooted in Adam's skull, arose over Adam's grave, and, long after, a miraculously

durable beam from this tree was raised upon the same hill, called Golgotha, *the place of the skull*.[45] It was upon this new tree of life that Christ
suffered so that the eternal life that Adam's sin had taken from humankind could be restored. The sacrifice of Christ in a sense restored the
cosmos to its original perfection.

This legend relates to the representations of Jesus crucified in a flourishing tree, its branches festooned with fruits, birds, and flowers. Sometimes Jesus sags pitifully upon a cross with huge grapevines and clusters
of grapes twining about him. In addition to associating Christ with the
vine, so long a sacred plant, this symbol suggests Dionysus, the pre-
Christian sacrificial savior and god of the vine who annually suffered,
died, and returned to life.

The image of Christ upon the Cross (or tree) at the earth's center,
saving all humankind, is clearly symbolically related to images of other
gods atop the axial pole or cosmic summit—Horus, Enlil, Varuna, and
so on. Golgotha is often shown as a mound resembling the Delphic omphalos. And although Christ's role as suffering victim is usually emphasized in these images, even the outstretched arms, often so thin and vulnerable, sometimes convey an all-embracing, sheltering love.

In medieval and Renaissance pictures, Christ is sometimes centered
in a bowl-like boat that clearly represents the cosmos with Chirst as the
axial pole. (One remembers that the ancient Middle Eastern cosmos
either floated upon water or was a "tent" immersed in water.) In one
such picture, the Virgin and Child sit in the middle of a little boat, their
outstretched arms suggesting at once comprehensive love, the Cross, the
boat's mast, and the cosmic axis (Fig. 21). In another, the Cross with
Christ nailed to it is a boat's mast (Fig. 22). At the top of the mast
perches the eons-old spirit-bird, here the Holy Ghost.

Nor is the idea of the watchful god at the cosmic center confined to
ancient Middle Eastern cultures or to those clearly influenced by them.
The image of the enclosed cosmos, sometimes with the watchful god at
the top, pervades North American Indian myth. The Delaware Indians'
sacred building called the Big House represented the cosmos itself. A
rectangular hut oriented according to the cardinal points, the Big House
had a massive central post supporting the roof, with the two faces of
Gicelemukaong, the Creator, sculpted on it. According to the anthropologist Werner Müller, this post represented Gicelemukaong "in his aspect
as centre post of the universe, the supporter of the whole structure of
creation."[46] Gicelemukaong sat in the twelfth highest layer of heaven

Fig. 21. The Virgin and Child stand in the middle of a boat, blessing all. The picture suggests the ancient cosmic egg and the earth-disc— deity at the central axis, floating on the primal sea. *After a miniature from a psalter, Yugoslavia. Former National Library, Belgrade.* (Erich Neumann, *The Great Mother: An Analysis of the Archetype,* trans. Ralph Manheim, Bollingen Series XLVII, Pl. 118. Copyright 1955 by Princeton University Press. Used by permission of the publisher.)

with his hand resting on the top of the center post. The floor of the hut represented the earth, the gabled roof the sky.

When the Cheyenne Indians of the Great Plains raised a lodge similar in meaning to the Delawares' Big House, they lashed bundles of brush to the central cross-poles for the "nest of the Thunder-bird," the all-knowing high god's special bird. [47]

MAKING THE CENTER HOLD

That cosmic centers appear so often in myth can be accounted for by the universal experience of a circular reality with oneself as the pole at the center; by children's experience of enclosed space over which powerful guardians preside; by the inevitable perception of a round world as one peers from a hilltop unobstructed by trees or as one stands at the bottom of a tall pine and peers straight up; by the fact that almost the simplest

Fig. 22. The crucified Christ is shown here as the axial pole for the spiritual cosmos. The boat approaches the heavenly Jerusalem, angels at the bow and St. Peter (the Church) enthroned in the stern. The ancient spirit-bird, in this case the Holy Ghost, surmounts the mast. After a manuscript drawing, Italy, fifteenth century. Page from the Codex Palatinus Latinus 412, *fol. 69ʳ, Vatican Library.* (Erich Neumann, *The Great Mother: An Analysis of the Archetype,* trans. Ralph Manheim, Bollingen Series XLVII, Pl. 120. Copyright 1955 by Princeton University Press. Used by permission of the publisher.)

man-made shelters are supported by a central pole; by the ancient experience of the sky as a dome; by the experience of smaller centers upon which attention converges and from which power flows (for instance, the campfire, the well, the home, the temple, the city); and by borrowing other peoples' symbols that complete one's own impressions.

But all such cosmic symbols arise from gratitude for the world's mysterious order and from the fervent hope that it will continue. For ancient people, only the will of the gods held up the sky-dome, hoisted the sun each day, restrained the seas, blew the clouds into place and sent them away, turned the seasons, and opened seedpods and wombs. Should those gods grow bored, angry, or exhausted, all would be lost. The sky-dome would fall; the surrounding waters would crush the cosmic bubble; or darkness, desert, snow, fire, or monster would snuff out life.

The story of the flood, in Genesis, suggests the human need for assurance that the cosmic order will last. After many months cooped up in the Ark, a miniature cosmos, Noah came forth onto the solid earth. His very first act was to build an altar to the Lord and offer up a sacrifice. "The LORD smelled the pleasing odor, and the LORD said in his heart, 'I will never again curse the ground because of man . . . neither will I ever again destroy every living creature. . . . While the earth remains, seedtime and harvest, cold and heat, summer and winter, day and night shall not cease' " (Gen. 8:20–22). The Lord was promising that, however human wickedness might anger him, he would never again ruin humankind's home. Virtually every ancient people sought gods with this power and this purpose: to make the center hold.

Meanwhile, the serpent hummed a little tune to himself.

8

Monsters as Images of Chaos

Monster!

It has two heads or ten or one hundred. Its skin is a vivid green, slick and damp, or its body is covered with warts or coarse, spiky hair or scales. Its tail, a great muscular whip, severs heads. Either a monster is ominously silent or it growls, snorts, shrieks.

A monster slithers, leaps, flies, lumbers, pounces. It moves like fire, molting corrosive feathers that sprout into snakes and scorpions. Its eyes bulge or are hooded or peer from the tips of long stems. It never simply kills. Its glance freezes men mid-leap, stuns them, turns them to stone. Its mouth is so big that, when it yawns, a bumpkin might fall in and be swallowed. Its razor teeth gleam; its fangs squirt poison. Its iron claws shred whatever they strike. Casually, it grinds its victims facedown in the mire, eats them like grapes, tears them limb from limb, turns them to frothing agony. Whatever it spies, it snorfs up in a moment and then oozes silently back into the sea or the earth, some would-be hero trapped whole in its deadly juices. No one will ever find his bones.

Kill it? Ha! Hunch deep within your locked house, and pray its eye does not fall in your direction. Only a hero from afar might have a chance, and then only with the aid of a magical helper.

The essential fact about monsters is that they come from beyond the wall. Just as in hero stories monsters belong to the dark forest beyond the town, so in god stories the monsters belong to the primeval chaos beyond the cosmos. In creation myths, the formidable stuff that the gods must subdue before they can make the cosmos is often a monster.

Sometimes a god even chops up a monster to make the cosmos of this stuff. Even an established cosmos under the care of powerful gods often goes awry because a monster has breached the cosmic membrane. Monsters of lesser species may be spawned in the untamed parts of the cosmos and one day encroach upon a town. The natural homes of monsters are deep lakes, salty oceans, remote mountains, distant planets, unknown galaxies, the old night to which we return when we enter sleep.

Because monsters come from beyond the cosmos and existed before it, only the most powerful gods can protect us from them. All the cosmic laws, whether social or physical, may be futile against their power. They are the creature, its stare blank and pitiless, that slouches toward Bethlehem to be born—snuffing order, civility, decency, compassion, all.

In a particular story, the chaos-monster may want gold or human flesh or a beautiful maiden to split to her waist, but in the West it always wants to destroy: to terrorize into stupefaction, to disrupt the daily round of toil and sweet rest, to kill, trample crops, spread fire and disease, ruin all human work and plans, empty the earth, swallow the sun.

Monsters are primeval energy—unchanneled, intractable. Against them there is no appeal. Neither Frankenstein's monster nor the Beast in *Beauty and the Beast* nor King Kong is a proper monster because these are creatures of the cosmos, their power undermined by their vulnerability to love and to compunction. Not so with a proper monster. One might as well reason with a tractor or plead with a bomb as with him.

In the folklore of the world's major cultures, monsters have long been one of life's great hazards. The main work of gods and mythological heroes is to slay monsters. Why? One may surmise with Joseph Fontenrose, in *Python: A Study of Delphic Myth and Its Origins*, that real experience long ago suggested this theme—the experience of Mesopotamian herdsmen and hunters with lions and wolves; of Africans and Indians with huge pythons, cobras, and crocodiles; of seafarers with sharks and other dangerous sea creatures.[1] But even if, as Fontenrose's evidence implies, the serpentlike monster of myths—often huge, winged, fire-breathing, associated with water—originated in Mesopotamia and spread from there throughout most of Asia and Europe, why did it spread so vigorously? Why do even isolated tribal peoples tell of heroes who rid the land long ago of cannibal ogres and boat-smashing monsters; of turtle-spirits that live in the lagoon and pull down the unwary; of angry ancestral spirits that go on destructive rampages, causing typhoons, diseases, and crop blights? Why do *we* find monsters so fascinating, so easy to half-believe in? We rarely battle lions, crocodiles, even sharks, to say nothing of Big Foot, King Kong, Dracula, the Hunchback of Notre Dame, Moby Dick, Darth Vader, and assorted ogres, dragons, demons. We seldom even encounter snakes, and yet they figure largely in our stories and dreams. Our children pore over pictures of dinosaurs, eagerly learn their difficult names, and, in museum shops, head straight for the small rubber brontosaurs and pterodactyls.

Monsters are all those forces that shred our serenity and threaten to overwhelm us. They are everything uncontrollable that we fear. We fear angry parents. We fear our own anger—that Incredible Hulk in all of us. We fear large animals, noisy machines. We fear dark, narrow places, strangers in our yard, jobs we cannot handle, unresponsive bureaucracies, marching mobs, lightning, earthquakes, rampaging rivers. We fear being defenseless and alone, bereft of love, choices. We fear disruption, disease, death, dissolution, the end of the world. But attempts to describe realistically the people and events that we fear seldom raise the hair on other people's heads. Even our friends shrug. Often we cannot even articulate our fear. It comes from a tangle of causes too complex, subtle, or discomfiting to describe.

Thus dreams and art, by using vivid symbols, best present our horror. The five-year-old child with a threatening mother may find himself pursued each night by a truck-sized tarantula whose name happens to be his mother's maiden name. James Thurber's line drawings of puffed-up, elephantine women ready to pounce upon tiny, cowering men sum up an array of complex relationships between ordinary-looking people. Paul Klee's painting of Sinbad shows one stumpy man teetering in a little dishlike boat upon a bottomless ocean; he pokes his puny spear at three formidable monsters risen from the deep. Courage, vulnerability—Klee's Sinbad is their essence. Dreams and art put our fears in communicable form.

Of course, as G. S. Kirk sensibly points out, one reason that monsters frequently appear in stories is that, from the dramatic point of view, they make the ideal enemy. "Slaying them creates a fundamental kind of suspense, in which danger and deprivation are satisfyingly replaced by safety and possession. . . . The more acute and apparently inhuman the danger, the greater the relief and satisfaction when it is overcome."[2]

The monsters of folklore acquire their particular characteristics in quite understandable ways. They tend to be enlarged composites of familiar animals whose sharp teeth and claws, ferocity, or seeming oddness make people uneasy. They may sport an unnatural number of eyes, heads, or breasts. They may combine human parts with those of fish, birds, lions, bulls, scorpions, or goats. Such monsters as griffins, demons, harpies, and sphinxes simply combine characteristics of animals that "the gods" did not mix (Figs. 23–25).

Fig. 23. The griffin combines the awesome features of the eagle and the lion. From very early times in Mesopotamia, this figure represented the thunderstorm. *Late Assyrian relief, ca. 1000–612 B.C., Nimrud.* (From an engraving in Austen Henry Layard, *Monuments of Nineveh, Second Series* (London: J. Murray, 1853). The original slab, in the British Museum, is badly damaged. Joseph Campbell, *The Hero with a Thousand Faces,* Bolllingen Series XVII. Copyright 1949 by Princeton University Press. Copyright © renewed 1976 by Princeton University Press. Pl. 21 adapted for use as a line drawing by permission.)

Fig. 24. Pazuzu, Mesopotamian demon of the southeast wind, brought dread diseases. The conception combines features of men, eagles, and scorpions. Pazuzu made his film debut in *The Exorcist, Part 2: The Heretic,* 1977. *Bronze, Late Assyrian, Dur Sharrukin, ca. 1000–612 B.C., from Lake Van culture in eastern Turkey. Musée de Louvre, Paris.*

People's reactions to the irregular, grotesque, or merely unusual in nature help to explain the symbolic power of monsters in folklore. People fear what the two-headed calf means, not the small creature itself. Even the Satan of medieval art does not look very formidable in himself, just peculiar or alien—a scorched rat, a frizzled bat, a black, hunchbacked dwarf, a cowering dog. What makes a cosmos is a widely shared confidence in its existence and a determination to protect it. Aberrants suggest

Fig. 25. This harpy combines a man's head, woman's breasts and torso, bat's wings, eagle's claws, and serpent's tail. In Greek myth, harpies were cruel, filthy monsters with women's heads and birds' bodies. *Germany, a sixteenth-century bestiary.* (Heinz Mode, *Fabulous Beasts and Demons* (Oxford, Eng.: Phaidon Press, 1975), Fig. 270. Copied by permission of the publisher.)

that some inimical force has got past the patrolling gods. The unsanctioned interloper is a threat even if, as in some cultures, it takes the shape of one's own child. Human twins are not "normal" and so, in many cultures, have caused alarm. Left-handed people are "sinister." Walleyes, a cleft palate, an unusual number of fingers, an odd color of hair, even a penetrating intellect make people uneasy. Epilepsy and madness terrify.

Folk cultures do not always view the freakish phenomenon as inimical to cosmic order. Its meaning may seem ambiguous, so that it is met with mixed contempt and respect, with mistrust and reverence. The freakish may even seem a good sign, perhaps even a gift of the gods. In any case, because it seems to come from beyond the natural world, it is seldom treated casually.

Typically, traditional monster-stories acknowledge the power of chaos (unsanctified, intractable energy, often malevolent) and reaffirm the superior power of the gods (order, justice). A great many stories treat the cycle of disorder and order: emerging from dark confusion; making and maintaining a clear, orderly system; falling back into darkness. This is our world's daily and annual cycle, the cycle of an individual life, of a culture, perhaps of the universe itself. Just as the god's power pulls all nature toward the cosmic axis in a harmonious dance, the monster's power works to scatter. Whether a story is upbeat or downbeat depends largely on where in the inevitable round the narrator has chosen to end his tale. Most monster stories are upbeat. The god conquering the monster is an emblem of the success repeated in each dawn, each spring, each birth, in each of the innumerable successful struggles during an individual's life and a culture's history. It is the grandest, most cheering image conceivable of the main drama in all life. The god conquering the monster was the central myth for the Mesopotamians, Canaanites, Egyptians, and Vedic Indians;[3] such later mythic systems as the Greek, Zoroastrian, Christian, and Norse adopted the motif.

These peoples envisioned in the remote past a dramatic conquest of original chaos and then a gradual regulation of chaos in lesser forms. In stories about the earliest times, so potent is the monster that he threatens the whole world or the gods' realm itself. Such monsters are the Egyptian Apep, the Babylonian Tiamat, the Judeo-Christian Satan, and the Norse monsters Fenrir and the world-serpent. Only one hero in all the world, a god, can stand against these beasts. In the Egyptian, Babylonian, and Judeo-Christian stories, victory over the chaos-monster brought a "more" perfect world than before and won a great boon for mankind.

In stories about later times, lesser monsters threaten not the whole world but a smaller realm such as a region or town, and human heroes may subdue such beasts. Classical Greek myths and medieval Christian tales afford numerous examples. The merely human villain enters a people's folklore fairly late. Still later, a human *group* representing chaos or evil may fight some other human group representing cosmic order. The Israelites subdued the Canaanites; the Christians, the Saracens. At this point, myth has given way to mythologized history. Yet, long after historical military campaigns have entered a culture's folklore, some monster stories persist. Even now, Nessie, Big Foot, and horrendous creatures from outer space loom in remote places, and their cousins rear up in our dreams.

The rest of this chapter first examines some of the primeval battles between cosmos-creating gods and the monsters representing chaos. Next, it shows how the actions of two human heroes, Beowulf and King Arthur, echo those of the gods in creation stories. Then, it explores the symbol of the monster as a cruel guardian. Finally, it seeks to explain our fascination with chaos.

APEP AND SET: EGYPTIAN CHAOS-MONSTERS

Egyptian mythology swarms with monsters, among them serpents associated with the earth, darkness, death, human helplessness. Some of them protect a dead person's boat as it sails through the monster-haunted lakes and tunnels of the underworld with its comatose cargo. The guardian serpents surround his helpless body, or they rear at the prow of his boat, keeping him safe from the many hostile monsters. But as soon as he begins to stir and tries to free himself, his protectors themselves grow hostile and must be subdued by charms and magic helpers.

One of the best known of ancient Egyptian monsters was Apep, or Apopis, the quintessential chaos-monster. Each morning after Re had sailed across the underworld in his sunboat and was about to create the cosmos anew by emerging into the upper world, Apep, the ferocious serpent of chaos and darkness, struck the sunboat. His aim was to swallow the sun. Were he to succeed, the world would end. Each day the battle had to be fought and Apep subdued. The Egyptians ceremonially rejoiced each morning when they saw that Re had won a day more for them.

But of all the battles fought between cosmic order and chaos in early and classical Egyptian mythology (ca. 3000–1700 B.C.), the richest by far is the story of the holy family: the king Osiris, his wife Isis, his treacherous brother Set, and Osiris' loyal, triumphant son Horus. In this story, although Set was a god, not a monster, so abominable was he that in later Egyptian mythology he came to be identified with Apep. Even in the early Coffin Texts (ca. 2250 B.C.), writes R. T. Rundle Clark, theologians viewed Apep as "a form of the essential hostile power, whose first form was the serpent dragon of the waters who was overthrown by the High God in primeval times. . . . [In Egyptian mythology] the hero and the enemy remain essentially the same whatever their names."[4]

The story follows the archetypal three-part pattern mentioned earlier: the establishment of order; the fall into chaos (treachery, destruction, suffering, struggle); the triumph of order.

Osiris, the king of Egypt during the First Time was a hero of the highest order, renowned not for military but for moral leadership; not for his physical might but for his power of persuasion in a great cause. He traveled throughout his kingdom, teaching his people to cease eating each other, even to stop quarreling. He made laws to help them live together in harmony. He showed them how to grow grapes, how to plant and sow grain, how to tend fruit trees. He taught them music and poetry. He taught them how to honor the gods and receive the gods' blessings. Osiris enhanced life in every way: physical, social, aesthetic, moral, religious. His actions perfected the cosmos. Under his wise and just reign, life thrived in the largest sense.

Enter Set. As Osiris was spreading the gift of his wisdom even beyond the borders of Egypt, his envious brother Set—associated with the desert wilderness beyond the influence of the Nile—hatched an evil plan. When Osiris returned, Set prepared a banquet, and at this grand affair, he offered an exquisite jeweled chest to anyone whose body it would fit. Though many lay down in the chest, they found themselves too short, too stout, or too lean. Then Osiris, who had a perfect body, lay down in it. It fit. Before he could arise, Set and his seventy-two evil attendants sprang forward, bolted the lid, sealed it with lead. Taken by surprise, Isis and the followers of Osiris could not fight their way through Set's henchmen.

That night in darkness, the plotters stealthily dumped the casket into the Nile. It bobbed out to sea. Set placed himself upon Osiris' throne. During Set's reign, corruption and discord rocked the realm. Drought, famine, and disease spread terror and death. The wilderness encroached upon the once green and fertile land. In short, the cosmos cracked.

Meanwhile, Isis was engaged in a desperate struggle to gather and save her husband's power. She tracked the chest's journey into Syria. Some time earlier, a flood had cast the chest upon the land, into a young tamarisk thicket. One growing tree had incorporated the chest in its trunk, and the king of Byblos had cut this fine tree for the central pillar in his hall. After much patient effort, Isis retrieved the chest, took it back to the marshlands in lower Egypt, and there secretly embalmed Osiris' body. Though comatose, Osiris in some sense still lived because his body was intact. Isis guarded it carefully.

But one day when Isis was off gathering food, Set in serpent form slid through the marshes and discovered the body. He stole it, chopped it into fourteen pieces, and scattered them the length of Egypt. With the help of Egypt's children, Isis contrived to find all the pieces except one crucial part. A wicked crab had eaten the penis. But the resourceful Isis sought out Egypt's finest craftsman and had him construct a wooden phallus. She reassembled the body. Then, so skilled was she in the arts of love and embalming that she enabled Osiris' body to engender upon her a son.

Isis' harrowing adventures continued. With time, in fact, their dramatic embellishments rather overwhelmed the original meaning of the story. What is important from the standpoint of the battle between order and chaos is that, when this son Horus grew up, he restored cosmic order by avenging Osiris' murder and establishing himself upon the throne. In one version of the story, the primeval hawk—also named Horus—descended along the cosmic axis to bring the good news to Osiris in the underworld, then ascended, still along the axis, past Re's own sunboat to the topmost point of the cosmos to proclaim the glorious return of justice and order. The image of the magnificent bird perched atop the pole and crying out the news parallels the image of the Benu-bird perched upon the staff, calling forth the original cosmic order.

In another version of the Osirian story, Osiris' son ascended the throne upon the Isle of Fire at the top of the cosmos. In some versions, once Osiris was restored, he established himself there. The stories all symbolize the same idea. As with the later stories of Varuna, Snorri Sturluson's Odin, and others, a just, all-seeing divinity patrolled the cosmos, binding it together with his moral authority.

Most versions of the Osirian story underline the triumph of life and order over death and chaos. Soon after Osiris fathered Horus, Osiris came to full life again but in the Other World; there he was Judge of the Dead, and through him all people could become immortal. Some later versions of the story stress in a second way the triumph of order. Although Set was allowed to live, he was forced to sail in the prow of Re's sunboat and fight Apep each morning. His position was rather like that of a chained dog. Thus was evil forced to serve good, the chaos-monster's energy made to serve the cosmic order. The Mesopotamian, Zoroastrian, and Christian versions of the combat story stress the same point.

TIAMAT: THE MESOPOTAMIAN CHAOS-MONSTER

In the Babylonian creation story, called the *Enuma elish,* the god Marduk battled the chaos-monster Tiamat. Marduk was not the story's original hero. The Sumerian god Enlil had earlier played that role, and perhaps others had preceded him. Nor did Tiamat begin as a monster inimical to order. She had begun as the great mother of the gods, associated with the primeval waters. By the early second millennium B.C., however, Mesopotamians saw her as on the side of chaos against her younger children. Chaos in this story is not boiling confusion but, in a sense, the opposite: blobby inertia. Indeed, one thinks of Tiamat as a great sprawling sow, full of milk, disinclined to move. When she finally was moved to action, she usurped the authority represented in the *Enuma elish* as properly held by her male descendants. Here is the story.[5]

Long ago, when only the realm of the gods existed, Tiamat's younger, more energetic descendants were scurrying around, making so much noise that the primeval gods began to find them tiresome. The noise grew worse and worse. Finally, Tiamat's husband Apsu, annoyed beyond endurance, plotted to kill the whippersnappers. But when the younger gods heard of Apsu's plan, they simply killed Apsu. Appalled, the other primeval gods aroused Tiamat herself against her descendants. Instead of reestablishing the old order, Tiamat set up herself and her new monster-consort Kingu as tyrants. Kingu even took possession of the Tablet of Destinies, a particularly shocking act because the Tablet was linked with supreme cosmic authority.

One of Tiamat's weapons against the younger gods was her own versatile fecundity. At will, she began to turn out fanged serpents and flame-belching dragons. Since the supremely intelligent Ea (god of sweet waters) had done most to rid the younger gods of Apsu by stunning him with a spell so that he could be killed, the other gods looked to Ea to subdue Tiamat in the same way. But even though the power of words was strong, Tiamat's power was stronger: Ea slunk away. Then the gods begged Ea's father Anu (god of the sky) to command Tiamat, in the name of their collective authority, to abide in peace. Anu, understanding the futility of that approach, refused. For a long time after that, the once bustling gods sat in glum silence. Finally, Ea's grandfather suggested that Ea's magnificent young son Marduk might be willing to fight on their behalf.

Yes, indeed, Marduk would go forth against his great-great-great-grandmother—for a price. He asked from Ea in advance the transfer of universal authority to himself. All the gods, including Ea, acquiesced, for their helplessness against Tiamat and her monstrous brood had made their lives insupportable. They conferred on Marduk both universal moral authority and the powers of compulsion to back up that authority: in a word, kingship.

So glorious was the youth mounted in his storm-chariot, brandishing not only arrows, club, and poison but also lightning and cyclone, that, as he advanced, most of Tiamat's monster-warriors fell back. Tiamat herself stood firm. Promptly swinging a great net, Marduk caught her in it, and when she opened her huge jaws to swallow him, he sent the winds to hold her jaws open and swell her body. While she hovered before him, helpless as a Goodyear blimp, he shot an arrow into her mouth. It went straight to her heart, slicing it in two. The old monster-mother fell dead. Splitting her body like a shellfish, Marduk set one half above as a heavenly roof, and the other below as the earth. Together the two cupped halves kept out the surrounding waters.

Marduk then regulated and furnished this sheltered place. He divided time into years, months, and days, establishing rules and ordinances. He founded shrines and handed them over to Ea. The Tablet of Destinies, which he had wrested from Kingu, he gave as a gift to Anu. From the blood and bones of Kingu, the most wicked god, Marduk made the human race. Thus the tremendous generative powers of the earliest beings produced the cosmos and the creatures within it.

SATAN: THE CHRISTIAN CHAOS-MONSTER

In Christian tradition, the chaos-monster and the creator of the cosmos also joined battle in the First Time, but this battle has continued during historical time. Before the earth existed, God ruled heaven, a magnificent realm of angels. Satan, an archangel filled with pride, persuaded one-third of the angels to rise up with him against God's just and generous reign.[6] The archangel Michael led the other angels in battle against Satan, casting him and his rebel forces into hell. Then God, in order to replenish his realm, created the earth and humankind. He endowed people with the ability to choose to follow him or, as Satan had chosen, to rebel. People would multiply, and those who proved worthy would, after their earthly lives, rise to heaven to join the angels. But Satan, growing ever more evil through his own freely committed evil acts, breached the wall of the garden that God had created for Adam and Eve. Taking the form of a serpent, he persuaded the human pair to disobey God.

The garden, though created by God as a perfect miniature cosmos, lost its significance when the corrupted pair had to leave. The human family increased and tilled the wilderness, yet such moral scruff were its inhabitants that in many ways the enlarged human space remained a wilderness. Because of Adam and Eve's Fall, a tough little chaos-monster starts working within the heart of each child at the moment of its conception, lacing its blood with poison. This world cannot become a completely harmonious realm because each person born belongs in part to the serpent; we are all the serpent's children. But God's untainted child Christ was born to drain off the poison, if we choose, so that, perfected, we can replenish God's heavenly realm. In this way, Christ more than restored God's perfect realm. His sacrifice made the cosmos—so much bigger and fuller than the old—"more" perfect.

The Christian story shares much with earlier stories depicting the conflict between order and chaos. Its pattern—order established, overthrown, reestablished—resembles that of the Osirian story. In both stories, the villain, once a beautiful celestial being of human shape, is later imagined as a serpent; and the perfect son eventually rises to rule over all in his father's name.

Indirectly, imagery from the *Enuma elish* helped to dramatize the Christian conflict. The gesture we know from medieval paintings of Saint Michael standing in resplendent armor, his foot on the vanquished Satan's neck, is Marduk's in the *Enuma elish*. When Milton in the late Renaissance pictured a great battle in heaven between Christ and Satan (*Paradise Lost*, Book VI), he was following the battle between Michael and Satan in the Book of Revelation; but in Milton's poem, Christ bears down upon Satan from a chariot, and brandishes in his right hand ten thousand thunders. Milton borrowed that image from Zeus' battle with the monster Typhon, which derives in turn from the *Enuma elish*.

Some scholars suggest that the Christian tradition differs radically from earlier stories of the god vanquishing the chaos-monster in emphasizing what is linear and progressive in time instead of what is cyclic. That is partly true, but, in fact, both linear and cyclic elements abound in pre-Christian as well as in Christian stories. Mesopotamians and Egyptians thought of the cosmos as a vast dwelling completed in the First Time and maintained by vigorous gods, but also as a system that the gods remade each year and each day. For instance, in an important Mesopotamian cult, the battle between Marduk and Tiamat was, at the beginning of each year, symbolically refought and the orderly world reconstituted. The king, taking Marduk's role, burned a lamb in which Tiamat's monstrous consort had been "realized." And Egyptian priests celebrated each dawn as another victory of Re over the serpent Apep.

The Christian story of vanquishing chaos is offered in many versions. One version ends with Christ's Crucifixion and Ascension, signifying the completion of cosmic harmony two thousand years ago. In another version, the story will end some day with Christ's Second Coming and earthly reign. The annual Easter celebration in which the Lamb of God is slain and then resurrected may be viewed as a reminder of the completed triumph or as a promise that such a triumph will some day occur, but whichever its interpretation, its strong cyclic element is clear. In still another interpretation of the story, the battle takes place within each individual, Satan urging him toward life-diminishing choices and God urging him toward life-enhancing choices. Christian time is complete, cyclic, linear, or "psychological," depending on how one interprets the story.

According to the Christian doctrine of the Fortunate Fall, although the little garden was indeed perfect, simple perfection is much less valuable than is struggling toward a remote and complex perfection in a world sections of whose protective walls are always collapsing. Satan's successful temptation of Adam and Eve, though it forced them to leave the beautiful enclosure, introduced them to a life whose challenges helped them to grow into truly human beings. Furthermore, in necessitating their reproduction, the Fall extended life to myriad people.

The relative merits of a serene eternal life in an earthly paradise and a life of struggle and death in the big, imperfect world have, of course, been pondered by people outside the Judeo-Christian tradition. For instance, in *The Odyssey*, the goddess Calypso offered her island-cosmos to Odysseus, she as Eve, he as Adam. The two stories, that of Calypso's island and that of Adam and Eve's garden, were written down about the same time. They share a common feature of the ancient Middle Eastern paradise, the spring with its four branching rivers (from the Sumerian myth about Dilmun, garden of the gods). In some ways, Calypso's paradise seems a bit more inviting: She displayed a number of domestic and sexual skills that Eve probably lacked, no angels lurked among her cedars, and Odysseus was free to eat whatever he fancied.

Yet Odysseus turned Calypso down. He had known, about as fully as any human can, the big world in which chaos recurrently lays waste men's lives and must be conquered again and again. Furthermore, he knew well that, upon his death, only Hades' insipid misery awaited him. Yet Odysseus chose adventure, chaos, and dusty death.

So would we all, and the serpent unlocked the garden gate for us. But Christ's followers believe that they will get an even better life, if they want it, than the life of this world. Like Apep and Tiamat, Satan has been forced to serve the god of order. A telling symbol of evil serving divine law is the tamed demon who works almost as Saint Michael's partner in illustrations depicting the weighing of souls (Fig. 26). Although the demon in some illustrations tries to cheat, Saint Michael's authority is the greater, and clearly the soul will get its just deserts.

OTHER CHAOS-MONSTERS

As one might expect, mythology yields many other versions of the god fighting the chaos-monster. For instance, even before Marduk slew Tiamat, the Sumerian god Ninurta slew Asag, the demon of sickness and disease, who had lived in the Kur, the underworld. A curious result of Ninurta's act was that the salty, primeval waters of the Kur rose to the earth's surface, preventing the fresh waters from reaching the crops in Sumer. It was as if slaying the demon of sickness aroused even more destructive forces. But Ninurta, equal to the crisis, heaped stones up over the Kur, forcing its waters down.[7] The Jewish legend about the foundation stone and the Roman legend about the soul stone, whether or not they derive from this Sumerian story, share with it the archetypal experience of frantically plugging a hole in the not-so-solid earth.

In classical Greek mythology, many heroes fought chaos-monsters. Zeus himself battled three great forces of disorder before establishing his reign forever. First, he defeated the Titans. Then, the great mother Gaea, enraged by the Olympians' harsh treatment of her children, the Titans, stirred up the Gigantes against Zeus. The Gigantes were huge earth-men, born of Uranus' blood as it soaked into the earth. So mighty were the Gigantes that Zeus needed the help of several Olympians and the hero Heracles to subdue them.

Lastly, Gaea sent forth Typhon, the worst threat of all—a horrendous, fire-flicking dragon with one hundred heads. Zeus first fought the monster from the sky, with lightning bolts. Zeus' lightning and Typhon's flame set afire such large parts of the world that most of the gods fled

Fig. 26. St. Michael and a demon weigh souls. The angel's chaste gown and bird wings signify his affinity with the celestial world. The demon's horns, claws, and tail, long associated with fierceness and sexual vigor, signify evil in Christian imagery. Divine law so curbs the demon's power that he must serve that law. *Altar panel, Spain, thirteenth century. Vich Episcopal Museum.* (Based on Pl. 28, *Spanish Frescoes*, published in the Unesco-Mentor Art Book series. Copyright © Unesco 1962. Copied by permission of Unesco.)

into Egypt. Then, descending to earth to fight the monster directly, Zeus finally killed him with thunderbolts and buried his still seething body under Mount Aetna. Altogether, it took one hundred years to conquer these monstrous forces of chaos and to establish Zeus' just and eternal reign.[8]

Joseph Fontenrose and other scholars believe that important Greek monsters, including Typhon and the cave-dwelling Python that Apollo killed, the labyrinth-dwelling Minotaur that Theseus killed, and several of the monsters that Heracles killed, are historically related to the chaos-monsters and death-demons fought by the gods of earlier cultures.[9]

The Persian cult of Ormazd (Mazda) helped shape some Christian versions of the battle between order and chaos. This cult lasted over a thousand years, from about the sixth century B.C. to the eighth century of our era, when the Moslem faith overwhelmed it. In one of the cult's many forms, Ormazd, the god of life and cosmic order, incessantly fought Ahriman, the demon of death and chaos. Ormazd was omniscient but, for the first twelve thousand years, not omnipotent. In the creation story, Ormazd created a universe full of life and warmth; in response, Ahriman created a universe so cold that even its two-month summers were icy. Ormazd created Ghaon, an earthly paradise full of roses and bright red birds; Ahriman created noxious insects. Ormazd created the holy city of Muru; Ahriman introduced lies and wicked counsel. And so on. Ormazd created a series of beautiful cities for mankind, each a small cosmos, verdant, peaceful, rich; Ahriman counteracted each gift with something destructive: wild animals that attack cattle; doubt, dissension, sloth, poverty.

Several subsidiary powers, rather like archangels, helped Ormazd to promote the natural and moral order. A corresponding group of demons—dark, malignant, many of monstrous appearance—assisted Ahriman. These demons strove to replace benevolent royal authority with crime, anarchy, tyranny. But according to the teacher Zoroaster (sixth century B.C.), after twelve thousand years, a final judgment would occur and Ormazd would win. Even the name of Ahriman would be forgotten. All beings human and celestial would promote virtue and harmony.[10] Ironically, it was Ahriman's evil machinations that, by evoking Ormazd's orderly defense, would enable Ormazd to perfect himself and the cosmos.[11]

This cult made available to Christian theology an explanation of evil in a god-created cosmos and a clear identification of harmonious order with good, of chaos with evil. It reinforced what Judaism also made available: an emphasis on linear, as opposed to cyclic, time; the view of history as a dramatic struggle between good and evil; the final judgment; the subsequent earthly reign of the god of order. The Persian story, in turn, had borrowed some of these themes from older cultures.

In Norse myth, the two chief gods Odin and Thor each battled fearsome monsters. After prodigious effort, Odin subdued the ravening wolf Fenrir and chained him in the underworld. Thor periodically fought the earth-serpent that gnawed at the main roots of Yggdrasil. In addition, all the gods had to stay alert against their primeval enemies the frost-giants, who kept scheming to get over the wall into Asgard. Fenrir, the earth-serpent, and the frost-giants were all explicitly chaos-monsters destined to succeed at last in destroying the gods' cosmos.

The pattern in each tradition, then, is of a very important god striving for harmony, peace, order, *a suitable home for humankind*, against an enemy of these purposes. Often this enemy is a monster older than the organizing god. The physical form of enemies not originally monsters often changes over time, to match their monstrous deeds. Such is the case with Tiamat, Set, Satan, the Gigantes whom Zeus fought.

In myths and legends about human heroes, the hero's function echoes that of the gods in creation stories. When the always vigorous forces of chaos threaten to overwhelm order, the hero temporarily pushes chaos back. Just as, in stories about shaping the cosmos, chaos is often personified as a monster, so in stories of human heroes battling lesser disruptions, these are disruptions often also personified as monsters. But occasionally a story with a human hero seems to go further, to echo *consciously* the original creation of the cosmos out of chaos, and the realm's subsequent defense. The stories of Beowulf and King Arthur are such stories.

BEOWULF AND KING ARTHUR AS GODLIKE SLAYERS OF CHAOS-MONSTERS

The Anglo-Saxon epic *Beowulf* (setting ca. sixth century, written eighth century) takes place on the bleak Danish islands, where past efforts to organize life have left but few signs upon the boggy wastes. Scattered rubble of a ruined agricultural settlement pokes through the snow; a crumbling barrow upon the windy moor marks the grave of some forgotten warrior. Historically, there was at this time no overarching civil authority; small bands of warriors, attached by personal loyalty to chieftains or "kings," made a kind of life by raiding each other, not just for plunder but for glory that would survive after they themselves had perished. To serve a strong king was to live in an orderly, centered world, to have, as the *Beowulf* poet wrote, power, a future, joy, glory. By contrast, he saw people who lived without a king's protection as wretches so alone, so poorly in command of their lives that they were often forced into slavery. To lose one's chieftain and one's place was worse than death; it was to be plunged into chaos.

In *Beowulf*, Hrothgar was a successful warrior-chieftain. To consolidate his success, he built in the icy wilderness a glorious meadhall, within whose safety his retainers could each night enjoy good fellowship and rest. In the poet's words, Hrothgar resolved

> To build a hall that would hold his mighty
> Band and reach higher toward Heaven than anything
> That had ever been known to the sons of men.
> [When the great hall was finished, Hrothgar,]
> . . . he whose word was obeyed
> All over the earth named it Herot.
> . . .
> [The bard's rejoicing songs rang loud,
> day after day, telling]
> Of the ancient beginning of us all, recalling
> The Almighty making the earth, shaping
> Those beautiful plains marked off by oceans,
> Then proudly setting the sun and moon
> To glow across the land and light it.[12]

After telling how the Almighty made the cosmos lovely with trees and quick with life, the poet turned to the parallel of the meadhall—also a safe, commodious shelter containing a large array of delights. For the poet, the meadhall was more than a safe place, more than a sign of great efficacy. He explicitly saw building the hall as a joyful reenactment of the original creation: Hrothgar had created a cosmos, with Herot as the axis and loyalty to himself as its moral center.

But even as the bard's songs joyfully recounted the Almighty's creation of the glorious earth and Hrothgar's creation of the glorious hall, the chaos-monster Grendel was snarling impatiently down in the dark earth. Explicitly, the poet links Grendel with hell. The hall was scarcely finished when

> . . . the monster stirred, that demon, that fiend,
> Grendel, who haunted the moors, the wild
> Marshes, and made his home in a hell

Not hell but earth. He was spawned in that slime,
Conceived by a pair of those monsters born
Of Cain, murderous creatures banished
By God, punished forever for the crime
Of Abel's death. The Almighty drove
Those demons out, and their exile was bitter,
Shut away from men; they split
Into a thousand forms of evil—spirits
And fiends, goblins, monsters, giants,
A brood forever opposing the Lord's
Will, and again and again defeated.[13]

When Grendel struck, ripping the latch and devouring groggy men, neither the aging Hrothgar nor his best warriors could stop him. The king sat humiliated and confused, drained of power. Desperately his followers appealed to an ineffectual clutter of old gods. And then—like the samurai hero of the film *Yojimbo*, like Oedipus striding into Thebes, like countless good guys of classic Western movies, like Christ himself—the shining Beowulf came from afar to restore the devastated little civilization. With his bare hands he pulled off Grendel's huge arm, mortally wounding him. When Grendel's mother arose from her lair and, violating the hall for the second time, gobbled more men, the remaining warriors were ready to abandon the hall and scatter to nameless fates. But Beowulf ventured out upon the frosty wastes and down the slippery chasms to the boiling lake. It was so thick with vicious serpents that their writhing almost wove a pattern on its surface. Alone, Beowulf entered that lake, struggled down, down to the enemy's lair. After a bloody battle so long that Beowulf's own men assumed him dead, he killed Grendel's mother. He had restored the great hall to peace and safety. The center held.

Like *Beowulf*, the Arthurian romances (twelfth through fifteenth centuries) envisioned a man of such godlike wisdom and physical power that he created for a time a cosmos within the wilderness. The story of how Arthur became king strongly suggests God's power flowing from the cosmic axis into the young Arthur himself, enabling him to restore God's badly tattered canopy. Before Arthur's day, wrote Malory in *Le Morte Darthur*, brigands robbed, raped, and murdered anyone who dared step forth, and bullying lords vied for power over the kingless land. God's earthly vicar, the Archbishop of Canterbury, asked the lords to gather at the holy center on Christ's own birthday to purify themselves by taking

Communion. He was preparing the world for a miraculous renewal. On Christmas morning, the miracle occurred. A great marble stone, surmounted by a steel anvil, appeared in the churchyard, a fine sword stuck fast in the anvil. Whoever could pull forth that sword would be God's choice as king.

The image echoes the ancient image of the cosmic axial pole, sometimes represented as a sword or spear, and the image of the god Odin plunging into a great hall's central pole (itself a symbolic cosmic axis) a sword that only his special warrior can remove.

In the Arthurian story, the assembled lords milled about the sword, tugged, stared, scratched their heads. On New Year's Day, the day of the world's annual rebirth, an ignorant, good-hearted boy doing an errand for his brother dislodged the sword. The boy was Arthur.

Arthur became a great king. Camelot, his hilltop castle with its Round Table, became a replica of the cosmic center. Arthur achieved a miracle. Out of moral and social chaos, he made a space within which people could build sane, orderly lives; he shaped a life-enhancing code of behavior, a social order, an enduring vision of justice. Both Arthur's accession and his rule suggest that, like Hrothgar, he was consciously represented as resembling a god shaping a cosmos. During Arthur's reign, he dispatched monsters, literal and symbolic; most important, he defended the True Faith against the Moslems, and defeated Lucius, the tyrannical emperor of the whole known world.

Yet for all the beauty and near-perfection of his realm, Arthur was a man, not a god; at the very beginning, he himself had unwittingly planted, at his world's root, the worm of its destruction. Shortly after Arthur was crowned king of England, a neighboring queen visited him. Arthur and the lady became so enamored of each other that for a month they shared the same bed. After the lady's departure, the young king was beset by a nightmare in which griffins and serpents attacked his realm, burning towns and killing all the people. In his dream, Arthur fought these monsters. Awakening deeply troubled, he rode out into the forest to hunt. There, the wizard Merlin revealed to Arthur his royal lineage and declared that God was extremely angry because Arthur had lain with his own sister. "On her ye have gotten a child that shall destroy you and all the knights of your realm."[14] This son was the wicked Modred; the prophecy, a true one. The chaos-monster, as in many stories, was akin to the hero himself.

When at last the evil Modred forced the confrontation between Arthur and Lancelot, a snake—that old chaos-monster was by then a well-established Christian symbol of evil—played a part in Arthur's end. Arthur's and Modred's forces stood by tensely as Arthur and Modred tried to negotiate an agreement. But a snake, slinking forth from a heath bush, bit a soldier; the startled soldier drew his sword to kill it. His action precipitated the battle in which Arthur suffered a fatal wound.

For all Arthur's godlike wisdom, he had been subject in his youth to such human imperfections as lust, heedlessness, stubbornness, and pride. He had held back chaos for many years, but he was only a man, and as Gilgamesh had learned long before, what is human must return to darkness and disorder. The griffins and serpents—the disintegrative forces in our own selves—did destroy his kingdom.

Yet the vision of justice remained. Arthur had changed the definition of the possible. This time, the monsters at once won and lost.

THE MONSTER AS CRUEL GUARDIAN

Monsters are one of the most confusing symbols in all mythology, because, despite their association with chaos and destruction, especially in the West, they do not exactly symbolize evil. In the ancient Middle East, monsters most often represented creative energy, the brute life-force that is at once the source and bane of *organized* life. Sometimes monsters would snatch the most prized forms of life—rosy babies, nubile maidens, robust young heroes—to reinvigorate the stock of primeval energy, and sometimes heroes would steal from some rich store of primeval life—a magical tree or spring—that a monster guarded. However, the early conflict was a clash between two manifestations of energy, not between good and evil in our sense. As the abstract concepts of good and evil emerged and as Western tradition tended more and more to repudiate the old understanding of death as the renewer of life, the meaning of the monster was simplified.

It is true, as I have suggested, that when an ancient deity fell into disrepute, its physical form tended to grow monstrous. But innumerable stories picture monsters as the guardians and repositories of primeval energy, not as personifications of evil. For instance, in Egyptian myth, the serpent, which ancient people often classed with monsters as unnatural, was the form in which divinity existed before there were gods and men, and the form to which divinity would one day return. In Greek tradition, such early beings as the revered founders of Attica and Athens had snakelike lower bodies. The Greeks viewed them as wilder or closer to the earth than later creatures, not as evil. In China, dragons have long been revered as representing water in all its forms—storms, the sea, winding rivers—the thing that sets all life in motion. In the East, though alarmingly unpredictable, many monsters are benevolent.

In the early stories of both Mesopotamia and Egypt, guardian spirits as well as demons might take monstrous forms, and the guardians and demons are often scarcely distinguishable in appearance and behavior. The Mesopotamian forest-guardian Humbaba is a case in point. I have also mentioned the Egyptian guardian-serpents that protected the dead until the soul tried to rise up and resume life in the afterworld, whereupon the serpents attacked the soul and had to be subdued. Egyptian myth also told of how Hathor, the benevolent mother-goddess, once became so angry with people that, taking the form of Sekhmet, a fierce lion-headed goddess, she set out to destroy humankind.

The blurred distinction between gods and monsters, guardians and destroyers, often arises from the fact that, long before the abstract concepts of good and evil had emerged, supernatural beings personified the powers of nature, both helpful and harmful. A particular natural "power" such as rain, sunshine, or fire is obviously sometimes helpful to people, sometimes injurious. Thus, a usually helpful being might be viewed as having destructive moods; he might be pictured as of monstrous appearance during these moods. Another reason for the blurred distinction is that a benevolent god might subdue forces necessary but often harmful, and then absorb these powers. The monster that a god subdues may, through long association, even come to represent that god's protective powers. And finally, a reason closer to home: Whatever possesses such ready might that we know it will truly protect us may turn against us. The storm-god, the macho husband, the beefy policeman, the professional soldier, the chained mastiff sometimes are indistinguishable from monsters.

Many clearly benevolent spirits in Egypt and Mesopotamia were envisioned as monsters, that is, as composite human beings and animals. Egyptian deities often combined human characteristics with those of such awesome animals as hawks, vultures, lions, jackals, bulls, and crocodiles. Mesopotamian guardian-spirits were sometimes depicted as composites in order to convey the powers of several animals.

The seeming contradictions dissolve when one perceives the ancient Middle Eastern monster as symbolizing the primal life-force—consuming as well as renewing the individual sheaves, melons, goats, and children that it sent forth. (Anyone who has watched a once sleek cat turn into a sack of bones as she bears litter after litter has seen a vivid instance of *the living being devoured in the service of Life.*) Early agricultural peoples believed that the living have only borrowed their life's energy. Organized life must break up for new life to come forth. The monster is this single life-destroying, life-renewing force.

Again and again in ancient art, paired monsters guarded some great source of life—the tree of life, the gates of paradise, the Ark of the Covenant, a temple's entrance, the cosmic center. Ferocious or fecund beasts served the same function as the guardian monsters. The symbol of the paired guardians appears to go back at least to the seventh millennium B.C., for in a shrine at Çatal Hüyük, in Anatolia, two leopards flanked the mother-goddess as she gave birth. Huge reliefs of winged bulls with human heads and of winged men with the heads of birds, bulls, or lions guarded Mesopotamian palaces and temples. Called *lamassu* or *kerubim*, these figures often stood in pairs, one on either side of the entrance (Fig. 27). The biblical cherubim that guard paradise derive from the Mesopotamian kerubim. In the Book of Ezekiel, the cherubim guarding paradise combine the characteristics of men, lions, oxen, and eagles (1:4–10). In Mesopotamian tradition, scorpion-men guarded the huge gate of Mashu, the mythical mountain range that Gilgamesh crossed.

At Mycenae, the dominant city of second-millennium Greece, two stone lions guarded the hilltop citadel (Fig. 28). One of the objects buried with the pharaoh Tutankhamen (ca. 1320 B.C.) is an ivory headrest representing Shu, god of the air, sitting on the earth and holding up the sky (Fig. 29). On either side of Shu sit two lions. They symbolize the mountains to the east and west of Egypt over which the sun rose and set, but they also guard the precious sky-pole personified in Shu. The lions flanking the entrances of American public libraries are descendants of all these Middle Eastern beasts.

On Romanesque and Gothic churches, grotesque gargoyles ward off evil. On Buddhist architectural monuments, the snakelike Nagas serve the same function. The fact that snakes have so often been classified as monsters in folklore and have played so large a part in myths needs explaining. Early Christians supposed that the prominence of snakes in other people's religious lore meant that the devil reigned in pagan minds, and it is common enough for one people to see other peoples' supernat-

Fig. 27. Stone "lamassu"—winged bulls with human heads—guarded Mesopotamian palaces and temples. Often placed in pairs, one on either side of the entrance, they signified primal energy tamed to serve the gods' divine order. *Late Assyrian, Dur Sharrukin, 721–705 B.C. Musée de Louvre, Paris.* (Heinz Mode, *Fabulous Beasts and Demons* (Oxford, Eng.: Phaidon Press, 1975), Pl. 63. Copied by permission of the publisher.)

Fig. 28. Over the main entrance to the royal citadel at Mycenae, two lions flank a pillar. The pillar probably was a symbol of Zeus, as sky-pillar, and was meant to honor him. Mycenae, Agamemnon's seat, was the most powerful city in Greece during the second millennium B.C. The Greeks borrowed the motif of the guardian lions from their eastern neighbors. The sky-pillar is a widespread motif. (*Gardner's Art Through the Ages*, rev. by Horst de la Croix and Richard G. Tansey, 6th ed. (New York: Harcourt Brace Jovanovich, 1975), Pl. 420. Copied by permission of photographer Alison Frantz.)

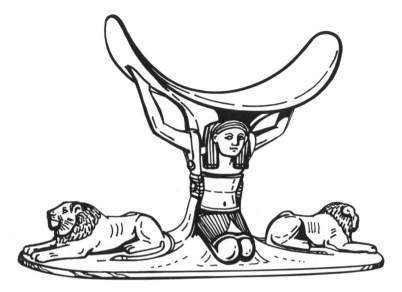

Fig. 29. Shu, the Egyptian god of air, helped to establish the cosmos in the First Time by raising and supporting the sky. This ivory headrest buried with the Egyptian king Tutankhamen (ca. fourteenth century B.C.) represents the god continuing to support it. The two lions, signifying the mountains to the east and west of Egypt, guard the sky-pole personified as Shu.

ural guardians as demons. But why so many snakes? Even early Mesopotamian monsters often had snake forms or horned snakes' heads, and the word "dragon" comes from a Greek word for snake.

Snakes unsettled the minds of ancient people outside the Judeo-Christian tradition as much as they unsettle our minds, and for some of the same reasons. We note with special misgiving the snake's peculiar but able form of locomotion. The creature seems unbound by natural laws. Its slither seems to take it in every direction at once. It can even wind itself up and spring, like an uncoiling arrow. Because the snake annually sheds its skin and comes out "new," it appears to be one of the few creatures able to regenerate themselves. Its dwelling within crevices, holes, and caves suggests the earth itself, where even in dry climates the primeval life-giving waters can be found and where the roots of the long-lived trees stay vigorous. But here too lies death.

Because the snake seems to possess powers that other creatures do not, ancient people of the Middle East and of Mexico inferred that, like the great monsters of the deep, it had existed before the cosmos. Middle Eastern people inferred, too, that it was subtle, wise, possibly evil, beyond the gods' dominion, certainly unknowable, dangerous, but perhaps able to convey the secret of longevity or regeneration. Indeed, R. T. Rundle Clark's catalog of serpents in ancient Egyptian lore neatly summarizes the symbolic meanings of the snake. Among important Egyptian snakes were the creator or earliest "manifestation of the emergent spirit"; the monster that had to be overcome before the world was truly in order; a serpent-god that encircled the world, protecting it from the disintegrative forces of the surrounding chaos; a guardian of the underworld; Apep, who personified the powers of darkness that had to be overcome at dawn; a fertility spirit; a water-god, especially one living within the caverns from which the Nile flood was thought to come; a primeval creature living in the depths of the earth or the water—uncanny, hostile to people, possibly very wise.[15] In short, in addition to the obvious power of some snakes to kill, they have seemed at once dangerous and valuable for their "special" power. They have long seemed to possess the elemental secrets of life, death, and regeneration.

The snake, then, like the ancient Middle Eastern monster generally, symbolized not evil but brute energy—dangerous, necessary. According to Clark, an early Egyptian myth describes how the high god curbed the power of the primeval snakes, but stresses that this power is very precious. These snakes are the forces of nature; the high god gave these forces direction through knowledge and then turned over to Osiris the job of controlling them.[16] Middle Eastern peoples often associated the snake with water and earth because these appeared to be the substances from which life sprang. These peoples often associated the snake with sacred trees and groves because these symbolized the rising and flourishing of life rooted in water and earth. The snake that stole the regenerative plant from Gilgamesh was not evil, just uncooperative, unimpressed by man's purposes. The gods clearly did not intend immortality for man; Gilgamesh had not been destined to make use of that plant. In some sense, the snake took what was more properly his than Gilgamesh's.

Another symbol that needs explaining is the monster lurking near a tree, sometimes a sacred, life-giving tree (see Chapter 7). In fact, a very frequent Middle Eastern motif was two griffins or other monsters guarding the tree of life. But in many stories, as guardian of a tree, a monster attacked an approaching human hero.

Sometimes in ancient stories, even when this monster guarded something sacred, the monster was called evil. The cause for the inconsistency is our profound ambivalence toward that which, in guarding *Life*, will destroy us, Life's ephemeral forms. In a Babylonian story, the hero Gilgamesh meant to cut down a cedar grove guarded by the monster Humbaba. This was not just any forest, and Humbaba was not just any monster. In the sun-blistered mud flats of Uruk, even a little tree tossed up by the flooding river was so precious that, in another story, Ishtar, goddess of fertility and life, rescued one and nurtured it in her sacred garden. A whole forest of fragrant cedar, then, was like paradise. Indeed, this forest was the "dwelling-place of the gods and the throne of Ishtar." One of the gods had placed Humbaba there to guard the sacred grove. When Gilgamesh arrived there, he gazed in rapture at the mountain of green, the caressing shade. And yet the young hero started chopping down the grove, because doing so would make a glorious exploit and, presumably, because in treeless Uruk the cedars would be much prized. Calling Humbaba ferocious, wicked, even evil, Gilgamesh killed him. But Humbaba was only evil in the sense of opposing Gilgamesh's purpose, in being frightening and alien, in being willing to take Gilgamesh's life, not in the sophisticated sense of thwarting Life itself.

Related to Humbaba was the Greek dragon guarding the Golden Apples in the Garden of the Hesperides. H. J. Rose calls this monster a faded symbol of the primordial serpent guarding the elemental life-force. The dragon guarding the golden fleece in the sacred grove had similar origins.

What all the tree-monsters, from the snake in the Sumerian huluppu tree to the Norse serpent three thousand years later, appear to have in common is that they impress particular men as alien, not cooperative with these men or their gods. It is true that some later tree-monsters attack the tree itself. For instance, in a Zoroastrian story, the Evil One tries to destroy the tree of immortality by shaping a lizard to kill it. The Norse serpent gnaws at the root of the cosmic tree, and the Greek Callicantzari at the base of its trunk. But in these stories the monster's meaning had drifted from an embodiment of Life's ruthless guardian to simply the evil destroyer.

The biblical serpent in the Garden of Eden reinterpreted an old theme. Long associated with the tree of life and with knowledge and trickery, the serpent had not before symbolized evil in the Judeo-Christian sense of thwarting the purposes of one righteous god. (In stories from the Greek tradition, from the Old Testament, and from early folk-lore generally, tricksters are frankly admired.) Nevertheless, even in the new version, the old theme is apparent. The biblical serpent vastly enriched life, qualitatively and quantitatively. He gave humankind the fruit of both the tree of knowledge and the tree of life. He freed human-kind from its infancy, its garden-prison, opening to people the chance to acquire a far more spacious life than they had known in the garden. He released the human seed. Without him, none of us, the descendants of Adam and Eve, would have existed. Clearly, most people given the choice would choose life, despite its anguish, over no life—or over the static, insipid life of the garden. From this viewpoint, whatever the snake's intentions, he was our benefactor.

That the monster, including the snake, is associated with the primordial energy of chaos accounts for its ambiguous character in myth, as a guardian of the life-force and at the same time as no friend of the presently living. Of course, whatever lives hugs itself and loathes what threatens it, but it must always at last lose to Life's cruel guardian.[17]

RELEASING THE SEED

> Whatever flames upon the night
> Man's own resinous heart has fed.
>
> William Butler Yeats

A grinning minister swoops in upon a Sunday school class of five-year-olds and snorts, "I'm the green-eyed monster with the thirteen tails! I fe-ed with gre-ed on lit-tle boys and girls!" The children squeal with delight.

Campers sit around the fire late at night telling each other stories of killer-bears, Big Foot, vampire bats, and insane hermits that chop up sleeping campers with rusty hatchets. Drawing together in their magic ring, feeling the black abyss brush the backs of their necks, the campers hold the ring together a little longer and a little longer with ever more terrifying stories. They are in bliss.

At a slumber party, teenage girls tell the story of the Lovers' Lane killer who has a steel hook for a hand. Some of the girls pull a blanket over themselves like a tent. Huddling there, screaming and giggling at once, they demand all the details.

An unamusing but related fact is that other people's disasters fascinate us. The sparkle in our eye as we read of earthquakes, floods, fires, epidemics, and mass murders is not just the welling up of sympathetic tears; beneath our sympathy lurks a queer excitement. When an accident occurs on the freeway, even the traffic in the opposite direction jams, the cumulative effect of drivers slowing down to stare. The lust to witness disaster so overwhelms the decency of some that, hurrying to the scene of a grisly crash or crime to stare, they impede the efforts of firemen, policemen, and ambulance attendants to rush the injured to hospitals.

Why, one might ask, would the same people who spend so much energy to deny their ephemerality seek to be reminded of it? The answer is really no more mysterious than the answer to why we enjoy hearing the storm when we are snug in our beds. Contemplating disaster from a safe distance stirs in us, yes, some sense of our fragility, but at the same time an exquisite awareness of our present safety. Finding ourselves, our homes, and our families intact when others are dramatically burnt and scattered makes us feel a bit like minor gods contemplating chaos from the top of the world-mountain; there we sit, suffering from vertigo but *safe*, hearts knocking within our still whole skins. Such an experience temporarily reconciles us to death. Why?

Sometimes the cosmic dome begins to feel more like an upside-down teacup beneath which we are trapped than like a spacious framework within which we can grow. Hunched there, we get bored or frightened. Oh, for a ferocious, middle-sized dragon skirling at the chimney. If none lurks nearby, we hallo one. We make a daring remark, press the accelerator, change jobs, or take up hang-gliding. In plunging ourselves into gratuitous danger, we are not seeking destruction. We are seeking the joy of having tempted and conquered chaos. Loosing and then subduing the monster is a freeing, exalting experience. We have even formalized teasing the monster in such ceremonial bashes as the Bacchanalia, the Saturnalia, Halloween, Midsummer's Eve, Carnival, Walpurgisnacht, New Year's Eve, the prenuptial bachelor dinner, even the Saturday night brawl. Most of these celebrations are a ritualized cracking of the cosmos just before a ritualized renewal of it or before a rededication of oneself to order.

The Greeks well understood the relationship between chaos and enhanced life. Dionysus, the god of the vine, came to be associated with all kinds of disorder induced through wine—with harmless asininity, yes, and with the destructive frenzy, but also with the creative power sometimes achieved when the mind breaks free of habitual attitudes. The rituals honoring Dionysus grew into the brilliant tragic dramas of the fifth century B.C. Typically, tragedy dramatizes the cracking of some essential order—usually domestic, political, and natural all at once—inducing such suffering in the hero and the audience that they are driven to redefine the essential. Tragedy often truly reconciles its witnesses to life's intrinsic limitations, leaving them with a profoundly joyful sense of harmony, of life's sweetness and humankind's potential nobility.

Similarly, times of personal or social upheaval, as painful and often killing as they are, seldom bring only evil. Sometimes when the monster is bearing down upon us and we are flinging all our bread and rubies in his path, we learn as if by revelation what is truly important. As we leap chasms and scale crumbling cliffs, we find our strength. Sometimes as the monster breathes his fire upon us, long dormant seeds of creative energy burst in us, and we turn to laugh in his teeth or stare him down.

In the 1960s, the American cosmos fell apart—three beloved leaders assassinated, Vietnam, mind-jellying drugs, Kent State, My Lai, Nixon's betrayal of his office. For many Americans, patterns broke, both the gracious and the essential. Whatever they had loved, trusted, *rested on*, all seemed to turn monstrous: parents, husbands and wives, the young, teachers, the local police, priests, statesmen, the FBI, their country itself, the "system." The sweet familiar turned savage and incomprehensible.

People broke into shouting groups, each unable to understand the others' language. Nothing made sense. Blood ran into their eyes, down the gutters, into the old obliterating seas. So much waste; so much beauty and goodness smashed. The unthinkable happened—again, again, again. The sun died, the sky fell. People lurched in the darkness, trying to clear their heads, but there was no place to sit and collect their thoughts even for a minute. They tried in whatever ways they knew to get into a little quiet space, to numb themselves enough to keep trying. Often it did not work. Some died.

Questions raced in their heads. Why is this happening? What should I do? What can I do? Is there anybody out there with a light? Always questions; no answers, maps, rules. Monster down the chimney, then no house. The gods themselves freaked out, abandoned them. Like cockroaches, monsters swarmed up and down the sky-pole, gnawing at it, befouling it.

Few who took part in the 1960s, and remember, would ever wish that time upon themselves again, but it was not all waste. Monsters, after all, pull down what is weak. In searching for ways to cure their anguish, people began to look with new eyes at blacks, the young, the elderly, women, homosexuals, the family, formal education, moral behavior, the purposes of government, the role of the United States in the world. People made important discoveries that had been long overdue.

As Odin chained the wolf Fenrir under the earth, Americans chained the monsters and began rebuilding their spacious dome. This time it would be better, they agreed. And it *will* be better for a time. The monsters are settling into sleep, storing energy for the next siege.

The threat of chaos and the periodic loosing of ferocious energy enhance human life as much as does the sense of a cosmic order. That is why monsters are such ambiguous symbols in mythology, why they sometimes guard the sacred tree, sometimes gnaw its roots; protect the helpless, gobble the maiden; bring life-giving rain and ruinous floods. Like the serpent that rose up the axial tree in the Garden of Eden, monsters bring at once bitter death and renewed life.

IV

CONQUERING DEATH

9

The Problem of Death

Die we must. How to live in the teeth of death has always been human-kind's greatest spiritual problem, for the thought of dissolution violates our sense of self, our sense of justice, even our sense of meaning. Many myths reconcile people to death. They do so in two ways: by showing why, despite a cosmos run by just and powerful gods, death is necessary; and by showing that, in some sense, we need not really die. This section explores these two themes.

WHY WE MUST DIE

Our need to believe in powerful protectors shapes our gods—analogous to parents but infinitely stronger and wiser. The most important function of the gods is to protect people from anxiety, pain, chaos, and, above all, death. And yet we do continue, with great regularity, to suffer and die. Because the gods let this happen, we must either assume that they are weak, neglectful, or wantonly cruel; or that they have provided ways for us to protect ourselves from death; or that death is just or illusory. These are our choices. Stories about why people must die comfort us by pro-tecting the reputation of our gods.

Such stories explain death in several ways: Every human death is the result of a specific act of magic; death is an irrevocable mistake, a phe-nomenon never intended by the gods; people grow tired or wear out, like all living things, and must rest; death is a necessary part of the great fertility cycle, nourishing the living and keeping the world from becoming overcrowded; not the gods but an evil being or the evil in people brought about suffering and death; death is an opportunity to join the gods in perfect bliss.

Death by Sorcery.		Some tribal cultures are very reluctant to believe in what we would call natural deaths. For instance, Australian aborigines, according to Kenneth Maddock, believed that most deaths were caused by "human acts, usually in the form of sorcery." People ensorcell (bewitch), went the belief, because they bear grudges. If everybody behaved better, there would be no motive for sorcery; people might even live forever.[1] In a three-volume study, *The Belief in Immortality and the Worship of the Dead*, Sir James Frazer reported similar beliefs among tribes in West Africa, New Guinea, Chile, Brazil, and Guyana, even when the dying person was aged or badly wounded.[2]

Death as a Mistake.		Stories about death as a mistake are widespread among Africans, Australians, Melanesians, and American Indians. The Zulu tell this story: The Old Old One sent the chameleon to men to say that they would not die. It dawdled along the way to eat purple berries. In one version, it basked in the sun, filled its belly with flies, and fell asleep. Meanwhile, the Old Old One, thinking better of his decision, sent the lizard off to tell men that they would die. The lizard did not loiter. When the chameleon finally arrived with his message, it was not efficacious because the lizard had gotten there first.[3]

Many other versions of the story about the two messengers are told in Africa. Often the message gets accidentally twisted. In the Ashanti version, God sent a goat to tell people that, though they would die, that would not be the end of them; they would come to live with God himself. But when God saw that the goat was stopping to nibble on a bush, he sent a sheep with the message. The sheep promptly went off to deliver it, but got it wrong, saying that death would be man's end.[4]

In a Melanesian story, the Good Spirit told his brother to go give men the secret of immortality, which was to cast off their skin every year so that their lives would be renewed. But the Good Spirit's wayward brother commanded men to die and told the serpents the secret intended for men.[5]

A Tlinket story explains that the Creator tried to make people out of rocks so that they would last, but making them this way was too slow. He decided to use leaves instead, and this is why people rot. A related story tells that the reason many people die in autumn, when the leaves are falling, is that people are made of leaves.[6]

Often death is said to have come about through the failings of a woman. In one of several Australian myths with this theme, a woman's disobedience caused death. Although women were forbidden to go near a certain hollow tree, they coveted the honey in a bees' nest there. One day a woman chopped into the tree to get at the honey. A huge bat—the spirit of death—flew out into the world.[7] In Moroccan Islamic tradition, people did not formerly die absolutely. After losing consciousness for a while, they revived. But the Prophet's daughter Fatima, when a child of her rival died this temporary death, begged the Prophet to have people die permanently. Because the Prophet loved her very much, he prayed to God to make death absolute. Later, when Fatima's own sons had been killed, she wailed, "Father, do not the dead live again?" "No," he said. "At your bidding, I prayed that death be final, and God answered the prayer."[8] In Western folklore, God had intended Adam and Eve to become immortal by eating fruit from the tree of life, but the serpent tricked the gullible woman into eating, instead, the fruit from the tree of knowledge (that is, knowledge of good and evil, with death regarded as the greatest evil). Then, helping himself to the fruit intended for human-kind, the snake attained immortality through the annual shedding of his skin.

The Gift of Rest.   All these stories save the gods' reputation as people's benefactors by blaming death on insurmountable problems or foolish creatures. The idea that people must die because they grow tired also affirms the gods' beneficence, but in a different way. The analogy is, of course, to sleep—the gods' role, that of wise parents sending the weary to rest. The underlying idea is that the tired spirits will awaken refreshed. In our own tradition, we "sleep" until judgment day and can even do so on Sealy innerspring mattresses so that we need not arise to face Christ our Judge with backaches.[9] In some cultures, the "sleeping" spirit returns in a new body. The fact that children often clearly resemble their grand-parents or other relatives surely promotes the belief in family spirit-banks and reincarnation, the sense that no life-essence is ever lost.

Death as Part of a Cycle.   The idea that death must occur if new life (including the plants and animals that feed us) is to come forth inter-twines with the complex idea that, through the round of fertility, we do not really die. Chapter 10, on survival through fertility, discusses the matter in detail. A story from the Mantras of Malaysia illustrates the insight that death is not an accident or mistake but a necessary part of the divine order. Long ago, people did not die. They only grew thin with the waning of the moon, and fat again when it waxed. But the population increased so alarmingly that a son of the first man asked his father what should be done. The first man said to let things go on this way, but his brother said, no, let men be like the banana tree, which dies as soon as it produces fruit. When the people submitted the question to the Lord of the Underworld, he decided on death. Since then, instead of renewing their youth like the moon, people have died like banana trees.[10]

Death as the Great Destroyer Thwarted by the High God.   Finally, in some traditions death arose not as part of God's plan but through a Great Destroyer (a principle of evil, a chaos-monster) who infected humankind with his poison. This explanation, as prefigured in the brilliant Osirian theology and later developed by the Zoroastrians, Christians, and Moslems, combines some of the other explanations in a highly sophisticated way: Although death was not intended by the high god, it cannot be reversed; people brought death upon themselves; death gives people a much-needed rest, after which they are restored to life in a new and better form. This explanation not only saves the reputation of the high god but affirms the soundness and perfection of the cosmos he created.

SAVING OURSELVES FROM DEATH

Our main purpose singly and collectively has always been *to survive in the largest possible sense.*

One way we forestall oblivion is by recording our names for posterity. Names have such fixing power for us that they seem almost magical. For as long as it remains known, a person's name confers on him a kind of permanence. T. Lamarr Caudle, Sue Sun, Gustavo Olivas, Daniel Boone, Jorge Orta, Bill Craddock, Izaak Perelman, Molly Babbage: As we hear the name, familiar or not, a living person seems almost to step from the shade and greet us.

From earliest historical times, we have felt that preserving our names is of the utmost importance. In the sealed chambers of Egyptian tombs, on the windswept wastes of Anatolia, in the monasteries of medieval Europe, in gigantic underground vaults of modern Utah, we have preserved our precious names and genealogies. They make a web across the void. Ancient books, scrolls, and tablets are full of names. All over the United States, volunteers of many faiths worked to gather and record every single name of the six million Jews who perished in the Holocaust so that these people would not be "lost."

But names are just the beginning. With fierce passion, we preserve our images, our seed, and our works. Our sense of identity lies not just in our names and faces nor in our singular, rather muddled consciousness nor in our puny, always dying physical selves, but in our acts, other people's appreciation of us, our influence on others, our membership in a family, nation, or ethnic group, our personal and family fame in both time and space. Panic seizes us, usually in the form of anger, if a wife or brother or old friend misremembers the trivial details of a shared experience. We seek for ourselves and those we cherish many kinds of permanence.

The will to conquer death pervades the central stories in every mythic tradition. That conquest is the main purpose, its achievement the highest value. The following chapters explore survival as the continuance of the life-force through fertility; as continuity of a family line; and as the immortal extension of one's personal, conscious self. The final chapter shows how the ancient story of Gilgamesh suggests still another kind of survival implied in all mythic systems—a survival ironically available only to mortals, never to the gods.

10

Survival Through Fertility

Unless a grain of wheat falls
into the earth and dies, it remains alone;
but if it dies, it bears much fruit.

John 12:24

Middle Eastern mother-goddesses are shown tenderly suckling babies; pouring life-restoring milk into the mouths of new arrivals in the Other World (Fig. 1); sprouting on their own generous bodies rows of egg-breasts, heaps of grapes, sheaves of barley, columns of sheep, deer, and honeybees (Fig. 30); or opening their arms in all-embracing love. Not so Coatlicue, the pre-Columbian Mexican mother-goddess. Her head, when she has one at all, is a grisly skull (Fig. 31). Sometimes she is shown beheaded, with serpents rising from her neck-stump. She often wears a necklace of skulls or human hearts, a skirt of serpents. She grasps the earth with the shredding talons of the eagle. The Mexican goddess of ripe maize Chicomecoatl wears an elaborate headdress composed of a human skeleton, and other Mexican goddesses associated with fecundity hunch like carrion crows, waiting.

Reflecting on these strange images, one remembers some peculiarities of more familiar mother-goddesses: The lovely Greek girl Persephone, abducted by Hades, was associated with the earth's fertility and with

Fig. 30. The goddess Artemis of Ephesus promotes abundance in all life. Her many breasts, clusters of grapes and other fruits, sheaves of wheat, and rows of lions, deer, sheep, oxen, and honeybees symbolize her generosity. *Alabaster and Bronze, Rome, second century of our era. Museo Nazionale, Naples.* (Erich Neumann, *The Great Mother: An Analysis of the Archetype,* trans. Ralph Manheim, Bollingen Series XLVII, Pl. 35. Copyright 1955 by Princeton University Press. Copied by permission of the publisher.)

death. Homer and Hesiod called her "that dread goddess." When Greeks died a quick and gentle death, it was said that Artemis, a *fertility* goddess, had struck them with an arrow. Her cousin Hecate, who could make the earth yield its plenty, became queen of the ghosts; at night she would

Fig. 31. The Aztec mother-goddess, Coatlicue, her own face a skull, emphasizes that only death makes possible the continuance of life. *Stone, Aztec, pre-Columbian. Muséo Nacional de Mexico, Mexico City.* (Erich Neumann, *The Great Mother: An Analysis of the Archetype,* trans. Ralph Manheim, Bollingen Series XLVII, Pl. 68. Copyright 1955 by Princeton University Press. Copied by permission of the publisher.)

appear at crossroads with a pack of hellhounds, striking terror into human hearts.

The gentle Egyptian mother-goddess Hathor once went on a binge, killing people for the joy of drinking their blood. When glorious Ishtar, the Mesopotamian goddess of fertility, invited the hero Gilgamesh to become her consort, Gilgamesh did not leap at the offer. Instead, he listed vigorous lovers she had chosen in the past—shepherds, gardeners, stallions, birds, lions—and recounted how, after taking her pleasure with them, she had had them killed, had turned them into blind moles, saddled and whipped them, broken their wings, thrown them into pits. It was rumored that the respected Norse goddess Freyja—bringer of such blessings as healthy children and rich harvests—roamed at night in the form of a goat, coupling with trolls and other evil creatures; that she used harmful magic on people; that she and Odin ghoulishly divided the dead between them. [1] The Hindu mother-goddess Kali is often shown with her long tongue hanging out, eager to gobble up her own children. The myths of Japan, Polynesia, and the Americas reveal a similar pattern. The deity of fertility and the deity of death are often identical.

FERTILITY, SEXUALITY, AND DEATH

Widespread customs related to increasing the food supply and promoting human fertility reveal strong links between fertility, sexuality, and death. People who live close to nature see killing, eating, propagating, and dying as locked into a single process. The point is often made in myths that either reproduction without death or death without reproduction would bring disaster. If the one must occur, then so must the other.

The first death and first generation are often causally linked. For instance, in a Greek myth, the first human beings arose from the ashes of the killed Titans; in Babylonian myth, Marduk made the earth, on which humankind was to live, out of Tiamat's corpse; in Norse myth, the corpse of the giant Ymir served a similar function. In East Indian myth, the first man and woman came from the corpse of a primeval being. The Eskimo story of the great mother Sedna belongs to a group of myths in which the death of a primeval being makes more life. Long ago, when Sedna was human, she and her father were at sea in his canoe during a heavy storm. Hoping to temper the storm, her father determined to sacrifice her. He cut off her fingers, toes, and limbs, and sank her corpse in the sea. Her fingers and toes became fishes; her limbs whales, walruses, and seals. Afterwards, she continued to live as the great mother in the underworld. [2] In the Judeo-Christian tradition, the very act that brought death upon Adam and Eve, eating the forbidden fruit, aroused their sexuality and led to procreation.

TURNING DEATH INTO LIFE: FERTILITY CULTS

Every culture has had to come to terms with the *quick* in life—its lovely leap, its speed, its pounce upon neighbors, its bloody and irrevocable fall. Coatlicue, the pre-Columbian mother-goddess, vividly symbolizes one of life's horrors: Life feeds on death. Not only must our leap in the sun end thus, but our own dance brings down other life mid-leap. The stalks of wheat, the buffalo, the lamb fall to fuel our motion. Do we anger the gods by killing their creatures? Will they make more life for us to feed upon? How can we make death *not* death?

The fertility cult long supplied an important answer. For modern Westerners, fertility cults are a source of either amusement or disgust. For many, such cult symbols as the erect penis and the splay-legged female offering her open vagina are clear evidence that pagans are lewd and nasty. According to Western folk tradition, Moses' difficulties in turning the Israelites from the Golden Calf to the true God arose because lascivious fertility cults were so much more fun than a serious, proper religion.

Such a view belittles both the Israelites and the fertility gods they kept returning to in hard, uncertain times. In a world of the Pill, supermarkets, and traffic jams, it is not easy to understand the needs of ancient peoples. In fact, their main purpose, like ours, was to survive in the largest possible sense; but they often expressed that purpose through a preoccupation with making food and children. Not to be thus preoccupied is a luxury peculiar to our own time. More people live today than lived from the beginning of our species to the opening of this century. For millenniums, the struggle to bear, feed, and protect children and to bring them to adulthood ended in defeat nearly as often as in success. To defy death meant to make abundant all life that supported human life; it meant to bring forth many people to help kill the bison, gather the acorns, sow the wheat, crush the grapes, build the shelter, smite the enemy, make more babies—all to ensure the survival of the group of which each person felt himself a part.

Moses' frustration stemmed not from the Israelites' seeking an excuse for promiscuity but from their cautious retreat, in moments of weariness, to the old, known ways of securing life as opposed to a newer, abstract, less immediately persuasive way. It strained the imagination to believe that some god in the sky would make from generations of slaves a great sovereign people, a people whose name would ring gloriously through time. It was easier to think an old, familiar god would help one cross the wilderness instead of falling there, without issue, into nameless dust. Many fertility gods had been efficacious in the past. They could help to produce not just children but whatever sustained life—water, grass, animals, seeds. In the Israelites' desolate circumstances—the desert, the loss of their known lives, the uncertain future—they returned sometimes to the older, simpler life-sustaining gods. People still do.

The concern with fertility has so much influenced mythology and mythic symbols that one can hardly overstate the case. The fertility cult venerates gods that promote chiefly physical life—food, children—by sanctioning the destruction of other physical life. In a continuous holy process, the living kill, and the dead make life in new forms. The fertility cult is a way of canceling death by turning one's mind to what demonstrably continues in life despite death, even a way of imaginatively transforming death into enlarged life. People observe that the river falls but rises again; the drought comes, then the rain; the sun dies daily, the moon monthly, the land yearly, but they all come back refreshed. In many cultures, people have believed that, by propitiating the river god or the sun god, they could ensure that return. Similarly, after people slaughter the animals, the animals seem to return the next year; to kill the buffalo frees its spirit so that it can go home to rest and then come again, refreshed. People cut the barley but, if they give some back to the earth, the earth brings forth more. The baby in the mother's belly draws on the mother's teeth, bones, and blood, but then the mother and the father see in the child a fresh version of themselves or of a grandparent, and they feel restored. Life feeds upon life, yes, but that means death makes life or the dying "return" to life and, therefore, death is not really quite death. Life may return in a different form, but it is not lost. In short, in the fertility cult, death becomes not the end but merely a pause, a rest, in the life cycle. Death is seen not as a disaster, an unsanctioned intrusion of chaos, but as a fit and appropriate part of the natural harmony established by the gods.

And yet, as in all mythic reconciliations with death, the harmony is not complete. Much anxiety and uncertainty remain. Sometimes the animals do diminish, the crops fail, the children die. Throughout the year the community urgently performs rites to establish rapport with the gods so that the gods will bless it with abundance and continue to see its valued members as lives to nourish, not as fuel for life in some other form. Sometimes it is wise to sacrifice particular living things to the gods to persuade the gods not to take other, even more valuable, ones. A duty of some fertility gods is to make the dead stay dead; once when Ishtar was very angry, she threatened not to perform that duty so that the dead would swarm out of the netherworld to steal the food from the living.[3]

FERTILITY CUSTOMS AMONG HUNTING PEOPLES

Fertility magic, which reaches into the dim past of our species, dominates the rites of both hunting peoples and early agricultural peoples. While many of the Advanced Paleolithic cave paintings of France and Spain were surely intended for simple hunting magic—for procuring the animals—some were probably intended for promoting and conserving the food supply. The male animals often have prominent genitals; sometimes, so do the females. At the end of a long dark passageway, a pair of modeled clay bison prepare to mate, and beneath them, in the once soft floor, many footprints suggest that men performed here a ritual dance.[4] Some human figures wearing animal heads closely resemble figures in the religious art of recent hunting cultures of Siberia, North America, and Africa; because this recent art is propitiatory and much of it accompanies rites to promote and conserve the food supply, we surmise that the same was true of much of the Advanced Paleolithic art.

Recent hunting cultures of Japan, Siberia, Lapland, Finland, and the Americas characteristically possessed myths reconciling the killed with the killers and performed rites canceling the death of the animals. Typically, the hunters believed that the animals, or "nature people," had lived on the earth before people came, and possessed special powers that people lacked. Among themselves, the animals often took human form and lived in houses like those of people. A well-known phenomenon among the remnants of hunting peoples is a divine being who rules and protects the animals. He may look like a particularly imposing reindeer, bear, seal—whatever the most important game animal—or like a human being. (Artemis as Protectress of the Hunt was probably once such a personage.) It is this being who gives people permission to hunt the animals so long as the people repay this generosity with tact, courtesy, gifts, and, above all, strict observance of the rites that help the living animals increase and restore the killed animals to life. If the hunters fail to treat the animals properly, this Animal Master withdraws the animals or otherwise brings misfortune upon the hunters.[5]

"The Feast of the Mountain Goats," a Tsimshian Indian legend recorded by Franz Boas, illustrates the hunters' view toward hunting. The people used to hunt mountain goats. Six brothers, very good hunters, would kill many goats but would take home only the choice fat, leaving the rest of the meat strewn about to decay. That practice bothered the goats very much because the bodies of goats left that way stayed dead. One early spring when the six brothers went hunting, they captured a kid and brought it home. The village children, playing with the kid, kept throwing it into the icy river, and, each time it would struggle out, they would push it into the fire to watch its hair burn. A young man named Really Black, drawn by the shrieks of laughter, rescued the kid, gently led it back to the mountains, and let it go.

That summer, friendly messengers from another tribe invited the people to build a new village near the mountains. When the people arrived at the new place, the whole friendly tribe came out of the big house to welcome them. Their welcoming dancers wore goatskin robes and head-dresses representing mountain goats. After everyone, by invitation, had entered the big house, a young man, addressing Really Black as "friend," asked Really Black to sit with him behind a certain sturdy post. As the seemingly friendly chief danced and his people sang, a mountain sprang up right in the middle of the big house, and what looked like a real mountain goat jumped down. He was the Prince of the Mountain Goats. Leaping in front of the people, he kicked the mountain. The whole big house fell, and everyone except Really Black was crushed to death.

The post behind which Really Black had been sitting became a spruce tree far up on a rocky mountain so steep that there was no way down. All night, Really Black wept in fear. Then his new friend appeared. He explained that the tribe had really been the Mountain Goats and that they had destroyed the people in vengeance for their improper treatment of the mountain goats they had hunted. The friend was the kid that Really Black had rescued from the children. "Because you took pity on me," he said, "I want to help you." Putting on his goatskin robe, he showed Really Black exactly how to jump from rock to rock. "And when you get down," he said, "pick out the bodies of all your relatives that you would like to live. Put the bodies in good order. Jump over them four times. Leave my robe hanging on the tree below. Then go home with your relatives."

Really Black found that, in his friend's robe, he could jump from rock to rock just as goats do. By following the young Goat's directions exactly, he brought his relatives back to life. The next day, Really Black and his relatives went to the mountains' to properly gather and burn the remains of the dead goats so that they could come alive again. Always after that, the people treated the goats in the proper way, and the Mountain Goats were very pleased.[6]

The same purpose of conserving the food supply and staying on good terms with killed animals accounts for a Tsimshian requirement that part of a killed salmon be thrown into the fire. Doing so transformed the salmon into a young spring salmon. Drinking water after eating salmon was important, too, for that was said to revive the fish. Tsimshian hunters were required to be especially solicitous of bears that they had killed. Before skinning the bear, the hunter sang the bear's mourning song. If a bearskin creaked as it was being dried over a fire, the bear felt chilly, and people were enjoined to add more fuel to the fire.[7] With similar consideration, northern hunters gave the whales they had killed a drink of fresh water, supposed to be delectable to ocean creatures. Sometimes, the animals' eyes were then sewn shut so that the animals would not have to watch themselves being butchered.[8]

The Hopi, for a long time primarily an agricultural people, do hunt antelope and deer. In Hopi legend, antelopes originated this way: When the Hopi emerged from the Underworld, they wandered from place to place. One day they had to leave a woman behind because, about to bear a child, she could go no farther. When they returned the next day to see how she was getting along, she had given birth to antelope twins and had herself become an antelope. Although the three animals wanted to stay there instead of going to the new camp, the Hopi compromised by taking them to a place where they could live in a hole in the ground. After that, the antelope mother was called the Mother of All Animals. The Hopi gave the antelopes prayer sticks and have done so ever since, so that both the antelope and deer may increase and be hunted by the Hopi.[9]

Traditionally, before a hunt, the announcer of hunts took prayer sticks and offerings of corn meal to the shrine of the Mother of All Animals. During the days of preparation, strict sexual continence was necessary. During the hunt, the men observed solemn rituals to promote the animals' breeding and increase. They offered prayer sticks not only to the Mother of All Animals but to the Sun and other helpful deities. Although hunters sometimes used bow and arrow, the approved way to hunt was to chase the animals till they were exhausted, then strangle them. Blood was not supposed to fall on the ground. Smothering the animals enabled their spirits to go home and come alive again.[10]

Hopi rituals for hunting sheep reveal the same respect for the animals, the same care taken to ensure that the animals' spirits will return to life. Of the animals caught, one male and one female were freed on the last day of the hunt in order to make more sheep. In all the hunting rituals, the animals' spirits were carefully placated so that they would not become angry. Special care was taken not to kill the animals' spirits. During the winter solstice, "prayer sticks [were] placed on shrines or buried in fields . . . to ensure fertility of all animals, whether wild or domesticated."[11]

Carleton Coon cites several rituals used by tribal hunting peoples to ensure continued abundance of game animals by proper treatment of the souls of those killed. The Alaskan Eskimo held an elaborate winter ceremony centered on the Bladder Feast. People saved the bladders of the sea animals they killed during the year, ritually lured the spirits of the animals back into their own bladders, and, during the feast, returned the bladders to the sea.[12]

The Ainu of Japan were similarly solicitous of the bears they hunted and ate. They viewed bears as gods visiting the world. In Ainu myth, all animals assumed human form when in their own country and lived in houses like those of the Ainu. The bear-god, an enormous bear-person called the Owner of the Bears, lived in a great house in the mountains. Each March, his deputies would go to visit the Ainu, bringing bearskins and bear meat. In return, each Ainu who had such a guest would honor it with particular hospitality. That is, after killing a bear, the hunters put its head and skin at the place of honor at the feast and arranged special tidbits of its own flesh before it. Then, according to belief, the bear returned to its own country and reported to the Owner of the Bears. If the traveler gave a satisfactory report of its treatment, the chief would send out more deputies the next year. Baby bears that the Ainu caught were kept for a year or two as greatly indulged pets before being killed. In the killing ceremony, precautions were taken to keep away evil spirits, and the man selected to kill the bear was chosen at the last moment to protect him from these spirits.[13]

In short, hunting peoples have characteristically viewed killing not as a glorious or desirable act but as a regrettably necessary encroachment on a dangerous realm. They take great care to help the animals' spirits survive and to stay on cordial terms with the species they hunt. They reconcile themselves to killing by believing that what they kill and eat by prescribed rules does not really die.

What about planting peoples? The next section takes up a prehistorical puzzle.

THE PREHISTORICAL "VENUSES"

Little figures of women, carved from bone or stone, stand among the Neolithic ax heads and scrapers in anthropological museums from Western Europe to East Africa to Central America. Most scholars agree that the earliest religious representations known, earlier even than the exquisite cave paintings of the hunters of the Advanced Paleolithic period (ca. 15,000–10,000 B.C.), are figures of women from a slightly earlier culture found from the Pyrenees to Russia. These figures, which appear long before any signs of agriculture, strongly suggest a fertility cult based on the mysterious power of the female to make new life. Although carved when obesity must have been rare, most of the figures are extravagantly fat. They possess opulent breasts, buttocks, and great bulging bellies; the artists tended to pay little attention to their heads and feet, much to the maternal organs. The most famous such figures are the "Venuses" of Willendorf, Lespugue, and Laussel.

The Venus of Laussel, a limestone relief, is especially haunting because she seems to prefigure the widespread Middle Eastern mothergoddesses associated with agriculture in historical times. These mothergoddesses, embodying the mysterious female ability to make new life, sponsored all the processes that make life and obliterate death by renewing life. Some of them, such as Demeter and Ceres, were closely associated with the chief food-crop. Like many representations of the historical goddesses, the Laussel Venus points to her genitals with one hand. In the other, she holds a bison horn. Often, representations of the historical goddesses, from the Egyptian cow-goddess Hathor to modern images of the Virgin, wear horns upon their heads or headdresses, or stand upon horns. (Horns have been associated, through cows, bison, goats, and so on, with fertility; with milk as a miraculous life-giving drink; with the virility of the goddess' consort; with beer, wine, and mead, drunk from horns by heroes and believed to inspire godlike courage and creativity; and later, more broadly, with bountiful nature in general, as with the horns of plenty that decorate many a Thanksgiving table. The association of the goddess with horns was reinforced by her independent association with the crescent moon.) The Laussel figure is even paired with that of a slim young man suggesting the consorts of the much later Middle Eastern goddesses.

During the Neolithic period, when many cultures were shifting gradually from hunting to a more settled agricultural life, ritual interest shifted from game animals to the fertility of the soil and the turn of the seasons. Probably, as American Indians have done, these peoples sometimes adapted hunting rituals to agricultural use.[14]

In the archaeological digs from this period, female figurines have turned up abundantly, suggesting that, as with historical agricultural communities, mother-goddesses played a large role in Neolithic religious expression. A great many such figures have been found in the Neolithic villages of Iran, Syria, and Mesopotamia. Although, of course, no irrefutable connection appears between them and the historical mother-goddesses, most scholars assume at least a common impulse.

Excavations at Çatal Hüyük, in Anatolia, are important because they have revealed one of the oldest known organized towns in the world. Although settlements existed on the site for thousands of years, Çatal Hüyük flourished around 6,000 B.C. Digs there have revealed many female figures that cannot possibly be interpreted as mere fertility amulets or erotically appealing dolls, as some scholars have interpreted the earlier figures, for those of Çatal Hüyük have been found *in place* in shrines. Sometimes the goddess's consort is represented as a youth or bearded man, sometimes as a bull, ram, stag, or boar—animals of dramatic strength, virility, and value to human life. In one large plaster relief, the goddess gives birth above three decorated bulls' heads. In shrines throughout the excavations, archaeologists have found the goddess and the bulls' horns. Clearly, in this Neolithic agricultural community the goddess of fertility dominated religious life, and the male contribution to reproduction was well understood.[15]

These Upper Paleolithic figurines suggest a strong appreciation of woman's fertility; an attempt to promote it; and an apotheosis of it in goddesses promoting not just human life but all animal life, possibly plant life, too. The great mother is one of humankind's most enduring mythic symbols.

EVOLUTION OF AGRICULTURAL DEITIES IN ANCIENT MYTH

From earliest historical times, fertility deities have promoted not just human or animal fertility but plant fertility as well. The earliest known documents on the subject view fertility as a power pervading all life *and associated with death.* Judging from the surviving stories, that association grew ever more rich and subtle, in Egypt and Greece evolving into religions offering personal immortality.

The Sumerian Inanna was the first historical fertility goddess, and one of the earliest known stories in the world tells of Inanna's descent to the underworld. The story reveals that many of the motifs we associate with the underworld were already established in the third millennium B.C. Here is the story.

From above the great sky-dome, the goddess Inanna decided, despite the great peril of the journey, to go to the netherworld. She donned her full regalia—crown, breastplate, gold ring, robe, and so on. Grasping her lapis lazuli staff, she said to her faithful vizier Ninshubur, "I have determined, despite the peril, to go to the netherworld. When I have arrived there, you must go to the house of the gods and rush about wailing and insisting upon my safe return so that I do not get trapped there and killed. If Enlil does not listen, you must plead before Nanna. If Nanna does not listen, you must plead before Enki. Father Enki, the lord of wisdom, will surely restore me to life, for he knows the food and water of life [that is, Enki has special life-promoting powers]."

Abandoning heaven and earth, her own realms, the goddess went to the netherworld. At the gate of its lapis lazuli palace, she called out, "Open up, gatekeeper. It is the goddess Inanna."

"But what can have brought the goddess Inanna to the land of no return?" asked the gatekeeper. [Inanna's reply, partly lost, is obscure.]

The gatekeeper went to tell Ereshkigal, queen of the netherworld and [perhaps significantly] Inanna's older sister, that Inanna was waiting, dressed in the seven special insignia of her authority. Ereshkigal gave him detailed instructions. Unlocking the seven gates, the keeper invited Inanna to enter. As she passed through the first gate, her crown was removed.

"Just a moment," she cried out. "What's going on here?"

"Hush!" was the reply. "Do not question the perfect rules of the netherworld." As she passed through the second gate, her rod was taken from her hand. "Just a moment," she cried out. "What's going on here?"

"Hush!" came the reply again. "Do not question the perfect rules of the netherworld." At each of the gates, another of her regal insignia was removed—the lapis lazuli stones around her neck, the sparkling gems upon her breast, the gold ring, the breastplate, and finally, the garment of authority that had covered her body. And each time, the reply to her alarmed protest was "Hush! Do not question the perfect rules of the netherworld." There she stood, naked, at the center of the netherworld.

Ereshkigal seated herself upon her throne and looked down upon her crouching sister, the great goddess, stripped of all her authority. The seven Anunnaki [Sumerian gods who determined the time of each person's death] fastened their eyes of death upon Inanna . . . .

Soon they scooped up her corpse and, without ado, hung it upon a stake.

There it hung for three days and nights, while Inanna's faithful vizier Ninshubur waited for her return to the upper world. When she did not return, he did exactly as she had instructed him. Scratching his eyes, he filled heaven with his cries for her release.

"Do not let such a precious power be lost," he wailed. "It would be like burying rich metal in the netherworld, like grinding lapis lazuli into rubble, like chopping up a living tree."

[Enlil's response, though obscure, was apparently equivalent to "So what else is new?"] So Ninshubur rushed away to plead before Nanna. Nanna gave exactly the same response. But when Ninshubur wept out his plea before Enki, Enki exclaimed, "This is terrible! My own daughter! The queen of all the lands!"

Urgently, Enki flicked some grime from under his fingernail and made from it the *kurgarru* and the *kalaturru* [two sexless creatures]. Entrusting to them the food and water of life, he gave them long, detailed instructions on how to restore Inanna's corpse to life. [Although most of these instructions have been lost, they included sprinkling this "food" and "water" sixty(?) times upon Inanna's dangling corpse.]

The *kurgarru* and the *kalaturru* did exactly as Enki had instructed. Inanna came alive again and hastily left the netherworld.

However, all was not exactly as before, for a crowd of death-demons swooshed out of the netherworld and surrounded her.

At the sight of the goddess, the faithful Ninshubur threw himself at her feet. [Apparently, the death-demons clamored to be given Ninshubur as her substitute, but Inanna dissuaded them because he had worked hard and well for her life.]

As Inanna moved from city to city in Sumer, the gaggle of demons swarmed eagerly around each faithful person who threw himself at her feet. Each time, she dissuaded them from taking that person. But then she came to the place where Dumuzi, her young husband, was. He, unlike the others, had not been mourning, nor did he throw himself at her feet. She found him lolling about on a high seat [perhaps her own] as if luxuriating in her death, and certainly unmindful of Inanna and the demons.

"Ha!" she cried to the demons. "Take him away." Dumuzi, bursting into tears, begged Utu, the sun-god, to save him.[16]

Here the tablet breaks off; the outcome is still unknown. Apparently, the only condition under which Inanna could be freed from death was that she provide a substitute for herself. Folklore reveals a pervasive belief that the dead may snatch the living as a way to regain some life for themselves. Vampire stories and stories of wistful old souls snatching their own grandchildren stem from this belief. In *The Odyssey* the dead waft like tattered curtains, not only without substance but without memory or even consciousness; only a drink of fresh blood can restore them briefly. Such visions seem to arise from the sense that, though all prefer life to death, the two states must be kept in balance; each life must be exchanged for or purchased with a death. More broadly, life flourishes only at the expense of other life. Also, many peoples have believed that, unless placated, the dead will be driven by envy and spite to harm the living.

That Enki's messengers used a magic formula to revive Inanna adumbrates later customs. Osiris, Dionysus, Adonis, and other fertility gods who had died were annually revived through rituals. In the Tsimshian myth about Really Black and the Mountain Goats, young Goat told Really Black a formula for reviving the goats' spirits and for reviving Really Black's relatives. When the veneration of fertility gods evolved, in ancient Egypt and, much later, in Thrace and Greece, into cults offering personal survival after death, the restorative formula was adapted to human funerary rites. The apostle Paul introduced a similar adaptation into the Christian rite of baptism: The initiate ritually accompanies Christ into death and is reborn "in" Christ, thereby becoming eligible, like him, for eternal life (Rom. 6:3–11).

Although the stories and rites about Inanna-Ishtar and Dumuzi-Tammuz are often obscure, both the stories and liturgies link fertility with death as well as with life. One could argue that in the story recounted above, the earliest known version of Inanna-Ishtar's descent to the land of the dead, the link may be incidental. The fertility goddess may just happen to have been the personage who contrived to go to the "land of no return" and actually return. But slightly later versions of the story, as well as many other stories and rites of these deities, linked them with death in a way that pointed up their functions: When the deities were threatened, life itself was threatened. Early in the Ishtar tradition, when Ishtar was detained and killed in the underworld, the processes of life ceased in the upper world:

> The bull springs not upon the cow,
> the ass impregnates not the jenny,
> In the street the man impregnates not the maiden.
> The man lies in his own chamber,
> the maid lies on her side.[17]

For millenniums, the concern with fertility dominated Middle Eastern myths. Most of the deities of classical mythology, including Zeus, of course, and even the virgins Athena, Hestia, and Artemis, originated as fertility deities. Tammuz was the prototype for young gods embodying the annual vegetation cycle—Baal, Adonis, Attis, Dionysus—who died or disappeared for part of the year and returned with the new growing season. These gods were once venerated because human life was thought to depend heavily upon their miraculous restoration; later, the plant world's annual recovery from death suggested that even people might, with the god's help, be vouchsafed a similar recovery from death. This shift in the god's meaning occurred most notably with the Egyptian Osiris and the Greek Dionysus.

Like Osiris, discussed in Chapter 8, Dionysus had become a great deal more than a vegetation god by the time much was recorded about him. The profusion of myths concerning him suggests his symbolic importance to the Greeks. Most of the stories fall into two groups, those about his early suffering, death, and regenerative power and those about his establishment as a god, specifically about the dreadful fates befalling people who questioned his divinity. Often, as in Euripides' tragedy *The Bacchae*, they were torn up and eaten by their own mother or child in a Dionysian frenzy.

In the classical version of Dionysus' story as told by Meyer Reinhold, Dionysus' mother was Semele, the daughter of the king of Thebes.[18] Semele did not know that her lover was Zeus himself. The jealous Hera, upon discovering the liaison between her husband and the young princess, disguised herself as Semele's nurse and persuaded the girl that she should learn her lover's true identity. Thus it happened that Semele tricked Zeus into making an irrevocable promise to reveal himself in the full splendor of his divinity. The anguished god knew the outcome in advance. When he showed himself as the high god, the girl fell dead as if struck by lightning. Rescuing the fetus of Dionysus from her burnt body, Zeus sewed it into his thigh, where he carried it until it was ready to be born. Having been born this way, Dionysus was Zeus' favorite, "truest" child.

This strange story obliquely points up Dionysus' origin as a fertility god. The story is one of several symbolizing that Dionysus was "twice-born," indicating his self-regenerating powers. Also, like many classical myths, the story contains echoes of primitive folklore about fertility. Semele was originally Zemelo, a mother-goddess of Asia Minor, who had "faded" into a mortal princess. In folk belief, lightning fertilizes the earth. According to Reinhold, the Greeks regarded places and people struck by lightning as holy. He also notes that in primitive folklore the thigh symbolizes male sexual power. The story continues.

Zeus tried to shield the holy child from Hera's jealous ferocity by entrusting him to Semele's sister and her husband, but Hera found the child and drove his guardians mad. Zeus then took him to a land where legend says that wine was discovered. Hera continued to pursue Dionysus. Dionysus suffered so much, indeed, that he seemed annually to die; yet suddenly, in the spring, he would reappear, the god of wine, just as the seemingly dead vines were sending out new shoots.

Driven insane by Hera, the young god pitched from one end of the known world to the other, establishing his worship and the cultivation of the vine. Wherever he went, droves of ecstatic women followed him, attracted, Reinhold writes, by this dramatic presentation of "the procreative forces in nature and man."

In myth, Dionysus' followers were Satyrs (half-man, half-goat) and Seleni (half-man, half-horse), whom Reinhold identifies as primitive fertility demons characterized by uncontrollable lust.

In a later version of Dionysus' story, it was the evil Titans who pursued the child Dionysus. They killed him, boiled him in a vat, and ate him. But Athena contrived to save his heart and bring it to Zeus. Zeus swallowed it, and Dionysus was reborn from this "seed."

So complex a symbol was Dionysus that dictionaries often simply call him the ancient Greek god of wine and drama, leaving the reader to wonder how wine and drama became linked. Slightly longer discussions of him may mention his orgiastic rites and then go on to link him, without explanation, to the ascetic Orphic cult. They may even state that some early Christians associated him with Jesus. So various and contradictory seem his meanings that a reader may well wonder if, in meaning everything, he meant nothing.

It turns out, however, that a common function bound together all the symbolic meanings of Dionysus. People believed that the god helped them to conquer death by moving them outside their own sack of bones. He seems to have begun as a Thracian god promoting fertility in plants, animals, and people. His early rites probably were intended to revive the dead god in the spring. As described in *The Bacchae* and other classical sources, the rites involved frenzied dancing, singing, wine drinking, and sexual abandon. They culminated in the seizure of some animal that the god's followers believed his spirit had entered, in ripping it to pieces and eating it raw. Through these rites, worshipers sought communion with the god through *ecstasis* (standing outside oneself) and *enthusiasmos* (having a god within oneself). The classical scholar W.K.C. Guthrie suggests that, although the Thracians probably believed they thus achieved literal immortality, the Greeks, to whom such an idea was alien, more likely believed this communion charged them temporarily with the reproductive powers of nature embodied in the god.[19]

As for Dionysus' connection with drama, one may say that drama can so effectively move actor and audience beyond their ordinary selves that such regulatory agencies as governments and established religions have repeatedly restricted it. Historically, it is known that sixth-century Athenian hymns to Dionysus, chanted by a chorus, evolved into dramatic presentations that became the classical Greek tragedy of the next century. Essentially a religious rite, tragedy celebrated man's reach toward the divine. It presented mortal, imperfect man falling to his doom with such grandeur that a witness could be proud of his own humanity.

The Orphic cult, one of the first religions in Europe to offer personal survival after death, tapped the story of humankind's origin in a fusion of Titan evil and Dionysian divinity. (The Titans, in eating Dionysus, had absorbed his divinity; when Zeus destroyed the Titans, the first men, who sprang from their ashes, also contained that divinity.) The cult taught that a person consists of an evil but mortal body and a divine, immortal soul, able, when the body dies, to achieve joyful freedom.

Here, then, is the curious link between the barbaric cult, classical Greek tragedy, and the ascetic Orphic cult: *the reach of ever-dying humanity toward the divine and permanent.* But how different are the three manifestations of that reach! Members of the Dionysian cult strove to partake physically of the god's divinity; tragedy presented the human striving toward godlike mastery and perfection as doomed but majestic; and the Orphic cult affirmed the possibility of successful divinity (that is, spiritual immortality) after physical death, especially for those who purified their souls by denying the body mastery in life.

Even after the Greeks had tamed Dionysus the fertility god, and after he had evolved into the god of exaltation, he did not lose his sinister side. In Guthrie's words, "Sanity, self-consciousness and limit were the very qualities that distinguished the Greek mind from its surroundings."[20] Dionysus was, after all, the god of wine, and the Greeks well understood the implications of wine. Dionysus was the god who lifted people out of their ordinary selves, moved them, in a rapture of confidence, toward unconventional acts. Dionysus, or wine, could move one toward harmless asininity, as seen in classical comedies, in Renaissance paintings of Bacchanalia, and in our own symbol of the drunk with the lampshade on his head. Or Dionysus could move one to destructive frenzy. In Greek stories, crazed imbibers sometimes tore a bystander to bits and devoured him. We associate such frenzies with barroom brawling, beating one's children, or driving the wrong way on a freeway at ninety miles an hour. Finally, Dionysus could push gifted people toward a creative insight or a glorious performance.

Often enough, the inspired artist is consumed, like Judy Garland, by the very energies that propel him to brilliance, or, like Robert Frost, he blasts the lives of those around him. Dionysus is, in a sense, the divine twin of the chaos-monster. In the inspired individual may burn exactly the same power, the same ruthless disregard for orderly, established life that burns in the chaos-monster. Surely Coatlicue, Dionysus, and the Old Serpent himself salute each other in the night. But in another important sense, artistic brilliance frees us all from death. Such masterpieces as Dante's *The Divine Comedy,* Michelangelo's *David,* Verdi's *Requiem,* or Beethoven's Ninth Symphony achieve not only a kind of immortality for their creators; such works lift all who love them out of their ordinary lives. For a time, at least, these works make death irrelevant.

Still, one cannot but be struck by the prominence in the Dionysus stories of breakdown and death, of the link between dissolution and sexuality and procreation. That same link occurs in the myths of peoples who have recently committed murder and sometimes practiced cannibalism in their efforts to promote more life.

FERTILITY RITES AMONG TRIBAL GATHERING AND PLANTING PEOPLES

People of the ancient Middle East vigorously pursued agricultural fertility as a way to push back death. But the versions we know of their "agricultural" myths are overlaid with much nonagricultural meaning, and their rites are known imperfectly. Fertility customs among recent tribal gatherers and planters suggest how the older customs may have evolved and how persistently and in what a variety of ways people associate enhanced life with death. Sir James Frazer's twelve-volume *The Golden Bough* (1890–1915) catalogued many cultures' rites, myths, and symbols, ancient and modern, concerning agricultural fertility. His survey showed the startling frequency with which cultures link agricultural fertility, human sexuality, and death. Since then, studies of particular cultures have yielded answers to questions arising from Frazer's survey, but the answers often leave an even more tantalizing trail of questions. The student of mythology moves here into a dark forest agleam with foxfire, the light itself mysterious.

But we can start with what is known. Like hunters, tribal gathering and planting peoples seek to establish rapport with the supernatural protectors of the life they destroy for food. As in the fertility rites and myths of hunters, so in those of tribal gathering and planting peoples, sexuality cancels death by making more life. Generally, the rites are meant to secure the help of the plants' protectors in growing the food and then their approval of killing the plants at harvest time. Some rites help the protectors make more life by sexually stimulating them. Methods include ceremonial dances imitating copulation; highly erotic chants; phalli of stone or wood set up in the fields; human sperm sprinkled on the earth; and sexual orgies.

But gatherers' and planters' rites and the ancient Dionysian rites share a peculiarity absent from the rites of hunters: They often involve not only sexual expression but also murder, dismemberment, and cannibaliam. Customs of the Asmat, a West New Guinean people, demonstrate this pattern.

HUNTING FOR "FRUITS" IN WEST NEW GUINEA

The Asmat of West New Guinea were in the 1950s one of the few peoples still practicing headhunting and cannibalism. Although they were exclusively hunters and gatherers, not planters, their main source of food was the starchy pith of the sago plant. Gerald Zegwaard, who lived among them for five years, recorded their myths on the origin of headhunting and the origin of the sago palm, and he described the related rituals. Again, the themes of sanctified killing, procreation, and vegetal abundance are connected. Here is how headhunting began.

Long ago Wounded Man (Desoipitsj) and his younger brother Parrot Man (Biwiripitsj) lived together. Because Wounded Man could not work and had to stay in all day, Parrot Man had to do the work for both. One day, Parrot Man brought home a pig and, as Wounded Man watched, beheaded it. "That's pretty impressive," Wounded Man said, "but to behead a man would be much more impressive."

The idea did not appeal to Parrot Man at all. "Besides," he asked, "where would I find one?"

"I'm right here," Wounded Man said.

Absolutely not! Parrot Man would not hear of it.

But Wounded Man kept insisting. Finally, he persuaded his brother that the idea was a good one. Parrot Man beheaded Wounded Man in the correct way and set aside the head. Then Wounded Man's head instructed Parrot Man, step by step, in the art of butchering. Parrot Man followed each step exactly.

Zegwaard writes that New Guineans, in butchering whatever they are preparing to eat—beast or person—follow the elaborate instructions included in the myth. The myth then shifts to Parrot Man living among other people, showing them how to butcher and prepare the bodies of people. (According to Asmat tradition, Parrot Man, a culture hero, taught the people many of their customs and rituals.) Although the bodies are eaten, the head, as will become clear, is ritually the most important part.

Another story tells that the sago palm originated when Parrot Man, on his way home one evening, sank into a bog. After a thunderstorm that night, a magnificent sago palm appeared on the spot where Parrot Man had disappeared. The people found his head in the bud, his arms in the branches.

According to Zegwaard, the Asmat think of people as like trees, their feet the roots, their trunk the tree's trunk, their arms the branches, and their head the fruit. They observe, of course, that new sago palms grow from fallen fruit. And *human* fruits—heads—in Aswat belief promote life. The most important function of heads is to aid a young man's proper bodily growth and sexual maturation. In a boy's initiation into manhood, a decapitated head is placed between his legs so that its germinative powers will transfer to him. Clusters of heads may be placed near sickly children. Apparently the heads are thought to stimulate plant growth, too, for the Asmat often hang clusters of heads near little stands of bananas, coconut, and sugar cane.

A third story tells that the starchy pith of the sago palm was very hard to knead until Parrot Man found a way to change its texture. One day he, his wife, and children went out to pound sago. Parrot Man felled a palm and began removing the rind. Then he called his son to lie down in the trunk. Cutting off the boy's head and setting it aside, Parrot Man pounded and mashed the boy's body with the sago pith. From that day on, the sago has been much easier to knead. Another benefit of that day was that, before the boy's head died, it taught Parrot Man the proper songs to sing on headhunting raids and at decapitation festivities.

Zegwaard thinks that the function of headhunting among the Asmat, though complex, is largely economic. The heads are supposed to promote strength and virility, qualities of particular value to the Asmat because only through frequent warfare does the group safeguard its territory and thus its supply of sago palms. Taken as a group, the stories, like the stories hunters tell about the food supply, link the abundance of food with sexuality, procreation, and death. They transform Parrot Man himself and his son into the main food source. Above all, they sanction killing and cannibalism.[21]

HAINUWELE AND OTHERS

Joseph Campbell observes that in myths of tribal planters from Southeast Asia through Oceania and into the Americas, a strange plot-pattern recurs: Long ago in the First Time, a supernatural being suffered death and dismemberment, but, instead of perishing, the body of this personage turned into the chief food crop. In some annual reenactments of these events, this being—embodied in an effigy, an animal, or even a person— is murdered or disappears but miraculously returns each year with the new growing season, in the form of the main food crop.

Anthropologists have recorded many fragments of such stories presenting the origin of wheat, barley, maize, manioc, taro, yams, and acorns. The stories sometimes suggest that, though the original murder was wicked and atonement necessary, the gods turned the murder into a boon for humankind, and the divine being continues to live in the Other World. In killing and eating the personage in the form of the food crop, the people are doing something sanctioned by the gods. The themes of guilt, atonement, and reconciliation haunt these stories.[22]

The most famous example of such a myth concerns Hainuwele, one of the three virgin spirits revered by the island people of West Ceram, New Guinea. The myth's special value lies in the fact that, when discovered by the anthropologist Adolf Jensen, it was still intact; thus, it illuminates the many fragmentary stories about the origin of foodcrops. Here is the story.

Long ago, the first people emerged from clusters of bananas. One of these people, Ameta, was out hunting one day when his dog chased a wild pig into a pond. The pig drowned. When Ameta retrieved it, he found a coconut sticking to its tusk, though no coco palms yet existed in the world.

That night a mysterious figure appeared to Ameta, instructing him to bury the coconut. He did so, and in three days a tall palm had shot up. In three more days it had blossoms. While trying to cut them in order to make himself a drink, Ameta cut his finger, spilling blood on a leaf. Three days later, he discovered that where his blood and the tree's sap had mingled on the leaf a face had appeared; in three more days, a body; and in three more, a little girl.

That night, the same mysterious figure told him to climb the tree, wrap the child carefully in a cloth, and bring her home. He did so. In three more days, the little girl had become a nubile maiden—Hainuwele.

Hainuwele possessed a remarkable talent: Instead of ordinary excrement, she produced such valuable objects as Chinese dishes and gongs. After a while, indeed, she had bestowed upon her father great riches. Hainuwele's generosity extended beyond her father. During an elaborate nine-day festival in which a maiden always stood at the center of the dance-spiral, distributing betel nuts to the dancers, Hainuwele distributed the customary nuts on the first night only. On the next night, she distributed coral, and on subsequent nights, such treasures as Chinese porcelain, great bush knives, copper boxes, gold earrings, and gongs. She gave these things not only to the dancers but to everyone present.

The people's initial pleasure did not last long. Quickly it soured into such extreme jealousy of Hainuwele's ability that they decided to kill her. On the ninth night, when Hainuwele had again been placed at the center of the great spiral, the men dug a deep pit. As the spiral turned, they pressed Hainuwele toward the pit and threw her in. Then they quickly buried her and trampled the place thoroughly in their dance.

Discovering the murder, Hainuwele's father dug up the maiden's body, chopped it into pieces, and buried these around the dancing ground. Quickly the pieces began turning into things that had not existed before, especially into the tuberous plants that have been the people's principal food ever since.

Satene, the second of the three revered virgin spirits, was so angry with the people for murdering Hainuwele that she told them she would no longer live among them. Building a great spiral gate on one of the dancing grounds, she said that, from now on, anyone who wished to come to her would have to try to get through the gate. All the people tried to get through. Those who succeeded remained people; those who failed became spirits or animals. That is how the many spirits and the pigs, deer, fish, and other animals came to inhabit the earth. [23]

The tale of the food plants' origin from a murdered human body has many Polynesian versions. The stories involve a girl and a snake or, on islands lacking snakes, a lizard or other reptile. [24] In a Tongan version, Eel, the male child of a human couple, lived in a pool. When he sprang affectionately toward his human sisters, they fled into the sea. Eel followed them. Once in the sea, Eel continued swimming until he came to Samoa, and there he settled again in a pool. When a virgin bathed in the pool, he made her pregnant. For that, the people decided to kill him. He told the girl to have the people give her his head after he had been killed, and to plant it. She did so. It grew into a new kind of tree, the coconut. [25]

American Indians also tell stories of vegetation-spirits from whose bodies food plants sprouted long ago. Several Arawaken tribes of the Amazon basin celebrate a religious festival called the Yurupary ceremonies. The anthropologist Otto Zerries recounts the myth:

> Yurupary was believed to be the son of a virgin who had no genital organs and who conceived him through drinking *kashiri* [an intoxicant]. A fish slit open her abdomen while she was bathing so that the birth could take place. The body of the child emitted light. . . . Yurupary grew rapidly. One day he killed and devoured some boys who had dis-

obeyed his dietary laws; and the men then intoxicated him with *kashiri* and threw him into a fire. From his ashes there grew a paxiuba palm; paxiubas are the "bones of Yurupary." In the course of the same night the soul of Yurupary climbed up the trunk of one of these trees to heaven.

The Yurupary rites are celebrated when the palm fruits ripen.[26]

Sometimes Yurupary rites and others closely related to them include a ritual whipping that, according to Zerries, is, from the circumstances, clearly a fertility ritual. He cites a myth, summarized by a sixteenth-century traveler, that helps explain the flagellation: "Once, during a time of great famine, the creator himself, Maire Monan, changed himself into a child, and was *beaten* by a group of starving children who were desperately searching for food themselves and who wanted to drive him away. Thereupon all manner of edible plants rained down upon them, and their hunger was relieved."[27]

In the rites as well as the myths of tribal planting peoples, violence occurs with astonishing frequency—not only beating and boxing but outright killing. The associated motifs—by now familiar—are vegetal abundance, human sexuality, death, and often cannibalism. Unlike hunters, who kill to eat, tribal planters kill for complex religious purposes, often killing people during rites to promote abundance of food. Although the pre-Christian Norse are known to have engaged in such practices and although festivals still widely celebrated in rural Europe and elsewhere suggest that the customs were once very widespread, the most recent instances have occurred among various peoples of Africa, India, Oceania, and the Americas.

The tribes of the Orissa region in eastern India regularly killed people in agricultural rites until the British suppressed the custom in the nineteenth century. The victims, called Meriahs, were usually bought as children and raised to adulthood for the purpose. The people from several villages would gather annually at a month-long festival of drinking, feasting, and dancing around the garlanded victim—in some districts working up to an impressive sexual abandon. At the festival's climax, the celebrants would dig a pit near the village idol, kill a hog, and drain its blood into the pit. Then they suffocated the Meriah in the blood. After the priest had cut a piece of flesh from the body and buried it near the idol as an offering to the earth, the people of each village would take a piece home and bury part of it near their idol, part of it near the village boundary. In some localities, each planter would bury some of the flesh in his own field.[28]

The mass human slayings and cannibalism of the Aztecs were tied ceremonially to the continued life of the sun, from which the Aztecs believed all life emanated. But the Aztecs also killed people in rites more explicitly vegetal. Small children were drowned to reinvigorate the dwarfish rain god—not, declares the anthropologist Walter Krickeberg, as food for the god but as surrogates of him. The rites of the vegetal gods Xipe and Tlazolteotl, celebrated in spring and fall, involved phallic dances and a ritual drama symbolizing the conception and birth of the maize. The victim representing Xipe was flayed, suggesting the husking of corn, and the skin was later worn by Xipe surrogates in other ceremonies. A rite in which the victim was tied to a frame and shot with arrows was called "scratching (the earth)" and "coupling with the earth"; its intention apparently was to prepare the earth magically for sowing.[29]

Ruth M. Underhill describes a Pawnee rite whose liturgy, she states, clearly links it to an Aztec rite. A captive virgin embodying Evening Star, the patroness of vegetation, was tied spread-eagled to a wooden frame and ceremonially killed by an arrow shot into her heart. Then every male shot an arrow into her body. The Pawnees viewed the girl as a messenger, not a victim. "Her soul went to her husband, Morning Star, who clothed her in the colors of the dawn and set her in the sky. Their reunion meant the renewal of growing things on earth."[30]

Among some tribal peoples, a girl or boy and girl are chosen to embody the fertility spirits and may be required to perform their first copulation as part of the ceremony. (The English Maypole festival was a remote cousin of such rituals.) According to the ethnologist Paul Wirz, the boys' puberty rites of the Marind-anim, a New Guinean people, involved a great deal of unrestrained copulation by everyone assembled except the boys themselves. Then, at the climax of the festival, each of the boys copulated with the girl chosen to embody the spirit. As the boy chosen to be last was performing, the props from a heavy wooden scaffold above the couple were knocked away, crushing them. Their bodies were then retrieved, cut up, roasted, and eaten.[31] In short, murder and cannibalism marked the boys' entrance into procreative life.

Surely all this killing among planting people needs explaining. One could, of course, suppose that the Meriahs were sacrifices in the standard sense: The offering of human life, as the thing most precious to people, might be thought to honor the gods most—an idea perhaps supported by a customary emphasis on the Meriahs' costliness. One might think of the Pawnee killing as sending the girl to notify her "husband" that it was time to reactivate vegetation and as reuniting a celestial husband and wife so that their renewed sexual activity could stimulate the crops. But most of the victims have not been propitiatory offerings or messengers to the vegetation spirit. They have *embodied* that spirit. What are we to make of the murder and, often, the eating of the god? Why would one kill and eat the spirit protecting the food? Of course the ritual killing often enacts the analogy between harvesting the crops and killing the spirit, between the cyclic waning of the vegetation and the cyclically absent vegetation spirit. But why?

Turning to the ancient Middle Eastern stories for clues seems at first pointless because in those stories the effect of the divine personage's death was quite different. The Middle Eastern deity's periodic death explained or embodied the periodic *decline* of the food crops. In the Persephone story, before the girl's abduction by the lord of the underworld, no annual decline had occurred. Nor does there seem to be any recorded suggestion that wheat or some other food crop first appeared after the death of Dumuzi-Tammuz-Attis-Adonis, the food arising in some primordial time out of the dead god's body.

Still, the story that Dionysus "invented" wine could be a late, rationalized version of a story in which grapevines originated from his corpse. And, yes, Mesopotamian liturgies did declare that the dead Tammuz returned annually in the form of the sprouting grain. In Egypt, the same was true of Osiris, a vegetation deity long before he became the Lord of Eternal Life. Even in New Kingdom times he was often pictured as a corpse from which grain sprouted. Furthermore, the places up and down Egypt where legend declared pieces of Osiris' body to have been buried were sacred places, beneficial to those seeking an enlarged life. In the story we know, the evil Set buried pieces of Osiris' body up and down Egypt so that it would be hard to reassemble. But the beneficial scattering does bear a queer resemblance to planting pieces of Hainuwele's body or even the bodies of the Meriahs.

In an Osirian mystery play performed about 2000 B.C. in Egypt, oxen trod barley on the threshing floor, symbolizing Osiris' dismemberment by Set.[32] Such a strange reenactment begins to make sense if one sees it in light of the Hainuwele story.

A myth from India of the second millennium B.C. "explained" why an intoxicating drink called "soma" was offered in Brahmanic rites. The myth, probably older than its contemporary myths about the gods as protectors of the cosmos, told of the gods carrying out the first, prototypical, sacrifice, which people must emulate in all sacrifices they make. This first sacrifice was the murder of their fellow god Soma, who had existed before all other life. His death brought forth all familiar life, vegetal as well as animal; pressing the soma plant—a cultic reenactment of the slaying—yielded a potion that made the gods immortal and made people immortal as a species, even though individuals would die. [33]

Reflecting on our own Christian traditions provides insight into the ceremonial slaying and cannibalization of a divine being. Easter commemorates God's generosity, Christ's miraculous absorption of evil and death, his regenerative powers, his triumphant sufficiency. As in the Hainuwele myth, Easter's central themes are guilt, atonement, and reconciliation.

Imagine that Christian communities annually chose a young man to embody Christ, and, amid wailing and lamentation, actually crucified him on Good Friday. (The Penitentes, a Christian cult in New Mexico, do annually relive Christ's Passion to the degree allowable by law, and on Good Friday bind one of their members to a cross.) The community would be viewing the man neither as victim nor messenger, nor would it be sacrificing the god to himself. It would be ritually reenacting a profoundly important event that occurred long ago, commemorating it (remembering it together), renewing the whole community's sense of the event's meaning. Having an "actual" Christ undergo, first, Christ's sorrow and pain and, then, on Easter morning, embody Christ's glorious triumph and human life's consequent enlargement would greatly heighten the community's experience. Instead of partaking of communion wafers and wine, symbols of the Savior's flesh and blood, the faithful might partake of the surrogate Christ's body. Although the community would not be able to return the young man to his ordinary life, neither the original Christ nor Hainuwele returned to life in that sense. Both went to the Other World but returned to our world in the form of greater life for their people.

It is a peculiar, unsettling vision; yet it does help make sense of stories like the Hainuwele myth. One sees in religions both familiar and exotic the fervent wish for closeness and communion with the god, the need to get him *into* the land, the sanctuary, the holy images, the roasted goat, the wheat, the maize, the bread and wine, the devotees' own bodies. Killing and eating whatever the god has entered is a way of making that god immanent, infusing the world with his holy presence.

Adolf Jensen believes that ritual killings associated with myths of the Hainuwele type and often erroneously explained as religious sacrifices are intended to reenact the divine event from which everything in our world began, in order to keep it fresh in memory. The cannibalism is the ritual remembrance that eating the food crop is eating the transmuted deity. Noting that puberty rites almost always involve the initiates' ritual death, Jensen calls the rites "reminders of the act of procreation . . . which originated . . . with the first mythic act of killing and of the fact that mortality is inevitably a part" of procreation.[34]

The central idea of the killed god, writes Joseph Campbell, is that the divine god "has become flesh in the living food-substance of the world: which is to say, in all of us, since all of us are to become, in the end, food for other beings." The idea affirms and embraces humankind's fate. The only way to live is to kill. The hunting cultures dealt with this fate by denying the full reality of death, but some planting societies found a way to reconcile themselves to death as a fact. Their rites, Campbell declares, extinguish the will of the individual to his own immortality "through an effective realization of the immortality of being itself and of its play through all things."[35]

Put plainly, these rites are a ceremonial recognition that *all* life rises out of, consumes, and then falls to other manifestations of *its own self.* The rites ceremonially welcome killing and dying as necessary phases in the perpetual renewal of life. The reenactment of the god's death, that is, the opening out of life, reaffirms the goodness of things as they are and helps to secure their continuance.

Again, familiar Western traditions illuminate the seemingly exotic ones. If sin were not such an overriding concept in the Judeo-Christian tradition, we might see the killing of the deity among tribal planting cultures as similar in significance to Eve's eating of the forbidden fruit. We might celebrate the event annually with a subdued but profound joy. Both the murder of the god and Eve's fateful meal resulted in the present world order. In the Fall, of course, no god suffered dismemberment or returned as food, either plant or animal. But in both events, immortal personages became mortal, that is, human, and through that change released life's seed. In both, life's new abundance was inextricably linked to death. In both, the themes of guilt, atonement, and reconciliation were central. The stories make the fact of death not a triumph of chaos but, forming a unit with abundance, a necessary and proper part of a well-ordered cosmos, even a boon.

LIFE'S ANSWER TO DEATH IN A CROWDED WORLD

Fertility rites have not totally disappeared from the Western world. We still engage in ceremonies that serve three basic purposes: to establish rapport with the divine source of the earth's plenty; to increase that plenty; and to offer thanks for it. Some rural communities even still participate in that mysterious rite so deeply buried in the past, the commemorative reenactment of the crop-spirit's murder. An example or two of each type of ceremony will suffice.

Even though the Judeo-Christian God explicitly gave humankind the open-ended right to use all plants and animals for food (Gen. 1:28–29), we still seek divine sponsorship for the processes involved. Long ago, the Church incorporated many ancient agricultural rites into the Christian liturgical year. It attached to saints' festivals various pre-Christian rites to protect crops from specific diseases, pests, and other disasters. The Easter festival absorbed rites celebrating the renewal of abundance and rites establishing divine protection of the crops and animals. The old fertility symbols of the egg and rabbit were given a new significance. Children in the American Southwest still bring animals to the priest at Easter to be blessed. A priest blesses the tuna fleet before it sails. Until recently at least, the vicar in a part of Yorkshire cut the season's first wheat, and the communion bread was made from it.[36]

Current rites to promote abundance take many forms. Couples who want children may light a candle at the altar of the Virgin. Less decorously, some rural folk in both Europe and the United States still believe that human nakedness and copulation in the planted field will spark the grain into action.

Many thanksgiving rites flourish today. The simplest, most familiar ceremonial thanks is the daily "grace" before meals. Annual thanksgiving rites often include ritual purification and atonement—explicit in the Jewish Passover and the traditional Christmas and Easter. The purpose is to thank God for one's continued life and good fortune and for the availability of everlasting life; and to make oneself worthy of God's future bounty by ritually cleansing oneself of past sins and pledging improvement. We feel some of the same significance in New Year's Day. In the traditional harvest celebrations of Thanksgiving and the Jewish Sukkoth, the community signifies its awareness of God's grace and its dependence on him for food and prosperity. Additionally, a priest may offer thanks for a bountiful harvest of grapes, wheat, whatever constitutes the region's chief food crop.

As for the ritual murder of the crop-spirit, the rural European custom of the "corn dolly" is the best-known example. From England to Russia, the custom survives of personifying the chief food crop in a divine being and killing it. W. Mannhardt collected an abundance of "corn-mother" lore from modern Europe, and Frazer's *The Golden Bough* draws heavily on this lore. Frazer recounts a custom in Hanover, for instance, in which the reapers converge on the last sheaf of wheat standing in the field and beat it with sticks, shouting at each other to hit "her."

> In some villages, the man who gives the last stroke at threshing is called the son of the Corn-mother; he is tied up in the Corn-mother [the last sheaf in the field], beaten, and carried through the village. [A wreath made of the Corn-mother] is dedicated in church on the following Sunday; and on Easter Eve the grain is rubbed out of it by a seven-year-old girl and scattered amongst the young corn. At Christmas the straw of the wreath is placed in the [ceremonial] manger to make the cattle thrive. Here the fertilizing power of the Corn-mother is plainly brought out by scattering the seed taken from her body . . . among the new corn; and her influence over animal life is indicated by placing the straw in the manger.[37]

Just as in Egypt 4000 years ago, so in modern Norway, Lithuania, Bavaria, and elsewhere, the grain-spirit is explicitly "killed" in reaping or threshing the grain.[38] In parts of Europe, "the corn-spirit is represented by a man, who lies down under the last corn; it is threshed upon his body, and the people say that 'the Old Man is being beaten to death.' . . . Sometimes the farmer's wife is thrust, together with the last sheaf, under the threshing-machine, as if to thresh her, and . . . afterwards a pretence is made of winnowing her."[39] "At the close of the harvest the Arabs of Moab bury the last sheaf in a grave in the corn-field, saying as they do so, 'We are burying the Old Man,' or 'The Old Man is dead.' "[40] According to the sociologist William Graham Sumner, in some French villages, the last of the wheat harvested was in recent times made into a human-shaped loaf, representing the wheat-spirit, and distributed and eaten by the villagers.[41] In the United States, a festive Easter dessert is a white cake shaped like a lamb and covered with white frosting and shredded coconut. It represents the Lamb of God, that is, Christ.

But such customs are vestiges. Today in large parts of the world, fertility rites seem remote indeed. We work to control our own fecundity, not to promote it. And while specialists increase our food supply by highly technical means, most of us are so detached from food production that we do not even know what newly sprouted wheat looks like or which part of the steer our steak comes from. We do not imagine that a Prince of the Chickens will be angry if we dump the giblets down the garbage disposer, and we rarely get close enough to the seed-grain to chant sexy lyrics over it. Beyond our lascivious pleasure in food, if we at all associate sexuality and death with eating, it is probably in thinking that too many juicy steaks and buttered rolls will make us fat and sexually unattractive or, some day, kill us.

Yet all the while we know in our bones what Coatlicue means. The same processes that make life make death, and those processes are always nudging us forward. Dyeing our hair, jogging, dressing young, chirping such slogans as "You're only as old as you feel" do not really fool us. We know what is coming. The joy we feel in the changing seasons is a wrenching joy. So reassuring in their beauty, their returning inexhaustible freshness, they nevertheless neatly mark out our time, ticking off our lives' own swift, unrepeatable seasons. We know, too, that as our children wax, we wane; that they at once enlarge our own lives and take our lives from us. We do not one day have to choose, as old Eskimo women did, to walk off into the snow and die to make room for the young, but only because our own snows engulf us soon enough.

Against these cold truths we seek the old comforts: discovering in a grandchild our own twinkling eye; in somebody's well-being our own influence. We want to feel that we have seeded ourselves, put something of ourselves into life's horn—whether our genes, our potatoes, our vision.

For many people, bearing children still appears to be the most satisfying way of defying chaos and death. Doing so is far less perilous than in the past, and far more so. Childbirth rarely results in the mother's death now, and most children will probably reach maturity. But children are no longer the natural boon they once were—the helpers in the yam patch, the providers for their aged parents. Considered economically, they are a pure liability; and they are much, much harder to rear than in a traditional society, where parents get help from grandmothers, uncles, and from a settled communal truth.

To guide a child toward responsible, satisfying maturity has always taken work and wisdom, yet that work used to be our plain daily work with which the older children helped, and that wisdom an old, unconscious wisdom possessed by all. Recently, one parent and then two started working at jobs away from home. The aunts moved to Philadelphia, the uncles to San Diego. Parents themselves often split. The unconscious wisdom no longer fits. When we dip into its magic well and bid our children drink, they see mud and half-dead toads, and laugh at us. We look into the cup, see that they are right, and, stunned, start dressing young. The once solid truth slides and blinks like disco lights.

Unless we are very lucky and skillful, our children may become strangers who twitch in tune with their peers and who refuse even to sit down and eat our Thanksgiving turkey. Later, they may drop in twice a year from across the globe or send a check at Christmas.

Despite these perils, many people still want children. For them, bearing children still expresses, as does no other act, the sense that life is good, that the cosmos will hold, and that working hard for twenty or more years to help it hold is worth their time and is likely to succeed. Or they just want to see their genes dance above them in the sunlight as they themselves sink into the pit.

Some few people, at least, soften death in another way once associated with traditional fertility rituals. They view all life and energy as an organic system in which, treated with care, nothing "really" dies. Like the hunting peoples, they try to think of all they consume as "holy," to be used respectfully, and, if possible, replenished or at least recycled, not squandered mindlessly.

This notion that one owes the physical world something for what, as a living being, one consumes and pollutes runs counter to the traditional Western view of humankind and its place in the world. The God of Genesis named man master of the plants and animals; they were his to use freely. The Western view has extended that permission to cover all the earth's resources, which have been thought of as gifts stashed around the cosmic Big House for people's serial delectation. We were so few and the earth so large that, when we struck down its bison, more thundered round the bend; when we dug its coal, we hit another vein; when we dumped our sewage into its rivers, it was washed away. The vision of an earth that could, like the snake, restore itself or could, like the wilderness, be left behind when one had used it up—this vision worked.

The Western view is most fully developed in the United States. Early on, we Americans got into the habit of strewing our trash in the vast and empty land as a way of asserting our presence, making the land not so strange. To defile something is to cancel its power to frighten. (People desecrate the altars of those they have feared, rape their women, mutilate their dead.) As this country grew in wealth and power, we began to think of our good fortune in an old, old way, as a sign of God's special favor, a sign of our natural superiority as a people. Ironically, we continued to embrace the part of Puritanism that suggested our superiority but, more and more, abandoned the Puritan thrift. Thrift seemed a mean virtue, unsuited to the lords of the world. Crowing "There's plenty more where that came from!" we urged each other to toss, pour, and burn. Mid-twentieth-century economic policy reinforced galloping consumption by urging us to use more goods because that made more jobs, and jobs made the economy boom. The sellers of electricity, steel, bottled lemon juice, and frozen waffles wooed us on TV, and sellers of expensive whiskey democratically assured all of us that we deserved the very best.

Then, in the 1960s, a different notion of humankind's place in the world emerged. It came from the "ecology" movement; from the new vision of the American Indians as a neglected minority with a valuable insight; and from the popularization of Eastern thought, especially the Vedanta philosophy, according to which all that lives—people, tumble-weeds, whooping cranes—is akin, or as Alan Watts would say, really "God" in disguise.

A series of emotionally charged symbols flashed before the public eye: strontium 90 in mothers' milk; Silent Spring; killer smog; dead fish float-ing in the fabled Rhine; gasoline lines; lists of endangered species; cancer maps. Growing numbers of people felt spooked. Was the Prince of the Mountain Goats shaking the mountain at the center of the Big House? A few people are beginning to suspect that, like Really Black's family in the Tsimshian story, we must atone for what we destroy, learn restraint, and help the earth recover what it spends to support our lives. This atti-tude is expressed in such gestures as recycling newspapers, in changes in utility companies' price scales and advertising, in wide-ranging environ-mental legislation. The motives are often highly practical, but behind them hovers a new image, an image of mythic power: the earth as seen from outer space—a globe blue, white, green, wrapped in a precious air sac and gleaming with light and life in the sterile, black space. To the modern imagination, the symbol is all the more compelling because, no mere artist's conception, it is a product of Science, a genuine photograph. The image evokes even from cynics gulps and gazes, the sense that the earth is truly a holy, miraculous gift; that it is *all* that stands between everything we hold dear and annihilation; and that it is finite and vulnerable. This image views with respect whatever is alive or might serve life: Construction of the great dam waited while we peered quizzically at the tiny snail-darter.

11

Survival Through a Family Line

We partly satisfy our hunger for immortal life by belonging to a continuing group and helping it thrive. We work for the good of our family, our neighborhood, our town, our country, the human species, the life on our planet, the planet itself—all things to which we feel ourselves akin. The fertility cult is, of course, one form of this concern with group survival. Two others are the belief in reincarnation (serial selves) and the veneration of ancestors. All three value the dead as the source of new life, and value the living as a source of extended life for the dead.

Another kind of group survival stresses not the cycle of life and death, not the dead as a source of renewed life, but the continuance of the family group upon this earth. The best expression of survival through the living family appears in the Old Testament. Because we all share the sense of posthumous survival through our continuing families and because the Old Testament, so important a part of Western tradition, is often badly misunderstood on this point, this chapter explains group survival in that text.

THE FAMILIAL SOUL

Much of the Old Testament should be read as the account of a chosen family's magnificent triumph over death. Although we generally know the stories, we tend to misread them because we are poorly acquainted with the *agent* of postmortem survival assumed in the Old Testament, the *familial soul*. The familial soul was what we all still mean by a "sense of family," but greatly heightened—the family's strength, its defining customs, its proud knowledge of having been chosen for God's blessing, its living members' sense of oneness with their forebears and descendants. The familial soul was the group consciousness of all this, perpetuated through the group's living members.

People's conceptions of posthumous survival, of course, grow out of their circumstances. Their gods often promise them, after death, a resplendent version of what the people most want in their everyday lives, be that the end of brutal toil or something more—survival of their personal, conscious selves, their fame, or their group. The people who became the Israelites were for a long time semi-nomadic tribes moving across the land to find forage for their animals and competing with their neighbors. Like most ancient peoples, they knew the wilderness and had ample evidence of how those before them had risen up and fallen back in the sand. This tribal people saw that a person's only chance for life at all was as a member of a group, and that the larger and more prosperous the group and the stronger its leader, the more likely its continuance. Thus, an Israelite's sense of identity was founded on his membership in a group, specifically a family headed by a patriarch.

Reasonably then, the early Israelites' conception of immortality resembled—in more glorious form—the perpetuation of the family line. By analogy with their more mundane hopes, they viewed survival in the *highest* sense as the perpetuation and growth of the family's "soul" through its succession of living members. The living head of the family, always male, had custody of this soul's essence; centered in his own person, it also pervaded everything that belonged to him—his children, wives, relatives, servants, sheep, camels, and other goods. When the patriarch felt his death approaching, he gathered his strength for one last great act: the transfer, through the "blessing," of the soul's essence to his chosen son. A prayer so efficacious as to be almost a prophecy, the blessing poured the patriarch's soul-power into that son. (The Russian folktale recounted in Chapter 1 echoes this notion; the dying giant breathed out his special power through the coffin crack into the body of the young hero.)

The family's soul manifested its vigor physically through each succeeding patriarch's prosperity and fecundity, and spiritually through the family's reverent sense of itself—its bonds with its forebears, the land, the rest of humankind, and, above all, with God. For the early Israelites, the continued vigor of this familial soul constituted life's highest purpose and greatest boon, a glorious triumph over death. The idea of individual conscious survival after death was not exactly unavailable to these people; it simply had so little to do with their everyday aims that their yearnings did not, as ours might, take that shape.

Although, for the Israelites, posthumous survival flowed from Abraham, the story began much earlier, with the inauguration of death. The first twelve chapters of Genesis present an escalating battle between the forces of life and death, culminating in God's covenant with Abraham. Out of a void, God had created a bright disc of teeming life with two godlike creatures presiding at its center. When Adam and Eve doomed themselves, God rescued humankind from annihilation by conferring upon the couple the power of procreation. When human wickedness polluted the whole earth, God—like creators in other mythic traditions similarly dissatisfied with their earliest efforts—decided to start anew. A good husbandman, God did not destroy the cosmos before he had stored its best seeds in the Ark. Then, pondering humankind's irremediable flaws, he made a crucial decision: Though individuals would of course perish as before, he would never again threaten the species.

EXTENDED LIFE FOR ABRAHAM

Not all high gods promise their people such restraint. Sometimes, annihilation by the angry god remains such a frightful possibility that every flood or famine, every blasting summer or iron winter, awakens the fear that this may be *it*. But God's sponsorship of human life went even further than his promise. In Abraham, he found a man he thought might be worth saving in a fuller, more personal sense, a man whose worth might even extend that fuller survival to many others. God's proposition to Abraham was this: "Go from your country and your kindred and your father's house" into an alien land "and I will make you a great nation, and I will bless you, and make your name great . . . and by you all the families of the earth shall bless themselves" (Gen. 12:1–3). God was saying, if you will leave your home and family for me, leave all that swells your life, all that seems to give it point and permanence, all that for you means survival beyond mere consciousness, I promise you a kind of survival that will reach far more deeply and broadly into the future than any sort you could achieve by yourself. Furthermore, I will make you the agent of a similar survival for all families. In short, if you will risk all for me, I will make you, and others through you, "immortal."

A self-contained, twentieth-century person might not comprehend the magnificence of this offer, especially if he is a person who views immortality as the posthumous survival of his personal consciousness. But Abraham understood, for God had offered a glorified version of a patriarch's dearest wish.

The extended survival that God promised Abraham echoes throughout the Old Testament in every blessing and every curse, every description of future good and ill. To bless meant to augment the familial spirit; to curse meant to blast it. To be blessed was to gather goods, live long, produce a large and fruitful family, be long known, and, above all, have a family line reaching far into the future under God's special care. For instance, here is God's blessing of Jacob: "The land on which you lie I will give to you and to your descendants; and your descendants shall be like the dust of the earth, and you shall spread abroad to the west and to the east and to the north and to the south; and by you and your descendants shall all the families of the earth bless themselves" (Gen. 28:13–14).

The grand theme running through the saga of Abraham's family is the survival of the familial soul. Because this soul comprised a special consciousness in a succession of men, its survival depended both on bearing sons in each generation and on unusual qualities of mind. Long after Abraham and his wife Sarah had passed the age of childbearing, God miraculously enabled Sarah to bear Abraham's son Isaac. When God later commanded Abraham to sacrifice the beloved child, he was asking Abraham to affirm in the most outrageous way possible his total commitment to God: Abraham, in thus demonstrating his extraordinary qualifications for posthumous survival, would be destroying the very means that God had promised and bestowed. Abraham's willingness helps account for God's later forbearance with Abraham's less worthy descendants: God's blessing of them implied not his endorsement of all they did but, rather, his firm commitment to the soul of Abraham that survived through them.

The theme of posthumous survival as a gift shared by a *group* accounts for the emphasis, in the next episode, on ethnic purity. God told Abraham to find a wife for Isaac from Abraham's stock in Mesopotamia instead of from the local people. A woman from within the Mesopotamian group would strengthen both the physical "seed" and, through her sense of identity, the spiritual consciousness that God had found and nurtured in Abraham; an outsider would weaken them. Ethnic purity advanced the survival of the group, including its dead members.

After Isaac's marriage, the saga moves to a series of betrayals by brothers, mothers, wives, uncles, sisters, daughters—stories believable and highly entertaining but, for a modern reader, disconcertingly peopled by characters so mean-spirited, so selfish, as to bear no apparent trace of the supposedly expanding familial spirit. An appropriate bearer of that spirit, one reasons, would eagerly embrace his solemn responsibilities toward his family, his fellow men, and God. He would see himself as a holy vessel abrim with the immortality of all. He would see past, present, and future as one; himself, his ancestors, his descendants as one; his family's purposes and God's as one. Not so Esau, Jacob, Rebekah, Rachel, Laban, the murderous brothers of Joseph—these pellet-hard snatchers and grabbers.

Well, yes. God had said that, although people generally were not very good, he would take them as they came. And if transferring spiritual values to children is notoriously uncertain, all the more to wives, the wives' relatives, and so on. As Abraham's *seed* flourished from generation to generation, the task became, more and more, ensuring the survival of his *spirit*. Indeed, that task is the great unifying theme of the Old Testament—in Moses' rallying of the Israelite slaves, in establishing the united kingdom of Israel and Judah, in the exhortations of the prophets, and in the Exile and the Diaspora. Survival of the seed would be worthless if Abraham's spirit perished.

Very early in the story, that spirit faltered. For instance, it is inconceivable that Abraham's grandsons might, as Abraham had done, badger God until he agreed not to kill everyone, good with bad, in an iniquitous city (Gen. 18). Abraham, his plain, generous mind fixed stubbornly on the principle of justice and the welfare of his fellow men, had simply worn God down until God promised. Those coming after Abraham, by contrast, fixed their minds on their own bellies, tents, and camels. Yet again and again, the person who became custodian of the familial soul was he who demonstrated at least his potential for understanding its holy significance.

Isaac's eldest son Esau, the presumptive custodian in his generation, early revealed his insufficiency. One day he returned from hunting, very hungry, to find his brother Jacob cooking a savory stew. Esau yearned for some of that stew. Why, sure, have some, said the sly Jacob—if you'll pay for it with your birthright. (The "birthright" meant the special rank that one son, usually the eldest, would inherit from his father. Its holder would become head of the family in its covenant with God; with the rank went special privileges and probable inheritance of the blessing.) So wholly did Esau's mind focus on his hollow belly that, thoughtless of even his future personal self, he eagerly chose the stew. Later, when he married two Hittite women instead of women from his own people, he again showed his meager understanding. Esau's paltry imagination could not extend his selfhood beyond his present comfort and his delight in the local girls.

Jacob's self-absorption was of quite a different order—slick, calculating, ambitious. When Isaac, a blind old man sitting in his tent preparing for death, asked that Esau come in to receive the great blessing, Rebekah easily got Jacob to impersonate Esau so that Jacob could receive it instead. Although Jacob was only too ready to put forth himself as the next patriarch, he showed no comprehension of the glorified spiritual survival God had offered his family, only of the goods and privileges falling to its chief custodian. However, in Jacob's ambition lay the possibility of spiritual enlargement. One evening as he was journeying toward his mother's family in faraway Mesopotamia, fleeing Esau's wrath, he lay down to sleep in the stony wilderness. Who knew what next? His circumstances suggest that he felt anxious, dejected, uncomfortable with his solitary, puny self. He could not imagine his future.

Then came the revelation that changed Jacob's life and the destinies of all who came after him. In a dream he saw a ladder reaching straight to heaven with angels moving up and down it. God himself stood at the top of the ladder. Appalled, Jacob saw God turning his attention far below to the dreamer himself, guilty and exposed. But instead of cursing him, God uttered a momentous blessing! Waking, Jacob said fearfully, "Surely the LORD is in this place; and I did not know it. . . . How awesome is this place! This is none other than the house of God, and this is the gate of heaven" (Gen. 28:16–17). Swept by relief, joy, and awe, Jacob made a vow: If God really does feed, clothe, and preserve me, and lets me return some day in peace to my father's house, I will dedicate myself to him. If he really does make me prosperous, I'll give him back ten percent of all I get.

Jacob set up a pillar, anointing it with oil, to seal his vow and signify his awareness that the place he had supposed an empty wilderness was truly God's own house.

What happened to Jacob was, on a personal scale, exactly analogous to the central event in many mythic traditions: the high god's creation of the spiritual cosmos. As seen in Chapter 7, the high god's power, traveling down the axial pole, infuses the wilderness with divinity, transforming it into the cosmos. In the ladder symbol, Jacob saw that what he had taken for a world merely of men's things and purposes was a holy place infused with God's presence. This revelation spurred Jacob's spiritual growth. From that time forth, the mean clutter of his mind began to reshape itself to purposes harmonious with God's own. About twenty years later, when the now wealthy Jacob was returning, at God's command, to his own land, an angel announced that from now on Jacob's name would be Israel, a name of honor.[1] Jacob had become the worthy custodian of the familial soul.

Of God's many gifts to Jacob, the best was Joseph, the long-awaited first son of Jacob's dearest wife. Like Abraham himself,[2] like Isaac, like Moses later, Joseph was the holy miraculous child snatched from death to save his entire people. (The figure of Jesus, though much more broadly interpreted, belongs to the same archetype.) Almost murdered by his jealous brothers, almost left to die in a dry well, falsely accused and imprisoned in Egypt, Joseph not only lived but used his tremendous gifts to save his family and all the Egyptians as well. Joseph's ingenuity so filled Egypt's granaries for the seven years' drought that, when the hungry Israelites sought help, Egypt had enough to feed them also. Combining Jacob's canny toughness with Abraham's intuitive spirituality and compassion, his sense of the *holy oneness* of things, Joseph added his own intelligence. Here, for the first time, is the gifted Jew of later history, the maligned stranger whose talents overcome great obstacles to enlarge the lives of those among whom he finds himself, a boon to the world.

In the first three generations of Abraham's family, the familial soul had centered in only one man at a time. By the fourth generation, however, this spirit so thrived that, though it resided chiefly in Joseph, it flourished also in his eleven brothers. Each became the head of a family that expanded into a tribe, and all these tribes together became the "children of Israel." Through this shared, vigorous, ever-growing identity, the Israelites—all the descendants of Abraham—emphatically conquered death.

A RAIN OF SPARROWS

> *For not one sparrow can [fall] &*
> *the whole Universe not suffer also*

In all its Regions, & its Father & Saviour
not pity and weep. [3]

Probably what most dismays modern readers about the Old Testament is
its disregard for the vast majority of human beings, those who happened
not to be patriarchs or kings—whether their children, wives, nephews,
servants, or subjects, or simply old women crouched in a wall's shadow.
Take, for instance, the Book of Job.

God let Satan test Job's allegiance by bringing upon this very virtuous
and very rich man a swift series of calamities. As Job's seven sons were
gathered at dinner, a messenger straggled in to announce that a ma-
rauding tribe had cut down Job's five hundred oxen, five hundred donkeys—and all the servants attending them. As the diners tried to absorb
this news, another messenger entered to say that a fire had consumed
Job's seven thousand sheep—and the shepherds attending them. Then a
third messenger arrived to say that an enemy tribe had rustled Job's three
thousand camels—and murdered the servants attending them. Scarcely
had the third messenger finished his account when a great wind out of
the wilderness smote the hall in which the sons sat, bringing the roof
down upon them. All seven sons were crushed.

The book is about Job, of course, not his sons or servants, and it
explores profoundly the meaning of misfortune. Yet while the story rolls
swiftly on, the minds of some readers keep turning back to those sons
and servants. They really died? They stayed dead? When Satan had finished hurling horrors at Job in the name of the test, the story goes, God
restored all that Job had lost, doubling the oxen, donkeys, sheep, and
camels—and providing seven new sons. (New servants are not mentioned, but presumably God provided plenty of them to tend the animals.) That the new sons were blandly presented as a restoration strikes
us with special horror. Those dead people had had, at least for the writer,
no value independent of their value to the patriarch Job. God had let the
original seven sons, to say nothing of uncounted servants, die just to
make a philosophical point. No big deal, apparently.

Nor is that view peculiar to this story. In most of the Old Testament,
children, servants, and others attached to a man were seen as possessing
no intrinsic value, only value derived from their relationship with that
man. They did not fully inhabit their own humanity. A glimpse at the
roughly contemporaneous *Odyssey* points up the startling difference in
attitude. There, the lowliest beggar or slave stood, by right, in his patch

of sunlight, sorting among his choices, unmolested by gods and heroes in their dealings with each other. Certainly, the powerful often violated his right, but in doing so they brought dishonor upon themselves. In the Old Testament, by contrast, those attached to a patriarch were mere extensions of him, without sovereign existence or meaning. For instance, when the greedy Achan deeply offended God by secretly taking some of the spoils of Jericho for his own use, not only did Achan have to be stoned and burnt but also his sons, daughters, oxen, donkeys, sheep, tents, all that pertained to him (Josh. 7). In the Book of Esther, not just the evil Haman was hanged but, at virtuous Esther's request, his ten sons as well (9:13–14). When some of Belshazzar's governors dealt harshly with the prophet Daniel, not only these men but also their wives and children were tossed to the lions (6:24). David had seven of Saul's grandsons slain not because they were guilty of anything but because David wished to punish Saul (II Sam. 21:1–9). Devout Jephthah felt obliged to sacrifice his daughter to God. Although the girl grieved to find her life ending so early, her death was treated as purely Jephthah's tragedy. (Judg. 11:30–40). The Sodomite mob, noisily bent upon sodomy, thumped at Lot's door, demanding the strangers he was sheltering for the night. But Lot, a blameless man and impeccable host, offered his two virgin daughters instead (Gen. 19:1–8). When Jehoiakim, king of Judah, burned the scroll upon which Jeremiah had recorded God's words, God punished not just Jehoiakim but also his servants and seed (Jer. 36:31). Virtuous Jehu, king of Israel, punished his wicked predecessor Ahab by directing that everyone remotely related to Ahab be chopped down, including Ahab's "great men," seventy sons, and all the family's other children, servants, and priests (II Kings 9–10).

The view that those attached to a powerful man were little more than his possessions is especially clear in an episode about David. As king of Israel, David virtually owned his people. Deciding to punish David for David's personal sin of pride (about having so many subjects), God gave him a choice of punishment. David first chose a pestilence for his people, rather than a punishment that would fall heavily upon himself personally. God set right to work and, before David reconsidered, had felled seventy thousand people.

Yet to see these stories, as modern readers often do, as pointless or inexplicably barbarous is unjust. The Israelites' disregard for individuals followed from the hard circumstances in which they had shaped their world-view. Their strength had arisen from their perception that meaning must center on the patriarch—on his extension through the group and on the group's validation through him. Individuals must be valued as their existence extended or diminished the familial soul centering on the patriarch.

It was quite reasonable, for the Israelites, that death in its largest sense be the exact obverse of life in *its* largest sense. Because the blessing of extended life, or "immortality," started with the perpetuation of the patriarch's seed, the curse of annihilation logically consisted of blasting the patriarch's family and followers, ruining anything that enlarged him in anyone's mind. The many curses uttered or prophesied in the Old Testament make this attitude abundantly clear. For instance, in the Book of Job, Bildad described the worst fate that could befall a man:

> He is torn from the tent in which he trusted. . . .
> In his tent dwells that which is none of his;
>   brimstone is scattered upon his habitation.
> His roots dry up beneath,
>   and he has no name in the street.
> He is thrust from light into darkness,
>   and driven out of the world.
> He has no offspring or descendant among his people,
>   and no survivor where he used to live.
>
> (18:14–19)

In punishing Cain for murdering Abel, God had cursed him with a kind of living death. Nothing Cain touched would thrive. Land he tilled would bring forth no life-giving fruits; whatever he chose to do would yield only trivial and transitory results. God had locked Cain into the dying part of himself, the singular consciousness in the mortal body.

No mode of conquering death is free. Each has powerful advantages and disadvantages. Each strikes a kind of bargain with death, giving up some valued part of life in order to secure some part valued even more. The virgin was tossed into the volcano to keep it from destroying the whole village. The young god was chopped up and planted to make food for all. The Greek or Scandinavian warrior-hero, knowing he must in any event spend eternity gibbering batlike in dusty caverns, sought a glorious death in war to secure an immortal fame. The ancient Egyptian, the medieval Christian, the Moslem—whoever has believed in personal salvation—has narrowed his earthly life to secure a much enlarged life in the Other World. The Israelites sacrificed personal dominion to the group's strength.

Later, as a growing social network permitted greater attention to the individual, Hebrew thought shifted. For instance, in the seventh and sixth centuries B.C., the prophet Ezekiel said that if a son were righteous, he would not be punished for his father's sins (Ezek. 18:14–20) and, indeed, that God would judge all men as individuals, each according to his own behavior (33:20). Because all too often individuals' fates on this earth did not conform with justice, Judaism moved in the next few centuries toward the concept of rewards and punishment after death, the subject of the next chapter.

Meanwhile, it is worth noting how Jewish views in the last two thousand years have bent but have not broken. While Jews have long believed in the Final Days (the coming of a Messiah and the resurrection of all good people in an earthly paradise), one might say that their chief aim is to make the *present* as much like the Final Days as possible: They still spend far more energy nurturing their living group and the Jewish spirit than preparing for those Final Days; and the spirit or "soul" of Jewishness is still close to Abraham's own spiritual qualities.

But do modern Jews see themselves as the "chosen" people? The view of one's group as a special people has always been widespread; it is common to provincial people of whatever time and place. Once, it helped a group survive. Generally, it works less well in our world, where groups who differ in many vivid ways, from skin color to basic values, must share the space and the water, must learn to cooperate or perish. Today, the attitude of universal brotherhood probably has more survival value than the notion of one's own group as preeminent.

But it is precisely in defining and promoting universal brotherhood that Jews have contributed most to civilization. To them, the term "chosen" has long implied chosen by God not for his favorite, privileged people but for a hard task: setting a moral example for all people. Some Jews would even say that as a people they chose themselves for this task. Keenly aware that their own ethnic identity has been both a source of enlarged life and of persecution to the point of attempted annihilation, the Jews have probably worked harder than any other group to foster brotherhood among *diverse* peoples and individuals. Brotherhood does not mean to them ironing people flat and making them hold hands like paper dolls. It does not mean pretending that "We are all just one big happy family around here." It means seeking justice for all people, even the morally outrageous. It means respecting, celebrating people's life-enhancing differences. The value Jews have traditionally placed on tolerance and liberality, the nurture of every person's talents, has served civilization well.

For many Jews, the idea of having been "chosen" has taken on painfully ironic overtones: chosen for the pogroms, chosen for the ovens. Who needs such an honor? But—a kindlier irony—the centuries of persecution have indeed made the Jews a chosen people in a sense close to the original meaning—survivors whose presence enlarges the lives of all. Jewish contributions to science, the arts, the civilizing notions of human dignity and universal brotherhood far surpass their modest numbers. The other peoples of the earth have in simple fact been blessed by the children of Israel.

12

Personal Survival in Another World

In the Big Rock Candy Mountains,
There's a land that's fair and bright,
Where the handouts grow on bushes
And you sleep out ev'ry night,
Where the box-cars are all empty
And the sun shines ev'ry day.
. . .

There's a lake of stew, and of whiskey, too,
And you can paddle all around in a big canoe
In the Big Rock Candy Mountains. [1]

Imagining a personal survival after death, usually in another world, is probably the oldest and surely the most nearly inevitable way that people reconcile themselves to death. The belief that individuals can survive death is apparently over thirty-five thousand years old. The earliest members of our species, the Neanderthalers, buried some of their dead with food and implements that could only be of use if the occupants of the graves were thought to have a personal afterlife of sorts. It is so hard for the human mind to imagine complete personal extinction that, even in cultures whose formal eschatologies—views on the final destiny of people and the world itself—discourage a belief in survival, individuals still may be buried with a knife, cup, or a few coins.

What people yearn to find after death reflects the obvious universal trials and delights of their mortal lives. Usually the Other World is a place very like what they know—with specific improvements. Whether the people be modern fundamentlist Christians, ancient Egyptians, or tribal New Guineans, they imagine comfort, safety, and happiness among their loved ones, plenty to eat, time to dance or sing and glorify the high god. They specify that they will not be troubled by pain, disease, grueling work, sorrow. Northern peoples imagine a heaven emphatically light and warm; those from vast, parched lands imagine walled gardens with shade, fountains, birds, flowers. Hunting peoples imagine many animals; farming peoples imagine plentiful servants that do the work or fruits and grains that swell untended from miraculously fertile soil.

People of many cultures believe that not everyone is destined for a happy afterlife. Sometimes, as with the Eskimos and Maori, all are thought to enter a world a bit sadder than this one.[2] Sometimes, all are thought to languish in a gloomy netherworld. More often, a person's happiness after death is thought to be determined by one of these conditions or a combination of them:

- The treatment of his corpse: whether burned, buried, or tossed in the bush; whether accompanied in the grave by such assorted aids as amulets, food, tools, wives, servants.
- The nature of his funeral: appropriate charms, prayers, offerings.
- His earthly rank or power.
- His membership in a cult; observance of rituals and taboos; submission to tattooing, circumcision, or some particular form of mutilation.
- His moral conduct.

The next section of the chapter explores some of these conditions.

THE IMPORTANCE OF A GOOD SEND-OFF

Concerning the first two conditions, the treatment of the body and the nature of the funeral, we of the Western mainstream might be surprised to find how much we share with people of other cultures past and present. People from ancient Mesopotamia to present-day Mexico have held that, without a proper abode and mortuary offerings by relatives, the dead would have to wander homelessly, feeding on offal in gutters or ravines. They might even become resentful and plague the living with disease and misfortune. Although we modern Americans seldom let our imaginations express our discomfort this fully and although we may say that we believe what determines a person's happiness after death is his moral conduct while alive, many of us nonetheless do behave as if the body's treatment and the funeral ritual were also important.

To us, drying the heads of the beloved dead and hanging them from the rafters may seem bizarre, but we too like to think that, if our beloved dead are physically near, we can communicate with them. We may take flowers to the grave, talk to the person within, and affectionately pat the marker stone as we leave. It seems appropriate to us that the United States government spend millions of dollars to bring home the bodies of Americans who have died abroad in wars and disasters. We share others' sense that the unburied or neglected dead are less at ease than those buried in hallowed ground near home where we can visit them. We chuckle at the ancient Egyptians' custom of furnishing graves with roast ducks, parlor games, and headrests, but our mortuaries offer such "Practical Burial Footwear" as street oxfords and the Ko-Zee, a slipper with "soft, cushioned soles and warm, luxurious slipper comfort."[3] We usually bury or burn our dead with their wedding ring, perhaps a Masonic Apron, a teddy bear, a copy of their favorite poem. It may seem quaint that, for the Papuans of northeast New Guinea, souls will drown unless they have been provided with money to pay a tollkeeper or that pre-Islamic Arabs provided the dead with a riding camel. We may read with scientific detachment that some Australian tribes perform rites to separate the immortal spirit from the mortal body so that the spirit can go off to a proper place instead of hovering about the body. But we, also, try to assist the soul in its difficult journey. Sometimes we place a cross or Bible in the hands of the dead. Some Christian funerals ritually help the soul find peace or boost it toward heaven. A modern Catholic may believe that his earthly behavior will determine his condition after death, but, given the choice of having a priest rub a spot of oil on his forehead or not, he would probably choose the oil. And very likely many non-Catholics, if hastily included in this sacrament of the Mother Church during a disaster, would be comforted.

Most of these customs arose from a common belief that the soul's welfare at least partly depends upon that of the body. Even though eschatological beliefs tend to move in time from the concrete to the abstract, many of the earlier customs flourish alongside the latter. Since the living really cannot know what is in store for the dead, the living do whatever occurs to their imaginations to comfort, protect, and appease the dead. Our efforts tend to be fluid and multiple, and we rarely trouble ourselves over incongruities. Our hope is that if one custom is not helpful, another will be.

YOU CAN TAKE IT WITH YOU!

The idea that social rank might affect a person's fate after death runs so counter to the Western sense of justice that we may find the notion not only surprising but revolting. Browsing in any survey of eschatological beliefs among early or tribal peoples, we may wince at how often a person's fate after death is thought to depend upon his earthly rank and power. For instance, the ancient Mesopotamians and others pictured a few eminent people as going to an island of the blessed but most people as residing in their graves or a dusty netherworld. The pre-Hellenic Cretans[4] and pre-Christian Norse apparently held similar views.

Such distinctions prevailed also among more recent peoples. For instance, the Aht of Vancouver Island pictured chiefs and slain warriors as awaking in sunny lands in the sky, the low-ranking dead as finding themselves beneath the earth in shabby houses. Aristocratic Incas went to the mansions of the sun, ordinary people to a place like the earth.[5] Many tribal cultures of Oceania and Africa also made these distinctions based on rank. In Tikopia in the southwestern Pacific, the distinctions in rank among the living held also among the dead.[6] The souls of powerful Solomon Islanders lived longer in the Other World than the souls of ordinary people.[7] Throughout Bantu Africa, souls of the rich remained rich; the poor, poor. Among Congo and Nigerian tribes, since the grandeur of one's funeral determined one's state in the Other World, the rich fared best.[8] According to the North Melanesians in the Gazelle Peninsula of New Britain, the rich spent their time in the Other World smoking, eating, and enjoying other pleasures; the souls of the poor, finding their way barred, would return home to wander, wild and miserable, in the forest. But if someone gave a feast in the poor person's honor and distributed money to the guests, the person's soul could return to the island of the blessed and be welcomed.[9] According to the Gilbert Islanders, only tattooed people, that is, generally people of free birth, would be admitted to the Other World. A monstrous giantess would eat the others.[10] Among the Tongans, only chiefs and their ministers could expect immortality.[11]

In fact, the belief that one's earthly fortune will simply continue in the Other World is deeply rooted not just in early and tribal cultures but in most mythic traditions that assert an afterlife, including our own.[12] The notion lies close at hand, and we shape our visions from what we know. Our little patch of experience tends to seem natural and right. One reason the notion still thrives in sophisticated cultures is that the gods are almost by definition just, and earthly fortune—despite our sincere sympathy for the less fortunate—does suggest to us the gods' favor. The rich find the judgment congenial, and the poor tend to see themselves through the eyes of the rich, as less worthy. A society in which both rich and poor believe themselves justly treated achieves a nice stability; harmony prevails because the poor, accepting their lot as divinely ordained, cooperate in serving the purposes of the rich.

A glance at two traditions officially emphasizing the distinction between earthly rank and personal value reveals the stubborn link between rank and posthumous felicity. In the ancient Egyptian tradition, the moral requirements for a happy afterlife were so rigorous and the posthumous dangers so terrifying that Egyptians sought elaborate magical assurance of success.[13] By the New Kingdom period, even a moral sloven could feel fairly snug tucked into his grave with a wad of papyrus scrolls asserting that he had not committed a certain list of sins. Any prosperous Egyptian could afford these scrolls.

The pattern is familiar to people of the Christian tradition. Jesus said wealth and virtue are so incompatible that a camel could squeeze through the eye of a needle more easily than a rich man could squeeze into heaven. Especially welcoming the poor and the lowly, Jesus promised that in God's kingdom many of the rich would be "last" and many of the poor "first" (Matt. 19:28–30). But during the Middle Ages, the virtues required for salvation were elaborated beyond most people's abilities to succeed, and the horrors of Purgatory and Hell elaborated beyond the imagination's endurance. The Church grew rich and powerful on the hopes of the prosperous to buy their way through the needle's eye. Although the poor could not really afford both sin and heaven, they offered their hens and cabbages along with their prayers.

The sixteenth-century Reformation repudiated the custom of exchanging goods and services for the promise of salvation. Calvin reiterated Paul's view that good works would not unlock heaven's gates: Only

God's grace and Christ's sacrifice could save people from damnation. Yet prosperous Calvinist merchants thought that surely earthly fortune must be a sign, at least, of one's acceptability to God. By the eighteenth century, Calvin's own followers had informally reestablished the association of earthly wealth, power, and rank with eternal felicity—this time without having to pay out a cent. One certainly would not want to thwart God's plans by much meddling with the lot of the poor. If he had meant them to sleep in feather beds, doubtless he would have given them geese.

Thus, one of Jesus' basic teachings was bent to the age-old certainty that one's rank on earth and in the Other World would be the same. Yet the notion of moral excellence as an important value independent of rank is also very old. In the Middle East, it had firmly established itself by the beginning of written history and had flourished alongside the vague notion that rank corresponds to the degree of the gods' approval. To kill one's neighbor and grab his vineyard was never acceptable, even if one were King Ahab and one's neighbor were Naboth the simple farmer. All societies embrace ideas about what is fair and not fair that apply to rich and poor alike. In all, the poor, even against their will, one day see that the rich are not always good, and they begin to ask dangerous questions: Why do the gods favor some people who break the gods' own rules? Why do the gods let good people suffer?

THE SANTA PROBLEM

Jolly old Santa brings lots of toys to good children. Wise (the white beard), generous (the bulging bag and belly), he comes like a kindly Judgment at the annual end of time, bringing children exactly what they deserve. Getting few toys means that Santa has spied out one's naughtiness. In sentimental stories, ragged, heartbroken children, always good, infer that the rich, snobbish children on the hill are their moral superiors, and poor parents stutter out excuses for Santa's neglect. The Santa problem is a child's version of the central problem in all religious ethical systems. Why do the gods, who established, sponsor, and maintain justice, so often let the evil prosper and the righteous suffer?

The Sumerians and then the Hebrews and Greeks struggled with the question. They viewed social rank and personal virtue as separate measures of a person's worth and recognized that he could stand high on one scale and low on the other. But they could offer no very satisfying explanation for the suffering of the righteous.

Earthly society, the Sumerians held, is analogous to divine order. A king might reason that, just as the gods had created people for their servants, he, the representative and favorite of the gods, could use his subjects as he pleased. But clearly that view did not go unchallenged, for Sumeria had both sacred and secular laws protecting the lowly from the high.[14] Just as the god Enlil had established the harmonious processes of nature—day for growing and working; night for rest; planting time and harvest time; birth and decay—he had established earthly society with its orderly ranking of authority—its laws for shielding the weak from the powerful, for protecting and exchanging property, for settling disputes; its customs promoting family harmony and agricultural success. The concept of "sanction"—authoritative permission in both the legal and the theological sense—expresses the Sumerian view that civil laws reflected divine laws and that proper kings would promote social harmony just as the gods promoted cosmic harmony. Because people of high rank represented the gods on earth, those who oppressed the poor marred divine order and surely angered the gods. In short, because the Sumerians distinguished might from right, they necessarily distinguished a person's rank from his moral worth.

Puzzling over why the innocent suffer in a universe defined as just, the Sumerian sages concluded that suffering is the result of humankind's sins and that, appearances perhaps to the contrary, no one is really guiltless. Foreshadowing the story of Job, a Sumerian poem presented a wealthy man, in every observable way wise and righteous, suddenly overwhelmed by misfortune. Instead of cursing his god or railing at cosmic injustice, the man prayed humbly that his god might lift these misfortunes. Moved, the god did so.[15]

Later, the Hebrews and the Greeks sought to save the gods' reputation for justice by blurring the assumed connection between fortune and the gods' favor. Although the Old Testament often had God pointedly heaping power, rank, and wealth upon his favorites and punishing the wicked by taking these things away, the Hebrews necessarily observed that impartial justice did not really prevail in the world. The Book of Job, written about the fourth century B.C., declared that suffering is not always the result of sin, that sometimes God's purposes in sending good or ill fortune lie so far beyond humankind's comprehension that people should simply take up whatever he lays upon them without assuming that he is rewarding or punishing them.

But, in fact, after eloquently exploring the problem of seemingly gratuitous suffering in a supposedly just world, the authors of the Book of Job gave up. Like its Sumerian counterpart of a thousand years before, it canceled its own point by restoring to Job what he had lost and showering him with extra wealth for his pains. Officially, the story said that good fortune is not a sure sign of divine favor, nor bad fortune of divine disfavor. Unofficially, it said, When you-know-who dumps on you, play along, and he'll come around later with the goodie bag. How the innocent farmer Naboth must have chuckled at that one as the city's elders and nobles were having him condemned and stoned to death so that King Ahab could turn Naboth's ancestral vineyard into a kitchen garden for the palace.

The Greeks even more than the Hebrews emphasized that though good fortune often signifies the gods' favor, the two should not be equated. The tragedies (fifth century B.C.) emphasized that at any moment the wheel might turn, flinging the fortunate to the depths. *The Odyssey* (ca. eighth century B.C.) suggested that only the grace of the gods, not intrinsic merit, separated the fortunate from the unfortunate. Homer sponsored the virtue of *aidos* in the fortunate, a special kind of conscience arising from that understanding. *Aidos* promoted not what we call magnanimity or noblesse oblige—attitudes implying condescension —but *respectful* generosity toward the unfortunate. And the sturdy self-respect of several lowly characters in *The Odyssey*, so different from the groveling humility long obligatory in the Christian tradition, suggests that some lowly Greeks of Homer's day actually felt themselves to possess a personal value quite separate from social rank, wealth, or power. *Aidos* was a magnificently humane concept, counseling modesty among the fortunate and self-respect among the unfortunate. But some righteous Greek slave might still wonder why he so rarely got the chance to exercise a bit of *aidos* himself.

A BRILLIANT SOLUTION TO THE SANTA PROBLEM

> *More acceptable is the character of one upright in heart than the ox of the evildoer.*
>
> Egypt, late twenty-second century B.C.[16]

The Egyptians invented the posthumous judgment in the early third millennium B.C., or earlier. One of the most brilliant ethical concepts of all time, the posthumous judgment envisions people awakening either immediately after death or all together at the end of time. Each person, whether in his restored body or as an immaterial spirit, stands before the gods, stripped of scepter, medals, polished boots, plumed hat, also of hoe, grime, and tatters, while divine authorities judge him on his virtue alone. The virtuous get a blissful afterlife; the wicked, extinction or prolonged, horrendous suffering. And unlike Santa, the gods never err. Every person does get exactly what he deserves.

How did the Egyptians come to invent the idea? If it is such a fine solution to the Santa problem, why were others so slow to discover similar solutions? What conditions seem congenial to this invention? On what did the Egyptian expect to be judged? How did he imagine the judgment scene itself? The answers clarify the Christian conception by giving it some points of comparison.

First, the invention could occur only in a society with a well-developed moral and civil code.[17] The concept of *maat*, intimately associated with the invention, embodied the Egyptians' profound respect for social harmony. *Maat* meant the social order and, more broadly, truth, justice, the fundamental law of the cosmos itself. In Egyptian myths, Maat was Re's daughter, guardian of both social and cosmic law. During the stable Old Kingdom period (roughly most of the third millennium B.C.), Egyptians revered the goddess and the well-known social and ethical principles that she sponsored. Moreover, should some clod fail to be awed by the goddess herself, he would soon be awed by the government's power to maintain *maat*.

Second, the invention of the posthumous judgment could occur only among people who believed that the posthumous fates of individuals could differ. Why Egypt's brilliant Eastern neighbors the Sumerians did not invent the concept or borrow it from Egypt lies in Sumerian beliefs uncongenial to the idea. The Sumerians did not surmise that anyone for any cause could achieve a blissful afterlife. Very early, they seized upon an aspect of death that we all recognize, death as the great equalizer. Their cosmogony, or creation theory, probably reinforced this view of death. Since the Sumerians saw their gods less as loving parents than as aristocrats seeking servants, they thought of a person as living only so long as the gods wanted his services and so long as he rendered them with meticulous zeal; and as dying when they found him of no further use.[18]

Two of Egypt's traditional views of the afterlife, unlike the main Sumerian view, early became associated with a final moral judgment. In one view, Osiris' death and resurrection in the Other World enabled his followers to be similarly resurrected. This cult offered immortality to whoever, having arrived before a divine tribunal, could show his innocence of offenses against *maat*. The other view of the afterlife belonged to the royal cult. Asserting pharaohs to be the incarnated sons of Re, this cult envisioned pharaohs as returning, upon death, to their divine father and sailing across the heavens with him each day in his splendid sunboat. Pharaohs did not have to prove their moral fitness, only their divine birth, and they possessed the ritual means to do so. But since the royal priests early incorporated Osirian material into the royal cult, scholars infer a widespread belief, in third-millennium Egypt, that one's earthly conduct, whatever his station, could affect his condition after death.

Two circumstances converged at the end of the Old Kingdom period to encourage the elaboration of a posthumous judgment: a traditional set of funerary customs promoting eternal happiness, and an unwonted social chaos undermining those customs. During the Old Kingdom period, a wealthy person who had maintained *maat* in his life, provided for his material posthumous needs, and had a proper funeral could expect eternal happiness. But those material posthumous needs were considerable, and meeting them was possible only in well-ordered society. As in our own folk tradition, Egyptians conceived of the soul variously as living within the tomb, as hovering in and near it but able to visit earthly haunts, and as living in the Other World. Unlike us, the Egyptians gave those separate notions separate identities. The welfare of the tomb-dwelling soul required not only the body's mummification, the carving of the person's statue, and magical rites to animate the figure, but also regular provisions, such as bread and beer, and the regular performance of protective liturgies and magical formulas conjuring up more food and drink.

In the orderly society of the Old Kingdom, these customs worked. But as royal control began to break down toward the end of the period, offenses against *maat* often went unpunished. The relatives and endowed priests attending a tomb's occupant sometimes scattered. A tomb was sometimes robbed, or the body tossed out and the tomb taken by others. Against such calamities—the ruin of one's eternal future—people began to seek protection from a source more dependable than the civil law: the high god himself. Tomb inscriptions still urged visitors to chant the helpful formulas and admonished would-be robbers, but declarations of the posthumous value of a moral life became more firm and detailed. In other words, hoping to gain better control of their posthumous fate, Egyptians began to emphasize ethical conduct more, the state of the tomb and corpse less.

During the Middle Kingdom period (ca. 2160–1580 B.C.),[19] the once-royal mortuary ritual apparently opened to anyone who could afford it, but it was combined with an impersonal posthumous judgment, a judgment based on morality alone. Scholars know details of this Egyptian judgment from the papyrus scrolls that prosperous Eyptians customarily buried with their dead during the New Kingdom period (ca. 1590–1090 B.C.). These scrolls contained prayers, rituals, charms, practical advice, and protestations of innocence to help the prosperous dead reach the Other World safely. Often abundantly illustrated, these documents show that the judgment had developed two parts, the weighing of the person's heart and a formal declaration of innocence before a divine tribunal. The *Papyrus of Ani* is the best, most complete version known. A picture in it shows Ani and his wife standing off to the left, anxiously awaiting the outcome of the judgment. At the center stands the balance with the two scales hanging from its beam. In one lies the symbol for the heart; in the other, a feather, the symbol of *maat*. The jackal-headed god Anubis adjusts the scales. The ibis-headed god Thoth, the divine scribe, prepares to record the verdict. Nearby crouches Am-mut, a monster, "devourer of the dead," composed of parts from the crocodile, the lion, the hippopotamus. Clearly, Am-mut pounced on those whose hearts were heavy with sins. In most illustrations of the judgment, after a favorable verdict, the deceased is led before the enthroned Osiris himself.

The Declarations of Innocence, the other part of the judgment, contain the dead person's testimony before a divine court. This testimony reveals the high moral ideals of second-millennium Egypt. For instance, the declarations assert that the person has not diminished physical life itself by murdering, encouraging murder, snatching milk from babies, mistreating cattle, or tampering with irrigation water. He has not hurt his fellow men by committing adultery or pederasty, by lying, gossiping, jumping to conclusions, being quarrelsome or greedy, frightening anyone, hurting poor people, defaming a slave to his master. In business transactions, he has not falsified the grain-measure, tinkered with scales, or practiced usury. He has not blasphemed the gods, neglected offerings to them, or taken either their property or the bread intended for the dead. At the end of the list, the person reciting it was to declare that all this was "right and true a million times."[20]

Later, when Greek and Roman settlements brought Christianity to Egypt, the holy family, resurrected savior, and posthumous judgment were already ancient concepts for the Egyptians. Probably the Egyptian Christians—the Copts—introduced the scales into the Christian judgment scene, with Saint Michael presiding instead of Anubis.[21] Other symbols of the Christian judgment—Saint Peter recording one's deeds in his great book, demons awaiting the Judgment's outcome, the saved soul's appearance before God himself—may have been influenced by the Egyptian Judgment, but, after all, their invention by any people with a king, a formal legal system, and a posthumous judgment seems natural enough. The jaws of hell devouring the damned, a favorite medieval theme, might seem a bit more likely to have come directly from the Egyptian scene, until one reflects that a common fate of the condemned in times past was to be thrown into a pit of lions, snakes, or other beasts.

POSTHUMOUS JUDGMENT OUTSIDE EGYPT

Although outside Egypt the idea of a posthumous judgment did not for many centuries achieve anything like the moral and visual richness of the Egyptian version, the idea was fairly widespread by the middle of the first millennium B.C. Both the Hebrews and the Greeks moved toward the notion of personal survival after death and, with that, toward a posthumous judgment.

Hebrew eschatology changed dramatically in the several hundred years between the composition of Genesis and the second century B.C., moving from a dim, insignificant afterlife for all to a future resurrection on this earth and a final judgment.[22] As in Egypt, a social calamity speeded the change by shaking confidence in the established means of posthumous survival. For the early Israelites, significant survival, as explored in Chapter 11, had meant survival of the family or community, and God had rewarded or punished his people in this world. From Abraham on, the Israelites saw Yahweh both as their special god and as the sole lord of the universe who would one day rule over all people. The Israelite prophets explained whatever trouble the group suffered as God's punishment of his people's disloyalty. That explanation worked fairly well until the overthrow of Judah in the mid-sixth century B.C., when most of its people were forced into exile. This calamity severely strained religious faith. People began to ask why all should suffer, innocent as well as guilty. What made the problem more acute for the Hebrews than for the Mesopotamians or the Greeks was that Yahweh had been gradually exalted as the omnipotent, universal, *just* God; the Babylonian exile seemed wholly inconsistent with his supposed power and concern for his people.

The circumstances called for no less than a new eschatology, one that could offer individuals more justice than they found in their earthly lives. Thus, Hebrew theology moved toward a doctrine of universal resurrection and final judgment at the end of time. By the mid-second century B.C., universal resurrection had become part of the Jews' accepted faith.[23] During the same century, the old prophetic belief that God would save the Israelites and punish their enemies evolved into a belief in a final universal judgment. In the following centuries, especially after the fall of the Jewish state in A.D. 70, the belief in a judgment focused more and more sharply on the individual.

In Greece, the very old, profoundly satisfying mystery cults, such as the Eleusinian cult, probably offered initiates a happy, presumably conscious afterlife. Although the benefit derived solely from initiation into the rites, not from personal behavior, the rites may have encouraged later Greek thought on personal survival and posthumous judgment.

In the Homeric picture of Hades, most souls drifted about half-consciously. Of everyone there, only Sisyphus, Tantalus, and Tityus were punished, and they more for having offended Zeus than for having sinned. The writings of Plato, a few centuries later, show that the small but influential Orphic cult had put forth the doctrine of metempsychosis, a series of incarnations in which people were rewarded or punished for forgotten acts in former lives. Orphism's solution to the problem of apparent earthly injustice is similar to that of Buddhism and Hinduism.[24] Sometimes, it was held that part of one's reward or punishment occurred in another world, before rebirth—an idea that promoted vivid fantasies about that world. Even though no clear divine judge or procedure emerged, the works of later Greek and Latin writers influenced by the Orphic doctrine reveal a well-established tradition of posthumous punishment. For instance, in *The Aeneid* (second half of the first century B.C.), Virgil divided the Other World into two parts, a paradise (the Elysian Fields) and a place of punishment (Tartarus), replete with the flames, demons, and dreadful tortures familiar to us as "Christian." Early Christian writers drew heavily upon this tradition.

THE CHRISTIAN COSMOS

Christianity's great appeal has ever been that it offers a happy posthumous survival to all, including the poor, the "peculiar," the outcast, the most degraded of sinners, *all*. In return, it requires repentance of sins, faith in Christ as one's savior from damnation, and service to Christ through charity toward the unfortunate. Most Christians have absorbed their faith through a cluster of symbols dramatizing the significance of each individual and the heart-pounding differences between his two possible fates.

A favorite Christian symbol is the cosmos itself: the ancient "bubble" or tent with the axial pole and, at the center, an added life-symbol—the Nativity, the Cross, the Virgin under a canopy, the tree of life, the fountain of life. The Christian cosmos sharpens the meaning of the old Middle Eastern image. The great shelter glows with God's concentrated purpose. Every single person has been made *safe*, his individual self indestructible. The middle tier, the earth, has become a liberal reformatory; here, through Christ's help, people may restore themselves to their original perfection, enabling them to take up their permanent lives in the upper tier as suitable replacements for the rebellious angels long ago cast out. The Nativity, the Crucifixion, and the other familiar symbols, because they make this restoration possible, become appropriately the middle tier's central events.

The monster-infested chaos that in some ancient conceptions surrounded the cosmic shelter is usually incorporated into the Christian cosmos as the lower tier. People who fail to prepare themselves for heaven do not simply perish; immortal whether they wish to be or not, they will descend to this netherworld to suffer forever. The monsters inhabiting the netherworld are no longer the personified brutal life-force from which organized life has emerged and to which it will return; they are *evil* beings that torture the damned.

Of all the Christian symbols, the Nativity is probably the most loved. Altar triptychs, canvases, crèches in front of churches and city halls, Sunday school tableaux, greeting cards, humble models in wood, clay, cardboard—Christians untiringly evoke this joyful scene. Whether proclaimed by baroque trumpets or floodlights, it quickens the most shriveled heart. Drawing upon the poignant experiences of childbirth and all-giving parental love, the Nativity represents the supreme gift of eternal life offered by the loving Father to whoever strives, however imperfectly, toward him. In the middle of the Nativity scene, before the shed's central pole, lies the Child in the manger. Divine light—variously represented by paint, gold leaf, strips of tin, an electric bulb wrapped in gauze, toothpicks covered with aluminum foil—emanates from the Child's body. The beams of God's Star, directly above, suggest the conelike armature of the sheltering cosmic tent. The longest beam, the axial pole, points directly at the Child. The poor shepherds, the racially assorted Magi, even the gently imbecilic oxen suggest the universality of God's saving love.

Many medieval paintings include three tiers: a life-symbol on the middle tier, heaven above, hell below. Medieval theaters, in which puppets or folk actors dramatized humankind's creation, fall, redemption, and final judgment, also suggested the cosmic image. The original purpose of the medieval puppet theater was to instruct the faithful in why a soul in the Christian cosmos moved up to bliss or down to horror. The puppet theaters of Eastern Europe sometimes had three levels, representing heaven, earth, and hell.[25] *Pageants*—moveable stages that evolved from dramatizations of the Resurrection and Nativity—sometimes displayed at one end a canopied box representing heaven and at the opposite end the jaws of hell from which smoke and "demons" issued. In writing metaphorically that all the world's a stage, Shakespeare was artfully reversing a tradition, one to which the Globe Theatre belonged. With its trapdoor into the "cellarage," its raised, partly concealed platform above the stage, and its star-studded canopy, the Globe represented the cosmos itself.

WASHED IN THE BLOOD OF THE LAMB

Like the Judaism from which it grew, Christianity viewed humankind as prone to sin.[26] Preaching, as did John the Baptist and others of the Jewish apocalyptic tradition, that this world's end and a day of judgment were fast approaching, Jesus exhorted people to *save themselves* by repenting their sins and sinning no more. The phrasing is important, for nothing in Jesus' preaching suggests that Jesus' own death would save anybody. He urged people to abandon whatever might distract them from the coming upheaval—worldly goods and ambitions, even families if need be.

The Gospels and other early Christian writings indicate that Jesus lifted his followers out of their ordinary states into the kind of love and fellowship that we achieve only during great crises, if ever. Together they prepared for a splendor promised after a coming dark time. The evidence suggests that Jesus was a brilliant, electrifying preacher, moved by love and urgency—and that he made a huge mistake in predicting the world's imminent collapse. But he had shown people how to live as members of a close community working toward a glorious common goal. He had exalted them.

The Christian problem ever since Jesus' death has been how to adapt this spirit to a world *not* about to end in catastrophe for the wicked and in glory for the righteous. One solution has been to believe that the big event is still just around the corner. But after a few bestrewings of earthly goods followed by a sunrise vigil—and then noon without one's loaf and night without one's rug—that belief tends to fray. Another solution has been to ignore the apocalyptic context in which Jesus preached (a doubly attractive choice because it denies that Jesus made a mistake) and browbeat oneself and one's fellows for not sustaining the pitch of love and virtue urged by Jesus. A third solution is to wholly reinterpret the nature and meaning of Jesus: He was really a god sent to be sacrificed. Each solution has its familiar place in institutional Christianity.

After their leader's puzzling death, Jesus' followers continued to try to live as he had preached and to await his return and the world's end. But passing time strained faith and made severe practical difficulties for the faithful. It may be possible to live for a few months, even longer, in a state of moral purity and intense loving awareness of one's fellow men, but as anyone who has been swept up in the Christmas spirit knows, most people cannot sustain such exaltation indefinitely. The watchers needed bread and onions. Some died without having seen the Second Coming. If Christianity was not to fail, it needed a theology that could help people to live with heightened compassion and righteousness, to serve the Christian community, but still to marry, to feed and clothe their children, to go quietly to their graves without having witnessed the Return. Their faith needed also a whole system of ritual purifications; then, when in the long course of their lives they inevitably fell into sin, they could cleanse themselves and rejoin the struggle for righteousness without fearing that even truly repented sins would drag them into hell.

The Church that emerged in the early second century saw Christ as saving the faithful from damnation *through his own death.* That startling view arose from the interpretation of Jesus espoused by Paul, an interpretation quite different from that of the original community of his followers in Jerusalem. In Paul's view, some sin committed by the earliest people and the continual sinning of subsequent generations had so spiritually damaged all humankind that a person's own moral efforts could not save him from hell. Only by sending a divine being into the world as the man Jesus could God rescue us. Paul saw Christ's death not as a perplexing interruption of Christ's messianic career but as the most significant part of his life, a divinely planned event by which Christ vicariously "paid" for our sins.

For Paul, the ceremony of baptism meant more than being cleansed or born again into the Christian community. In baptism, he wrote in his *Epistle to the Romans*, a person's sinful self is ritually crucified with Christ, united with him in death, burial, and resurrection into eternal life.[27]

Paul's conception of survival after death drew upon the life-enhancing cults widespread in the Middle East. It resembles, for instance, that of the Osirian cult, in which the devotee achieved eternal life by being "assimilated" into the resurrected Osiris. Egyptian tomb paintings of the deceased bear the green face, ceremonial staff, and flail of Osiris himself, and the inscriptions hyphenate the person's name with that of Osiris. But the Christian did not have to wait until physical death for his eternal "Christ-life" to begin.

When the Romans overthrew the Jewish state in A.D. 70, the Mother Church in Jerusalem fell. The Pauline version of Christianity, which had spread far into Gentile lands, became the dominant form. Although Paul naturally supposed that sincere Christians would emulate Christ by doing good works, he stressed that good works had no power to save, that only faith in Christ as their Savior could win people salvation. Gradually a view arose of Christ not as the Judge on a fast-approaching judgment day but as God's Son dwelling in heaven, acting continuously as a loving intercessor for sinners before God.

The Church did not see itself "as the company of the Elect, awaiting reward; rather it had come to see itself as a divinely founded institution having the pastoral care of the faithful from their birth or baptism on to their death." The whole elaborate structure that we know as the medieval Church—its hierarchy, its sacraments, its complex system of penance and absolution—grew to offer spiritual support not only to the spiritually inclined or to those capable of an intense short-term spiritual commitment but to ordinary people living in a chaotic age.[28] In these new circumstances, the Church reaffirmed the partial efficacy of good works, especially as officially prescribed for atonement of confessed sins, but Christ remained and still remains the Lamb whose holy blood cleanses the repentant sinner.

THE CHRISTIAN SENSE OF GUILT

In the reshaping of Jesus' thrilling message to a world that had not ended after all, something very peculiar happened to that message. Christianity does promise a blissful afterlife to those who are free of sin and does offer lovingly to wash away people's sins in the blood of the Lamb. But the underside of this offer has been an insistence, unique among major religions, on universal depravity. The message is that all people urgently need saving from their sins and that only Christianity can do the job. Traditionally, attaining a happy survival has been the Christian's main concern, his sins the great impediment. Many innocuous people have lived in terror that they would spend eternity in hell suffering for their sins instead of in heaven among the blessed. Two images of man dominate Christian art and rhetoric: the helpless suppliant for mercy and the industrious climber toward salvation. Strikingly, both bend under a heavy load of guilt.

Christians certainly have no monopoly on the sense of guilt. Guilt and its cousin shame are the common property of humankind. Indeed, shame—the sense of having alienated someone whose approval one needs—is not even confined to people; pet dogs and cats clearly demonstrate this painful emotion. Whatever creatures yearn for approval and affection are subject to shame, for all such creatures of course fear disapproval and rejection. And the sense of guilt is a kind of internalized, sophisticated shame, shame before the judge within. The most powerful socializing agents, from parents to states to religions, properly use these deep needs to render people tractable. But Christianity has used the sense of guilt in an often corrosive way: It promised the sinless a glorious posthumous survival; declared all humankind by its own efforts ineligible; threatened a horrible punishment of sinners; and then offered a miraculous possible way out of the nightmare—Christ's loving absorption of others' sins.

Each part of this harrowing drama found expression in a popular symbol or tableau painted, sculpted, eloquently described in churches throughout the Christian world: heaven, hell, the Fall, the Crucifixion, the Resurrection. Because these symbols have shaped people's lives for many centuries, they are worth our attention.

Visions of heaven have been as happy as the human imagination could make them, given the awkward need to express an unknown, nonmaterial bliss, often for an unsophisticated audience. Christian visions of heaven range from gentlefolk strolling in an enclosed garden, to a city of pearly gates and golden streets; from blessed music-makers, whether banked choirs or solitary harp-pluckers on fluffy clouds, to great family reunions. In many paintings the blessed gather in a garden around some holy life-symbol, such as Christ or a fountain representing at once the fountain of life and the baptismal font. Sophisticates have understood these scenes as symbols of exquisite, intangible delight; and many people living in brutish misery have surely found the pictorial harmony comforting and have trusted that, if ever they attain such a state, their souls will become exalted enough to appreciate it.

But could one attain heaven? Something called original sin, a legacy bequeathed to us by Adam and Eve, had, according to the Church, rendered us all *by nature* too sinful to be eligible for heaven. Significantly, the Fall has inspired far more art than has heaven, including some of the most poignant scenes in Christian culture. The scene is heavy with guilt and dramatic irony. Often, while the fresh young couple flank the tree of life, smiling out at the viewer, the serpent slithers above them, biding his time. In another version, he has already caught the woman's eye. Eve reaches for the fruit or, having eaten it, offers it to Adam. In still another version, the two prone figures, sickeningly like snakes, undulate toward the fruit. In the next scene, the so recently radiant couple cringe, turning their eyes from each other, and try to hide. And in the next, an angel shoos the sinners from the garden. Their dim, shrunken forms bowed by shame, express the new relationship between people and God. Gazing, we shudder, children again, fallen from grace, sinking into the swamp of guilt and shame, drowning in the terror of abandonment.

The story of the Fall comes of course from Jewish tradition, and this tradition passed to Christianity the idea that people are by nature prone to sin. But to say that we are by nature prone to sin is in a sense only a mournful way of expressing something true by definition. Because the purpose of ethical standards is to improve conduct on whatever scale a society has invented, the standards are usually more austere than actual conduct. If a society invents difficult standards for itself, most of its members will fail to meet them. Should changing conditions happen to make the established standards easy to meet, raising the standards regains for its members the painful but customary sense of human shortcomings. Westerners play a dangerous game: We spur ourselves toward an ever higher moral performance by setting very high standards, then wound ourselves and others with guilt and shame when we fail to meet those standards.

The Christian concept of original sin expresses the tautology even more lugubriously than does the Jewish view of human nature. Original sin, a kind of moral venom that infected Adam and Eve as a result of their fall, has, according to Pauline doctrine, transmitted itself undiluted from them to all their descendants. However strenuous, however seemingly successful our efforts to lead virtuous lives, we fail to meet God's requirements for salvation because original sin infects each infant at the moment of conception.

Then, lest the traditional Christian decline to play a game rigged against him, tableaux of the Last Judgment and of hell afforded numerous peeks at the destiny suitable to one of his iniquity. A large majestic Christ would descend on the judgment day, the earth would crack and yield up its dead, and Christ would instantly turn over the hordes of deep-dyed sinners to demons. The demons would goad them into hell's jaws, as sharp-toothed as those of the Egyptian monster Am-mut, but much larger, able to gulp scores of sinners at once. In pictures, the jaws of hell often gape below the judgment panel, the sinners tumbling in helter-skelter, offal tossed into a hole.

Numerous panoramic visions of hell, in art and sermons, show what happens next. Demons, demonstrating the meaning of the phrase "working like demons," bustle about, cheerily engrossed in their tasks: flaying people, boiling them in oil, roasting them on spits. Every moment of the agony, say the sermons, is compounded a thousand, thousand times beyond earthly understanding. Brains bubble in their pans; rats and worms gnaw tender parts; monster-dogs rend limbs; monster-eels tunnel through decaying orifices, playing peekaboo with their own tails. All the while, the damned are perfectly conscious and, in addition to the physical horrors, suffer incomprehensibly vast spiritual agonies of abandonment, grief, remorse.

While such scenes are by no means exclusively Christian, traditional Christian art and rhetoric have laid particular stress on them. Today, although many branches of Christianity have put aside the horrors of hell as unsuited to a religion of love and forgiveness, some Catholics and fundamentalists continue to teach them. The message is that sin is pervasive, its result likely to be a lengthy experience of the utmost horror.

Theologically, of course, a doctrine of *irremediable* insufficiency will not work. The Nativity is a symbol of God's miraculous cure for human imperfections. But a wrenching sadness underlies even this happy scene: This Child so tender, so innocent, was born to bear the punishment that all we sinners should rightfully suffer. God sent this baby as a sacrifice, to hang on the Cross and suffer *in our stead*. To require such an atonement as this, our guilt must be great indeed.

To many Christians, expressions of divine love convey a similar message. The Virgin, that Mother radiating universal love, and the Egyptian Isis, that other gracious, loving mother, differ sharply in symbolic meaning. Isis served all living people by helping to restore the harmony, justice, and prosperity that Osiris had established; she helped save the dead by reviving Osiris so that the dead could gain life from him in the Other World. Her great love and strength, like the Virgin's, enhanced life but did not, like the Virgin's, save anyone from his just punishment. The Virgin's love saves us first by having borne and nourished the Savior and then, especially in later tradition, by urging forgiveness and mercy, not justice, for all repentant sinners. Like the infant Christ, she conveys not our value but our intrinsic, humanly irremediable guilt, our inadequacy to save ourselves.

The most important event in the whole drama of Christianity is Christ's absorption of our sins. Tableaux of this event underscore Christ's suffering for us, binding us to him in a bloody tangle of guilt, sorrow, shame, wrenching love and gratitude. In ten thousand representations the horror builds, his suffering like nails pounded into our flesh. The crown of thorns is jammed onto his head, raking his flesh; as he drags his own cross through the street, he is whipped, kicked, spat upon. The most painful symbol of Christ's love and our blame, our insufficiency, is the Savior nailed upon the Cross. Christ's bloody, twisted body, over the centuries sagging in ever more painful and vulnerable postures, must baffle many non-Christians as an image of peculiar horror. This image smites viewers from nave, plaza, roadside shrine, master's canvas, Sunday school wall, kitchen, and bedroom. *All for us. Instead of us.*

Some people free themselves from the horror by turning resentfully away. ("I never asked anyone to do that for me!") Others stop seeing. But the image has not lost its power. It continues to bring the tenderhearted to their knees to weep out their guilt, their sorrow for their imperfections, their pledges of virtue and devotion. Whether Westerners be Catholics responding to the image of the crucified Christ or Protestants responding to the image of the plain cross, the response is the same: Jesus died for us. How he loved us! I must try harder to be worthy of that love. And under that response: My sins made this awful thing necessary; *we killed Jesus.* Many, suffering horribly for commonplace imperfections, have thrown themselves before Christ in an agony of helpless self-hatred. That Jesus died a long time ago does not, in their minds, mitigate their own, our, blame; for our present wickedness, the wickedness of all people rolling on to time's last tick, will continue to make necessary that writhing on the Cross. In some sense, Christ still hangs there because we still sin, and each day of our lives our new sins pound new nails into his flesh. "Every word of sin is a wound in His tender side. Every sinful act is a thorn piercing His head. Every impure thought, deliberately yielded to, is a keen lance transfixing that sacred and loving heart." [29]

A civilization that imbues its members with so strong a sense of guilt must, in some, produce frenzied efforts to shake it off. People may repudiate what makes them feel guilty and yet not be able to free themselves from the feeling. (Flannery O'Connor's novel *Wise Blood* makes the point painfully convincing.) Since it seems elementally wicked to deny what has been from one's most impressionable years one's "Savior," some people may turn their anger in upon themselves, praying abjectly for forgiveness, cursing themselves, so tightening the screws on their impulses to rebel that the major effort of their lives becomes controlling the seething monster within. ("I don't know why I do it. I seem to have a devil in me!") Or upon contemplating the writhing Savior and finding the guilt intolerable, they may discover that the ones "really" responsible for his suffering are not ordinary Christian sinners like themselves but the Jews, the Infidels, the Russians, the blacks, the young. The devil inside moves out, into whoever distinctly unlike themselves crosses their path, and whacking the devil in other people is in every way more satisfying than whacking him in oneself.

Indisputably, the religion that set out to wash away our sins in the blood of the Lamb has comforted and improved large numbers of people, but it has drenched many in a sense of guilt, and "Christian" wrath has battered many "devils." A sense of insufficiency is neither good for the person it troubles nor for his neighbor.

But the Pauline image of man the helpless sinner, as suggested earlier, did not push out the other dominant Christian image of man the industrious climber toward salvation. The next section shows how that conception has evolved.

CLIMBING JACOB'S LADDER

> *We are climbing Jacob's ladder,*
> *Soldiers of the Cross. . . .*

Every rung goes higher, higher,
Soldiers of the Cross. . . .
Sinner, do you love your Jesus?
Soldiers of the Cross. . . .
If you love Him, why not serve Him?
Soldiers of the Cross. . . .

A hymn

Christianity has never seen humankind only as piteous and insufficient. Everything that God made is good, and even fallen humankind is part of God's creation. Furthermore, Christianity has always held that each person is going to live with himself—his unique, conscious self—forever, and that his own choices will shape his happiness for all time. This phase of Christianity sees the individual as supremely important and effective. The vision drew on two powerful pre-Christian forces in Western thought: Greek humanism and the Judaism of the last centuries before Christ. The Greeks saw people not as servants or glorifiers of the gods but as beings intrinsically valuable. In behaving with dignity, courage, or generosity, the Greeks held, a person honored not the gods but himself and his humanity. The notion that people *could* achieve a godlike excellence of mind and body invited them to reach for excellence.

Meanwhile, Judaism had affirmed not only a personal survival after death but affirmed also the individual's profound effect on the quality of that survival. One could secure one's own eternal felicity by following religious laws and easing others' earthly woes.

The Greek and the later Judaic traditions converged in a Christian view of the individual as valuable and efficacious. Over the centuries, the doctrine of salvation through one's own efforts has had a far stronger attraction than Paul's and, later, Calvin's denial of the doctrine. The doctrine is so deeply embedded in our culture that in a variety of ways it affects the religious and nonreligious alike. Most important, it has engendered the myth of the Superself.

According to this myth, everyone, even the poor, the untalented, the seemingly helpless, can control his final fate. The value of that belief is so great as to be incalculable. Not only does it reconcile us to unavoidable troubles; it predisposes us to good cheer, self-reliance, and persistence in the face of adversity. Countless people, sure that virtue will be rewarded and vice punished in an afterlife, have passed through the world confident that their griefs are not heartbreaking by-products of impersonal processes but have been ordained by a loving God for their improvement;

that God will wash all griefs away in the afterlife; and that a person's efforts to bend the world a bit toward his vision of heaven will open heaven to him. These beliefs have made people's lives rich and meaningful to them and often beneficent to their neighbors.

Furthermore, the Superself myth, in assigning the individual great potential worth, fosters twin institutions—representative government and public education—that do extend personal power. Representative government demands educated citizens. Although public education cannot develop the best in every person, it does give large numbers of people the means to participate in their society, and it does awaken in some the desire to develop themselves. Representative government and the free ventilation of ideas provide an orderly way to improve ideas and to promote the social stability needed for elaborate projects. To be sure, our raising of the individual to such heights results in much loud honking by the fatuous, the self-indulgent, the pretentious—but also for many people, lives of otherwise impossible fullness; and for a few, lives that bestow on the rest of us the gifts of untrammeled genius.

All great myths—those that help people make good lives—exact a price. Our habit of investing people with power that they often do not really command confuses us. The United States contains not one Superman disguised as Clark Kent but many Clark Kents disguised as Superman. Americans say, "You can do anything you really want to" and "If you really try, you'll succeed." Faithfully we buy books explaining how to be happy, popular, rich, beautiful, slim without exercising more or eating less; how to speak fluent German in two weeks; how to raise our children and our I.Q.s. Our sense of what is possible has an extraordinary amplitude. We tend to believe not only that effort is good for its own sake but that effort or even confidence alone ensures success. We are all going to be the best, all dance on the pinhead.

When we fail to achieve what we have expected, we may preserve our sense of efficacy by explaining that we did not try hard enough, and then go off to find something we are better at. No harm done. But too often, when a person does not meet unrealistic expectations, he and others conclude that he is lazy, burdening him with a sense of guilt in a culture that takes moral failure very seriously. When we know full well that he is trying, yet failing, we are so discomfited that we often pretend he is succeeding. The American educational system often awards the mediocre and the outstanding alike, fostering mediocrity. ("Because psychology is such a tough graduate program to get into, I don't jeopardize

the chances of my psych majors by giving any of them less than an A.")
In such a muddled atmosphere, when we do clearly fail, we tend to
collapse in helpless despair.

Another cost of the Superself myth is that it encourages rashness. In
rueful moods, we characterize Western civilization of the Protestant era
as Faustian, after the legendary scholar so restless for universal knowledge
and technical mastery that he paid for a twenty-year spree with eternal
damnation. During that spree, for the adolescent joy of doing what he
could do, Faust changed the Rhine's course, summoned Helen's spirit
from the dead, played crude magical jokes on the Pope, and looped the
loop among the planets. Sometimes in a similar exercise of power and
greed, we broadcast deadly chemicals intended to take the ping out of
our gasoline, the bugs off our broccoli. We more readily turn our minds
to producing atomic energy than to disposing of its deadly wastes. Making
something happen now is more to our taste than pondering its effect
twenty or two hundred years from now. Critics warn that our heedlessness may doom all life.

Obviously, we must learn to behave more responsibly than has been
our custom, but we might also give our characteristic zest its due. Most
members of "contemplative" Eastern societies are really too poor, sick
and uneducated to know and enjoy the benefits of contemplation. These
millions have no choice but to shuffle resignedly from day to day, their
greatest hope not a better life but a final release from life. To foster the
contemplative response may be best where climate, soil, and debilating
diseases relentlessly cancel human effort; in our luckier circumstances,
however, the experimental habit of mind still seems, for all its risks,
preferable.

Perhaps not Faust, after all, but Hamlet is the figure who says most
to us about ourselves. Both the Faust and the Hamlet in us stem from
the Superself myth, but the latter may be the more dangerous precisely
because it has undermined our zest. Although we have always held the
individual responsible for his own fate, he became more emphatically so
with the loosening of Church authority in the Renaissance. Whereas the
clergy, sacraments, and saints of the medieval Church had been one's
conduits to God, with the Reformation each Protestant became in effect
his own conduit, listening for God within himself. Protestants held that
God had created each person sufficient, through reading and reflecting
on the Bible, to understand and heed God's will.

In secular thought, too, people grew more independent, more intensely aware of the private world within their own skulls—and more preoccupied with the implications of that privacy. The brooding Hamlet, so tortured by the burden of solitary introspection, catches the imagination again and again, not only in English-speaking countries but throughout the Western world. Clever, charming, analytical though he be, Hamlet is insufficient because he cannot move outside himself. He lacks both robust convictions and the ability to love wholeheartedly anyone but himself. There he stands, unsupported, unsupporting.

Many Western minds, whether Catholic or Protestant, religious or secular, large or small, have, like Hamlet's, trembled at their own solitude, at the burden of living alone in that vast inner space. Some have thought of God as peering from afar, while they heave themselves seal-like over the sharp rocks, never knowing whether their absurd, gelatinous selves will finally *do* or will be thrust into hell's fire. Gerard Manley Hopkins's cry is the cry of many: "O the mind, mind has mountains; cliffs of fall / Frightful, sheer, no-man-fathomed" ("No Worst, There Is None"). But many, like Camus, suspect worse, that even the god is a mirage, and the solitary journey not a test but the sum and meaning of it all.

Despite the Neoclassical interruption of the late seventeenth and the eighteenth centuries—with its reassertion of the communal, the shared, the generic—our awareness of each person's singularity has on the whole deepened since the Renaissance. In fact, the sense of solitude had reaffirmed itself even more strongly by the end of the eighteenth century with the commonplace speculation that perhaps *only* one's self existed, that other people and all the moiling world were mere dreams invented by one's mind. The individual had become in speculation not just his own Pope, his own world, but his own crack-brained god, living quite alone with his disordered dreams, not the controller yet the sole source of all.

Today, many of a less philosophical bent can see well enough that the world exists. They just cannot get very excited about it. Generations before them went climbing Jacob's ladder, higher, higher, ever higher, but not they. Climbing is tough work, and they suspect they know what they would find up there. Squinting in the thin air, one would see no God, no heaven—only the swaying ladder and one's own spent self clinging to it in otherwise vacant space. The literature of the last two centuries is full of cosmic abandonments, betrayals, expressions of shock and dismay. Characters helplessly witness the collapse of their meaningful world. They cry out that, contrary to John Donne's assertion, *every* man is an island. A striking number of characters either think of themselves as wandering alone in the snow or actually perish that way.[30]

Although our singularity has never seemed more true than it does today, the late twentieth century has domesticated it. No big deal. Some shrug, work enough to keep the paychecks coming, slip through their lives by watching TV, eating out, taking up and putting down a series of attitudes, projects, lovers, none very disturbing for long. Yet a pervasive unease suggests that, without knowing how, people want to do something significant. Even the extreme narcissism so evident in the past decade tends to express itself in efforts to connect, if temporarily, with other people.[31] These efforts range from casual copulations to encounter sessions in which the nude participants loll in hot tubs, touching toes, or shut themselves up together for a weekend to lay before one another, in stupefying detail, the contents of their minds.

To be sure, each person is irrevocably singular. He cannot even share his child's earache, only remember his own. Each person does wander through his shadowy, puzzling life alone, often hungering for the impossible contact, the revelation. All are unhoused, vulnerable. Many twentieth-century people are existentialists—whether or not they have heard the word—spinning a kind of meaning as they go along, out of their personal experience. Each one makes his way through the void of time by the light of his singular consciousness, and waves to the other people in the dim light of their collective glimmers.

But that light is real and precious. We may agree with the Hindu philosopher that one person's effort is unlikely to improve the world for long. We may suspect that the "soul" dies with the body. We may believe that the earth, the universe itself, is dying. But the ancient Egyptian god Re thought it worthwhile to battle Apep every single night in order to make one day more, and the Egyptians rejoiced for that one day. To believe in the eternal life of individual souls or in the permanence of one's acts is not the only path to a meaningful life on this earth. Perhaps few people today see themselves as ever standing before the Great Judge and perhaps most muddle through the anomie of our age, but they sometimes come upon a truth that their forebears knew: Individuals become significant and effective as they spend themselves for something larger than themselves. The human community is still there.

STAR WARS AND JUDEO-CHRISTIAN ESCHATOLOGY

Judeo-Christian eschatology expresses what were long our dearest hopes about human life. Since that myth is the fullest, most powerful expression of those hopes, it surely influences many Western stories in ways both obvious and subtle. This chapter's final section shows how the myth shaped the popular movie *Star Wars* and then suggests how attitudes exemplified by that movie affect people whether or not they still believe in the myth.

When the movie opens, young Luke Skywalker is living on a remote farm with his plain-minded aunt and uncle, his inauspicious beginnings like those of many traditional folk heroes, including Jesus working in his foster father's village stall. Luke's first name suggests luck, light, and Saint Luke; his last, the great Waterwalker and risen Skywalker Himself. Luke's blond hair haloes an innocent, blue-eyed face, a Sunday school portrait of purity.

Though polite and industrious, Luke finds himself oddly restless. Suddenly, like a heavenly father, Ben (Obi-Wan) Kenobi enters Luke's life. Ben Kenobi is a mysterious godlike personage, who, though thought to have been dead for years, reappears when much needed. Through his influence, Luke, still dressed in his simple white farming tunic, is catapulted into a hero's role. Luckily, Luke has made himself a crack pilot by tinkering with jalopy spaceships, as boys will do of an evening when the farm chores are finished. Evil forces have conquered the Empire, tyrannizing over all the worlds of the galaxy, and Princess Leia needs a select company of great pilots willing to fly to almost sure death in order to free the galaxy. Luke answers the call.

The movie's arch-villain, tall, black-carapaced Lord Vader, sweeps across the screen like Lucifer, once the highest ranking angel but now evil incarnate. Lord Vader's eyes are hooded, his mouth an ugly black grid, his hands gloved in shiny black. The usually expressive parts of a person's body that we scan in trying to begin a relationship with him are covered. Lord Vader's appearance and the low angle from which he is photographed suggest a large, elegantly cruel machine—perhaps a Lincoln Continental—bearing down upon a small victim. His first name, Darth, suggests dearth and death's dark dart. His last name suggests father (the traditional evil father-substitute that the young hero must fight) and invader. As Satan invaded the garden, Lord Vader has invaded the Empire.

When Darth Vader enters a room, the room itself seems to wheeze, a curiously horrible detail. One imagines that his shriveled soul, hunched within the shiny carapace and strangling on his own toxin, is drawing upon every life in the closed space. The effect is rather like that of Satan got up as an elegant gentleman but with one shocking anomaly, the goatish hooves or bull's tail, or like Dracula with his long canines, but worse. In all three cases, the symbol indicates both monstrous power and weakness. Goats and bulls are virile, but they are less than man; bats can fly and, in folklore, have sharp teeth whose bite turns people into the walking dead, but God's wholesome sunlight blinds them.

Lord Vader operates from the space station Death Star, a sterile steel globe resembling a modern hell. Monstrous whackers, zappers, and chompers lurk on scaffolds and in dimly lit corridors. A trapdoor drops good guys into a slime-filled tank. If its tentacled beast should fail to crush them, walls that move like a steel sandwich turn them into pressed meat.

Like the traditional hero, Luke journeys to death's realm. His face, blank as a grape, and his "aw, gee" dialogue point up his innocence of thought or experience. Although he would hardly seem a match for all this concentrated evil, the viewer need not despair. Because uncluttered, Luke's head has plenty of room for the Force (supernatural power), which the disembodied voice of Ben Kenobi pumps into it at desperate moments. The Force works itself in Luke not through knowledge or chains of reason, but through bursts of intuition. Filling Luke's head at the crucial instant, it causes him to shut down the banks of sophisticated computers in his spaceship and simply make a split-second guess when to release the bomb that pulverizes the Death Star.

Armageddon over, the movie's Last Judgment takes place in the huge temple of a remote jungle-paradise. Luke and Han Solo, a mercenary loner turned good guy (the disreputable hero so attractive to Americans), walk a long carpet through a throng of noble admirers to the dais of the white-robed Princess Leia. She decorates the two heroes with medals and chaste kisses, while the crowd cheers.

The *Star Wars* plot follows the widespread pattern of the hero struggling against great odds to save something life-enhancing by battling the villain. It echoes specific details of our eschatological myth—the images of Christ and Satan, probably the images of the final judgment, hell, and paradise. But our tradition shaped the story also in two less obvious ways, its treatment of moral efficacy and of time.

Because everywhere the young person's task is to achieve mastery and because, whatever our ages, we often identify his success with *human* success, a youth makes a very attractive hero. Furthermore, pitting a youth against an older, shrewder villain heightens the audience's sympathetic involvement. We all want assurance that the world is just, and assigning the winning role to an inexperienced youth suggests to every boy facing the formidable old world that, with courage and perseverance, he will suffice. But our own tradition goes further: The Judeo-Christian sense of character equates innocence with goodness, knowledge with evil. Jesus and, before him, Adam and Eve are the models.

In the story of Jesus, stepping out of the carpenter's stall to make our salvation possible, efficacy was compatible with innocence because his power came not from worldly experience but straight from God. In the everyday world, however, innocence is perilous to both the innocent person and whomever else his untried judgment happens to affect; also, except in the obtuse, innocence is mercifully brief. Important acts have both good and bad results, and exercising responsibility means living with inevitable guilt, choosing among *kinds* of guilt. Our popular stories, in echoing our central myth, often avoid coming to terms with these facts. "Wholesome" stories such as *Star Wars* circumvent facts in several ways, slightly reshaping elements of the traditional heroic life-pattern: by concentrating on young people; by giving the young hero a special skill or technical knowledge to make his survival plausible and to counterbalance his social blandness (the "Lindbergh" hero); and by assigning the untainted hero a superhuman guide, for instance, God himself, the angels, a kindly Providence, or, as in *Star Wars*, the Force. All stand for the divine wisdom that protects and rewards the youth for that purity.

The magical potency of innocence, for Americans, shows up in more than popular fiction. For at least a century, during every national disgrace, journalists have declared that at last we have lost our innocence, come of age, and so on. For as long as possible, we pause on the edge of conscious guilt, ignoring the buzz of critics and hugging our innocent dream-self. Then, in one hasty gesture, we prop that dream-self on a shiny leaf, plunge shuddering into the swamp, jump out, shake ourselves off, and, blank-eyed as ever, pick up our dolly again. Because, in American myth, our innocence is the source of our power and of the continued protection of Providence, we continue to insist on that innocence.

Our refusal to assimilate guilt hampers our moral integration. When we call in sick so that we can go to a terrific party, we say, "Well, a person owes himself a day off now and then." When American soldiers blew up a Vietnamese village, they "liberated" it. When a commissioner appointed to protect coastal land is found to have accepted large sums of money from developers and subsequently to have voted in their favor, he explains that if he had for a moment considered the money bribes rather than the gifts of friends, he would not have touched it. A recent President, discovered in a web of lies, betrayal of his political supporters, manipulation of governmental agencies, and falsification of evidence, explained that his actions had been appropriate because he had not undertaken them in a dishonest spirit.

Star Wars exemplifies both the great Western concern with good and evil and the American sense that efficacy flows less from experience than from innocence. The movie also exemplifies the Western sense of time. For the Eastern philosopher, time is an endless round, earthly life essentially unchanging, meaningless except as the soul's training field. For the Westerner, on the other hand, history is a great moral struggle occurring only once, culminating in the permanent establishment of good. As mentioned earlier, the tendency to isolate a segment of a natural cycle that begins with a struggle and ends with a harmonious resolution is widespread, not unique to cultures whose religions posit a final judgment and triumph of good. But Western eschatology reinforces the tendency.

Ordinary Westerners today, like most people who have recorded their views, see justice as a cosmic law, not a human invention. Not only in such movies as *Star Wars* but in our fantasies about our own lives, we insist that justice prevail. Even if it is not prevailing now, our traditional eschatology encourages a vague assumption, whatever our religious views, that fitting rewards and punishments will be doled out "at the end." Today, however, as our faith in an afterlife recedes, we are anxious for those deeply engrained expectations to fulfill themselves on earth. The wish collides with a harsh fact: Old age usually brings not triumph but loss, loneliness, confusion. Sometimes, instead of facing that fact, we try to deny it with such terms as the "golden years." Many of us, especially when young, half-expect, against all evidence, that a normal, proper life here on this earth moves toward some splendid reward or revelation analogous to seeing the face of God and being blessed by him. Then, during our strong, prospering middle years, a suspicion sharpens: "Is this all?" Panic-stricken, we start grabbing more goodies in an attempt to somehow swell our lives. It is possible, as the poet Yeats advised, to integrate the knowledge of approaching death into a good life:

No longer in Lethean foliage caught
Begin the preparation for your death
And from the fortieth winter by that thought
Test every work of intellect or faith,
And everything that your own hands have wrought,
And call those works extravagance of breath
That are not suited for such men as come
Proud, open-eyed and laughing to the tomb.[32]

But we most often try to deny old age and death until they accost us in the street.

To lose faith in one's eschatological myth while clinging to the hopes it engenders makes one appallingly vulnerable to unhappiness in middle and old age. But the dangers go beyond the personal. Vaguely moving our expectations of a cleansing cataclysm and subsequent perfect world from a mythic future into ordinary earth-time has produced such notions as that World War I would be the last war, the war that, once and for all, would make the world safe for democracy; and that, after World War II, some glorious thing called the postwar world would miraculously appear. Sunday supplements featured this world: elegant, elevated freeway cloverleafs with streamlined cars whizzing along them and, below, on miles of rolling sward, clusters of young, shapely people dressed in Flash Gordon suits, as if at a very spacious garden party. To the unsophisticated mind, the tinted pictures suggested that the war itself would produce this strange green peace.

A more sinister result of moving our myth into earth-time is a sharpened periodic hankering for war, for simply blowing up civilization's intractable problems and starting fresh. Ironically, the steady, wearing fear of atomic war led to a release of tensions in the "Do it!" fantasy: pressing the button to bring on universal atomic war. In the 1950s, books and movies ran to the literal horrors of the catastrophe itself. Later, they moved to the eerie blankness of the world after the catastrophe, and then to black humor: "So what if the world blows up? This season's TV isn't worth watching anyway." More recently, rampant inflation, oil shortages, and other large, frightening problems wear our patience. ("Why all this pussyfooting talk, talk, talk? I say go in there and blast the hell out of the bastards!") Meanwhile, the loss of shared values dismays us—employees who feel no obligation to their jobs, citizens who do not vote, strangers who routinely victimize the unwary, newspapers that publish instructions for making nuclear weapons; above all, families that are little more than temporary consuming units. The family has always been the primary teacher of affection, self-esteem, empathy, the civilizing values. Not just in the underclass but in all classes, many families are no longer serving this function.

We do not know how to solve these problems. Our ready-made vision of cataclysm followed by joyful perfection leaps to mind. The cataclysm in *Star Wars* is just right: exhilarating combat involving great heroes, minimal suffering of innocent bystanders, and glorious success. We would do well to remember that even God, in the flood myth, discovered that no dramatic solutions exist.

WHAT NEXT?

All forms of conquering death, of extending life beyond what is given to us individually on this earth, are ways of joining our dying selves to something that continues. In emphasizing procreation and fertility, we focus on the energy that the dying transfer to the living. In emphasizing the continuance of our group, we focus on that group's physical and spiritual survival on this earth. In emphasizing personal survival after death, we focus on the individual soul revived by divine miracle either in another world or upon this earth at time's end.

For complex reasons, many people today do not find these kinds of posthumous survival convincing. We see as many reasons for not having children as for having them. Families, neighborhoods, whole cities disintegrate around us. We doubt a personal resurrection. Nor have other kinds of posthumous survival sparked much interest. Most Westerners who seek comfort in the Eastern idea of reincarnation make of it a trivialized Western fantasy; they tend to chat coyly about their dimly remembered lives as Roman dignitaries or Elizabethan courtiers. In a quintessentially modern Western twist on reincarnation, a few people want their corpses frozen, in hopes that, when medical science has further advanced, they can be thawed as their very own selves and cured of their mortal disease, to totter alone for a few more years through a world that they probably could neither serve nor find meaningful. It is Cain's fate they seek.

Great deeds as a kind of immortality? In a vast culture where celebrities fall upon each other like autumn leaves and where the sense of history is so muddled that college students can think Darwin was burned at the stake and can ponder whether the Holocaust was a figment of Jewish imagination, few of us imagine ourselves contributing anything that would immortalize our names and shape the lives of others long after we have perished. Again and again, we are thrown back upon the only certainty in our lives, our selves with their hardened arteries, narrowing vision, puzzlement. Is it any wonder that we have our faces lifted, take "self-improvement" courses, overeat, sift through people for someone who will "understand" us, and deny our approaching deaths? We are trying *as always* to enlarge and extend our lives. That we choose such trivial ways says not so much that we are trivial as that we cannot find something of larger, more lasting value than ourselves to serve.

But the ancient story of Gilgamesh suggests an answer, a kind of survival implied in all mythic systems, a survival ironically available only to mortals, never to the gods. This book's final chapter traces Gilgamesh's discovery of the great secret.

13

Gilgamesh and the Great Secret

The Epic of Gilgamesh is about a king who found the thought of death so horrible that he pursued the "secret" of immortality to the world's rim. He died, just as we shall, yet he did discover that secret. It is available still to all mortals. For modern readers who recognize in Gilgamesh's story their own, understanding its remote origin sharpens the thrill of knowing the story and poignantly suggests the brotherhood of our species.

As the Babylonian national epic, the narrative dates from the second millennium B.C., but parts of it are much older. Gilgamesh was probably a real king of Uruk, the dominant city of Sumeria in the late fourth millennium B.C. Some episodes come from the Sumerians; a few are known only through the Akkadians, a people who spoke a different language from the Sumerians' and lived higher on the Euphrates River; other episodes date from a later time, when the Babylonians dominated lower Mesopotamia. The Babylonians joined the episodes in an epic.

In the mid-nineteenth century, a British expedition discovered the library of Assurbanipal (seventh century B.C.), a great king of the Assyrian Empire. Among the stacked clay tablets in his library, the team found most of this epic. The adventure of sorting, translating, and comparing tablets continues to this day. Despite gaps in the text, it makes a powerful, unified narrative demonstrating the stages in every person's understanding of mortality, in his experience of grief, and, if he is lucky, in his conquest of death.

Here is a brief version of the story.[1]

Gilgamesh, the young king of Uruk, reveled in his great vigor and his absolute power over his people. The men of Uruk muttered in their houses that, instead of protecting his people like a wise shepherd, he stalked about banging on the city's drum for amusement, shouting orders, gathering up the young men, even the boys.[2] Worse yet, he treated himself to a night with each bride before her new husband lay with her.

Finally, the people appealed to the gods for help against their king's arrogant oppression. Seeking a way to channel Gilgamesh's energies into actions less destructive to his people, the gods created Enkidu, a man Gilgamesh's physical equal, a fitting companion for him. At first, Enkidu roamed the hills with the wild animals, startling trappers, terrifying them with his speed and size. He filled in pit-traps, rescued beasts caught in snares, and destroyed the snares. A trapper went into Uruk to ask that a temple harlot come out to tame the wild man.

The harlot placed herself at the animals' watering hole, and on the third day, along with the rabbits and gazelles, Enkidu came to drink. The harlot, flashing her "woman's power," felled the ecstatic Enkidu. After he had lain with her for a week, gratefully learning from her an assortment of delights, his former animal friends ran from him in terror, and he found that he had lost much of his own animal swiftness.

A whole week of imaginative lovemaking could well be exhausting, but that meaning was not the story's intent: "Enkidu was grown weak, for wisdom was in him, and the thoughts of a man were in his heart."[3] Baffled, he crept back to sit at the harlot's feet. She said, "You have become like a god." The implication seems to have been that human sexuality, with its tenderness and conscious intimacy, separates people from wild animals. And very generally women do tend to "humanize" men because men's sexual need is strong and women welcome men who are affectionate and thoughtful. After the harlot had tempered Enkidu's brute strength, his power could be used for constructive human purposes.

The temple harlot told Enkidu about Uruk, where people dressed in fine robes and smelled good, and about the glorious Gilgamesh. Enkidu felt himself already yearning toward Gilgamesh as a possible companion.

The harlot took Enkidu to the shepherds' tents as a sort of halfway house, for he had lived wholly as an animal, sucking milk and grazing. Although the shepherds treated Enkidu kindly, their customs baffled him. While they looked on, the harlot gently instructed the delighted

Enkidu in the eating of bread and wine, in grooming his body, and in wearing clothes. For a time, he served as the shepherds' watchman, using his still extraordinary powers to protect the sheep from wolves and lions. Then a man from Uruk came to say that again Gilgamesh was tyrannizing over the townspeople. Turning white with anger, Enkidu said, I will change that.

Striding into the city just as Gilgamesh was going toward the bridal house to deflower another bride, Enkidu barred the door against the king. In the ensuing fight, the startled Gilgamesh discovered an opponent as strong and brave as he, a person worth respect. Quieted, the two men arose as friends.

The relationship between them, though only sketched, clearly involved mutual love and respect. Gilgamesh was brash, adventurous; Enkidu more prudent, humane. One day Enkidu reminded Gilgamesh that, though Gilgamesh's mother was a goddess, he had not been given immortality. Still, Enkidu said, you should not be sad, because the gods have granted you good fortune above all other men. You have won many battles. You have great strength and supreme power over all people. But take care to follow Shamash [the Sumerian lawgiving god, the judge] and not abuse your power.

Gilgamesh, thinking of his mortality, was only half-listening to the last part. You know, he said, I still have not stamped my name on brick as the doer of some great exploit so that my glory will live beyond me. And a great exploit would be to set up my name among the other famous names in the sacred cedar forest . . . even build a big monument there . . . even kill Humbaba, the cedar guardian.

Enkidu gasped. Kill Humbaba! The god Enlil had put the ferocious monster there to guard the forest. They could get themselves killed.

So what, Gilgamesh shrugged. We all have to die some time. I'll tell you what. Even though you should properly go first because I am your lord, I'll go first, and you can tuck yourself behind me, shouting, "Forward. There is nothing to fear." For Gilgamesh at this stage in his life, death was little more than the great cliché, his impatience like that of the young motorcyclist told to wear his helmet on the freeway.

Enkidu had promised to stick with his friend; despite his foreboding, he agreed to go.

Gilgamesh, in his prayer to Shamash before the journey, was somewhat more mindful of death's reality. He said, Certainly I undertake this

journey as one who knows about death. Haven't I stood many times at
the city wall, watching the bloated bodies bob down the river? But I must
make a name for myself. Help me!

Shamash listened. . . .

As the two young men drew close to their destination, first one and
then the other was struck with panic. Merely touching the forest-gate
numbed Enkidu's hand—from fear, from Humbaba's magic, or from
both. Enkidu begged Gilgamesh to stop right there.

Turn back, Gilgamesh asked, after going all this way? Just stick close
to me, little coward-brother. Follow me, for though I am not foolhardy,
I am brave.

They plunged deep into the forest, and Gilgamesh felled the first
cedar. From far off, Humbaba, hearing the noise, roared, Who has
pierced my woods and cut my cedar?

Now it was Gilgamesh's turn. At Humbaba's roar, he fell down in a
dead faint.

Neither man was a coward. Although they had tried valiantly to bol-
ster each other's courage, they were clearly no match for this huge,
fanged beast. In a sharp, new way, Gilgamesh understood his vulnerability to death. But Shamash rushed in, his howling winds beating at Humbaba like scorpions, dragons, serpents, rendering him helpless.

When Humbaba pleaded with the two men for mercy, the usually
generous Enkidu counseled Gilgamesh not to give it; from some prior
experience, he knew Humbaba's treachery.

Upon their killing the monster, Gilgamesh's reaction was a familiar
one when a great victory follows stupefying terror: Now we are glorious
heroes, and completely undamaged; killing monsters is not so tough after
all.

But Enkidu's reaction was another familiar one: Killing is not free;
we are mortal creatures, and we have killed a holy guardian; we will pay
for this.

Not right away, as it happened. They returned to Uruk, where Ishtar
[the goddess of love, fertility, and war] found their exploit most impressive. What a big, strong, handsome, brave man was Gilgamesh. The
very sight of him steamed her eyeballs. Besides, he would make such fine
babies.

Come be my husband, she crooned. I, the glorious goddess, offer
myself. What an honor, my offer; what a sumptuous gift, myself! Oh,
lucky man.

In case Gilgamesh might waver, Ishtar threw in some bonuses: a throne that would kiss his very feet, a chariot of lapis lazuli and gold, the obeisance of kings, ewes that would drop twins, goats that would drop triplets. . . .

Keep the stuff, Gilgamesh said. I know you. Your lovers find you "a castle which crushes the garrison . . . a sandal that trips the wearer."[4] They have an odd way of ending up broken or lying in pits or harnessed and drinking muddy water or changed into blind moles burrowing deep in the earth.

Boiling with fury, the spurned goddess went straight to her father Anu, god of the firmament, and threatened that if he did not send a special beast, the Bull of Heaven, to kill Gilgamesh, she would call up the hosts of the dead to swarm over the land and gobble up all the food of the living. Anu knew she could.

Okay, okay.

The dreadful Bull of Heaven killed a hundred young men with his very first snort. But by this time the two heroes had had some experience with monsters. Working almost as one, they dispatched the divine bull. The city held a joyful feast.

Yet Enkidu had been right about killing. And though Humbaba and the Bull of Heaven were monsters, both had, after all, been in the service of gods. Soon Enkidu sickened, and before the eyes of his helpless friend, wasted away.

From a prophetic dream, Enkidu knew what was coming, and told Gilgamesh. A feathered, batlike demon would smother him and take him off to the underworld. He would become such a creature himself, skulking around in the darkness, eating dust and clay. Even the finest lives would come to this, only this. Gilgamesh heard his friend's words.

Enkidu died. Upon discovering that his friend's heart had really stopped, Gilgamesh tore his own clothes in anguish. Since part of grief's first horror is that the sun shines as usual and people chatter as if the world's true light had not guttered, he vowed that everyone in Uruk must mourn. For seven days he keened over his friend's body, thinking that somehow Enkidu could not be finally dead. Only when the worms began to fasten on what was left of the beloved friend did Gilgamesh let go and bury him. Then, in a frantic effort to put something beautiful and undying in the great void made by Enkidu's death, Gilgamesh summoned all the goldsmiths and stoneworkers to make a splendid statue of Enkidu in gold and lapis lazuli.

Here was the royal Babylonian equivalent of the death masks, locks of hair, marble plaques, and tinted photographs through which the grieving in many cultures seek to keep their beloved dead alive to them. Ironically, one of the most heartbreaking aspects of grief is the knowledge that one's excruciating but *vivid* appreciation of the lost one will fade, and that that process will complete his death. Through the formal memorial, we seek to hold both the person's life and his death in our minds and learn to reconcile these incompatible facts.

Compounding Gilgamesh's grief was the certainty that the same fate awaited him. The whole procession of lives, shining, frisking, full of purpose, and then stilled, stinking, scattered—it was vile, unthinkable. With us all, the death of someone we love is what makes death most real to us, and we think over and over, if this is true, there is no way for me to endure this day and tomorrow and the next.

When the grieving mind howls within its prison, perfumed robes and soft divans provide no solace. Time to move. Having heard vaguely of one man to whom the gods had granted eternal life, Gilgamesh set off to find that man and learn the "secret" of eternal life. With desperate energy, he set out from the city, crossed the grasslands, climbed into the mountains. He let his hair go long and matted. When his clothes wore out, he tossed animal skins on his body. When he came upon splendid lions rejoicing in life, unmindful of his grief, he fell upon them in reckless fury, hacking with ax and sword.

At the edge of the known world, Gilgamesh found the great mountain Mashu whose tunnel was guarded by terrible Scorpions, half-man, half-dragon. So what? He moved toward them. Impressed, they let him pass, the first living man to cross that boundary.

After trudging many leagues through the dark tunnel, Gilgamesh emerged in the dazzling garden of the gods. There stood Siduri, a mysterious divine woman, as if stationed there to answer his question. Could she tell him how to find the man Utnapishtim to whom the gods had granted immortality?

Yes, she could—but gently, simply, she told Gilgamesh what Enkidu himself had once said: He would not have eternal life. He should go home and live the best life that mortals can. Do this, do that. Gilgamesh twitched. Now, what about the directions to this Utnapishtim's dwelling? Siduri said that Urshanabi, Utnapishtim's ferryman across the waters of death, might be able to take Gilgamesh across, and told him the way to the crossing.

When Gilgamesh got there, he fell upon the boat's tackle for reasons not clearly explained, shattering it with ax and dagger. With extraordinary restraint, Urshanabi said, You have just destroyed what kept me safe from the waters of death, but if you will cut a large number of poles and help me prepare them, we might be able to push our way across with them this one time.

Although the water journey was a grueling one, they succeeded. Gilgamesh found the immortal Utnapishtim and his wife leading a bland domestic life devoid of drama. Gilgamesh noticed the blandness, but he did not reflect on how the expectation of death shapes our daily purposes, sharpens our zest for each moment, and inspires our noblest, most brilliant works.

As Siduri had done, Utnapishtim made a speech. He told Gilgamesh that nothing lasts; that human life, like the dragonfly's life, is a brief flutter in the sun. The immortal couple gently mocked him: Because you, as a mortal man, cannot even stay awake for more than a day at a time, you are surely ridiculous to reach for eternal life. Sleep is, after all, a little death and bodies wear out. . . .

Not so!

They shrugged. Soon the exhausted Gilgamesh dozed. . . .

Ho! Must have blinked off there for a minute.

Indeed, yes. Gilgamesh had slept for seven days, and each day Utnapishtim's wife had put a loaf of bread by his head. The startled Gilgamesh awoke to find his head ringed with six loaves in six stages of staleness. So he really was just a man, and his quest had failed.

Kindly, the couple helped Gilgamesh wash the journey's grime from his still beautiful body and gave him fresh clothes. Almost as an afterthought, the woman suggested to her husband that they might direct Gilgamesh to a certain life-restoring plant.

Yes? Yes? Gilgamesh begged for details. As if it mattered little, they complied.

A second difficult water journey with Urshanabi yielded the plant. Gilgamesh dove to the bottom of a pool and brought it up. Then he started homeward, full of joy, dreaming of the plant's great benefits. First, I shall feed some of it to the old men,[5] he exulted, so that they become young again. Then I shall eat some of it myself.

Of course, Gilgamesh lost the plant, for everyone had said that mortal men shall remain mortal. While he was bathing, a water snake rose up and ate it. Taking Urshanabi's hand, Gilgamesh sat down and wept.

Then he arose and, with Urshanabi—whose livelihood had been ruined when Gilgamesh had destroyed his tackle—began the journey back to Uruk and his people.

Gilgamesh thought his quest a failure, and it is usually treated as such. But his intention to feed the plant first to the old men suggests otherwise. It suggests that Gilgamesh had finally learned the wisdom that Enkidu had tried to teach him, the secret that Siduri had plainly spoken to his unheeding ears, the understanding that the ferryman Urshanabi had shown when Gilgamesh destroyed the ferryman's living, the great truth manifest in the conduct of Utnapishtim and his wife toward the impatient hero.

As a young king of absolute power, Gilgamesh had followed his moment's whim. Scarcely aware of his people as feeling beings, he had moved among them like a boy poking lizards with a stick. Then, somewhat as the temple harlot had awakened Enkidu to his humanity, Enkidu had opened Gilgamesh to his, introducing him to gentleness, restraint, the joy of friendship.

Love for another person, by breaking the self's hard kernel, does of course make one vulnerable to pain, but combined love and suffering begin the growth toward compassion. When a person suffers a great loss that other people understand, they often treat him kindly. As his head clears and the pain settles in, he gropes toward those outstretched hands. His wonder at people's gratuitous kindness becomes a new appreciation of them. Then, when other people in turn need help, he is likely to understand and to do what he can.

People had treated the suddenly needy Gilgamesh with great kindness. After a while, the thought did occur to him that people generally felt the same pangs as he and that he might help them. In a profoundly important sense, Gilgamesh began conquering death when he started seeing other people as somewhat like himself and when their welfare started concerning him as much as his own. He could neither extend their lives nor his own *in duration*, as he had meant to, but he could extend them in other ways. Returning to Uruk, he might choose life-serving work, work that other people could take up when he had perished. He might learn something fine, and teach it to his children. Having truly accepted the inevitability of his own death, he could move beyond his singular dying self into more rewarding pursuits. Ironically, the vulnerability of a conscious mortal, if others respond kindly, nourishes his altruism, opening to him a life more spacious than any that an immortal god could know.

It was now possible for Gilgamesh to heed the advice Siduri had given in the garden: "Fill your belly with good things; day and night, night and day, dance and be merry, feast and rejoice. Let your clothes be fresh, bathe yourself in water, cherish the little child that holds your hand, and make your wife happy in your embrace."[6] Simple, obvious, universal though this ancient wisdom is, it still is the hardest wisdom to receive, and it still is the most precious. To attain it is to live well and to conquer death. Whether one's culture finds "immortal" life in melting back, after death, into a great vat of quiet bliss, in personal glory, in a perpetuation of one's line, or in a happy afterlife, the best way truly to extend one's life is to enjoy life's innocent sensuous pleasures, to cherish and teach the young, to concern oneself with other people, with all life wheeling through time. Whatever our century or our circumstances, these things are possible.

Notes

INTRODUCTION: WHAT MYTH IS AND WHAT IT DOES

1. Although scholars explain the functions of myth in various ways, I have followed Joseph Campbell's classification, with minor changes, because it seems most helpful and most nearly comprehensive. See, for example, *The Masks of God: Occidental Mythology* (1964; rpt., New York: Viking Press, 1970), pp. 519–22.

2. Fred Rogers, of the television program *Mister Rogers' Neighborhood*, suggested these views on Superman and the Incredible Hulk (*Mister Rogers Talks to Parents about Superheroes*, a program filmed at Station WQED, Pittsburgh, probably in early 1980). Bruno Bettelheim, in *The Uses of Enchantment: The Meaning and Importance of Fairy Tales* (New York: Knopf, 1976), argues persuasively that fairly tales help children grow in confidence and understanding. A similar claim can be made for other forms of fantasy.

3. R. W. B. Lewis's *The American Adam: Innocence, Tragedy, and Tradition in the Nineteenth Century* (Chicago: University of Chicago Press, 1955) traces this myth in the works of major American writers from Emerson and Thoreau to Henry James. That the myth inspired earlier Americans is clear from David Ramsey's "Oration, July 4, 1778" (in H. Niles's *Chronicles of the American Revolution*); Crèvecoeur's "What Is an American?" 1782; Freneau's *The Philosopher of the Forest*, No. 10, 1782; Royall Tyler's play *The Contrast*, 1787; and Jeremy Belknap's *The History of New Hampshire*, vol. 3, 2nd ed., 1813.

4. See, for instance, Gunnar Myrdal, "Racial Beliefs," in *An American Dilemma: The Negro Problem and Modern Democracy* (1944; rpt., New York: Harper and Row, 1962).

5. My main source is Malcolm X (a.k.a. Malcolm Little), *The Autobiography of Malcolm X* (New York: Grove Press, 1965), pp. 165–69. A few details of the

story and its background come from Raphael Patai, *Myth and Modern Man* (Englewood Cliffs, N.J.: Prentice-Hall, 1972), pp. 183–86.

6. Elizabeth Gould Davis, *The First Sex* (New York: Putnam's, 1971), pp. 34–36.

7. Mircea Eliade, *The Sacred and the Profane: The Nature of Religion*, trans. Willard R. Trask (New York: Harcourt, Brace and World, 1959), pp. 32–34; Sir Baldwin Spencer and Francis James Gillen, *The Arunta* (London: Macmillan, 1927), vol. 1, p. 338.

8. Susanne K. Langer, *Philosophy in a New Key: A Study in the Symbolism of Reason, Rite, and Art*, 3rd ed. (Cambridge, Mass.: Harvard University Press, 1957), especially Ch. 2.

9. G. S. Kirk, *Myth: Its Meaning and Function in Ancient and Other Cultures* (Berkeley and Los Angeles: University of California Press, 1970), p. 40.

10. James Joyce used these words to define the stuff of tragedy. Joseph Campbell applied them to myth in *The Masks of God: Primitive Mythology* (1959; rpt., New York: Viking Press, 1970), p. 50.

11. Kirk, *Myth: Its Meaning and Function in Ancient and Other Cultures*, pp. 37–39.

1: WHERE WE GET UNIVERSAL SYMBOLS

1. The dreams recorded in this chapter come from college students in an introductory mythology class taught by the author. During the first week, before any discussion of symbols, students were asked to write down one of their most memorable dreams.

2. Adapted from George Dorsey, *The Mythology of the Wichata* (Washington, D.C.: Carnegie Institution, 1904), pp. 88–102.

3. Adapted from Elsie Clews Parson, *Tewa Tales*, vol. 19 of *Memoirs of the American Folklore Society* (New York: American Folklore Society, 1926), pp. 99–104.

4. A myth adapted from R[onald] M. Berndt and C[atherine] H. Berndt, *The World of the First Australians* (Sydney: Ure Smith, 1964), pp. 339–40.

5. Adapted from Franz Boas, *Tsimshian Mythology* (Washington, D.C.: Government Printing Office, 1916), pp. 58–63.

6. Adapted from Bernard Guilbert Guerney, ed., *A Treasury of Russian Literature* (New York: Vanguard, 1943), pp. 38–40; and Charles Downing, *Russian Tales and Legends* (London: Oxford University Press, 1956), pp. 28–35.

7. Adapted from Parson, *Tewa Tales*, pp. 195–210.

8. Joseph Campbell, *The Flight of the Wild Gander: Explorations in the Mythological Dimension* (New York: Viking Press, 1969), pp. 20–25. But, of course, some of the similarities in European and Eastern stories came from much earlier contacts between the two cultural areas. For instance, Mycenaean Greeks who had settled in Asia Minor after the collapse of Mycenaean power incorporated Eastern themes into Greek stories. Later, after Alexander the Great had conquered the Persian Empire and part of India, Greeks poured into Asia. Great centers of Greek culture, most notably the cosmopolitan Egyptian city of Alexandria, flourished far from the Greek peninsula. And some of India's rich folklore

found its way into European tales through such writers as Babrius and Avianus. Babrius, a Graeco-Roman, put many of Aesop's fables—from India and other parts of the Orient—into verse, and the Roman Avianus (fl. ca. A.D. 400) translated them into Latin. The collections of both writers were tremendously popular in medieval Europe. The Indian *Pancatantra* (ca. 300–500 of our era), a lively collection of tales, legends, and fables, came to medieval Europe through a thirteenth-century Latin version, in turn from a Hebrew one, the Hebrew one from an Arabic one, and the Arabic one from a Middle Persian one. See Thomas George Tucker, *The Foreign Debt of English Literature* (New York: Haskell House, 1966), pp. 34, 129; and Dorothee Mellitzki, *The Matter of Araby in Medieval England* (New York: Yale University Press, 1977), p. 106.

9. Johannes Wilbert, *Folk Literature of the Warao Indians: Narrative Material and Motif Content* (Los Angeles: Latin American Center, University of California Press, 1970), p. 26. I have summarized the story from pp. 395–98.

10. Erich Fromm, *The Forgotten Language: An Introduction to the Understanding of Dreams, Fairy Tales, and Myths* (New York: Rinehart, 1951), p. 7.

11. Leopold Caligor and Rollo May, *Dreams and Symbols: Man's Unconscious Language* (New York, London: Basic Books, 1968), pp. 12–13.

12. Carl G. Jung and K. Kerenji, *Essays on a Science of Mythology* (Princeton: Princeton University Press, 1949), pp. 97–117.

13. Fromm, *The Forgotten Language*, pp. 18–19.

2: SYMBOLIZING THE SOURCES OF LIFE

1. R[onald] M. Berndt and C[atherine] H. Berndt, *The World of the First Australians* (Sydney: Ure Smith, 1964), pp. 204–5.

2. Thorkild Jacobsen, in Henri Frankfort et al., *The Intellectual Adventure of Ancient Man: An Essay on Speculative Thought in the Ancient Near East*, (1946; rpt., Chicago: University of Chicago Press, 1977), p. 171.

3. Robert Hughes, *Heaven and Hell in Western Art* (New York: Stein and Day, 1968), p. 94.

4. *Time*, (Jan. 31, 1977), pp. 43–44.

5. N[ancy] K. Sandars, redactor, *The Epic of Gilgamesh*, rev. ed. (New York: Penguin Books, 1972), p. 62.

6. J. A. MacCulloch, "Festivals and Fasts (Celtic)," *Encyclopaedia of Religion and Ethics* (1951).

7. H[ilda] R[oderick] Ellis Davidson, *Gods and Myths of Northern Europe* (Baltimore: Penguin Books, 1964), pp. 165–66.

8. James Houston, *Eskimo Prints* (Barre, Mass.: Barre Publishers, 1971), p. 70.

9. Franz Boas, *Tsimshian Mythology* (Washington, D.C.: Government Printing Office, 1916), pp. 58–63.

10. Of course these values often broke down, as many instances in both poems attest; and Odysseus' revolting treatment of Polyphemus (Book 9) suggests that creatures viewed as savages were fair game for brutality.

11. R[obert] T[homas] Rundle Clark, *Myth and Symbol in Ancient Egypt* (1959; rpt., London: Thames and Hudson, 1978), pp. 55–56.

12. Samuel Noah Kramer, *Sumerian Mythology: A Study of Spiritual and Literary Achievements in the Third Millennium B.C.*, rev. ed. (1961; rpt., Philadelphia: University of Pennsylvania Press, 1972), pp. 33–34.

13. Davidson, *Gods and Myths of Northern Europe*, pp. 190–96.

14. E. A. Wallis Budge, *Osiris and the Egyptian Resurrection* (1911; rpt., New York: Dover, 1973), vol. 2, p. 260.

15. Arnold Whittick, *Symbols, Signs and Their Meaning and Uses in Design*, 2nd ed. (London: Leonard Hill, 1971), pp. 33–39.

3: SYMBOLIZING THE MYSTERY OF DEATH

1. The earliest evidence of belief in an afterlife comes from Neanderthal graves of about 35,000 B.C., roughly 32,000 years before recorded history. The food and implements laid beside the bodies in some graves strongly suggest such a belief.

2. R[obert] T[homas] Rundle Clark, *Myth and Symbol in Ancient Egypt* (1959; rpt., London: Thames and Hudson, 1978), p. 31.

3. H. J. Rose, *A Handbook of Greek Mythology, Including Its Extension to Rome* (1928; rpt., New York: E. P. Dutton, 1959), pp. 79–80.

4. James Thayer Addison, *Life Beyond Death in the Beliefs of Mankind* (Boston, New York: Houghton Mifflin, 1932), pp. 1–6.

5. George Bird Grinnell, *The Cheyenne Indians: Their History and Ways of Life* (New York: Cooper Square Publishers, 1962), vol. 2, p. 91.

6. Arnold Whittick, *Symbols, Signs and Their Meaning and Uses in Design*, 2nd ed. (London: Leonard Hill, 1971), pp. 197–202.

7. "Islāmic Myth and Legend," *Encyclopaedia Britannica* (1974).

4: WHAT HEROES DO

1. Jakob Ludwig Karl Grimm and Wilhelm Karl Grimm, *Household Stories, from the Collection of the Bros. Grimm*, trans. Lucy Crane (1886; rpt., New York: Dover, 1963), p. 132.

2. *Ibid.*, p. 89.

3. Dante Alighieri, *The Inferno*, trans. John Ciardi (New York: Mentor, 1954), p. 28 (I, 1–9).

4. Edmund Spenser, *The Faerie Queen*, vol. 1 (Oxford: Clarendon Press, 1961), pp. 6–8 (I, 1, vii, x, xii). I have modernized the use of the letters *v* and *u*.

5. For a more detailed treatment of the quest motif in myth and early literature, see Joseph Campbell, *The Hero with a Thousand Faces*, 2nd ed. (1968; rpt., Princeton: Princeton University Press, Bollingen, 1972). My discussion owes much to his.

6. Mathew Arnold, "Stanzas from the Grand Chartreuse," in *The Norton Anthology of English Literature*, Major Authors Edition, 3rd ed. (New York: Norton, 1975), pp. 2184–99 (ll. 85–87).

7. Matthew Arnold, "Dover Beach," in *ibid.*, pp. 2183–84 (ll. 21–37).

8. Matthew Arnold, "The Scholar-Gypsy," in *ibid.*, pp. 2177–82 (ll. 142–80). Arnold addresses the Scholar-Gypsy ("Thou"), who, according to Joseph

Glanvill's *Vanity of Dogmatizing* (1661), left Oxford in the seventeenth century to wander the countryside with a band of gypsies. Upon meeting some former friends, the young man told them enthusiastically that he was learning from the gypsies a special traditional wisdom and that, when he had absorbed it all, he would share it with the world (from Arnold's note). Arnold pictures the Scholar-Gypsy as living on, still serenely pursuing this one purpose.

5: THE HEROIC LIFE-PATTERN

1. Masson-Oursel and Louise Morin, "Indian Mythology," *New Larousse Encyclopedia of Mythology*, trans. Richard Aldington and Delano Ames, 2nd ed. (London, New York: Hamlyn, 1968), p. 326.
2. Charles Downing, *Russian Tales and Legends* (London: Oxford University Press, 1956), pp. 64–74.
3. My main sources for the pattern are Jan de Vries, *Heroic Song and Heroic Legend*, trans. B. Timmer (London, New York: Oxford University Press, 1963), pp. 211–17; and Joseph Campbell, *The Hero with a Thousand Faces*, 2nd ed. (1968; rpt., Princeton: Princeton University Press, Bollingen, 1972), pp. 321ff. Because Lord Raglan's *The Hero: A Study in Tradition, Myth, and Drama* (1936; rpt., New York: Vintage, 1956) includes numerous striking examples, it is of some value despite the book's frequent lapses in logic and scholarship.
4. My main source is Mark P. O. Morford and Robert J. Lenardon, *Classical Mythology*, 2nd ed. (New York: David McKay, 1977), pp. 342–48.
5. John R. Swanton, *Tlinket Myths and Texts* (Washington, D.C.: Government Printing Office, 1909), pp. 41–42.
6. Laurette Sejourné, *Burning Water: Thought and Religion in Ancient Mexico* (1956; rpt., Berkeley, Cal.: Shambhala, 1976), p. 56.
7. E.T.C. Werner, *Myths and Legends of China* (New York: Farrar and Rinehart, 1922), pp. 305–6.
8. Ruth M. Underhill, *Red Man's Religion: Beliefs and Practices of the Indians North of Mexico* (Chicago: University of Chicago Press, 1965), p. 189.
9. Masson-Oursel and Morin, "Indian Mythology," p. 348.
10. Louis Ginsberg, *Legends of the Bible* (Philadelphia: The Jewish Publication Society of America, 1909–13), pp. 87–88.
11. Martha Beckwith, *Hawaiian Mythology* (1940; rpt., Honolulu: University of Hawaii Press, 1970), pp. 480–83.
12. See Bruno Bettelheim's *The Uses of Enchantment: The Meaning and Importance of Fairy Tales* (New York: Knopf, 1976). Part of my discussion is based on Dr. Bettelheim's perceptions.
13. See "Hero Tales," in *Tales of the North American Indians*, sel. and annot. by Stith Thompson (Cambridge, Mass.: Harvard University Press, 1929), pp. 78–125.
14. R[obert] T[homas] Rundle Clark, *Myth and Symbol in Ancient Egypt* (1959; rpt., London: Thames and Hudson, 1978), pp. 150–54.
15. N[ancy] K. Sandars, redactor, *The Epic of Gilgamesh*, rev. ed. (New York: Penguin Books, 1972), pp. 97–117.
16. Joseph Fontenrose, in *Python: A Study of Delphic Myth and Its Origins*

(Berkeley and Los Angeles: University of California Press, 1959), pp. 247–52, suggests that the journeys of Greek heroes derive ultimately from eastern stories of the vegetation god killed "temporarily" by a lion, boar, or other ferocious creature representing chaos and death; and that the vegetation god's involuntary journeys to the underworld were transformed into the hero's bold assault on the chaos-monster in his own lair. Although I find Fontenrose's view valuable, it seems to me by no means necessary in accounting for the journeys.

17. Sejourné, *Burning Water*, pp. 69–71.

18. Almost any collection of a culture-group's myths contains a few samples. The stories selected by Stith Thompson, in *Tales of the North American Indians*, pp. 126–49, make a fair sampling for North American Indians.

19. S[amuel] G[eorge] F[redrick] Brandon, *The Judgment of the Dead: The Idea of Life After Death in the Major Religions* (New York: Scribner's, 1967), p. 182.

20. George Dorsey, *The Mythology of the Wichata* (Washington, D.C.: Carnegie Institution, 1904), pp. 88–102.

21. Homer, *The Odyssey*, trans. Albert Cook (New York: Norton, 1967), p. 176 (XIII, ll. 79–80).

22. Recent novels centering on the theme of the underworld journey and subsequent return include William Styron's *Sophie's Choice*, John Cheever's *Falconer*, Saul Bellow's *Mr. Sammler's Planet*, John Gardner's *Resurrection*, Ralph Ellison's *Invisible Man*, E. M. Forster's *Passage to India*, James Joyce's *Ulysses*. Novellas include D. H. Lawrence's *The Man Who Died*, Joseph Conrad's *The Heart of Darkness*, Leo Tolstoy's *The Death of Ivan Ilych*. Short stories include John Barth's "Night-Sea Journey," Flannery O'Connor's "The Artificial Nigger," Katherine Anne Porter's "Pale Horse, Pale Rider," D. H. Lawrence's "The Horse-Dealer's Daughter." Poems include T. S. Eliot's "The Journey of the Magi."

23. Campbell, *The Hero with a Thousand Faces*, p. 322.

24. Beckwith, *Hawaiian Mythology*, pp. 482–83.

25. Thompson, in *Tales of the North American Indians*, pp. 78–125.

26. In *The American Monomyth* (Garden City, N.Y.: Doubleday, Anchor, 1977), Robert Jewett and John Shelton Lawrence argue persuasively that the American monomyth, as exemplified by *Star Trek*, Superman, and the Lone Ranger, dramatizes the hero's defense of innocent communities against malevolent attacks rather than dramatizing the move from childhood to maturity, and that it involves the hero's renunciation of sexual union. These American heroes, they suggest, are popular replacements of the Christ-figure.

6: IMAGES OF COSMOS AND CHAOS

1. R[obert] C[harles] Zaehner, *The Teachings of the Magi: A Compendium of Zoroastrian Beliefs* (1956; rpt., New York: Oxford University Press, 1976), pp. 39–40.

7: Cosmic Centers as Images of Physical and Moral Order

1. Snorri Sturluson, *Prose Edda of Snorri Sturluson: Tales from Norse Mythology*, trans. Jean I. Young (1954; rpt., Berkeley and Los Angeles: University of California Press, 1964), pp. 25–27.

2. Wallace Stevens, "Anecdote of the Jar," *Poems by Wallace Stevens*, sel. and intro. Samuel Morse French (New York: Vintage, 1959). p. 21.

3. H. J. Rose, A *Handbook of Greek Mythology, Including Its Extension to Rome* (1928; rpt., New York: E. P. Dutton, 1959), p. 17.

4. James Joyce, A *Portrait of the Artist as a Young Man* (1916; rpt., New York: Random House, Modern Library, 1928), pp. 11–12.

5. R. T. Rundle Clark, *Myth and Symbol in Ancient Egypt* (1959; rpt., London: Thames and Hudson, 1978), pp. 235–37.

6. Hermann Trimborn, in Walter Krickeberg *et al.*, *Pre-Columbian American Religions*, trans. Stanley Davis (New York: Holt, Rinehart, Winston, 1969), pp. 65–70.

7. Mircea Eliade, *Shamanism: Archaic Techniques of Ecstasy*, trans. Willard R. Trask (London: Routledge and Kegan Paul, 1964; New York: Bollingen Foundation, 1964), pp. 259–85.

8. H. R. Ellis Davidson, *Gods and Myths of Northern Europe* (Baltimore: Penguin Books, 1964), p. 88.

9. Quoted by E[dward] O[swald] G[abriel] Turville-Petre, *Myth and Religion of the North: The Religion of Ancient Scandinavia* (1964; rpt., Westport, Conn.: Greenwood Press, 1975), p. 245.

10. Snorri Sturluson, *The Prose Edda of Snorri Sturluson*, pp. 35–47.

11. J. C. Lawson, *Modern Greek Folklore and Ancient Greek Religion* (1910), cited by Arthur B. Cook, *Zeus: A Study in Ancient Religion* (New York: Biblo and Tannen, 1964–65), vol. 2, pt. 1, pp. 50–57.

12. Trimborn, in Krickeberg *et al.*, *Pre-Columbian American Religions*, p. 66.

13. Edmund Nequatewa, *Truth of a Hopi: Stories Relating to the Origin, Myths, and Clan Histories of the Hopi* (1936; rpt., Flagstaff, Ariz.: Northland Press, 1967), p. 17.

14. "Romulus," xi, *Plutarch's Lives*, trans. Bernadotte Perrin (Cambridge, Mass.: Harvard University Press, 1914), vol. 1, pp. 119–21.

15. Aniela Jaffe in *Man and His Symbols*, ed. Carl G. Jung (Garden City, N.Y.: Doubleday, 1964), p. 242.

16. "Romulus," xx, *Plutarch's Lives*, pp. 151–550.

17. *Ibid.*, xxvii–xxix, pp. 173–85.

18. *Reuben Levy, The Social Structure of Islam* (2nd ed. of *The Sociology of Islam*) (Cambridge, Eng.: Cambridge University Press, 1969), pp. 462–63.

19. "Islāmic Myth and Legend," *Encyclopaedia Britannica* (1974); Philip Hitti, *History of the Arabs from the Earliest Times to the Present*, 6th ed. (London: Macmillan; New York: St. Martin's Press, 1956), p. 100.

20. S[amuel] G[eorge] F[redrick] Brandon, *The Judgment of the Dead: The Idea of Life After Death in the Major Religions* (New York: Scribner's, 1967), p. 115.

21. Louis Ginsberg, *Legends of the Bible* (Philadelphia: The Jewish Publication Society of America, 1909–13), p. 542.

22. George Every, *Christian Mythology* (London, New York: Hamlyn, 1970), p. 52.

23. *Ibid.*, p. 50.

24. Hamilton A. Tyler, *Pueblo Gods and Their Myths* (Norman: University of Oklahoma Press, 1964), pp. 105–11.

25. Ruth M. Underhill, *Red Man's Religion: Beliefs and Practices of the Indians North of Mexico* (Chicago: University of Chicago Press, 1965), p. 209.

26. See, for instance, Richard J. Clifford, *The Cosmic Mountain in Canaan and the Old Testament* (Cambridge, Mass.: Harvard University Press, 1972), pp. 1–25.

27. Joseph Campbell, *The Masks of God: Oriental Mythology* (1962; rpt., New York: Viking Press, 1970), pp. 106–7.

28. Joseph Campbell, *The Masks of God: Occidental Mythology* (1964; rpt., New York: Viking Press, 1970), pp. 76–85; and Clifford, *The Cosmic Mountain*, pp. 16–18.

29. Cook, *Zeus: A Study in Ancient Religion*, vol. 2, pt. 1, p. 187.

30. *Ibid.*, pp. 190–92.

31. Adapted from Charles Hose and William McDougall, *The Pagan Tribes of Borneo* (1912; rpt., New York: Barnes and Noble, 1966), vol. 2, p. 137.

32. Arnold Whittick, *Symbols, Signs and Their Meaning and Uses in Design*, 2nd ed. (London: Leonard Hill, 1971), p. 342.

33. H. J. T. Johnson, "Regalia," *Encyclopaedia of Religion and Ethics* (1951).

34. Werner Müller, in Krickeberg *et al.*, *Pre-Columbian American Religions*, p. 194.

35. Clark, *Myth and Symbol in Ancient Egypt*, p. 58.

36. Samuel Noah Kramer, *History Begins at Sumer* (1956; rpt., Garden City, N.Y.: Doubleday, Anchor, 1959), pp. 89–93.

37. Snorri Sturluson, *The Prose Edda of Snorri Sturluson*, p. 46.

38. *Ibid.*, pp. 63–64.

39. Shakti M. Gupta, *Plant Myths and Traditions in India* (Leiden: E. J. Brill, 1971), pp. 50–55.

40. Whittick, *Symbols, Signs, and Their Meaning*, p. 324, following Dietrich Sekel, *The Art of Buddhism*, trans. Ann E. Keep (Baden-Baden and London: Methuen, 1964), p. 102.

41. Sherman E. Lee, *A History of Far Eastern Art*, rev. ed. (New York: Abrams, 1973), p. 84.

42. Underhill, *Red Man's Religion*, p. 33.

43. "Islāmic Myth and Legend," *Encyclopaedia Brittanica* (1974).

44. 'Abd al-Malik ibn Hishām, *The Life of Muhammad*, trans. Alfred Guillaume (London, New York: Oxford University Press, 1955), pp. 181–87.

45. Sabine Baring-Gould, *Curious Myths of the Middle Ages* (1868; rpt., New Hyde Park, N.Y.: University Books, 1967), pp. 379–84.

46. Müller, in Krickeberg, *et al.*, *Pre-Columbian American Religions*, p. 36.

47. E. Adamson Hoebel, *The Cheyennes: Indians of the Great Plains* (New York: Holt, Rinehart and Winston, 1960), pp. 14, 86.

8: MONSTERS AS IMAGES OF CHAOS

1. Joseph Fontenrose, *Python: A Study of Delphic Myth and its Origins* (Berkeley and Los Angeles: University of California Press, 1959), pp. 217–18.
2. G. S. Kirk, *Myth: Its Meaning and Function in Ancient and Other Cultures* (Berkeley and Los Angeles: University of California Press, 1970), p. 191.
3. Fontenrose, *Python*, p. 218.
4. R. T. Rundle Clark, *Myth and Symbol in Ancient Egypt* (1959; rpt., London: Thames and Hudson, 1978), p. 223.
5. Adapted from E. A. Speiser's translation in *Ancient Near Eastern Texts Relating to the Old Testament*, ed. James B. Pritchard, 3rd ed. (Princeton: Princeton University Press, 1969), pp. 60–72, 502.
6. The story, which evolved over time, is based in part on Rev. 12, 20–21, and on the apocryphal Wisdom of Solomon 2:24. Although the Book of Revelation calls the celestial rebel "Satan," "Devil," "dragon," and "serpent," Christian tradition usually envisions him as a splendid angel who, only after his rebellion, took the forms of serpent, devil, and dragon. His character as archvillain owes something to the Old Testament angel "the Satan," who tempted or tested Job. In a general way, Satan's metamorphosis parallels Set's; once worshiped in Upper Egypt as a beneficent God, Set early became evil, but not until later did he tend to be identified with the serpent Apep.
7. Samuel Noah Kramer, *History Begins at Sumer* (1956; rpt., Garden City, N.Y.: Doubleday, Anchor, 1959), pp. 172–73.
8. Meyer Reinhold, *Past and Present: The Continuity of Classical Myths* (Toronto: Hakkert, 1972), p. 69.
9. Fontenrose's whole book, *Python: A Study of Delphic Myth and Its Origins*, documents that thesis. See also H. J. Rose, *A Handbook of Greek Mythology, Including Its Extension to Rome* (1928; rpt., New York: E. P. Dutton, 1959), pp. 56–60, 214; and Jan de Vries, *Heroic Song and Heroic Legend*, trans. B. Timmer (London, New York: Oxford University Press, 1963), p. 223.
10. *New Larousse Encyclopedia of Mythology*, trans. Richard Aldington and Delano Ames, 2nd ed. (London, New York: Hamlyn, 1968), pp. 315–18.
11. R[obert] C[harles] Zaehner, *The Teachings of the Magi: A Compendium of Zoroastrian Beliefs* (1956; rpt., New York: Oxford University Press, 1976), pp. 30–31.
12. *Beowulf*, trans. Burton Raffel (New York: New American Library of World Literature, Mentor, 1963), pp. 25–26 (ll. 64–95).
13. *Ibid.*, p. 26 (ll. 101–14).
14. Sir Thomas Malory, *Le Morte Darthur* (New York: Heritage Press, 1955), pp. 28–31.
15. Clark, *Myth and Symbol in Ancient Egypt*, pp. 239–43.
16. *Ibid.*, pp. 243–45.
17. The myths of some American Indians treat the relationship between order and chaos very differently from the myths recounted in this chapter. But,

clearly, that relationship is for these people equally important, and their stories about it are magnificent. Interested readers can sample the stories in Hamilton A. Tyler's *Pueblo Gods and Their Myths* (Norman: University of Oklahoma Press, 1964), "The Emergence," pp. 103–8. Tyler's bibliography is a fine source for further reading.

9: THE PROBLEM OF DEATH

1. Kenneth Maddock, *The Australian Aborigines: A Portrait of Their Society* (1972: rpt., Middlesex, Eng.: Pelican Books, 1974), p. 158.
2. Sir James George Frazer, *The Belief in Immortality and the Worship of the Dead* (London: Macmillan, 1913), vol. 1, pp. 32–51.
3. *Ibid.*, p. 60.
4. *Ibid.*, p. 64.
5. *Ibid.*, p. 69.
6. John R. Swanton, *Tlinket Myths and Texts* (Washington, D.C.: Government Printing Office, 1909), pp. 80–81, 18.
7. Maddock, *The Australian Aborigines*, p. 161.
8. Wilson Dallam Wallis, *Religion in Primitive Societies* (New York: F. S. Crofts, 1939), p. 206.
9. Jessica Mitford, *The American Way of Death* (1963; rpt., New York: Fawcett World Library, Crest, 1964), p. 47.
10. Frazer, *The Belief in Immortality*, vol. 1, p. 73.

10: SURVIVAL THROUGH FERTILITY

1. H[ilda] R[oderick] Ellis Davidson, *Gods and Myths of Northern Europe* (Baltimore: Penguin Books, 1964), p. 115.
2. Cottie A. Burland, "Primitive Societies," in Arnold Toynbee, Arthur Koestler *et al.*, *Life After Death* (London: Weidenfeld and Nicolson, 1976), p. 43; and *Tales of the North American Indians*, sel. and annot. Stith Thompson (Cambridge, Mass.: Harvard University Press, 1929), pp. 3–4.
3. E. A. Speiser, trans., *The Epic of Gilgamesh*, Assyrian Version, Tablet VI, pp. 108–11, in *Ancient Near Eastern Texts Relating to the Old Testament*, ed. James B. Pritchard, 3rd ed. (Princeton: Princeton University Press, 1969), p. 84.
4. N[ancy] K. Sandars, *Prehistoric Art in Europe*, in *The Pelican History of Art*, ed. Nikolaus Pevsner (Baltimore: Penguin Books, 1968), p. 60.
5. Adolf E. Jensen, *Myth and Cult among Primitive Peoples*, trans. Marianna Tax Choldin and Wolfgang Weissleder (1951; trans. and rpt., Chicago: University of Chicago Press, 1963), pp. 135–46.
6. Franz Boas, *Tsimshian Mythology* (Washington, D.C.: Government Printing Office, 1916), pp. 131–35.
7. *Ibid.*, pp. 448–49.
8. Ruth M. Underhill, *Red Man's Religion: Beliefs and Practices of the Indians North of Mexico* (Chicago: University of Chicago Press, 1965), p. 121.

9. Ernest Beaglehole, *Hopi Hunting and Hunting Ritual* (New Haven, Conn.: Yale University Press, 1936), p. 4.

10. *Ibid.*, pp. 5–7.

11. *Ibid.*, p. 24.

12. Carleton Stevens Coon, *The Hunting Peoples* (Boston: Little, Brown, 1971), p. 344.

13. *Ibid.*, p. 342.

14. Walter Krickeberg, in Walter Krickeberg *et al.*, *Pre-Columbian American Religions*, trans. Stanley Davis (New York: Holt, Rinehart, Winston, 1969), pp. 162ff; Otto Zerries, in *ibid.*, p. 276; Underhill, *Red Man's Religion*, pp. 159, 173; and Wilhelm Dupré, *Religion in Primitive Cultures: A Study in Ethnophilosophy* (The Hague, Paris: Mouton, 1975), p. 103.

15. Marija Gimbutas, *The Gods and Goddesses of Old Europe, 7000 to 3500 BC: Myths, Legends and Cult Images* (Berkeley and Los Angeles: University of California Press, 1974), pp. 176, 216.

16. Adapted from Samuel Noah Kramer's translation in *Ancient Near Eastern Texts Relating to the Old Testament*, pp. 52–57.

17. E. A. Speiser, trans., Akkadian "Descent of Ishtar to the Nether World," in *ibid.*, p. 108.

18. Meyer Reinhold, *Past and Present: The Continuity of Classical Myths* (Toronto: Hakkert, 1972), pp. 117–27.

19. W.K.C. Guthrie, *The Greeks and Their Gods* (1950; rpt., Boston: Beacon Press, 1955), pp. 145–82.

20. *Ibid.*, p. 173.

21. My information on the Asmat, including their myths, is from Gerald A. Zegwaard's "Headhunting Practices of the Asmat of West New Guinea," in *Melanesia: Readings on a Culture Area*, eds. L. L. Langness and John C. Weschler (Scranton, London, Toronto: Chandler, 1971), pp. 254–78.

22. Joseph Campbell, *The Masks of God: Primitive Mythology* (1959; rpt., New York: Viking Press, 1970), pp. 170–225.

23. Adapted from Campbell, *The Masks of God: Primitive Mythology*, pp. 173–76. Campbell's account comes from Adolf Jensen, *Das religiöse Weltbild einer frühen Kulture* (Stuttgart: August Schröder Verlag, 1949), pp. 34–38.

24. Campbell, *The Masks of God: Primitive Mythology*, pp. 198–99.

25. Edward Winslow Gifford, *Tongan Myths and Tales* (Honolulu: Bernice P. Bishop Museum, 1924), pp. 181–83.

26. Zerries, in Krickeberg *et al.*, *Pre-Columbian American Religions*, p. 281.

27. Zerries, in *ibid.*, p. 285.

28. Maj. Gen. John Campbell, *A Personal Narrative of Thirteen Years Service amongst the Wild Tribes of Khondistan for the Suppression of Human Sacrifice* (London: Hurst and Blackett, 1864), pp. 54–55.

29. Krickeberg, in Krickeberg *et al.*, *Pre-Columbian American Religions*, pp. 50–51.

30. Underhill, *Red Man's Religion*, pp. 192–93.

31. Recounted by Joseph Campbell, *The Masks of God: Primitive Mythology*, pp. 170–71.

32. E[dwin] O[liver] James, *Seasonal Feasts and Festivals* (New York: Barnes and Noble, 1961), p. 65.

33. Jensen, *Myth and Cult among Primitive Peoples*, pp. 174–75. Jensen's information comes from H. Lommel, "Mithra und das Stieropfer," *Paideuma*, vol. 3 (Bamberg, 1949), p. 207ff.

34. Jensen, *Myth and Cult among Primitive Peoples*, pp. 162–69.

35. Campbell, *The Masks of God: Primitive Mythology*, p. 180.

36. E[dwin] N[icholas] C[ollingwood] Fallaize, "Harvest," *Encyclopedia of Religion and Ethics* (1951).

37. *The New Golden Bough: A New Abridgment of the Classic Work*, ed. Theodor H. Gaster (New York: S. G. Phillips, 1959), pp. 401–2.

38. *Ibid.*, p. 429.

39. *Ibid.*

40. *Ibid.*, p. 404.

41. William Graham Sumner, *Folkways: A Study of the Sociological Importance of Usages, Manners, Customs, Mores, and Morals* (1906; rpt., New York: Blaisdell, 1940), p. 338.

11: SURVIVAL THROUGH A FAMILY LINE

1. The name "Israel" is variously translated, most often as "He strives with God." The entry for "Israel" in *Encyclopaedia Judaica* (1971) calls it a name of honor given Jacob because he has "striven with God and with men and hast prevailed."

2. See p. 104.

3. William Blake, *Jerusalem*, in *The Complete Writings of William Blake with All the Variant Readings*, ed. Geoffrey Keynes (London: Nonesuch Press; New York: Random House, 1957), p. 648. The statement did not express Blake's own views. He used it ironically, to express the sentiments of many Christians in his day. Nor does it reflect accurately its ultimate source, Matt. 10:29: "Are not two sparrows sold for a penny? And not one of them will fall to the ground without your Father's will." But that Blake understood the evolution of popular Christian thought is attested by the fact that his statement was seized upon and has often been quoted without intended irony in the past two centuries. His words appear, out of context, in William Neil's *Concise Dictionary of Religious Quotations* (1974), and today one often hears sincere allusions to God's grief over the fall of every sparrow.

12: PERSONAL SURVIVAL IN ANOTHER WORLD

1. Bob Miller, in *The Fireside Book of Favorite American Songs*, ed. Margaret Bradford Boni (New York: Simon and Schuster, 1952), pp. 112–15.

2. Cottie A. Burland, "Primitive Societies," in Arnold Toynbee, Arthur Koestler *et al.*, *Life After Death* (London: Weidenfeld and Nicolson, 1976), pp. 43, 47.

3. Jessica Mitford, *The American Way of Death* (1963; rpt., New York: Fawcett World Library, Crest, 1964), p. 46.

4. S[amuel] G[eorge] F[rederick] Brandon, *The Judgment of the Dead: The*

Idea of Life After Death in the Major Religions (New York: Scribner's, 1967), pp. 77–78.

5. James Thayer Addison, *Life Beyond Death in the Beliefs of Mankind* (Boston, New York: Houghton Mifflin, 1932), p. 87.

6. Raymond Firth, *Tikopia Ritual and Belief* (Boston: Beacon Press, 1967), pp. 25–27. Firth and other scholars point out that, among tribal peoples, eschatological beliefs are even more varied and fluid than in the major religions. Readers should not suppose that the beliefs cited in these pages are the only ones held by these peoples. See Firth's Chapter 15, "The Fate of the Soul."

7. Sir James George Frazer, *The Belief in Immortality and the Worship of the Dead* (London: Macmillan, 1913), vol. 1, p. 351.

8. Addison, *Life Beyond Death*, pp. 85–86.

9. Frazer, *The Belief in Immortality*, vol. 1, pp. 405–6.

10. Sir James George Frazer, *The Belief in Immortality and the Worship of the Dead* (London: Macmillan, 1924), vol. 3, p. 49.

11. Sir James George Frazer, *The Belief in Immortality and the Worship of the Dead* (ca. 1922; rpt., London: Dawsons of Pall Mall, 1968), vol. 2, p. 85.

12. Even so, some peoples that assume one's earthly fortune simply continues in an afterlife do think that supernatural forces respond to a person's earthly morality. Presumably, then, such a people may view one's posthumous rank as indirectly "earned." Guy E. Swanson's chapter, "The Supernatural and Morality," in *The Birth of the Gods: The Origin of Primitive Beliefs* (Ann Arbor: University of Michigan Press, 1960), demonstrates that societies with significant differences in personal wealth tend to link morality and supernatural sanctions.

13. See, for example, Siegfried Morenz, *Egyptian Religion*, trans. Ann E. Keep (Ithaca, N.Y.: Cornell University Press, 1973), p. 131.

14. See Samuel Noah Kramer, *History Begins at Sumer* (1956; rpt., Garden City, N.Y.: Doubleday, Anchor, 1959), chs. 8, 14, 15.

15. *Ibid.*, pp. 112–18.

16. "The Instruction for King Meri-ka-Re," trans. John A. Wilson, *Ancient Near Eastern Texts Relating to the Old Testament*, ed. James B. Pritchard, 3rd ed. (Princeton: Princeton University Press, 1969), p. 417.

17. Brandon presents a scholarly, detailed history of the posthumous judgment in Egypt. The following pages owe much to his discussion in *The Judgment of the Dead*, pp. 6–48.

18. *Ibid.*, pp. 50–55.

19. Scholars differ somewhat on dates for ancient Egyptian periods. In this section, I follow Brandon's dates.

20. "The Protestation of Guiltlessness," trans. John A. Wilson, in *Ancient Near Eastern Texts Relating to the Old Testamant*, pp. 34–36. Of course, Egyptian morality went a good deal further than these declarations, as shown by the instructions on behavior that fathers often prepared for their sons: These express sophisticated ideals of justice, generosity, civility, and tact. Wilson's translations of some of these appear in the same book, pp. 412–24.

21. Brandon, *The Judgment of the Dead*, pp. 120–23.

22. This section draws on "Eschatology," *Encyclopaedia Judaica* (1971) and Brandon, *The Judgment of the Dead*, pp. 56–75.

23. Brandon, *The Judgment of the Dead*, p. 64.
24. *Ibid.*, p. 91.
25. Bil Baird, *The Art of the Puppet* (New York: Macmillan, 1965), pp. 64–67.
26. For a full, scholarly discussion, see Brandon, *The Judgment of the Dead*, pp. 98–135. My discussion draws on his.
27. *Ibid.*, pp. 105–7.
28. *Ibid.*, pp. 107–10.
29. James Joyce, A *Portrait of the Artist as a Young Man* (1916; rpt., New York: Random House, Modern Library, 1928), p. 154.
30. Many recent short stories use snow as a symbol of sterile singularity, a loss of value, especially of meaningful connections: James Joyce's "The Dead," Ernest Hemingway's "The Snows of Kilimanjaro," Willa Cather's "Paul's Case," F. Scott Fitzgerald's "The Ice Palace," Ted Hughes's "Snow." Novels include D. H. Lawrence's *Women in Love* and Margaret Drabble's *The Ice Age*. In their very different ways, Hans Christian Anderson's tale "The Snow Queen" and Randall Jarrell's poem "90 North" use the same symbol. Examples of anomie in Western literature, philosophy, and social commentary of the last two centuries are too numerous to need citation.
31. Although the phenomenon of widespread narcissism, as Christopher Lasch cogently demonstrates in *The Culture of Narcissism*, has developed over the past two centuries, it has recently taken startlingly extreme forms.
32. From "Vacillation," *The Variorum Edition of the Poems of W. B. Yeats*, eds. Peter Allt and Russell K. Alspach (New York: Macmillan, 1957), pp. 500–501 (ll. 27–34).

13: Gilgamesh and the Great Secret

1. Readers will find a beautiful English prose redaction of the epic, about sixty pages, by N[ancy] K. Sandars in a Penguin paperback, *The Epic of Gilgamesh*, rev. ed. (New York: 1972). In addition to Sandars, I have used E. A. Speiser's translation from the Akkadian texts in *Ancient Near Eastern Texts Relating to the Old Testament*, ed. James B. Pritchard, 3rd ed. (Princeton: Princeton University Press, 1969), and Alexander Heidel's translation in *The Gilgamesh Epic and Old Testament Parallels* (Chicago: University of Chicago Press, 1949). Quotation marks in my summary indicate Sandars's words, not dialogue.
2. For what purpose is not clear; perhaps, general rowdiness.
3. Sandars, *The Epic of Gilgamesh*, p. 65.
4. *Ibid.*, p. 86.
5. Although the line contains a small gap and translators' guesses vary slightly, Gilgamesh's first thought clearly was to share the plant with his people.
6. Sandars, *The Epic of Gilgamesh*, p. 102.

Bibliography

Addison, James Thayer. *Life Beyond Death in the Beliefs of Mankind.* Boston, New York: Houghton Mifflin, 1932.

Alighieri, Dante. *The Inferno.* Trans. John Ciardi. New York: Mentor, 1954.

Arnold, Matthew. *The Poems of Matthew Arnold.* Ed. Kenneth Allott. New York: Barnes and Noble, 1965.

Baird, Bil. *The Art of the Puppet.* New York: Macmillan, 1965.

Baring-Gould, Sabine. *Curious Myths of the Middle Ages.* 1868; rpt., New Hyde Park, N.Y.: University Books, 1967.

Beaglehole, Ernest. *Hopi Hunting and Hunting Ritual.* New Haven, Conn.: Yale University Press, 1936.

Beckwith, Martha. *Hawaiian Mythology.* 1940; rpt., Honolulu: University of Hawaii Press, 1970.

Beowulf. Trans. Burton Raffel. New York: New American Library of World Literature, Mentor, 1963.

Berndt, R[onald] M., and C[atherine] H. Berndt. *The World of the First Australians.* Sydney: Ure Smith, 1964.

Bettelheim, Bruno. *The Uses of Enchantment: The Meaning and Importance of Fairy Tales.* New York: Knopf, 1976.

The Bible. Revised Standard Version.

Blake, William. *Jerusalem.* In *The Complete Writings of William Blake with All the Variant Readings.* Ed. Geoffrey Keynes. London: The Nonesuch Press, New York: Random House, 1957.

Boas, Franz. *Tsimshian Mythology.* Washington, D.C.: Government Printing Office, 1916.

Boni, Margaret Bradford, ed. *The Fireside Book of Favorite American Songs*. New York: Simon and Schuster, 1952.

Brandon, S[amuel] G[eorge] F[rederick]. *The Judgment of the Dead: The Idea of Life After Death in the Major Religions*. New York: Scribner's, 1967.

Budge, E. A. Wallis. *Osiris and the Egyptian Resurrection*. 2 vols. 1911; rpt., New York: Dover, 1973.

Caligor, Leopold, and Rollo May. *Dreams and Symbols: Man's Unconscious Language*. New York, London: Basic Books, 1968.

Campbell, Maj. Gen. John. *A Personal Narrative of Thirteen Years Service amongst the Wild Tribes of Khondistan for the Suppression of Human Sacrifice*. London: Hurst and Blackett, 1864.

Campbell, Joseph. *The Flight of the Wild Gander: Explorations in the Mythological Dimension*. New York: Viking Press, 1969.

————. *The Hero with a Thousand Faces*. 2nd ed. 1968; rpt., Princeton: Princeton University Press, Bollingen, 1972.

————. *The Masks of God: Occidental Mythology*. 1964; rpt., New York: Viking Press, 1970.

————. *The Masks of God: Oriental Mythology*. 1962; rpt., New York: Viking Press, 1970.

————. *The Masks of God: Primitive Mythology*. 1959; rpt., New York: Viking Press, 1970.

————. *The Mythic Image*. Princeton: Princeton University Press, 1974.

Clark, R[obert] T[homas] Rundle. *Myth and Symbol in Ancient Egypt*. 1959; rpt., London: Thames and Hudson, 1978.

Clifford, Richard J. *The Cosmic Mountain in Canaan and the Old Testament*. Cambridge, Mass.: Harvard University Press, 1972.

Cook, Arthur B. *Zeus: A Study in Ancient Religion*. 2 vols. New York: Biblo and Tannen, 1964–65.

Cook, Roger. *The Tree of Life: An Image for the Cosmos*. New York: Avon, 1974.

Coon, Carleton Stevens. *The Hunting Peoples*. Boston: Little, Brown, 1971.

Davidson, H[ilda] R[oderick] Ellis. *Gods and Myths of Northern Europe*. Baltimore: Penguin Books, 1964.

Davis, Elizabeth Gould. *The First Sex*. New York: Putnam's, 1971.

De Vries, Jan. *Heroic Song and Heroic Legend*. Trans. B. Timmer. London, New York: Oxford University Press, 1963.

Dorsey, George. *The Mythology of the Wichata*. Washington, D.C.: Carnegie Institution, 1904.

Downing, Charles. *Russian Tales and Legends*. London: Oxford University Press, 1956.

Dunne, John S. *The City of the Gods: A Study in Myth and Mortality*. New York: Macmillan, 1965.

Dupré, Wilheim. *Religion in Primitive Cultures: A Study in Ethnophilosophy*. The Hague, Paris: Mouton, 1975.

Eberhard, Wolfram. *Guilt and Sin in Traditional China.* Berkeley and Los Angeles: University of California Press, 1967.

Eliade, Mircea. *The Sacred and the Profane: The Nature of Religion.* Trans. Willard R. Trask. New York: Harcourt, Brace and World, 1959.

————. *Shamanism: Archaic Techniques of Ecstasy.* Trans. Willard R. Trask. London: Routledge and Kegan Paul, 1964; New York: Bollingen Foundation, 1964.

Eliot, Alexander. *Myths.* New York: McGraw-Hill, 1976.

"Eschatology." *Encyclopaedia Judaica.* 1971.

Every, George. *Christian Mythology.* London and New York: Hamlyn, 1970.

Fallaize, E[dwin] N[icholas] C[ollingwood]. "Harvest." *Encyclopaedia of Religion and Ethics.* 1951.

Firth, Raymond. *Tikopia Ritual and Belief.* Boston: Beacon Press, 1967.

Fontenrose, Joseph. *Python: A Study of Delphic Myth and Its Origins.* Berkeley and Los Angeles: University of California Press, 1959.

Frankfort, Henri. *The Art and Architecture of the Ancient Orient.* 2nd rev. impression. Middlesex, Eng., Baltimore: Penguin Books, 1958.

———— et al. *The Intellectual Adventure of Ancient Man: An Essay on Speculative Thought in the Ancient Near East.* 1946; rpt., Chicago: University of Chicago Press, 1977.

Frazer, Sir James George. *The Belief in Immortality and the Worship of the Dead.* 3 vols. London: Macmillan, 1913–24. Vol. 2, ca. 1922; rpt., London: Dawsons of Pall Mall, 1968.

————. *The New Golden Bough: A New Abridgment of the Classic Work.* Ed. Theodor H. Gaster. New York: S. G. Phillips, 1959.

Fromm, Erich. *The Forgotten Language: An Introduction to the Understanding of Dreams, Fairy Tales, and Myths.* New York: Rinehart, 1951.

Gehman, Henry Snyder, ed. *The New Westminster Dictionary of the Bible.* Philadelphia: The Westminster Press, 1970.

Gifford, Edward Winslow. *Tongan Myths and Tales.* Honolulu: Bernice P. Bishop Museum, 1924.

Gimbutas, Marija. *The Gods and Goddesses of Old Europe, 7000 to 3500 BC: Myths, Legends and Cult Images.* Berkeley and Los Angeles: University of California Press, 1974.

Ginsberg, Louis. *Legends of the Bible.* Philadelphia: The Jewish Publication Society of America, 1909–13.

Grimm, Jacob Ludwig Karl, and Wilhelm Karl Grimm. *Household Stories, from the Collection of the Bros. Grimm.* Trans. Lucy Crane. 1886; rpt., New York: Dover, 1963.

Grinnell, George Bird. *Blackfoot Lodge Tales.* New York: Scribner's, 1917.

————. *The Cheyenne Indians: Their History and Ways of Life.* 2 vols. New York: Cooper Square Publishers, 1962.

Guerney, Bernard Guilbert, ed. *A Treasury of Russian Literature.* New York: Vanguard, 1943.

Guillaume, Alfred. *Islam.* 2nd ed. Middlesex, Eng., New York: Penguin Books, 1956.

Gupta, Shakti M. *Plant Myths and Traditions in India.* Leiden: E. J. Brill, 1971.

Guthrie, W[illiam] K. C. *The Greeks and Their Gods.* 1950; rpt., Boston: Beacon Press, 1955.

Haldar, Jnanranjan. *Links Between Early and Later Buddhist Mythology.* Calcutta: Grantha Parihrama Press, 1972.

Hall, James. *Dictionary of Subjects and Symbols in Art.* Rev. ed. New York: Harper and Row, 1979.

Handy, E. S. Craighill. *Polynesian Religion.* Honolulu: Bernice P. Bishop Museum, 1927.

Hawks, Jacquetta. *The Atlas of Early Man.* New York: St. Martin's Press, 1976.

Heidel, Alexander. *The Babylonian Genesis.* 2nd ed. Chicago: University of Chicago Press, 1951.

———. *The Gilgamesh Epic and Old Testament Parallels.* Chicago: University of Chicago Press, 1949.

Hitti, Philip. *History of the Arabs from the Earliest Times to the Present.* 6th ed. London: Macmillan; New York: St. Martin's Press, 1956.

Hoebel, E. Adamson. *The Cheyennes: Indians of the Great Plains.* New York: Holt, Rinehart and Winston, 1960.

Hogg, Garry. *Cannibalism and Human Sacrifice.* London: Robert Hale, 1958.

Holmberg, Uno. *Finno-Ugric, Siberian.* Vol. 4 of *The Mythology of All Races.* Ed. John Arnott MacCulloch. New York: Cooper Square Publishers, 1964.

Homer. *The Odyssey.* Trans. Albert Cook. New York: Norton, 1967.

Houston, James. *Eskimo Prints.* Barre, Mass.: Barre Publishers, 1971.

Hughes, Robert. *Heaven and Hell in Western Art.* New York: Stein and Day, 1968.

ibn Hishām, 'Abd al-Malik. *The Life of Muhammad.* Trans. Alfred Guillaume. London, New York: Oxford University Press, 1955.

The Interpreter's Bible: The Holy Scripture in the King James and Revised Standard Versions with General Articles and Introduction, Exegesis, Exposition for Each Book of the Bible. Vol. 1. New York: Abingdon Press, 1952.

"Islāmic Myth and Legend." *Encyclopaedia Britannica.* 1974.

James, E[dwin] O[liver]. *Seasonal Feasts and Festivals.* New York: Barnes and Noble, 1961.

Jensen, Adolf E. *Myth and Cult among Primitive Peoples.* Trans. Marianna Tax

Choldin and Wolfgang Weissleder. 1951; trans. and rpt., Chicago: University of Chicago Press, 1963.

Jewett, Robert, and John Shelton Lawrence. *The American Monomyth*. Garden City, N.Y.: Doubleday, Anchor, 1977.

Jung, Carl G., ed. *Man and His Symbols*. Garden City, N.Y.: Doubleday, 1964.

————, and K. Kerenji. *Essays on a Science of Mythology*. Princeton: Princeton University Press, 1949.

Joyce, James. *A Portrait of the Artist as a Young Man*. 1916; rpt. New York: Random House; Modern Library, 1928.

Kirk, G[oeffrey] S[tephen]. *Myth: Its Meaning and Function in Ancient and Other Cultures*. Berkeley and Los Angeles: University of California Press, 1970.

Kramer, Samuel Noah. *History Begins at Sumer*. 1956; rpt., Garden City, N.Y.: Doubleday, Anchor, 1959.

————. *Sumerian Mythology: A Study of Spiritual and Literary Achievements in the Third Millennium B.C.* Rev. ed. 1961; rpt., Philadelphia: University of Pennsylvania Press, 1972.

————, trans. "Sumerian Myths and Epic Tales." *Ancient Near Eastern Tests Relating to the Old Testament*. Ed. James B. Pritchard. 3rd ed. Princeton: Princeton University Press, 1969.

Krickeberg, Walter, *et al. Pre-Columbian American Religions*. Trans. Stanley Davis. New York: Holt, Rinehart, Winston, 1969.

Langdon, Stephen Herbert. *Babylonian Menologies and the Semitic Calendars*. London: Oxford University Press, 1935.

————. *Sumerian Liturgies and Psalms*. Philadelphia: Museum, University of Pennsylvania, 1919.

Langer, Susanne K. *Philosophy in a New Key: A Study in the Symbolism of Reason, Rite, and Art*. 3rd ed. Cambridge, Mass.: Harvard University Press, 1957.

Lee, Sherman E. *A History of Far Eastern Art*. Rev. ed. New York: Abrams, 1973.

Levy, Reuben. *The Social Structure of Islam* (2nd ed. of *The Sociology of Islam*). Cambridge, Eng.: Cambridge University Press, 1969.

Lewis, R[ichard] W[arrington] B[aldwin]. *The American Adam: Innocence, Tragedy, and Tradition in the Nineteenth Century*. Chicago: University of Chicago Press, 1955.

Little, Malcolm. *The Autobiography of Malcolm X*. New York: Grove Press, 1965.

MacCulloch, J. A. "Eschatology." *Encyclopaedia of Religion and Ethics*. 1908–26.

Maddock, Kenneth. *The Australian Aborigines: A Portrait of Their Society.* 1972; rpt., Middlesex, Eng.: Pelican Books, 1974.

Malinowski, Bronislav. *Argonauts of the Western Pacific: An Account of Native Enterprise and Adventure in the Archipelagoes of Melanesian New Guinea.* New York: E. P. Dutton, 1953.

Malory, Sir Thomas. *Le Morte Darthur.* New York: Heritage Press, 1955.

Mellitzki, Dorothee. *The Matter of Araby in Medieval England.* New York: Yale University Press, 1977.

Mitford, Jessica. *The American Way of Death.* 1963; rpt., New York: Fawcett World Library, Crest, 1964.

Mode, Heinz. *Fabulous Beasts and Demons.* 1973; 1st English ed. London: Phaidon Press, 1975.

Moore, Clifford Herschel. *Ancient Beliefs in the Immortality of the Soul with Some Account of Their Influence on Later Views.* New York: Cooper Square Publishers, 1963.

Morenz, Seigfried. *Egyptian Religion.* Trans. Ann E. Keep. Ithaca, N.Y.: Cornell University Press, 1973.

Morford, Mark P. O., and Robert J. Lenardon. *Classical Mythology.* 2nd ed. New York: David McKay, 1977.

Myrdal, Gunnar. *An American Dilemma: The Negro Problem and Modern Democracy.* 1944; rpt., New York: Harper and Row, 1962.

Neil, William. "Animals." *Concise Dictionary of Religious Quotations.* Grand Rapids, Mich.: William B. Eerdmans, 1974.

Nequatewa, Edmund. *Truth of a Hopi: Stories Relating to the Origin, Myths, and Clan Histories of the Hopi.* 1936; rpt., Flagstaff, Ariz.: Northland Press, 1967.

Nethercot, Arthur. *The Road to Tryermaine: A Study of the History, Background, and Purposes of Coleridge's "Christabel."* New York: Russell and Russell, 1962.

Neumann, Erich. *The Great Mother: An Analysis of the Archetype.* Trans. Ralph Manheim. 1955; rpt., Princeton: Princeton University Press, 1972.

New Larousse Encyclopedia of Mythology. Trans. Richard Aldington and Delano Ames. 2nd ed. London, New York: Hamlyn, 1968.

Ogot, Bethwell A. "On the Making of a Sanctuary: Being Some Thoughts on the History of Religion in Padhola." In *The Historical Study of African Religion with Special Reference to East and Central Africa.* Eds. T. O. Ranger and I. N. Kimambo. London: Heinemann, 1972.

Parson, Elsie Clews. *Tewa Tales.* Vol. 19 of *Memoirs of the American Folklore Society.* New York: American Folklore Society, 1926.

Patai, Raphael. *Myth and Modern Man.* Englewood Cliffs, N.J.: Prentice-Hall, 1972.

Plutarch's Lives. Trans. Bernadotte Perrin. Vol. 1. Cambridge, Mass.: Harvard University Press, 1914.

Reinhold, Meyer. *Past and Present: The Continuity of Classical Myths.* Toronto: Hakkert, 1972.
Robinson, Herbert Spencer, and Knox Wilson. *The Encyclopaedia of Myths and Legends of All Nations.* Ed. Barbara L. Picard. 1950; rpt., London: Kaye and Ward, 1962.
Rose, H[erbert] J[ennings]. *A Handbook of Greek Mythology, Including Its Extension to Rome.* 1928; rpt., New York: E. P. Dutton, 1959.

Sandars, N[ancy] K. *Prehistoric Art in Europe.* In *The Pelican History of Art.* Ed. Nikolaus Pevsner. Baltimore: Penguin Books, 1968.
————, redactor. *The Epic of Gilgamesh.* Rev. ed. New York: Penguin Books, 1972.
Sejourné, Laurette. *Burning Water: Thought and Religion in Ancient Mexico.* 1956; rpt., Berkeley, Cal.: Shambhala, 1976.
Speiser, E. A., trans. *"Akkadian Myths and Epics." Ancient Near Eastern Texts Relating to the Old Testament.* Ed. James B. Pritchard. 3rd ed. Princeton: Princeton University Press, 1969.
Spencer, Sir Baldwin, and F[rancis] J[ames] Gillen. *The Arunta.* Vol. 1. London: Macmillan, 1927.
Spenser, Edmund. *The Faerie Queen.* Vol. 1. Oxford: Clarendon Press, 1961.
Strommenger, Eva. *5000 Years of the Art of Mesopotamia.* Trans. Christina Haglund. New York: Abrams, 1964.
Sturluson, Snorri. *The Prose Edda of Snorri Sturluson: Tales from Norse Mythology.* Trans. Jean I. Young. 1954; rpt., Berkeley and Los Angeles: University of California Press, 1964.
Sumner, William Graham. *Folkways: A Study of the Sociological Importance of Usages, Manners, Customs, Mores, and Morals.* 1906; rpt., New York: Blaisdell, 1940.
Swanson, Guy E. *The Birth of the Gods: The Origin of Primitive Beliefs.* Ann Arbor: University of Michigan Press, 1960.
Swanton, John R. *Tlinket Myths and Texts.* Washington, D.C.: Government Printing Office, 1909.

Thompson, Stith. *Tales of the North American Indians.* Sel. and annot. by Stith Thompson. Cambridge, Mass.: Harvard University Press, 1929.
Toynbee, Arnold, Arthur Koestler, *et al. Life after Death.* London: Weidenfeld and Nicolson, 1976.
Trevelyan, George Macaulay. *English Social History: A Survey of Six Centuries, Chaucer to Queen Victoria.* New York: David McKay, 1942.
Tucker, Thomas George. *The Foreign Debt of English Literature.* New York: Haskell House, 1966.

Turville-Petre, E[dward] O[swald] G[abriel]. *Myth and Religion of the North: The Religion of Ancient Scandinavia.* 1964; rpt., Westport, Conn.: Greenwood Press, 1975.

Tyler, Hamilton A. *Pueblo Gods and Their Myths.* Norman: University of Oklahoma Press, 1964.

Underhill, Ruth M. *Red Man's Religion: Beliefs and Practices of the Indians North of Mexico.* Chicago: University of Chicago Press, 1965.

Wallis, Wilson Dallam. *Religion in Primitive Societies.* New York: F. S. Crofts, 1939.

Werner, E[dward] T[heodore] C[hambers]. *Myths and Legends of China.* New York: Farrar and Rinehart, 1922.

Whittick, Arnold. *Symbols, Signs and Their Meaning and Uses in Design.* 2nd ed. London: Leonard Hill, 1971.

Wilbert, Johannes. *Folk Literature of the Warao Indians: Narrative Material and Motif Content.* Los Angeles: Latin American Center, University of California Press, 1970.

Wilson, John A., trans. "Egyptian Myths, Tales, and Mortuary Texts." *Ancient Near Eastern Texts Relating to the Old Testament.* Ed. James B. Pritchard. 3rd ed. Princeton: Princeton University Press, 1969.

Yeats, William Butler. *The Variorum Edition of the Poems of W. B. Yeats.* Eds. Peter Allt and Russell K. Alspach. New York: Macmillan, 1957.

Zaehner, R[obert] C[harles]. *The Teachings of the Magi: A Compendium of Zoroastrian Beliefs.* 1956; rpt., New York: Oxford University Press, 1976.

Zegwaard, Gerald A. "Headhunting Practices of the Asmat of West New Guinea." In *Melanesia: Readings on a Culture Area.* Eds. L. L. Langness and John C. Weschler. Scranton, London, Toronto: Chandler, 1971.

Zimmer, Heinrich. *Myths and Symbols in Indian Art and Civilization.* Ed. Joseph Campbell. Princeton: Princeton University Press, 1946.

Index

Note. Because this book is organized thematically, the index does not include general themes. It comprises names of characters in myth, legend, and tale; mythic systems; places and peoples; writers and their works.

Abraham: founder of Islam, 133, 146, 166–67; founder of Judaism, 255–57; peril to, as infant, 104
Achan, 261
Achilles, 36, 64, 91
Adam, 39, 171–73; earth formed from body of, 43; in Islamic tradition, 167. *See also* Adam and Eve
Adam and Eve, 38, 129, 189, 190, 215, 255, 283, 294; Fortunate Fall, 190, 206, 221. *See also* Adam
Addison, James Thayer, 66
Adonis, 232, 233, 244
Aeneas, 133; journey to underworld, 114
Aeneid, The (Virgil), 277
Afterbirth Boy, 100, 118
Agamemnon, 80, 86, 202
Ahab (king of Israel), 261, 270, 272
Ahriman, 130, 193
Ainus, 227

Alexander, 13, 91, 123; conception, 99
Allah, 166
American myth, 292–98; American prodigality, 251; land of opportunity, 10; New World, 5–6, 70, 81; 1960s, 208–9; socially binding quasi-myths, 86; Superself myth, 287ff. *See also* Finn, Huck; *Star Wars*; Washington, George
Am-mut, 275
Andromeda, 97–98
"Anecdote of the Jar" (Stevens), 134
Annunaki, the, 231
Antigone, 101
Anu, 187–88, 303
Anubis, 275–76
Apep, 62, 183
Aphrodite, 48
Apollo, 102, 193
Apsu, 187
Arandas, 9

Arnold, Matthew, 82–83, 85
Artemis, 86, 216, 224; of Ephesus, 219 (Fig. 30); fertility goddess, 233
Arthur, King, 3, 5, 91, 111, 133; Arthurian romances, 26, 76; conceived in incest, 101; death, 68, 123; godlike destroyer of chaos, 196–98
Aruru, 39, 47
Asgard, 69, 70, 142 (Fig. 7), 194
Ash Boy, 14, 109
Asmats (New Guinea), 237–39
Athena, 97, 110, 119, 234; fertility goddess, 233; unnatural birth, 101
Attis, 93, 233, 244; conception, 99
Australian aborigines, 9, 214. See also Arandas
Aztec Indians: blood sacrifices, 52, 243; creation myth, 43

Baal, 233
Babylonian myth, 43. See also Gilgamesh, The Epic of
Bacchae, The (Euripides), 233, 235
Bacchanalia, 207
Balder, 116–17
Beauty and the Beast, 178
Belief in Immortality and the Worship of the Dead, The (Frazer), 214
Belshazzar, 261
Benu bird, 47, 48, 155, 156 (Fig. 12)
Beowulf, 67; godlike slayer of chaos-monster, 194–96
Beowulf: summarized, 194–96
Big Foot, 179, 183
Big House, the: Delaware Indians' sacred building, 173–74; Tsimshian Indians, 225, 251
Bildad, 262
Black Muslims, 6–8
Blood Clot Boy, 100, 118
Boas, Franz, 224–25
Bogart, Humphrey: heroic type, 93
Boone, Daniel, 92
Borden, Lizzie, 87
Buddha, 55, 102, 131; enlightenment

under Bodhi tree, 162–63, 164 (Fig. 15); meaning modified over time, 162; unnatural birth, 101
Buddhism, 277
Bull of Heaven, 303
Bunyan, Paul, 13
Buslayevich, Vasili, 91–92

Cactus Flower Girl, 4, 24–25, 67, 111
Cain, 86, 87, 262, 297
Callicantzari, 141–43, 163, 205
Calvin, John, 269–70, 287
Calypso, 118–19, 190
Campbell, Joseph, 239, 309 n.1, 310 n.8
Camus, Albert, 94, 290
Cassady, Neal, 93
Castalia, 34
Çatal Hüyük, 50, 200, 229
Catch-22 (Heller), 94
Cecrops, 133
Chandragupta, 103
Charlemagne, 13, 105, 111, 121, 141; return after death, 123
Cherubim, 167, 200
Chicomecoatl, 218
Chomsky, Noam, 28
Christ. See Jesus Christ
"Christabel" (Coleridge), 77
Christian Mythology (Every), 146
Christianity: the Annunciation, 49; Copts, 49; early development, 278–82; Easter, 50; Eucharist symbolic drinking of Christ's blood, 51; the Fall, 15, 40, 188–91, 246, 283–84; doctrine of Fortunate Fall, 190, 206, 216; Holy Ghost, 48; Judgment Day, 66
Christmas, 247; fir tree as symbol, 170, 172 (Fig. 20b)
Church of the Holy Sepulcher, 147
Clark, R. T. Rundle, 138, 158, 184, 204
Clytemnestra, 80
Coatlicue, 218, 220 (Fig. 31), 222, 236, 248

Conrad, Joseph, 78–79
Coon, Carleton, 227
Copts, 49
Corn dolly, 248
Crete: Zeus' birthplace, 152, 153
Crockett, Davy, 95
Cronus, 99, 104
Cuchulainn, 99, 102, 106; conceived in incest, 101; son of a god, 100

Danaë, 28, 96, 98
Daniel, 261
David (king of Israel), 91, 146, 261
Deliverance (Dickey), 77
Delphi, 34; as cosmic center, 152–53
Demeter, 42, 44–45, 228
Devil, the, 16. *See also* Satan
Dilmun (Mesopotamian garden of the gods), 36, 113
Dionysus, 80, 100, 237; annual revival, 232; associated with Christ, 173, 235; associated with Orphism, 235; journey to Hades, 115; meaning changed, 233, 235; sacrificial savior, 93; story summarized, 233–36; symbol of relationship between enhanced life and chaos, 207–8; twice-born, 101
Divine Comedy, The (Dante), 76, 114–15, 236
Djed column, 137–38
Donne, John, 291
Dracula, 179, 293
Dumuzi, 231–32, 244. *See also* Tammuz

Ea, 187–88
Earhart, Amelia, 123
Easter, 190, 245, 247, 248–49
Eden, Garden of, 171–72, 205–6, 209
Eel (Polynesian god), 35, 241
Egyptian myth. *See* Osirian cult; Re
Eleusinian cult, 277
"Eli, the Fanatic" (Roth), 85
Elijah, 123

Elysian Fields, 65, 277
Enki, 230–32
Enkidu, 39, 113, 300ff.
Enlil, 131, 160, 187, 230–31, 271, 301
Enuma elish, 151–52, 189; summarized, 187–88
Ereshkigal, 230–31
Eros, 49
Esau, 257–58
Eskimo, 221, 227
Esther, 261
Eve, 246. *See also* Adam and Eve
Ezekial, 263

Faerie Queen, The (Spenser), 76–77
Fafnir, 105, 112
Fard, Wallace D. (founder of Black Muslims), 6–7
Fatima, 215
Faulkner, William, 80
Faust, 5, 13, 289–90
Fenrir, 183, 194, 209
Finn, Huck: as outlaw hero, 93
First Sex, The (Davis), 8
Fountain of Youth, 36
Frankenstein's monster, 178
Freud, Sigmund, 28
Freyja, 100, 221
"Frog Prince, The," 35
Fromm, Erich, 28, 30
Frost, Robert, 11, 236

Gabriel, 66; Mohammed's guide, 166
Gaea, 191
Ganges River, 38
Garland, Judy, 236
Gayōmart, 130
Genesis: transformation of chaos to order in, 8
Ghaon, 193
Gicelemukaomg, 131, 173–74
Gilgamesh, 15, 39, 65, 76, 111, 155, 204, 205, 220–21; nourished by eagle, 106; quest for immortality, 113–14; Sumerian story of huluppu tree, 56

Gilgamesh, The Epic of, 92, 299ff.
Gods and Myths of Northern Europe (Davidson), 140
Golden Bough, The (Frazer), 237, 248
Golgotha, 173
Grendel, 129, 195–96
Griffin, 180 (Fig. 23)
Guthrie, W.K.C., 235

Hades (Greek god of underworld), 44–45, 218
Hades (Greek underworld), 277
Hagar, 34
Hainuwele, 239–41, 244–46
Halloween, 207
Ham (son of Noah), 6
Haman, 261
Hamlet, 289–90
Hansel and Gretel, 13, 75, 106–7
Hardy, Thomas, 78
Harpy, 182 (Fig. 25)
Hathor, 53, 54 (Fig. 1), 138, 199, 220, 228
Hawthorne, Nathaniel, 77
Heart of Darkness (Conrad), 79
Hecate, 219–20
Hel (Norse underworld), 66
Helen, 114; conception, 99
Helios, 46
Hell, 269, 277, 284
Hemingway, Ernest, 94
Henny-Penny, 137
Hera, 102, 233–34
Heracles, 3, 15–16, 91, 99, 100, 102; apotheosized, 123; journeys to Hades, 114; rescue by shepherd, 106
Hermes, 97
Hermod: journey to Hel, 116–17
Herod, 5, 15, 104
Herot: symbolic cosmic axis, 195–96
Hesiod, 152, 219
Hesperides: Garden of the, 37, 65; Golden Apples of the, 44, 205
Hindu myth, 50; Jar Festival, 38
Hinduism, 277

History of Far Eastern Art, A (Lee), 164–65
Hitler, Adolf, 93
Hoasoro, 27
Hobbits, 3
Holy Ghost: as white dove, 48, 175 (Fig. 22)
Homer, 219, 272. See also Iliad, The; Odyssey, The
Hopi Indians, 226–27
Hopkins, Gerard Manley, 290
Horus (the Divine Falcon), 113, 131, 186
Horus (son of Osiris), 37–38, 184–86; as bull, 50; conception, 99, 100; divine aid to, as infant, 101; journey to land of the dead, 112–13
Houyhnhnms, 11
Hrothgar, 129, 195–96
Huckleberry Finn (Twain), 78
Humbaba, 111, 199, 205, 301–2
Hyperboreans, 65, 97

Iliad, The (Homer), 14, 49, 92
Ilya of Murom, 22–24, 27
Imam, the Hidden, 123
Inanna, 56, 232; journey to underworld, 230–32. See also Ishtar
Incredible Hulk, 4, 179
Indo-Europeans, 43, 140
Indra, 91
Isaac, 256–58
Isaiah, 160–61
Ishmael (son of Abraham), 34
Ishtar, 36, 103, 205, 224, 233, 302–3. See also Inanna
Isis, 54 (Fig. 1), 99, 101, 184–86, 285
Islam, 145–46, 166–67; Judgment Day, 67; Sidra tree, 166
Israelites, 222–23, 254–59. See also Judaism

"Jack and the Beanstalk," 109
Jacob, 163, 256–59
Jason, 51, 80, 106, 112

Jehoiakim, 261
Jehu, 261
Jeremiah, 261
Jericho, 34
Jesus Christ, 5, 81; associated with Dionysus, 173, 235; conception, 48, 99; as dove, 48; Easter, 245; as feminist, 86; infant Son of God, 35; in Islamic tradition, 166; journey to underworld, 115–16; Lamb of God, 190, 249, 281; like Luke Skywalker, 292; meaning modified over time, 162, 269, 279ff.; as miraculous child saved from death, 259; Nativity, 278–79; Pantocrator, 167, 168 (Fig. 17), 284; peril to, as infant, 104; Redeemer, 189–91, 281; sacrificial savior, 93, 278ff.; symbolic center of cosmos, 131, 173–75, 175 (Fig. 22)
Jews: Holocaust, 217; mythologized slayers of Jesus, 86. *See also* Judaism
Job, 260, 262, 271–72
John the Baptist, 279
Jonah, 3, 67, 117
Joseph (son of Jacob and Rachel), 4, 121; brothers' attempts to kill, 105, 257; as miraculous child saved from death, 259
Joyce, James, 81, 135
Judaism, 193, 253–64, 287; Ark of the Covenant, 200; the Messiah, 161; posthumous judgment, 276–77
Judas, 87, 116
"Judas Iscariot" (Spender), 116
Judeo-Christian myth: creation of woman, 7; the Garden, 78, 171–72, 205–6; trees of life and of knowledge, 55
Jung, Carl: "Archetypes," 28–30

Ka'ba, 38, 146
Kalevala, 117
Kali, 221
Karna, 99; son of a god, 100

Kauwa-auwa, 9–10, 55
Kenobi, Ben, 292
King Kong, 178
Kingu, 187–88
Kirk, G. S., 14–15, 179
Kiva: as image of cosmos, 143
Khomeini, Ayatollah Ruhollah, 123
Kramer, Samuel Noah, 160
Krishna, 104, 131; rescued by shepherd, 106

Lamassu, 200, 201 (Fig. 27)
Langer, Susanne, 11
Leda, 99; incest, 101
Legends of the Bible (Ginsberg), 146
Leia, Princess, 292–93
Leisure World, 130
Lévi-Strauss, Claude, 28
Lilith, 56
"Lindbergh" hero, 294
Little Red Riding Hood, 14, 75
Loch Ness monster, 36, 183
Loki, 116–17
Lot, 261

Maat (Egyptian goddess), 273
MacArthur, Douglas, 90, 122
Maddock, Kenneth, 214
Malik, 167
Mamuru, 21
Mara, 163
Marduk, 43, 151–52, 189–90, 221; story summarized, 187–88
Marind-anims (New Guinea), 243
Mary, the Virgin, 48, 285; associated with crescent, 53, 228; Queen of Heaven, 168–69, 169 (Fig. 18); at symbolic center of cosmos, 131; treading on serpent, 170 (Fig. 19)
Mashu, 304
May, Rollo, 28–29
Maypole, 243; related to Celtic festival of Beltane and Midsummer, 42
Mecca, 34, 132; symbolic earth-center, 146

Medea, 15, 51, 106, 112, 121
Medusa, 80, 97–98
Melville, Herman, 78–79
Meriahs, 242–44
Merlin, 197
Mesopotamia: ancient cosmos, 148–49 (Fig. 8); boat journey to underworld, 67; Inanna's journey to underworld, 230–32; rich source of myth, 26–27, 43. See also *Gilgamesh, The Epic of*; Sumerians
Michael (archangel), 171–72, 189, 191; weighing souls, 192 (Fig. 26), 276
Midgard, 69, 142 (Fig. 7)
Midsummer's Eve, 207
Minotaur, 112, 193
Mithra, 43
Modred, 197–98
Mohammed, 133, 146; Night Journey of, 166–67
Mormons, 11, 86, 133–34
Morte Darthur, Le (Malory), 196–98
Moses, 7, 35, 80, 81, 93, 112, 147–48, 222, 257; ambiguous death, 123; in Islamic tradition, 166; as miraculous child saved from death, 259; "Moses motif," 103; peril to, as infant, 104
Muhammad, Elijah. *See* Black Muslims
Müller, Werner, 158, 173–74
Mundus, 132, 144–45
Muru, 193
Mycenae, 200; guardian lions at, 202 (Fig. 28)

Naboth, 270, 272
Namaka-oka-paoʻo, 105
Navajo Indians: emergence myth, 40–41
Neanderthalers, 265
New Guinea, 237–39, 243
New Year's Eve, 207
Ninshubur, 230–31
Nixon, Richard M., 208
Noah, 15, 71, 176

No-Cha, 100, 102
Norse myth, 43, 53, 69–70, 71, 88, 140–41, 161–62, 194, 242; blood sacrifices to Odin, 52; Hel, 66; journeys to underworld, 67–68, 116–17; Snorri's conception of cosmos, 142 (Fig. 7); Valhalla, 65–66; Yggdrasil, 55. See also *Prose Edda of Snorri Sturluson*; Odin
Numbakula, 9
Nut (Egyptian goddess), 53, 54 (Fig. 1), 138

Odysseus, 80, 91, 121, 190–91; journey to Hades, 114; symbolic death and rebirth, 118–19
Odyssey, The (Homer), 14, 49, 92, 190–91, 232, 272
Odin, 52, 66, 116, 161–62, 186, 194, 197, 209; bloodthirsty, 221; cloaked stranger, 102, 108; at symbolic center of cosmos, 131
Oedipus, 13, 15, 112; father's two attempts to kill, 105; incest, 101; infancy, 103–4; rescue by shepherd, 106
Olympus, Mount, 144
Omphalos, 132, 152–54, 154 (Fig. 11), 173
One Flew Over the Cuckoo's Nest (Kesey), 94
Ormazd, 42, 129–30, 193
Orpheus, 112
Orphism, 50, 235, 277
Osirian cult, 15, 216. *See also* Osiris
Osiris, 30, 37–38, 46, 64, 99, 112–13, 159, 204; annual revival, 232; as bull, 50; sacrificial savior, 93; shift in meaning of, 162, 233, 274–75; story summarized, 184–86; vegetation god, 244
Our Town (Wilder), 135

Papyrus of Ani, 275
Paradise Lost (Milton), 189

Paris, 106
Parrot Man, 238–39
Parson, Elsie Clews, 28
Passover, 247
Paul (apostle to Gentiles), 232, 269–70, 280–81, 284, 286; *Epistle to the Romans*, 281
Pawnee Indians, 243
Pazuzu, 181 (Fig. 24)
Pelias, 5, 80, 106
Persephone, 44–45, 114, 218, 244
Perseus, 3, 28, 80, 121; heroic life-pattern of, 96–98
Peter (recorder of Christians' deeds), 276
Phoenix, the, 42–43
Piaget, Jean, 28
Plato, 277; world of Forms, 47
Plutarch, 144–45
Poseidon, 119
Prometheus, 13, 35, 52; blood of, 51
Prose Edda of Snorri Sturluson, 133, 141, 161–62
Psyche, 114
Ptah, 47; as bull, 50
Ptolemaic cosmos, 40
Puritanism, 251
Python (Fontenrose), 178, 193

Quetzalcoatl, 48; Aztecs' expectation of return of, 123–24; journey to underworld, 117

Raven, 35, 46, 48
Re, 5, 46, 50, 186, 273, 274; battle with Apep, 62, 190, 291; divine father and producer of infant Horus, 101
Really Black, 225–26, 232, 251
Rebekah, 257–58
Reinhold, Meyer, 233–34
"Revelation" (O'Connor), 87
Robin Hood, 76, 93
Romulus, 144–45; ambiguous death, 123; nourished by wolf, 106; son of a god, 100
Rose, H. J., 65, 135, 205

Samson, 91
Santa Claus, 160, 270
Sargon, 103
Satan, 16, 37, 93, 183, 191, 317 n.6; Christian chaos-monster, 188–89; Darth Vader's resemblance to, 292–93; Job's tester, 260; in medieval art, 179
Saturnalia, 205
Satyrs, 234
Saul, 261
Sedna, 221
Semele, 80, 101, 115, 233–34
Set, 37, 101, 112–13, 184–86
Seth, 171–72
Shabazz, the, 7
Shakespeare, William, 279
Shamanism (Eliade), 139–40
Shamash, 111, 301–2
Sheol, 115, 117–18
Shu, 200, 203 (Fig. 29)
Sidra tree, 59, 166
Siduri, 304–5, 307
Sigmund, 108
Sigurd, 103, 112; guardian's attempt to kill, 105
Sinai, Mount, 146, 147–48
"Sinbad" (Klee), 179
Sipapu, 41, 132, 147
Sisyphus, 277
Skywalker, Luke, 111, 292–93
Sleeping Beauty, 35, 107, 130
"Soliloquy in a Spanish Cloister" (Browning), 87
Solo, Han, 93, 293
Soma, 245
Spider Grandmother, 24–25, 111
Star Trek, 13, 91
Star Wars, 78, 111, 292ff.
Stranger, The (Camus), 94
Stupa, 163–65, 165 (Fig. 16)
Styx, 36

Sukkoth, 248
Sumerians, 12
Sumeru, 144
Sumner, William Graham, 248
Superman, 4, 91, 109, 288; "Moses motif," 103
Svyatogor, 22–24, 30
Sycamore fig, in Egyptian myth, 53–55, 54 (Fig. 1)

Tammuz, 93, 183, 232, 233, 244. See also Dumuzi
Tartarus, 277
Telemachus, 4, 109–11, 121
Thanksgiving, 86, 248
Theseus, 5, 14, 15–16, 91, 100, 112, 193; father's attempt to kill, 105; in Hades, 114; reared in obscurity, 108
Thor, 91, 140, 194; associated with oak tree, 55
Thoth, 59, 101, 275
Tiamat, 43, 187–88, 221
Titans, 43, 221, 234–35
Tlazolteotl, 243
Tlinket Indians, 35; hero Root-stump, 100
Trimborn, Hermann, 138–39
Troy: Norse earth-center, 133
Tsicomo, Mount, 158
Tsimishian Indians, 35; "The Feast of the Mountain Goats," 224–26, 232, 251

Underhill, Ruth, 243
Uppsala, 34, 141
Urshanabi, 304–6
Uruk, 205, 299–300
Utnapishtim, 304–6

Vader, Lord Darth, 179, 292–93
Väinämöinen: conception, 99; journey to underworld, 117
Valhalla, 65–66
Vampires, 232, 293

Varuna, 161, 186
Vedanta, 251
Vedas, 161
Venus of Laussel, 228
Virgil, 114–15
Volsunga Saga, 44, 100, 108, 140; incest in, 101; Volsung dynasty founded by Odin, 100

Warao Indians (Orinoco Delta), 27
Washington, George, 5, 84–85, 86, 91
Watts, Alan, 251
Wilbert, Johannes, 27
Wirz, Paul, 243
Wise Blood (O'Connor), 286
Wonder Woman, 4
Wuthering Heights (Brontë), 78

Xipe, 243

Yacub, Mr., 7
Yahweh: conception modified over time, 162. See also Israelites
Yeats, William Butler, 80–81, 295–96
Yellow Corn Girl, 20–21, 27, 28, 30, 44
Yggdrasil, 55, 58, 141, 144, 194
Ymir, 43, 88; ancestor of gods and men, 53, 221
Yojimbo (film), 196
Yurupary, 241–42

Zamzam, 34, 132, 153; symbolic earth-center, 146
Zegwaard, Gerald, 238–39
Zerries, Otto, 241–42
Zeus, 46, 49, 52, 80, 96, 99, 101, 119, 152–53; associated with bulls, 50; battle with Gigantes, 191; battle with Titans, 43, 191; battle with Typhon, 189, 191–92, 193; father of Dionysus, 233–35; fertility god, 233; meaning modified over time, 162; nourished by goat, 106; peril to, as

infant, 104; rescue by shepherd, 106; sacred oaks at Dodona, 152; umbilical cord, 153–54

Zeus (Cook), 141, 153–54

Ziggurats, 150–52, 151 (Fig. 10)

Zoroastrianism, 42, 193, 205, 216

Zu-bird, 56

Zuni Indians: emergence myth, 37